KU-517-388

KA 0257295 8

THE SUBVERSIVE GOSPEL

THE SUBVERSIVE GOSPEL

A New Testament Commentary of Liberation

TOM HANKS

Translated from the Spanish
by John P. Doner

THE PILGRIM PRESS
Cleveland, Ohio

The Pilgrim Press, Cleveland, Ohio 44115

Printed in the United States of America on acid-free paper

05 04 03 02 01 00   5 4 3 2 1

Library of Congress Cataloging-in-Publication Data

Hanks, Thomas D.

The subversive gospel : a New Testament commentary on liberation / Tom Hanks ; translated from the Spanish by John P. Doner.

p. cm.

Includes bibliographical references.

ISBN 0-8298-1398-5 (alk. paper)

1. Bible. N.T. – Commentaries. I. Title.

BS2341.2.H35 2000

225.8′305 – dc21

00-045306

The paradigm of the incarnation is now more meaningful to me and to others in Latin America than that of the Exodus. The Christology "from below" that helped theologians rediscover the historical dimensions of faith and the life of Jesus Christ is continually revitalized by a Christology "from above" that understands that it really is the Triune God who chooses to walk on our paths in order to change them and us. — NANCY E. BEDFORD

John's critique of Rome . . . did more than voice the protest of groups exploited, oppressed and persecuted by Rome. It also required those who could share in her profits to side with her victims and become victims themselves. But those who from the perspective of the earth and sea were Rome's victims John saw from the perspective of heaven to be the real victors.

— RICHARD BAUCKHAM

Contents

Preface

As originally conceived and developed in Spanish, this work has aimed to encourage and promote the reading and study of the New Testament book by book. The Bible continues to be honored as the privileged source for divine wisdom for many throughout the world who have never read it. However, even for those who "read it daily" (in devotional booklet excerpts) and hear it expounded weekly from the pulpit (in excerpts following the ecumenical lectionary), comprehension remains minimal. Commonly we blame the Bible for being so "difficult." However, were Shakespeare similarly studied (a paragraph from *Hamlet* one week, a page from *Macbeth* the next, then a brief selection from *Romeo and Juliet* accompanied by a censured sonnet), a century of reading would only produce similar befuddlement. As someone introduced to inductive Bible study in my undergraduate days in InterVarsity Christian Fellowship at Northwestern University (1952–56), I have a lifelong antipathy to the dominant methodologies involving devotional excerpts and sermonic hopscotching in the Bible. Everyone acknowledges that the first principle of sound interpretation (of any literature) is to study a text in its context, but singularly in the case of the Bible, very few apply the principle.

In the academic world of biblical scholarship, of course, the Bible is studied fervently book by book, but alas, the questions dominating such study commonly reflect the agendas of the Renaissance (authorship, authenticity, date, historicity, traditional theological puzzles), which privileged white males in privileged academic centers seem infinitely competent in perpetuating until everyone is bored with the Bible and convinced that whenever the books were written by whomever, they are largely irrelevant to contemporary church and society. In the present work above all I have sought to *change the fundamental questions* that should concern us if we read the books of the New Testament. For each book I indicate in an introductory paragraph what I understand to be the scholarly consensus regarding date, authorship, and historical context. For those who disagree or want more detail, the bibliographies offer more-than-adequate data for my own and alternative positions. Despite my evangelical background, after forty years' struggle with the data, I have come to accept the common scholarly consensus regarding dates and authorship, perhaps still leaning a bit to the early side of the spectrum on dates and allowing for maximum input from the traditional authors. However, such questions are not my area of expertise, and the conclusions of this work would not basically be affected should someone opt for the even earlier dates often advocated by evangelical and fundamentalist scholars, or for the somewhat later dates often advocated by those on the far side of the scholarly consensus (for instance, the majority in the Jesus Seminar).

Especially if you just picked up this book expecting to find what your favorite Hollywood movie star thinks about religion, I would emphasize that in the Spanish original and in my own teaching I recommend what I call the "didactic order" for reading both the New Testament and this introductory companion. My translator and my publisher finally convinced me that this kind of reference book on the New Testament is best presented in the traditional canonical order, so my preferred didactic order appears in an appendix. I would not be so naïve as to try to tell biblical scholars where to start reading (being humble types, we all look first in the bibliography to see if any of our works are included). But if you have never read the New Testament, I would urge you to experiment—creatively if you insist—with the didactic order. It is designed to start with things short, simple, and basic and to save the postdoctoral graduate stuff for when you are ready for it. That means starting with 3 John, the shortest book in the New Testament, and focusing on the theme of friendship in biblical theology. If you insist on starting your reading of the New Testament with Romans 9–11 and Paul's mature views on predestination, but then find it dull or shocking, discouraging and difficult, don't say I didn't warn you!

If your tradition obliges you to begin your study with Matthew's genealogy and persevere in canonical order until Revelation, you should at least realize that Matthew was in no way responsible for the problems your tradition got you into. Matthew was well aware that Mark wrote his Gospel first, and thus used Mark as a major source (along with Q). And Paul knew perfectly well that Romans was the last of his letters, not first, as in our canonical disorder. If you find my didactic order patronizing, insulting, or confusing, but recognize that the canonical disorder is seriously misleading, you might opt for the chronological order (see appendix A). However, my own preference for earlier dating of James and Jude, increasingly accepted by scholars, probably does not yet represent the consensus view. And the wide range of dates assigned for any one book by consensus scholarship makes it impossible to achieve precision regarding chronological order.

Authorial linguistic quirks that some Spanish readers have found frustrating include the following:

- I don't believe in defining terms, since I consider human words unique and dynamic (like human persons), and "definitions" a hoary white male control mechanism. Descriptions (not definitions) of a few words that may prove especially perplexing are included at the beginning, but generally I have sought to use synonyms in the context when introducing a new term.

- Since in Spanish we have no equivalent to the muddle in English represented by the word "right/eous(ness)," I avoid it like the plague and prefer to translate the Spanish literally as "justice" or "liberating justice." Why allow proper seating arrangements in the eighteenth-century French Parliament (monarchists on the right) to provide incessant linguistic advantage to wealthy oppressors today? Part of my personal linguistic asceticism is a kind of subversive fasting from the entire semantic field of "right" in English. I except inevitable references to the literal "right" hand, but even there I would insist on the danger of common metaphorical uses in theology. Why should Jesus, the friend of the poor, always be portrayed as sitting at the "right hand" of a god who incessantly tells us to heed the deluge of TV political ads paid for by millionaires and do the "right" thing: vote for a millionaire who has the "right" stuff, nominated in great part by other millionaires for whom anything remotely associated with the "liberal/left" is anathema?

- Since evangelicals and traditionalists commonly react allergically to the whole set of terms common in biblical study since the Renaissance (criticism, lower/higher criticism, authenticity, pseudonymity, etc.), I have sought to avoid them in this work. While no longer bothered by that particular allergy, I still sympathize with related concerns to treat the Bible with respect, even reverently, and see no advantage to imposing categories foreign to those of the authors and so misleading for ordinary modern readers. Also avoided is the term "family" (since the New Testament speaks only of "house[holds]" and never of "family values").
- In addition to the above linguistic asceticism, I seek to encourage a kind of conceptual asceticism, avoiding convenient labels such as "conservative" and "liberal." While liberating Israelite slaves in the Exodus, obviously neither God nor Moses could properly be labeled as "conservatives," but neither were they being simply "liberal" reformers putting a patch on the oppressive and violent status quo! However, at Sinai and thereafter, the Hebrew Bible portrays God and Moses as seeking to conserve the radical gains of the Exodus and create norms for viable community in the desert and in the Holy Land. Such a process of radical change followed by strenuous efforts to conserve the gains is evident repeatedly throughout history. Hence, I would hope that "taking the Bible seriously" would rather liberate us from the kind of false dichotomies and grossly misleading labels that too often serve as a substitute for careful analysis, coherent thought, and faithful praxis.

Although the word itself occurs only once in the Bible, "asceticism" is the "methodological wedge" employed for interpreting the New Testament in a significant recent work (see Leif E. Vaage and Vincent L. Wimbush, eds., *Asceticism and the New Testament,* 423). For more than twenty years in my own approach as a Bible professor in Latin America, I have advocated using "oppression" as the key "hermeneutical wedge" for interpreting scripture. Like a stone tossed into a pool, this approach leads to widening circles of concerns: beginning with the option for the poor so often explicitly voiced in both the Hebrew Bible and the New Testament, but then challenging us to consider the sick and handicapped, women, sexual minorities, Jews (the question of anti-Semitism, or more accurately, anti-Judaism in the New Testament), racial prejudice (especially the use of texts to defend slavery and racism), ecology, and peace.

In this work I do not repeat the evidence (never refuted) from my earlier book and *Anchor Bible Dictionary* article on poor/poverty in the New Testament that oppression (represented in scripture by more than twenty roots and occurring more than five hundred times in the Bible) is a fundamental structural category of biblical theology, and that oppression is viewed in scripture as the basic (not only!) cause of poverty in that epoch.[1] Although grateful for the many friendly citations of my book in later works, my major frustration has been the way so many excellent works on poor/poverty continue to neglect biblical teaching about its basic cause (oppression) and thus propose compassion, generosity, and charity (rather than liberating justice and fundamental structural change) as the appropriate solution (see the otherwise excellent works of Craig Blomberg and Ronald Sider, evangelicals cited in the general bibliography). Granted, biblical scholars and theologians, working alone, are ill-equipped to carry out specific work on the kind of viable and efficacious measures that are needed (and the twentieth century abounded in examples of fundamental structural changes that did much more harm than good). But where scripture so emphatically and repeatedly reflects one perspective, it is difficult to remain content with trumpets that give forth such uncertain sounds and reflect such superficial analysis of the root problems.

The category of oppressed and marginalized "sexual minorities" similarly functions in this work as a kind of hermeneutical wedge in the analysis of the New Testament books. The saint or sinner who perseveres soon will discover what a variety of persons and groups may be referred to with this phrase. My own ever expanding list now includes twenty-five subcategories of sexual minorities, which may describe any individuals or groups that do not represent the modern family, the standard married couple with offspring: unmarried adults (often gay, lesbian, or bisexual in orientation), childless couples, widows, divorced persons, single parents, polygamists, eunuchs, prostitutes, virgins, "bastards" (as the King James version translated literally), and so forth. Traditionally, biblical scholars tend either to ignore this common element in the texts or superficially reduce the texts to prooftexts for the traditional Augustinian sexual ideology. Even those who seek to explore or elaborate a bit commonly impose their heterosexual ideology, reflecting majority propaganda, and assume that avoiding marriage and procreation implies total sexual abstention, or "just saying no." However, the evidence that persons with this alternative lifestyle actually managed to live without any sexual fantasies, erotic/wet dreams, masturbation, or homoerotic activities is never supplied. Recent studies of eunuchs in antiquity remind us, however, that although they did not procreate, they often married and engaged in all sorts of other sexual activities (see below under Matt. 19:12).

José Míguez Bonino, in commending my earlier book, warned that "nobody . . . will find total comfort in these pages"—and even more is that true, I'm sure, of the present work. No author attempting to refocus attention on so many neglected but controversial areas can pretend to infallibility on so

1. Thomas D. Hanks, *God So Loved the Third World: The Biblical Vocabulary of Oppression*, trans. James C. Dekker (Maryknoll, N.Y.: Orbis, 1983); Thomas D. Hanks, "Poor/Poverty" (New Testament), *ABD*, 5:414–24.

many difficult questions. My concern, however, has not been to pontificate regarding the proper interpretation of a given text, but more fundamentally, to change the basic questions we raise and concentrate on in our reading and study of the New Testament. A reader might well conclude that I am naïve and basically mistaken in my conclusions. Many have concluded that a careful reading of the New Testament demonstrates rather that Paul and other authors are properly cited to uphold the divine right of kings, slavery, racism, anti-Semitism, homophobia, subjugation of women, and bourgeois complacency regarding the poor, and that hence the New Testament (or entire Bible) should be relegated to the purgatory of once important but no longer relevant works. For me, such honest disagreement about transcendent questions is much preferable to the endless monographs about whether Paul really wrote 2 Thessalonians—investigations commonly undertaken with a pretense of a "scholarly objectivity" that disdains others supposedly contaminated by their obviously political agendas.

Perhaps the most common complaint about my work has been that it represents only my interpretations, speculations, or hypotheses and that I should repeatedly make clear the purely hypothetical character of my unqualified affirmations (as opposed to supposedly "solid facts" represented in certain other writings on the Bible). However, when we interpret the literature and history of the ancient world, virtually any significant affirmation we make represents a hypothesis of greater or lesser degree of probability. Readers of all persuasions would find it insufferably boring were I to refer repeatedly to the hypothesis that Jesus or Paul really lived (and were not simply inventions of early church propaganda). Evangelicals and fundamentalists would be the first to object were I to refer continually to Jesus' resurrection or virgin birth as "hypotheses." Yet in the world of biblical scholarship we find much more overwhelming support for the admittedly hypothetical "Q" source than we do for Jesus' resurrection or virgin birth. At the other end of the theological spectrum I encounter similar complaints: any suggestions that Jesus or any New Testament authors may well have been persons of homosexual or bisexual orientation is viewed as "novelistic" speculation, while the alternative hypothesis that they were "normal heterosexuals" but mysteriously sexually celibate, or just never managed to find an appropriate soulmate of the opposite sex, is assumed to be "fact." Most commonly, of course, such questions about human sexuality are ignored by biblical scholars; hence, in order to change the questions we need to propose alternative hypotheses.

My conviction, stemming from long, often painful, personal experience, is that the kind of disturbing hypotheses abounding in this work gain credence not so much by scrutinizing and weighing each one in isolation, but rather as we face a whole series of questions and hypotheses that have been "off the map" for traditional scholarship. Whether it be stylistic criteria for distinguishing sources in the Pentateuch or historical problems resulting from rigid views of biblical inerrancy, fundamentalists often appear to win a debate conducted in TV sound bites by getting us to focus in an isolated way on a single verse or problem. But many solutions that appear convincing when applied to isolated phenomenon are totally inadequate when we view the entire range of evidence (a process that may take months or years of study, and work in the original languages rather than translations).

However, though I have sought to change the questions and encourage serious interface between the New Testament and fundamental problems and concerns in the modern world, I have never been among those who think that modern relevance of the Bible is best promoted by maximizing historical skepticism and viewing it as a mere collection of legend, myth, and ecclesiastical propaganda. Admittedly, my bibliographies abound in works that commonly would be labeled "evangelical." In part this reflects the context of my background, friendships, and life work, but perhaps even more the economic reality that in our capitalistic consumer society the major consumers of detailed exegetical commentaries are evangelicals; hence, publishers produce and market not what necessarily represents the "scholarly consensus" but what will bring in the most profits. We thus find ourselves affirming that the scholarly consensus overwhelmingly rejects traditional Pauline authorship of the pastoral letters (a consensus including evangelicals such as Howard Marshall), while providing bibliographies that may seem overloaded with works that deny that conclusion. However, since mainly evangelicals like to read and write about the pastorals, if you want linguistic or grammatical detail about some point in 1 Timothy, probably you will find yourself wading through pages of evangelical exegesis (often quite helpful where hidden evangelical agendas do not obscure significant questions).

In this area of basic philosophical presuppositions and historical methodology, in recent years I have been particularly encouraged by the work of N. T. (Tom) Wright. Obviously much cleverer than I, in recent years he has managed to become a virtual cult figure and guru in scholarly evangelical circles, while affirming and supporting many of the positions for which I was condemned as a "Marxist" or "communist" when my first book in English was published (1983). He generally abandons the Neoplatonic concepts of "ethics" and "morals" and prefers the biblical term "praxis" (see my comments about "walk" and "way" in Ephesians, 1–3 John, etc.). Wright recognizes that in biblical theology the "Exodus paradigm" is fundamental for interpretation (a hallmark of Latin American theologies since Medellín in 1968), which involves posing as fundamental the questions of oppressors and oppressed. He affirms that "salvation" in the Bible commonly refers to integral liberation, including a socio-economic-political dimension for individuals and society. This was something I was properly taught at Wheaton Graduate School (an evangelical academic stronghold) back in 1956–57), but when I repeated what for me had become a platitude in the 1980s, it was viewed by many as my most serious "heresy."

I find Wright's contention that Israel in the New Testament views itself as still in "exile" intriguing and helpful, but not totally convincing (the resulting "paradigm of the exile," however, provides the same focus on oppressors and oppressed that we find in the Exodus paradigm). I share many scholars' questions about Wright's conclusions that in Mark 13 Jesus did not refer to his second coming. However, for a multitude of fundamental questions regarding philosophy and historical methodology, I find Wright expressing conclusions similar to my own. This he does, however, with eloquence, wit, clarity, abundant bibliography, and all the proper qualifiers—generously sprinkled with those delightfully cautious double negatives ("not entirely impossible that...") so beloved by British scholars. Much of what so many of my own students and readers have found lacking in this present volume they can find in Wright (for an excellent introduction, see the work on Wright edited by Carey C. Newman in the general bibliography).

I am deeply indebted to a large number of extended family and household members, an international network of friends and colleagues, to my translator John P. Doner, and of course to the staff at Pilgrim Press, my very patient and courageous publisher. However, the controversial character of the questions raised and the answers herein suggested has meant that many who have contributed most would be deeply embarrassed (if not fired!) to find themselves singled out for special mention. Since they have nothing more to lose, I will specifically thank the several homeless streetpeople who have faithfully attended the Bible course in the First Methodist Church in Buenos Aires, and also the members of the Metropolitan Community Church both here and in Mexico City, where much of this material was first intensively and repeatedly scrutinized and debated.

Tom Hanks
thanks@thanks.wamani.apc.org
www.othersheep.org

Abbreviations

→	For more detail or related treatment, see (for subjects treated in this volume)
//	Parallel biblical passages
AB	The Anchor Bible
ABD	*The Anchor Bible Dictionary*
HCSB	HarperCollins Study Bible (with NRSV text)
ICC	International Critical Commentary
JB	Jerusalem Bible
JSNTSup	Journal for the Study of the New Testament Supplement Series
KJV	King James Version
NCBC	New Century Bible Commentary
NICNT	New International Commentary on the New Testament
NIGTC	New International Greek Testament Commentary
NIV	New International Version
NRSV	New Revised Standard Version
Q	Quelle, from the German for "Source": texts absent from Mark, but occurring in both Matthew and Luke (e.g., the Sermon on the Mount/Plain, Matthew 5–7 // Luke 6), probably edited ca. 60 C.E., and thus representing the most original form of many of Jesus' teachings (see appendix A, p. 259 below, for related dates).
WBC	Word Biblical Commentary

Glossary

Deconstruction. This term is not used in this work in the more technical sense of postmodern linguistics, but in the more general sense, as opposed to purely negative destruction, of a dismantling of thought or rhetoric (whether intentional or subconscious), thus illuminating the tensions and apparent contradictions, with the goal of positive reformulation (or synthesis where dialectically opposed affirmations are involved) (→Romans).

Praxis. Greek word used in the title for the "Acts" of the Apostles, and common in German (i.e., for designated hours of work: "praxis" of a physician), whence developed as the central concept in Marxist philosophy (free human activity to change the world) and later in Latin American liberation theologies (which rejected traditional notions of theory—interminably debated—and eventually applied to practice). Latin American thinkers insist that theology *take praxis as the starting point,* with theology functioning as the posterior critical reflection on praxis; in modern linguistics this approach is developed in the understanding of the "hermeneutical circle" (the interplay or dialectic between action and interpretation); in this work (like many others—see Tom Wright in the general bibliography), praxis (as a Greek biblical term) is preferred to the nonbiblical categories of morals and ethics (Greek philosophical constructs alien to the Bible that gravely distort biblical interpretation).

THE SUBVERSIVE GOSPEL

Chapter 1

MATTHEW

A Log Cabin Publican? Good News for Sex Workers!

Outline

Structure: Narrative + Five Discourses (cf. the Pentateuch)

Prologue. Liberating the new Liberator: birth, infancy (// Moses, Exodus 1–2)	1–2
1. *Narrative:* How Jesus' ministry began	3–4
Discourse: Sermon on the Mount: perfecting love for enemy-oppressors	5–7
2. *Narrative:* Ten miracles: solidarity with the sick and marginalized	8–9
Discourse: Twelve missionaries sent to oppressed Israel: their simple lifestyle	10
3. *Narrative:* Conflicts with local Jewish oligarchies	11–12
Discourse: Seven subversive word pictures portray God's just new order	13
4. *Narrative:* Jesus' alternative counterculture community in formation	14–17
Discourse: Keeping the space safe in the fictive kinship communities	18
5. *Narrative:* Toward Jerusalem: escalating conflict with local oligarchies	19–22
Discourse: God will judge oppressors: local oligarchies and empire	23–25
Conclusion. Liberating the Liberator: death, resurrection, universal mission	26–28

Commentary

1. Introduction: "Anti-Semitic" Judaism?

Just as Mark probably "signed" his Gospel with the scene of a young man who fled naked (Mark 14:51–52), Matthew apparently paints a self-portrait when he writes,

> Every scribe who has become a disciple for the realm from heaven is like the master of a household who brings out of his treasure first what is *new* [Jesus' good news] and then what is *old* [Moses' law/the Torah]. (Matt. 13:52)

Since those who identified with Jesus' "way" continued to be a sect within Judaism during the first century C.E., it would be anachronistic to think of Matthew as a Jew who became a "Christian." Consequently, we should understand his harsh expressions against certain "Jews" not as an expression of anti-Judaism (much less modern racially based anti-Semitism), but as a prophetic denunciation against other sectors within Judaism, especially the Pharisees.[1]

According to early patristic tradition, Matthew was written by the toll collector Matthew/Levi whom Jesus called to discipleship (Matt. 9:9), who then immediately threw a banquet to introduce Jesus to other toll collectors (despised collaborators with the Roman Empire who worked in the customhouses), including in the invitation even sex workers, their equally marginalized friends (9:10–13 // Mark 2:13–17; Luke 5:27–32; cf. Matt. 5:46; 11:19; 18:17; 21:31–32).

The name Matthew (*Mattiyah* in Hebrew) means "gift of Yah[weh]/God," but in Greek *Matthaios* sounds similar to "disciples" (*mathētai*), those who "become/make disciples" (*mathēteuō*), a key word in the Gospel (see "disciple all nations," 28:19). Matthew probably was written for a mixed church (Jewish-Gentile) in Syrian Antioch (4:24; Acts 13:1) at a time of much persecution (Matt. 5:10–12). The Antiochene church, founded by Hellenistic Jews, had a long tradition (since Paul's ministry, 46–65 C.E.) of reaching out to Gentiles.

The memoirs of the former publican (toll collector—perhaps the scribe of 13:52 in his later years) may have been edited in final form by another Jewish Christian (scribe [13:52]?). Whatever the process, Matthew has a markedly Jewish but emphatically Christian character: in 13:52 the new, unexpectedly, has priority over the old. Matthew uses Mark (written ca. 69 C.E.), as well as our earliest source Q (ca. 60 C.E.). Q consisted of the teachings that Matthew has in common with Luke (e.g., the sermon of Matthew 5–7 // Luke 6 [Luke ca. 80]). In addition to Mark and Q, Matthew contains much of its own and unique material, commonly indicated by M. The date for Matthew's final editing and publication may be ca. 85 C.E., after news about the destruction of Jerusalem (70 C.E.) became widely disseminated (21:41; 22:7; 24:15–16).

Most modern scholars find it difficult to accept as author of the Gospel Levi, the toll collector, especially because they cannot imagine that a disciple and eyewitness of Jesus' ministry would have taken over so much from Mark (a secondary source). However, according to patristic tradition, Mark represents the eyewitness testimony of Peter, who plays a uniquely large role in Matthew (see below). Moreover, literary habits of ancient authors and scribes regarding use of earlier documents differed from our modern capitalistic norms that emphasize originality and respect for copyrights to protect authors' economic

---

1. Luke T. Johnson, "The New Testament's Anti-Jewish Slander and the Conventions of Ancient Rhetoric," *Journal of Biblical Literature* 108 (1989): 419–41; Scott McKnight, "A Loyal Critic: Matthew's Polemic with Judaism in Theological Perspective," in *Anti-Semitism and Early Christianity,* ed. Craig A. Evans and Donald A. Hagner (Minneapolis: Fortress, 1993), 55–79.

interests in the market.[2] Consequently, even if our present Matthew does not proceed directly from the pen of the toll collector Levi, the Gospel still may preserve memoirs/traditions from this disciple, which formed the basis of the patristic tradition of Matthew as author. The Gospel's originality is evident in the author's remarkably creative theological and homiletic use of earlier documents (Q and Mark), as well as in the materials peculiar to Matthew (M).

Whoever the author, the emphatically Jewish character of Matthew is undeniable. Matthew so respects Jewish sensibilities that he prefers to speak of the "realm from heaven" (not "of God") and changes the reference to two men in a bed (Luke 17:34 = Q; KJV) to two men in a field (Matt. 24:40; cf. the "beloved slave" of Luke 7:2, but "son/slave" [Greek: *pais*] in Matt. 8:6). In addition, Matthew

- begins with a genealogy (1:1–17, "Abraham" and "David")
- emphasizes the law/Torah (5:17–20; 23:1–3)
- cites nine Hebrew scripture texts as prophecies Jesus fulfilled (2:5b–6, 15b, 17–18, 23b; 4:14–16; 8:17; 12:17–21; 13:35; 21:4–5; cf. 3:3; 13:14; 26:54, 56; 27:9–10).
- refers to specifically Jewish acts of piety (bring gifts to the temple altar, 5:23–24)

Matthew presents Jesus as the son of Abraham and of David (1:1, 17), the new Moses who ascends a mountain to receive and communicate divine revelation (5:1–2; 7:28–29), and collects Jesus' teaching into five great sermons, parallel to the five books of Moses. Matthew alternates Jesus' five great discourses with five narrations. The ten miracles in Matthew 8–9 (mainly healings) contrast impressively with the ten plagues of the Exodus. At the same time, however, Matthew is also emphatically Christian, emphasizing Jesus as the Christ/Messiah, Son of God, and Human One (literally "Son of Man") and (in texts taken over from Mark) underscores titles of divinity and even worship offered to Jesus.

2. Literary Genre

Even in conservative and evangelical circles, Robert H. Gundry's erudite commentary has provoked questions and discussions concerning the literary genre and historicity of the traditions Matthew preserves. Against the great majority of contemporary scholars, Gundry defends the tradition of Matthew as author and an early date (ca. 60–62).[3] Gundry concludes, however, that in addition to historical traditions taken primarily from Mark and Q, Matthew also includes elements of "midrash" (homiletical and theological creativity that do not reflect historical data—see Jesus' parables).[4] Another evangelical,

---

2. Robert H. Gundry, *Matthew: A Commentary on His Handbook for a Mixed Church under Persecution* (Grand Rapids: Eerdmans, 1994), 621.

3. Ibid., 599–622.

4. Ibid., xxiii–xxx (1994 edition). Perhaps the American conservative evangelical storm over Gundry (including his forced resignation from the inerrantist Evangelical Theological Society) was

Donald A. Hagner, defends the fundamental historicity of all that Matthew includes, without claiming that he wrote with the technical precision of a modern historian.[5]

Since 1985 the famous Jesus Seminar, a self-selected American group (seventy-four reputable scholars, but mainly of radical bent), has managed to utilize the mass media to disseminate their conclusion that very little in the four Gospels has any historical basis (the Seminar has voted that less than 20 percent of sayings the Gospels attribute to Jesus are authentic). Mainline and conservative critics point out that the conclusions of this self-appointed group do not represent the scholarly consensus.[6] However, literature (such as Jesus' parables) may be inspired and a source of divine wisdom, even when not pretending to measure up to modern expectations of scientific historiography. Whether Matthew includes much, little, or no midrash, the historical basis of Jesus' life is solidly grounded in the other Gospels, as well as in the historical elements Matthew shares with them.

3. *From "the Poor in Spirit" to "the Least of These My Brothers"*

Careful readers have observed that in Luke's Gospel, Jesus addresses his first beatitude to his disciples as "you poor" (Luke 6:20), while in Matthew he speaks of "the poor in spirit" (Matt. 5:3). Luke includes Jesus' discourse in which he cites Isaiah to specify that his mission is to proclaim good news to the poor and liberation for the oppressed (Luke 4:18–19, quoting Isa. 61:1–2 + 58:6)—a fundamental text for Latin American liberation theologians. At first glance, Matthew thus makes Jesus' option for the poor less offensive and thus appears more "conservative" than Luke.

A more careful reading, however, reveals that Matthew also is quite radical. "Spirit" in the Bible is not immaterial but is God's force, often invisible like the wind, a hurricane, or the cause of earthquakes. Matthew, who addressed a sect including a few affluent members, clarifies that God's blessing is promised not only for the poor but also for those who manifest solidarity with them in times of persecution, since such solidarity involves putting your life at risk (see Matthew's two Joseph paradigms: Mary's husband, 1:18–2:25; and Joseph of Arimathea, 27:57–61—an example of structural inclusion).

---

due in part to the fact that his interpretation of Matthew as including elements of midrash left open the door for someone to accept the inerrancy of the entire Bible and at the same time conclude that nothing in it represents history, including the tradition of Jesus' virginal conception and birth, one of the five "fundamentals" for fundamentalists (though hardly such in biblical theology—see under Luke). Inerrantists thought that with their view of inspiration they had everything of significance to them nailed down, but Gundry's questions regarding literary genre and midrash in Matthew indicated that with biblical inerrancy alone nothing is nailed down.

5. Donald A. Hagner, *Matthew 1–13*, WBC 33A (Dallas: Word, 1993), xliii.

6. Raymond E. Brown, *An Introduction to the New Testament* (New York: Doubleday, 1997), 820–23; Craig L. Blomberg, *Jesus and the Gospels* (Nashville: Broadman & Holman, 1997), 184–85; Ben Witherington III, *The Jesus Quest: The Third Search for the Jew of Nazareth* (Downers Grove, Ill.: InterVarsity, 1995), 42–57; Luke T. Johnson, *The Real Jesus* (San Francisco: HarperSanFrancisco, 1996); Paul Copan, ed., *Will the Real Jesus Please Stand Up?* (Grand Rapids: Baker, 1998); see also N. T. Wright's three volumes in the general bibliography.

Throughout his entire Gospel, Matthew develops the sense of "poor in spirit" whenever he speaks of solidarity and justice in the new community, but above all when he describes the final judgment with his unique criterion of separation: solidarity with the poor, the needy, and the persecuted (structural inclusion: Jesus' first and last teaching). In Jesus' original teaching, transmitted orally, the needy "brothers and sisters" (Matt. 25:31–46) probably referred to *any human in need.* However, when Matthew included Jesus' parable in his Gospel, his own linguistic usage and emphasis on the church resulted in a more concrete nuance of a "Christian brother" in need. Such a specific application was especially appropriate because of the oppression and persecution that the church in Antioch was suffering when Matthew wrote. This concrete application to Christian "brothers" (persecuted, missionaries?—see Acts 8:1–4), however, is not exclusive or preferential, but should be understood as paradigmatic for any humans in need (see God's Exodus liberation of Israel; Luke's parable of the good Samaritan; Gal. 6:10).

Many liberation theologians thus recognize in Matt. 25:31–46 a text even more radical than Luke 4:18–19. In this parable Jesus insists that at the final judgment "correct ideas" or proper theology (believing that God is one, or triune, or that Jesus is God incarnate) will not matter. The Judge inquires only about the works of loving solidarity done for humans in need. Religious people commonly devote immense energy, even resorting to "holy wars," to defend their "orthodoxy." Jesus, however, insists that in the final judgment all that will matter is their "orthopraxis"—sacrificial solidarity with humans in need ("take up your cross"). This revolutionary parable of Jesus, preserved only in Matthew (M), subverts all human ideologies and religions.[7]

Dennis Duling summarizes well the vocabulary that describes the numerous types of poor in Matthew:[8]

1. forced laborers, 5:41 (implied)
2. day laborers (*ergatēs*): 20:1, 2, 8, perhaps 9:37–38; 10:10
3. slaves/servants (*doulos*): 8:9; 10:24–25; 13:27–28; 18:23, 26–28, 32; 20:27; 21:34, 36; 22:3–4, 6, 8, 10; 24:45–46, 48, 50; 25:14, 19, 21, 23 (2x), 30; 26:51; slave/son (*pais,* adopted?): 8:6, 8, 13; 12:18 (Isa. 42:1); 14:2; 17:18; 21:15.
4. peasants, urban poor, and destitute:

    crowd(s) (*ochlos*): fifty references(!), including women, slaves, peasants, sick and physically challenged, eunuchs

    tenant farmers (*geōrgos*): 21:33

    poor (*ptōchos*): literal in 11:5; 19:21; 26:9–11; cf. 5:3, "in spirit" (allies)

    receivers of alms (*eleēmosunē*): 6:1–6; 19:21

---

7. Xavier Pikaza, *Hermanos de Jesús y servidores de los más pequeños (Mt 25, 31–46)* (Salamanca, Spain: Sígueme, 1984).

8. Dennis Duling, "Matthew and Marginality," in *SBL 1993 Seminar Papers* (Atlanta: Scholars Press, 1993), 653. See also shepherds (*poimenes,* cf. Luke), which for Matthew is always a positive metaphor: 9:36; 10:6 and 15:24 ("lost sheep"); 25:32; 26:31 (Zech. 13:7).

Social Stratification in the Herodian Period[9]

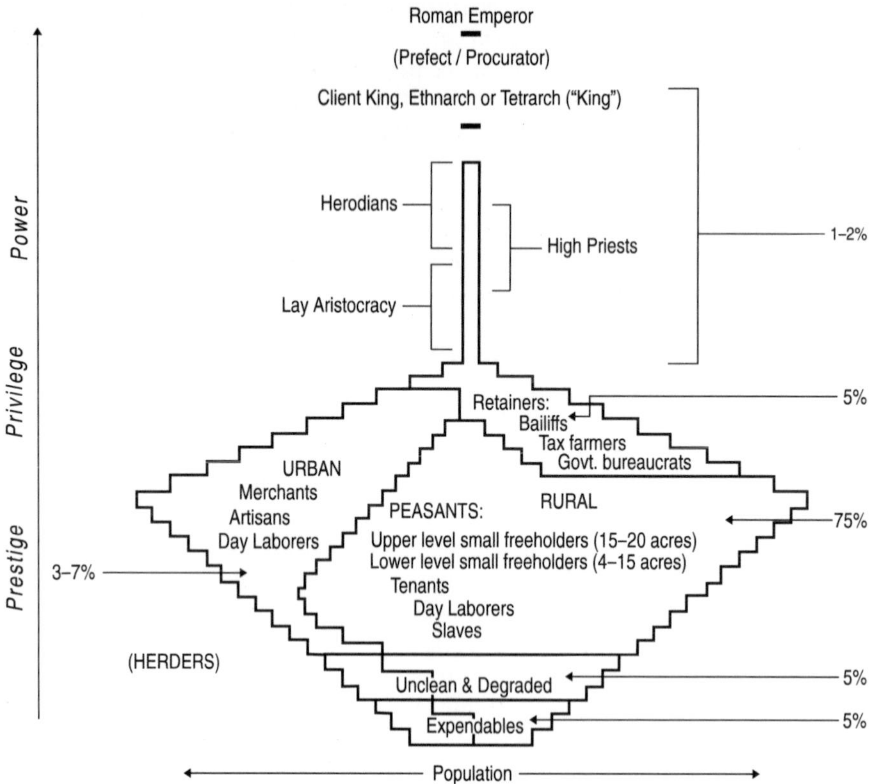

Also, only Matthew indicates that the *meek* will inherit *the earth* (5:5), a reference to the Jubilee Year (Leviticus 25) as an image of the realm from heaven (Matt. 6:12; 18:21–35; Luke 4:18–19).[10]

To what extent does Matthew reflect the dominant biblical perspective that views oppression as the fundamental cause of poverty?[11] Granted, the more obvious technical vocabulary for oppression is not common in Matthew (see "unjust/oppressors," 5:45; "injustice, wrong, harm," 20:13). However, when

9. The diagram is from Duling, "Matthew and Marginality," 651, and is used with permission. It is modified slightly from D. Fiensy, *The Social History of Palestine in the Herodian Period,* 158, based on G. and J. Lenski, *Human Societies,* 203, influenced by G. Alfödy, *Die römische Gesellschaft.*

10. Marcelo de Barros and José Luis Caravias, *Teología de la tierra* (Madrid: Paulinas, 1988); Roy H. May, *Los pobres de la tierra* (San José, Costa Rica: DEI, 1986); ET, *The Poor of the Land* (Maryknoll, N.Y.: Orbis, 1991); Sharon H. Ringe, *Jesus, Liberation, and the Biblical Jubilee* (Philadelphia: Fortress, 1985); Christopher J. H. Wright, "Jubilee, Year of," *ABD,* 3:1025–30.

11. Thomas D. Hanks, *God So Loved the Third World: The Biblical Vocabulary of Oppression,* trans. James C. Dekker (Maryknoll, N.Y.: Orbis, 1983), 33–39.

we recognize that persecution constitutes a religiously motivated expression of oppression in Matthew, his affinity with the Exodus paradigm becomes clear, since being persecuted for practicing liberating justice (5:10–12) forms the inclusion linking the final Beatitude with the first on those who show solidarity with the poor (5:3), while promise to the meek who are to inherit land (5:5) relates to the mourning of those who have lost their land due to exile and other mechanisms of oppression (5:4). Matthew is well aware of judicial mechanisms of oppression (see the more powerful "legal opponent, oppressor," 5:25). His narrative of Herod's violent oppression (2:16–20) shows his awareness of the social-political realities under Roman rule (see 5:40–41, 43–46). Matthew's denunciation of the scribes and Pharisees refers to mechanisms of oppression with metaphor ("burdens," 23:4) and synonyms ("robbery," 23:25; "lawlessness," 23:28) and concludes with indignant denunciations of violence (23:29–30). Violent oppressors are denounced as "serpents, offspring of vipers" (23:33; cf. 3:7, 10). Like →Mark, Matthew makes clear the link between the oppression and violence characteristic of the local temple-based political-religious oligarchy (23:38) and the destruction of the temple (24:15–28) and cosmic judgment (24:29–25:46; see oppression synonyms in 24:9, 12, 21, 29, 48–49; cf. the poor, oppressed, and weak in 25:35–39). As in James (5:1–9), so in Matthew, Jesus' decisive final intervention constitutes liberating justice for the poor and all the oppressed, including the Gentile nations (Matt. 12:15–21).

4. *The Realm of Heaven as God's Liberating Justice*

As John P. Meier points out, Matthew lacks the word that corresponds to the terms "morals" or "ethics," both categories of Greek philosophy. For Matthew the equivalent general category is that of "justice" (commonly but misleadingly rendered "righteousness" in English versions).[12] However, justice in Matthew (and the Bible as a whole) normally refers to the kind of liberating justice with which God acted to liberate the Hebrew slaves in the Exodus, which serves as the fundamental paradigm in biblical theology (3:15; 5:6; 6:33; cf. human justice in 5:10, 20; 6:1; 21:32; esp. 25:31–46).[13] Such liberating justice represents "God's will" (12:46–50), revealed to the disciples in Jesus' five discourses in Matthew, and is the fundamental characteristic of the realm of God (6:33; see also "realm *of God*" in 12:28; 19:24; 21:31, 43; Matthew, of course, prefers the synonym "realm *from heaven,*" used thirty-three times). Because he presents liberating justice as the fundamental characteristic of God's promised new order, Matthew's good news of the realm (4:23; 9:35; 24:14; cf. 26:13) is similar to Luke's "good news to the poor" (4:18).

12. John P. Meier, "Matthew, Gospel of," *ABD,* 4:640.

13. This was Jose P. Miranda's fundamental point in his classic liberationist study *Marx and the Bible: A Critique of the Philosophy of Oppression* (Maryknoll, N.Y.: Orbis, 1974). Miranda's understanding of "justice/righteousness" in the Bible as normally referring to God's liberating justice (from oppression) has been confirmed in the investigations of Karen Lebacqz, *Six Theories of Justice* (Minneapolis: Augsburg, 1986); *Justice in an Unjust World* (Minneapolis: Augsburg, 1987).

Careful examination of Matthew, where justice terminology (*dik-* words) is common (twenty-eight uses: twenty-six positively and two negatively [with the alpha privative, to signify "oppress," or "injustice"]), actually supports the picture from Q and →Mark, where *dik-* words are virtually absent. Thus, while in Luke's version of the Sermon on the Mount/Plain (Q), Jesus says, "Blessed are *you* who hunger now, for *you* will be satisfied" (Luke 6:21a), in Matthew's version Jesus says, "Blessed are *those* who hunger and thirst for liberating justice [*dikaiosunēn*], for *they* will be filled" (Matt. 5:6). The changes from "you" to "they" and the addition of "for liberating justice" are best explained as Matthew's own editorial additions that adapted Jesus' original teaching (Q) to later communities that included prosperous members who needed to learn to practice solidarity with the poor. Similarly, Luke reports Jesus as saying simply, "Seek God's realm and these things will be given to you as well" (Luke 12:31), but in Matthew's better-known version Jesus says, "Seek *first* God's realm *and his liberating justice* (*dikaiosunēn*) and *all* these things will be given to you as well" (Matt. 6:33). Again, while theoretically Jesus might well have made both statements verbatim, meticulous scholarship supports the conclusion that such additions probably represent the Gospel writers' interpretations and adaptations to their later contexts.

Matthew's context, like Paul's in Galatians and Romans, clearly reflects acute conflict with persecuting elements within Judaism (Matthew 23), and this would explain this evangelist's more proactive linguistic strategy to recapture the *dik-* words and use such justice language polemically against the persecutors, but with the Hebrew Bible meaning to reflect the Exodus paradigm and signify God's liberating justice for the poor and oppressed. Perhaps the best key to Matthew's proactive linguistic strategy and his intended meaning for the *dik-* terminology is his unique and climactic parable of the separation of the sheep and goats (Matt. 25:31–46). In this parable, which also is the hermeneutical key to his theology as a whole, the "just/righteous" (*dikaioi*, vv. 37, 46) are those more comfortable and affluent who put their lives at risk during a time of persecution to demonstrate loving solidarity with the hungry, thirsty, homeless, naked, sick, and imprisoned. Like the Liberator God of the Exodus, they function as salt and light to manifest God's liberating justice to the weak and oppressed.

The other clue to Matthew's subversive linguistic intentions in using *dik-* words is his literary device of inclusion whereby he introduces and closes his narrative with references to a Joseph who practices this kind of liberating justice: Joseph, who sided with Mary when she was accused of sexual immorality (1:19, the first *dik-* word in Matthew), and Joseph of Arimathea (27:57–60), who risked his social status to ask Pilate for Jesus' crucified body. Mark says only that Joseph of Arimathea was "honorable" (Mark 15:43), but Luke specifies that he was "good and just" (Luke 23:50). Matthew implies the wealthy Joseph's surpassing justice by honoring him with the name of "disciple" (Matt. 27:57; see 5:20).

Other uses of *dik-* words in Matthew include 3:15 (Jesus submits to John's baptism "to fulfill all justice"), 5:10 ("Blessed are those who are persecuted for practicing liberating justice, for theirs is the realm from heaven"), 5:20 ("the justice of the scribes and Pharisees"—ironic, as in →Mark 2:17), 6:1 ("Be careful not to do your acts of piety/justice publicly"), and 21:32, to Jewish religious-political authorities in the temple ("For John came to you to show you the way of liberating justice").

5. The Weak, Sick, and Physically Challenged

In his narrative portions between Jesus' five great discourses, Matthew continually shows us Jesus' compassion and solidarity (especially by touch) with the weak, the sick, the unclean, and the physically challenged. In his descriptions of Jesus' praxis, Matthew shows how Jesus' solidarity leads to miraculous healings:

- 4:23–24, "curing every disease (*noson*) and every sickness (*malakian*)... they brought to him all... afflicted (*kakōs*) with various diseases (*nosois*) and pains (*basanois*), demon-afflicted, moon-afflicted ["lunatics" = epileptics?], and paralytics, and he cured them"
- 8:16, "spirits... sick (*kakōs*)"
- 9:35, "curing every disease (*noson*) and every sickness (*malakian*)"
- 14:14, "sick (*arrōstous*)"
- 14:35, "sick (*kakōs*)"

Duling[14] also summarizes the specific kinds of those "involuntarily marginalized":

1. blind (*typhlos*): 9:27, 28 (two men); 11:5; 12:22; 15:14 (4x); 15:30–31; 20:30 (two men); 21:14
2. mutes (*kōphos*): 12:22 (2x; "blind and"); 9:32–33; 15:30–31
3. lame (*chōlos*): 11:5; 15:30–31; 18:8; 21:14
4. deaf (*kōphos*): 11:5
5. deformed (*kyllos*): 15:30–31
6. paralytics (*paralytikos*): 4:24; 8:6; 9:2 (2x), 6
7. demoniacs (*daimonizomenos*): 4:24; 8:16, 28–34; 15:21–38
8. epileptic (*selēniazomenos*): 4:24 (lit., "lunatic," crazed by the moon)
9. lepers (*lepros*, unclean): 8:2; 10:8; 11:5; 26:6
10. woman with hemorrhage (unclean): 9:20–22

14. Duling, "Matthew and Marginality," 653–54.

Furthermore, Matthew tells us how Jesus touched the body (unclean) of Jairus's daughter and raised her (9:25). In the Bible an illness represents the invasion of death's power, which is not unrelated to illnesses. Duling indicates that in Matthew, Jesus is invoked as "Son of David" principally in the cases of healing (see Isaiah 35).[15]

Traditional studies of the Gospels question or defend the historicity of the events (did it really happen? did it occur precisely in this way? or was it a trick, a coincidence, or only a psychosomatic healing?), or impose on the text philosophical (deistic) categories and questions (was it really "supernatural"?). Commonly ignored is the hermeneutical key (Matt. 25:31–46) of Jesus' praxis in solidarity with the physically challenged. Consequently, today few church buildings are accessible for them, and few worship services are signed for the deaf, or make available texts in Braille for the blind.[16] In addition, few church members avoid the common negative labels and words that injure.

6. *Women and Sexual Minorities*

Matthew emphasizes God's liberating justice, perhaps especially because he was a despised toll collector who celebrated his acceptance as Jesus' disciple with a banquet for other marginalized friends: publicans and prostitutes (9:9–13). Only Matthew informs us that women shared the table with Jesus—women of bad reputation.[17] Since toll collectors were despised and marginalized by the other Jews, these "apostate traitors," not surprisingly, developed an intimate relationship with the local sex workers. Near the end of his Gospel, in a denouncement of the hypocritical leaders, Matthew allows his euphemism ("sinners") to become quite explicit (21:31–32):

> Jesus said to them, "Truly I tell you, the *tax collectors* and *prostitutes* are going into the realm of God ahead of you. For John came to you in God's way of liberating justice and you did not believe him, but the *toll collectors* and *sex workers* believed him."

We must ask why Matthew, a young Jew and well instructed in the scriptures, ever would have chosen the despised profession of toll collector in Capernaum. If, however, he realized that he was attracted to persons of the same sex (in modern psychological terms, had a "homosexual orientation"), how a young pious Jew ends up marginalized as a toll collector is quite understandable. Since Jewish priests were expected to marry, the priesthood did not offer itself as a convenient closet for pious priestly descendants of homosexual orientation. The relationship with the local sex workers, then, would not have been due to heterosexual attraction but because both groups were

15. Ibid., 654 n. 48.

16. Nancy L. Eiesland, *The Disabled God: Toward a Liberation Theology of Disability* (Nashville: Abingdon, 1994); Nancy L. Eiesland and Don E. Saliers, *Human Disability and the Service of God: Theological Perspectives on Disability* (Nashville: Abingdon, 1998).

17. Duling, "Matthew and Marginality," 655; cf. Kathleen E. Corley, "Were the Women around Jesus Really Prostitutes? Women in the Context of Greco-Roman Meals," *Society of Biblical Literature 1989 Seminar Papers*, ed. David J. Lull (Atlanta: Scholars Press, 1989), 487–521.

marginalized targets of society's contempt. All this, of course, is a hypothesis, but alternative hypotheses (Matthew was 100 percent heterosexual, but just never found the right woman?) all look considerably less likely. At any rate, Matthew, who emphasizes the law and liberating justice, also highlights Jesus' choice to include among his disciples and friends toll collectors and sex workers, both disgustingly "unclean/dirty" in his society.

To open his Gospel, however, Matthew first dons gray pinstripe and necktie to reassure us of his conservative credentials with what at first appears to be a rather boring genealogy (1:1–17)—undoubtedly quite comforting to the original Jewish readers. Just as the reader is nodding off, however, Matthew starts slipping a series of four women's names into what had come to be an exclusively male club. Even more shocking, our toll collector lacks the taste to choose only mothers with a good reputation (Sarah, Abraham's wife?), but seems fixated on scandalous women: (1) Tamar, who pretended to be a harlot in order to produce a son with her father-in-law Judah (Genesis 38); (2) Rahab, the Gentile sex worker of Jericho (Joshua 2); (3) Ruth, the Moabite, unclean Gentile, who seduced the pious Boaz, in accord with the tradition of levirate marriage (book of Ruth); and (4) Bathsheba, Uriah's wife, who after David's adultery and Uriah's death became the king's eighth wife (2 Samuel 11).

Does all this properly prepare the reader for Jesus' birth—"illegitimate," a "bastard" son, as his contemporaries believed—into a sexual minority excluded from Hebrew worship (Deut. 23:2)? Joseph marries Mary, already pregnant, although he knows the child is not his own, and with his gesture of solidarity and liberating justice, frees them from the worst shame and punishment (Deut. 22:20–24 prescribes the death penalty). In ancient times shepherds were not known as paragons of sexual purity and virtue, but Luke's angels announced Jesus' birth to them first—an obvious faux pas. Not to be outdone, Matthew similarly celebrates Jesus' royal birth by summoning pagan astrologers—a profession of even more dubious sexual reputation. All (three?) apparently were unmarried and had traveled for two years claiming to be guided by a star. In the New Testament only Matthew explicitly refers to Jesus as conceived and born of a virgin (see under Luke), but questions regarding the possibly midrashic genre of this portion of Matthew leave even some defenders of biblical inerrancy with questions (see above, Literary Genre).

The strange circumstances of Jesus' birth, however interpreted, left him and Mary vulnerable to abusive language (John 8:41; Mark 6:3). That would explain Jesus' strong prohibition of abusive language in the Sermon on the Mount, which Warren Johansson concludes refers to the contemptuous language commonly directed against sexual minorities: "But I say to you, if you are angry with a brother or sister, you will be liable to judgment; and if you call your brother 'faggot' [Greek: *raka;* Aramaic: *reyqa'*], you will be liable to the council [Sanhedrin]" (Matt. 5:22).[18] Abusive expressions like "faggot" or

18. Warren Johansson, "Whosoever Shall Say to His Brother, *Racha,*" in *Homosexuality and Religion and Philosophy,* ed. Wayne R. Dynes and Stephen Donaldson, Studies in Homosexuality

"sissy," so common in patriarchal societies, continue to contribute to suicides, especially of young lesbians and gays (cf. the sins of the tongue in the chapter on James).

Immediately after the Sermon on the Mount (chaps. 5–7), Matthew narrates ten miracles (chaps. 8–9), mainly healings (cf. the ten plagues of the Exodus). The first tells how Jesus "cleansed" a leper, and in the second Jesus responds to an unclean Roman military officer whose beloved slave had become paralyzed (8:5–13 // Luke 7:1–10 = Q). Jesus offered to accompany the centurion to his home, but he declined the offer. Such Roman military officers, having chosen a career abroad that involved leaving potential wives in Italy (convenient cover for those who didn't want a wife anyway), commonly took a young male slave as a lover[19] (→Luke).

Significantly, Jesus neither pries into the privacy of the relationship nor even dispatches them to a priest for a bit of "ex-gay torture," but simply heals the youth with a word from a distance. By blessing the Capernaum centurion's relationship with his beloved slave, Jesus flaunted the common prejudices of his culture and furthered his reputation as a "friend of toll collectors and sinners" (Matt. 11:19). Luke informs us that this centurion had sponsored the construction of the synagogue in Capernaum (Luke 7:5), and in 1968 archaeologists discovered that the north side of Simon Peter's large house was below the balcony of the synagogue.[20]

Matthew basically follows Mark in showing how Jesus sought to protect women with a prohibition against divorce (19:1–9 // Mark 10:1–12), but Matthew establishes an exception in cases of *porneia,* irresponsible sexual conduct. Then, only in Matthew, Jesus expounds his version of the "science of eunuchology" (Matt. 19:11–12). Perhaps the purpose of the law of Moses that prohibited the participation of eunuchs in worship (Deut. 23:1) was to eliminate the pagan practice of this type of "sacrifice." After the Exile, when many male Israelites suffered castration as prisoners of war, Third Isaiah proclaimed that God accepts eunuchs (Isaiah 56:1–8). The good reputation of Nehemiah, probably a eunuch as indicated by his court function in Persia, may have helped produce Third Isaiah's radical new message of inclusion. Jesus, however, takes us a step further, pointing out the existence of three types of eunuchs: those born so, those who suffer castration, and those who choose

---

12 (New York: Garland, 1992), 212–14; reprinted from *Dabiron and Gay Books Bulletin* 10 (1984): 2–4.

19. Michael Gray-Fow, "Pederasty, the Scantian Law and the Roman Army," *Journal of Psychohistory* 13 (1986): 449–60; Donald Mader, "The *Entimos Pais* [Beloved Slave] of Matthew 8:5–13 and Luke 7:1–10," in *Homosexuality and Religion and Philosophy,* ed. Wayne R. Dynes and Stephen Donaldson, Studies in Homosexuality 12 (New York: Garland, 1992), 223–35; Tom Horner, *Jonathan Loved David* (Philadelphia: Westminster, 1978), 122; James E. Miller, "The Centurion and His Slave Boy" (paper presented at the annual meeting of the Society of Biblical Literature, San Francisco, November 22–25, 1997).

20. Virgilio C. Corbo, "Capernaum," in *ABD,* 1:866–69; for contemporary significance, see under Luke. Only Matthew explicitly links the episode about the centurion and his beloved slave with Peter's house (8:5–13, 14–17; but cf. the Capernaum synagogue and Peter's house in Mark 1:29 and Luke 4:38!).

not to marry for the sake of God's realm. These diverse eunuchs should not be despised but accepted as the new model in God's realm—and they included unmarried leaders like Jesus and Paul, who took the place of Israel's married priests. As in modern India, the word "eunuch" in the Bible may well be a euphemism, a generic term for various types of sexual minorities, especially those who do not marry or have children.

At the end of his Gospel, Matthew follows Mark, indicating that the first notice of the resurrection was given to Mary Magdalene and the other Mary (Matt. 28:1–10; Mark 16:1–8 (+ 9); cf. Matt. 27:56, 61; Mark 15:47; John 20:1–18). Mary Magdalene, from whom Jesus had cast out seven demons (Luke 8:2), had followed him from Galilee (Mark 15:40–41). She was unmarried, with her own economic resources and an independent life. The fact that Mary traveled in the company of single men and shared their table would have given her a bad reputation in her patriarchal cultural context. According to much later ecclesiastical tradition, Mary Magdalene was a prostitute, a coherent hypothesis, given her lifestyle. At any rate, any mention of husband and children is lacking, and for this reason she appears in a sexual minority in the Gospels. Her privileged relationship with Jesus, as the first witness and apostle of the resurrection, became an important theme in the apocryphal literature. Matthew, by insisting that toll collectors and prostitutes would have priority in entering into the realm of God (21:31–32), may thus support the identification of Mary Magdalene as a prostitute—similarly, when he injects prostitutes into Jesus' genealogy at the beginning of his Gospel and at the end features Mary of Magdala (a town of ill repute). This literary technique of repeating or returning to the end of a text the theme of the beginning, quite common in the Bible, is called "inclusion."

In *The Gospel of Mary,* an apocryphal book written ca. 100–150 C.E., Mary Magdalene and Martha argue with Peter and his brother Andrew concerning authority in the church. Later tradition identified Mary both with the adulteress woman in John (8:1–11) and the prostitute of Luke (7:35–50). Numerous contemporary feminist studies seek to refute the tradition that Mary Magdalene was a prostitute.[21] However, would it not be better to follow the example of Jesus and Matthew/Levi and defend the dignity not only of women in general but also that of sex workers?

The great commission at the end of Matthew (28:18–20), directed only to the male disciples, corresponds to the genealogy at the beginning of the Gospel (1:1–17). The genealogy in 1:17 is a literary genre that, traditionally, includes only men. However, Matthew subverts the genre, injecting four "unclean"

---

21. Richard Atwood, *Mary Magdalene in the New Testament Gospels and Early Tradition* (Bern, Germany: Lang, 1993); Esther de Boer, *Mary Magdalene: Beyond the Myth,* trans. John Bowden (Harrisburg, Pa.: Trinity, 1997); Susan Haskins, *Mary Magdalen: Myth and Metaphor* (New York: Harcourt, Brace, 1993); Carla Ricci, *Mary Magdalene and Many Others: Women Who Followed Jesus,* trans. Paul Burns (Minneapolis: Fortress, 1994); Jane Schaberg, "How Mary Magdalene Became a Whore," *Bible Review* 8, no. 5 (October 1992): 30–37; Mary R. Thompson, *Mary of Magdala: Apostle and Leader* (Mahwah, N.J.: Paulist Press, 1995).

women into Jesus' genealogy. Similarly, when we read the great commission in the light of its preceding context, clearly it is not intended to exclude women. On the contrary, Jesus here forgives his repentant male disciples and invites them to work together in the apostolic and missionary proclamation already initiated by the women. Consequently, although the great commission is addressed to male "losers," by no means does it exclude the faithful women.

When Matthew himself (source M) refers to women, they almost always represent sexual minorities (see also his parable of the ten virgins, 25:1–13). The only exception is Pilate's wife, who affirms Jesus' innocence (27:19). The "mother of the sons of Zebedee" (20:20) apparently abandoned her husband, Zebedee, to accompany Jesus (27:55–56; cf. 4:21–22). Matthew incorporates several positive accounts of women from Mark, but his own focus is on the women and men who represent sexual minorities. Feminist studies have done well to emphasize Mary of Magdala's significant leadership role, but this role may be maintained without prejudice against her sexual minority status, even if this involved the profession of sex worker (see further under Luke).

7. Peter and Mrs. Peter: Scandals for the Vatican?

Matthew's ill-deserved reputation as some kind of traitorous Log Cabin (Re?)publican stems largely from misunderstanding his teaching about Torah and about Peter as the rock (legalistic Protestant fundamentalism worldwide and centuries of Vatican bigotries are a lot to blame on any Gospel writer!). Following Mark, Matthew indicates that Peter had a mother-in-law, which has compelled even apologists for Vatican sexual ideology finally to concede that in all probability (miracles being ever possible), Peter must have been married (Matt. 8:14–15 // Mark 1:29–31). Perhaps overwhelmed with his "sexual minority" status within the twelve apostles (as the only married apostle), Peter apparently left this wife for a time to itinerate with Jesus (see Luke 14:20, 26; 18:28–29). Some twenty-five years later, however, Paul indicates that Peter traveled accompanied by a wife (1 Cor. 9:5). In the Gospels only Peter's mother-in-law is mentioned; only Paul refers to Peter traveling with a wife, but leaves her nameless (following the patriarchal tradition, the Vatican has long hesitated to name her a saint or ordain women priests).

The multiplication of the loaves and fishes, the only miracle recorded in all four Gospels (Mark 6:31–44 // Matt. 14:13–21 // Luke 9:10–17 // John 6:1–15), is followed by the sign of Jesus walking on the water (Mark 6:45–52 // John 6:16–21). This miracle is omitted by Luke, but Matthew includes it (14:22–27) and then records that Peter tried to imitate Jesus and almost drowned (Matt. 14:28–33). The waters over which Jesus and Peter walked represent the forces of chaos, oppression, persecution, and violence ("the gates of Hades") that threatened the existence of the new community. Peter, the "rock" upon which the church is constructed, almost disappears in the tempestuous sea. Peter trying to walk on the sea may also remind us of his efforts to dominate the tumultuous desires of the heart, at times more effective in destroying lives and communities than the exterior forces of persecution (Matt. 15:19–20).

In addition, only Matthew narrates the miracle concerning the coin that Peter found in the mouth of the fish and that Jesus commanded him to use to pay the temple tax for both of them (17:24–27). This may look like pro-Vatican favoritism on Jesus' part, but fishers of the period had to pay almost ruinous taxes.[22]

Matthew is the only Gospel that speaks explicitly of the "assembly/church" (*ekklēsia,* 16:17–19; 18:17), a mixed community that includes both the good and the bad (13:24–30, 47–50; 22:1–14), and of course, only Matthew includes Jesus' famous words to Peter. After Peter confesses Jesus as the "Christ/Messiah" (following Mark 8:27–30; // Luke 9:18–21), Jesus describes Peter as the "rock," the foundation of the new sect, with authority to bind and to loose (Matt. 16:18–19). In this context Peter's authority refers to norms of behavior in the new community, and in Acts 10–11 Peter accepts the Gentiles who believe in Jesus without obligating them to be circumcised. Later, however, Jesus confers on the entire church a similar authority of binding and loosing, and the norms of conduct thus established imply decisions of including or excluding members (Matt. 18:15–20).

After centuries of controversy, most scholars now agree that Jesus does designate Peter-Cephas as the rock (Greek: *petra;* Aramaic: *cefa*). However, the notion that Peter would have successors (popes) is absent in the text, and the history of the new sect in the first four centuries offers no support for the idea of the popes as successors to Peter.[23] And how could Peter, the only married apostle, become the first for a tradition of popes who are forbidden to marry?

Peter fulfilled his foundational function for the new sect with the keys when he opened the door of the realm, for the Jews on Pentecost (Acts 2) and for the Gentiles with the conversion of Cornelius (Acts 10–11). Later, however, both James's authority in Jerusalem (Acts 15) and that of Paul in Antioch (Gal. 2:11–14) appear to be superior to that of Peter. After the death of the apostles, the authorities of the new sect in the first centuries were Christ himself (1 Cor. 3:11), the apostolic testimony preserved in the New Testament (Eph. 2:20; Rev. 21:14), the Holy Spirit and the ministry of the prophets (Eph. 2:20; 4:11), and the entire community of the people of God (the church), with their elders, teachers, and other leaders (1 Pet. 5:1).

8. The Law

Matthew's perspective on Torah is diverse and complex to the point of rigorous dialectic (or blatant contradiction).[24] If Matthew really intended simply to

---

22. K. C. Hanson, unpublished paper cited in Duling, "Matthew and Marginality," 654 n. 51.

23. Raymond E. Brown, *An Introduction to the New Testament* (New York: Doubleday, 1997), 221–22.

24. Blomberg, *Jesus and the Gospels,* 249–51; Brown, *Introduction to the New Testament,* 179; N. T. Wright, *Jesus and the Victory of God* (Minneapolis: Fortress, 1996), Jesus' "redefinition of

attack antinomianism by emphasizing the divine authority of the law in every jot and tittle (Matt. 5:17–20), obviously he would be much more wed to Torah than Paul, who affirmed that the law functioned basically "to empower sin" (Rom. 7:5, 13) and that Christians are "free of the law" (Rom. 7:6; Gal. 5:1). Matthew, however, is more subtle and subversive, since he presents Jesus as affirming the authority of the law, but himself fulfilling it (5:17–20); and in the same sermon he also has Jesus radicalize and internalize the law (5:21–48). Later in Matthew, Jesus details the law's essential elements: love for God and for neighbor (22:34–40; 19:18–19), the Golden Rule (7:12), mercy instead of sacrifice (9:13; 12:7), liberating justice, mercy, and faithfulness (23:23).

Jesus' praxis and teaching, in fact, frequently transcend the law: he rejects the law's multiple prescriptions concerning unclean food (15:10–20; cf. Mark 7:18–19); prohibits vengeance, oaths, and divorce (5:31–39); and insists on the purity of the heart instead of preoccupation with externals (15:1–20; cf. 5:21–30). From his "But *I* say to you . . . " (5:21–48) we move through Matthew to Jesus' final words, which contain the phrase "everything that I have commanded you" (28:18–20), making clear that Jesus' own words, no longer those of Moses, have become the supreme norm. Both in the five discourses, which replace or reinterpret the law of Moses, and in Matthew's narrations Jesus imprints on his disciples' minds "the will of the Parent" that now transcends the five books of Moses' law and best enables his disciples to "reflect critically" on their praxis.

In his final discourse, however, Jesus again echoes the positive pro-Torah perspective of 5:17–20 (structural inclusion) and surprisingly refers to the authority of the scribes and the Pharisees who sat on "Moses' seat" (23:1–3). Whether that seat simply was a metaphor or a real seat in certain synagogues, Jesus probably did not commend their authority to *interpret* the books of Moses but to their *possession of the manuscripts* and the social control over the reading of them.[25] Before the invention of the printing press, the scarce copies of the manuscripts were expensive. In Matt. 23:1–3 Jesus recognizes that his followers, a poor messianic sect within first-century Judaism, had to have recourse to the scribes and the Pharisees to know the content of the books of the Pentateuch. But throughout Matthew's Gospel Jesus denounces the distorted interpretations of the scriptures commonly committed by the scribes and Pharisees.

In this final discourse, however, Jesus' climactic parable is the separation of the goats from the sheep in the final judgment (25:31–46), the decisive "hermeneutical key" to Matthew's theology of law and gospel. Jesus here makes clear that when God finally judges, no one will be excluded from the realm for the lack of compliance with some cultic detail of Leviticus, but only for the lack of compassion and loving solidarity expressed in a praxis of

---

Torah" (consistent with his redefinition of nation and family), 287–303, 432; Hagner, *Matthew 1–13,* 102–10, "hyperbole"; Gundry, *Matthew,* 78–82, a "forceful attack on antinomianism."

25. Mark Allan Powell, "Do and Keep What Moses Says (Matthew 23:2–7)," *Journal of Biblical Literature* 114, no. 3 (1995): 419–35.

liberating justice with the poor, the oppressed, the weak, and the needy (see also 28:20).[26]

Bibliography

Atwood, Richard. *Mary Magdalene in the New Testament Gospels and Early Tradition.* Bern, Germany: Lang, 1993.

Balch, David L., ed. *Social History of the Matthean Community: Cross-Disciplinary Approaches.* Minneapolis: Fortress, 1991. Includes studies concerning gender roles.

Barros, Marcelo de, and José Luis Caravias. *Teología de la tierra.* Madrid: Paulinas, 1988.

Bird, Phyllis A. *Missing Persons and Mistaken Identities: Women and Gender in Ancient Israel.* Minneapolis: Fortress, 1997.

Blomberg, Craig L. *Matthew.* The New American Commentary 22. Nashville: Broadman, 1992.

Boer, Esther de. *Mary Magdalene: Beyond the Myth.* Trans. John Bowden. Harrisburg, Pa.: Trinity, 1997.

Boring, M. Eugene. "The Gospel of Matthew." In *The New Interpreter's Bible,* 8:88–505. Nashville: Abingdon, 1995.

Carter, Warren. *Matthew and the Margins: A Socio-Political and Religious Commentary.* Sheffield: Sheffield Academic Press, 2000.

Corley, Kathleen E. "Were the Women around Jesus Really Prostitutes? Women in the Context of Greco-Roman Meals." In *Society of Biblical Literature 1989 Seminar Papers,* ed. David J. Lull. Atlanta: Scholars Press, 1989.

Corbo, Virgilio C. "Capernaum." *ABD,* 1:866–69.

Crosby, Michael H. *House of Disciples: Church, Economics, and Justice in Matthew.* Maryknoll, N.Y.: Orbis, 1988.

Duling, Dennis C. "Matthew and Marginality." In *Society of Biblical Literature 1993 Seminar Papers,* 642–71. Atlanta: Scholars Press, 1993.

Good, Deirdre. "Eunuchs in the Matthean Community." Paper presented at the Society of Biblical Literature annual meeting. Boston, 1999.

Gray-Fow, Michael. "Pederasty, the Scantian Law and the Roman Army." *Journal of Psychohistory* 13 (1986): 449–60.

Gundry, Robert H. *Matthew: A Commentary on His Handbook for a Mixed Church under Persecution.* Grand Rapids: Eerdmans, 1994.

Hagner, Donald A. *Matthew 1–13.* WBC 33A. Dallas: Word, 1993.

———. *Matthew 14–28.* WBC 33B. Dallas: Word, 1995.

Hanks, Thomas D. "La navidad según San Mateo." *Misión* 5 (December 1986): 3–4.

Haskins, Susan. *Mary Magdalen: Myth and Metaphor.* New York: Harcourt, Brace, 1993.

Howell, D. B. *Matthew's Inclusive Story.* JSNTSup 42. Sheffield: Sheffield Academic Press, 1990.

Humphries-Brooks, Stephenson. "Indicators of Social Organization and Status in Matthew's Gospel." In *Society of Biblical Literature 1991 Seminar Papers,* ed. Eugene Lovering Jr., 31–49. Atlanta: Scholars Press, 1991.

26. Pikaza, *Hermanos de Jesús.*

Johansson, Warren. "Whosoever Shall Say to His Brother, *Racha,*" In *Homosexuality and Religion and Philosophy.* Studies in Homosexuality 12, ed. Wayne R. Dynes and Stephen Donaldson, 212–14. New York: Garland, 1992; reprinted from *Dabiron and Gay Books Bulletin* 10 (1984): 2–4.

Johnson, Luke T. "The New Testament's Anti-Jewish Slander and the Conventions of Ancient Rhetoric." *Journal of Biblical Literature* 108 (1989): 419–41.

Keener, Craig. *A Commentary on the Gospel of Matthew.* Grand Rapids: Eerdmans, 1999.

Lapide, Pinchas. *The Sermon on the Mount: Utopia or Program for Action?* Trans. Arlene Swidler. Maryknoll, N.Y.: Orbis, 1986.

Lebacqz, Karen. *Six Theories of Justice.* Minneapolis: Augsburg, 1986.

———. *Justice in an Unjust World.* Minneapolis: Augsburg, 1987.

Levine, Amy-Jill. "Matthew." In *The Women's Bible Commentary,* ed. Carol A. Newsom and Sharon H. Ringe, 339–49. Louisville: Westminster John Knox, 1998.

Mader, Donald. "The *Entimos Pais* [Beloved Slave] of Matthew 8:5–13 and Luke 7:1–10." In *Homosexuality and Religion and Philosophy,* ed. Wayne R. Dynes and Stephen Donaldson, 223–35. Studies in Homosexuality 12. New York: Garland, 1992.

May, Roy H. *Los Pobres de la tierra.* San José, Costa Rica: DEI, 1986. ET, *The Poor of the Land.* Maryknoll, N.Y.: Orbis, 1991.

McKnight, Scott. "A Loyal Critic: Matthew's Polemic with Judaism in Theological Perspective." In *Anti-Semitism and Early Christianity,* ed. Craig A. Evans and Donald A. Hagner, 55–79. Minneapolis: Fortress, 1993.

Meier, John P. "Matthew, Gospel of." *ABD,* 4:622–41.

Miller, James E. "The Centurion and His Slave Boy." Paper presented at the annual meeting of the Society of Biblical Literature, 1997. To be published in *Theology and Sexuality,* 2001.

Overman, J. Andrew. *Church and Community in Crisis: The Gospel According to Matthew.* Valley Forge, Pa.: Trinity, 1996.

Pikaza, Xavier. *Hermanos de Jesús y servidores de los más pequeños (Mt 25, 31–46).* Salamanca, Spain: Sígueme, 1984.

Pitre, Brant James. "Marginal Elites: Matthew 19:12 and the Social and Political Dimensions of Becoming 'Eunuchs for the Sake of the Kingdom.'" Paper presented at the Society of Biblical Literature annual meeting, Boston, 1999.

Powell, Mark Allan. "Do and Keep What Moses Says (Matthew 23:2–7)." *Journal of Biblical Literature* 114, no. 3 (1995): 419–35.

Ricci, Carla. *Mary Magdalene and Many Others: Women Who Followed Jesus.* Trans. Paul Burns. Minneapolis: Fortress, 1994.

Saldarini, Anthony J. "Asceticism and the Gospel of Matthew." In *Asceticism and the New Testament.* Ed. Leif E. Vaage and Vincent L. Wimbush, 11–27. New York: Routledge, 1999.

Schaberg, Jane. "How Mary Magdalene Became a Whore." *Bible Review* 8, no. 5 (October 1992): 30–37.

———. *The Illegitimacy of Jesus: A Feminist Theological Interpretation of the Infancy Narratives.* San Francisco: Harper & Row, 1987.

Stanton, Graham N. *A Gospel for a New People: Studies in Matthew.* Edinburgh: T. & T. Clark, 1992; Louisville: Westminster John Knox, 1993.

Thompson, Mary R. *Mary of Magdala: Apostle and Leader.* Mahwah, N.J.: Paulist Press, 1995.

Wainwright, Elaine. "The Gospel of Matthew." In *Searching the Scriptures,* vol. 2, *A Feminist Commentary,* ed. Elisabeth Schüssler Fiorenza, 635–77. New York: Crossroad, 1994.

———. *Shall We Look for Another: A Feminist Rereading of the Matthean Jesus.* Maryknoll, N.Y.: Orbis, 1998.

Weber, Kathleen. "Plot and Matthew." In *Society of Biblical Literature 1996 Seminar Papers,* 400–431. Atlanta: Scholars Press, 1996.

Wilson, Nancy. *Our Tribe: Queer Folks, God, Jesus, and the Bible.* San Francisco: HarperCollins, 1995.

Wright, Christopher J. H. "Jubilee, Year of." *ABD,* 3:1025–30.

Chapter 2

MARK

Good News for the Sick and the Physically Challenged

Outline

1. Preparation, 1:1–13: John the Baptist's proclamation; Jesus' baptism and temptation

2. Jesus' Ministry in Galilee, 1:14–7:23

   Jesus proclaims his good news to the poor, 1:14–15

   Call of Peter and Andrew, James and John, 1:16–20

   An exemplary (hectic) day in Capernaum, 1:21–34

   Evangelistic/healing ministry throughout Galilee (leper cleansed), 1:35–45

   Conflict with regional religious-political authorities, 2:1–3:6

   Popularity, designation of twelve apostles, 3:7–19

   Jesus' conflict with his mother and brothers, 3:20–21, 31–34 (the scribes' slander, 3:22–30)

   Five parables depict God's just new order, 4:1–34

   Four miracles anticipate God's just new order, 4:35–5:43

   Unbelief in Nazareth, mission of the twelve apostles, 6:1–13

   Herod has John the Baptist executed, 6:14–29

   Three miracles: Jesus feeds (five thousand), walks on water, heals, 6:30–56

   Conflict with the Pharisees about their traditions, 7:1–23

3. Jesus' Ministry beyond Galilee, 7:24–8:30

   Three miracle stories: two healings, feeding of four thousand, 7:24–8:10

   Conflict: the ideologies (yeast) of the Pharisees and of Herod, 8:11–21

   Jesus heals a blind man, 8:22–26

   Peter outs the closeted Messiah, 8:27–30

4. Toward Jerusalem, 8:31–10:52

   First passion announcement, 8:31–33

   Conditions for discipleship, 8:34–9:1

   Transfiguration: martyrdom and glorification anticipated, 9:2–13

   Jesus heals a "demonized" epileptic, 9:14–29

   Second passion announcement, 9:30–32

   Seven teachings: authentic greatness, use of Jesus' name, solidarity with the disciples, scandals, divorce, children, a wealthy young man, 9:33–10:31

   Third passion announcement, 10:32–34

   Call to sacrificial service, 10:35–45

   Jesus heals a blind man, 10:46–52

5. Passion Week in Jerusalem, 11:1–13:36

   Festive but humble entry, 11:1–11

   Jesus expels traders from the temple, 11:15–19

   Day of questions: Conflict over Jesus' subversive authority

   Sign of the barren fig tree, 11:12–14 and 20–26

   Three questions, plus Jesus' decisive fourth, 11:27–12:40

   A poor widow's offering in the temple, 12:41–44

   Coming consummation of God's just new order, 13:1–36

6. Jesus' Death and Resurrection, 14:1–16:8

   Contrasts: male conspiracy and betrayal; a woman anoints Jesus, 14:1–11

   Passover supper with eucharist, 14:12–26

   Disciples' failures: Jesus prophesies Peter's three denials, 14:27–31

   Agony in Gethsemane while three disciples sleep, 14:32–42

   Oppressive, corrupt authorities, 14:43–15:39

   Jesus' arrest and Mark's escape, 14:43–50

   Jesus before the Jewish Sanhedrin, 14:51–65

   Peter's three denials, 14:66–72

   Jesus before the Roman governor Pilate, 15:1–16

   Jesus mocked, tortured, and crucified, 15:17–39

   Even faithful women flee (as Mark had done), 15:40–16:8

   The empty tomb: God's promise versus human failures, 16:1–8

   [Later addition: Jesus' appearances, 16:9–20]

Commentary

Mark not only is the oldest but also the shortest of our four canonical Gospels (sixteen chapters, some twenty pages; cf. Matthew 1–28; Luke 1–24; John 1–21). However, Mark is not always the most concise, often providing significant details omitted by Matthew and Luke. Who was this creative genius who, shortly before the fall of Jerusalem (70 C.E.), wrote our oldest Gospel (69 C.E.?), which then served as the basic source for both Matthew and Luke? Though not an apostle, Mark probably reveals his identity as an eyewitness, at least of Jesus' arrest, when, as his Gospel states, all the male apostles "deserted him and fled" (14:50). Mark then adds, "A certain young man was following [Jesus], wearing nothing but a linen cloth. They caught hold of him, but he left the linen cloth and ran off naked" (14:51–52).

Perhaps never has such a serious book been "signed" in such a scandalous form. This may indicate that Mark, after a difficult life with considerable mischief and many persecutions, maintained his humility and sense of humor. Ironically, his Gospel's scroll may have suffered a fate similar to that of its author—losing its "cloak"—in that the final verses, 16:9–20, are a later addition. Possibly they cover the Gospel's "nudity" after the disappearance of an original conclusion, perhaps due to the persecution and flight of the author or original recipients. Most specialists, however, now conclude that 16:1–8 represents Mark's original conclusion.[1] Like Mark himself, Jesus is seen in this Gospel as being characteristically "in a hurry": "immediately" (*euthus*) occurs forty times in Mark, although this is not faithfully reflected in our modern translations (see 1:10, 12, 18, 20, 21, 23, 28, 30; cf. 1:37–38). Like Mark, this "hurried" Jesus ends up with the cultural shame of being naked (15:20, 24), but crucified. Mark presents Jesus not only as somewhat in a hurry but also as a man of action, of few words, with a focus on healing miracles as the fundamental element of his praxis. Nevertheless, when Mark includes elements of Jesus' teachings, they are worthy of special attention because often Mark's version appears to represent the original and most radical form of Jesus' teaching.

If Mark was Paul and Peter's companion, we can understand why his Gospel has such a strong focus on Jesus' redeeming death, the theme that dominates the second half of the Gospel (8:31–16:8, after Peter's confession). With but little exaggeration, Mark's Gospel has been described as a passion narrative with a preface. Therefore, to think of Mark as a biography is not accurate.

---

1. Andrew T. Lincoln, "The Promise and the Failure," *Journal of Biblical Literature* 108, no. 2 (summer 1989): 283–300; Joel F. Williams, "Literary Approaches to the End of Mark's Gospel," *Journal of the Evangelical Theological Society* 42, no. 1 (March 1999): 21–35. Mark alone, as read by his original readers, may not have appeared so shockingly unclad. However, when canonically enthroned in company with Luke, Matthew, and John (all royally decked with their elaborate accounts of Jesus' resurrection appearances), poor Mark began to look like Adam and Eve fresh in the flesh from Eden: an emperor with no clothes! This would have prompted anxious theologians and scribes to hastily stitch their fig leaf "proper conclusions" (Mark 16:9–20 and a kind of Calvin Klein "brief" alternative; see NRSV, HCSB notes).

Nor may Mark be characterized as work of modern, scientific historiography. Rather, Mark created a new literary genre, based on historical events, but (as with all history) selecting and interpreting his data, a proclamation of the "good news" to the poor (explicitly affirmed in Luke 4:18, but already implicit in Mark 1:1). This new literary genre (Gospel), created by Mark's inspired genius, was then adapted by Luke and Matthew, who added much more teaching, birth narratives, and Jesus' postresurrection appearances.

To understand Mark's intention we must observe closely certain characteristics of the *structure* of the Gospel (see the outline above). Mark included blocks of material concerning Jesus' praxis (especially miracle stories) and teachings already brought together in oral traditions, as well as Peter's teaching.

1. The Oppressed Poor and Liberating Justice

Only Mark explicitly says that Jesus himself was a carpenter (6:3; cf. Matt. 13:55, "*son* of a carpenter," less offensive to elitist Greek prejudice against manual labor). Mark employs the word "poor" (*ptōchos*) only five times in three contexts (10:21, the young rich man; 12:42–43, the widow's offering; 14:5, 7, the anointing at Bethany). However, a careful reading will uncover many indirect references to poverty: the lifestyle of John the Baptist (1:6; cf. 6:17, 27) and of Jesus himself (6:3; 11:12; cf. 14:65; 15:15, 19); the voluntary privations of his disciples (1:18, 20; 2:23–25; 6:8–9, 36–37; 9:41; 10:28–31). The low socioeconomic level of the "multitudes"[2] and their surroundings are reflected in Jesus' teaching (2:21, the use of old patched clothing; see 5:2–3, 5; 7:11–13; 8:1–2; 12:1–2). Such evidence supports Paul's explicit affirmation: "For you know the generous act of our Lord Jesus Christ, that though he was rich, yet for your sakes he *became poor,* so that by his poverty you might become rich" (2 Cor. 8:9). This process of impoverishment, confirmed by the birth narratives added in Matthew and Luke, culminates in the crucifixion, where Jesus was stripped of his clothing, tortured, abandoned by his male friends, and even deprived of his awareness of God's presence (Mark 15:34). Guided by such evidence, Wolfgang Stegemann concludes, "The movement . . . within Judaism in Palestine associated with the name of Jesus was a movement *of the poor for the poor.* . . . Probably neither Jesus nor his first disciples were professional beggars, yet they shared the desperate situation of many of their fellow country folk—particularly in Galilee—barely avoiding utter poverty."[3] Jesus' identification as a carpenter in an insignificant Galilean village suggests the situation of a day laborer.

Mark probably wrote his Gospel from Rome for poor churches of Syria, occupied by the Romans (and paying crushing taxes to the empire), in a period of war and persecution (67–70 C.E.) and before a significant number of more affluent members would have joined. The infrequency of explicit references

2. Ched Myers, *Binding the Strong Man: A Political Reading of Mark's Story of Jesus* (Maryknoll, N.Y.: Orbis, 1988), 120; Thomas D. Hanks, "Poor/Poverty (New Testament)," *ABD,* 5:416–17.

3. Wolfgang Stegemann, *The Gospel and the Poor* (Philadelphia: Fortress, 1984), 23–24.

to the poor/beggars (*ptōchos*) in Mark (five times; cf. ten times in Luke) is quite compatible with indications of the overall poverty of the region. Endless comments about water are not necessarily to be expected of the fish who swim in it! Although Mark and his cousin Barnabas seem to come from rather prosperous families, undoubtedly the young man who lost his garment the night of Jesus' arrest experienced more severe deprivations during his years of labor as an itinerant, unmarried missionary. Mark's teaching about oppression and poverty, then, remains quite close to Q, our earliest and most radical source (→Luke).

Perhaps Mark's clearest text linking common mechanisms of oppression with the plight of the poor is Jesus' denunciation of the scribes who "devour widows' houses" (12:40), immediately followed by his comments about the poor widow's sacrificial offering (12:41–44; cf. the temple purification, 11:15–18). However, Jesus also denounced Gentile rulers who typically lorded it over their subjects (10:42). The parable of the sower refers to oppression (*thlipsis*) and persecution resulting from the proclamation of the good news to the poor (4:17), and the rich young ruler is reminded of the sin of defrauding (10:19). Above all, although Mark does not resort to technical terminology, both John the Baptist's and Jesus' arrest and death are portrayed as cruel examples of oppression and institutionalized violence (6:14–29; 8:31; 9:31; 10:33–34; 14:1–15:47; see also Simon from Cyrene, 15:21). Recent sociological studies amply document the oppressed status of ordinary inhabitants of Palestine ("the crowds," thirty-eight times in Mark), crushingly taxed by both the local political-religious oligarchy and the Roman overlords (see the incendiary question about taxes to Caesar, 12:13–17).

All the more remarkable, then, is the virtual absence of explicit terminology referring to God's expected liberating justice. Technical justice terminology (*dik-* words), virtually absent in pristine Pauline theology (→1 Thessalonians), is similarly scarce in both Q and Mark, our earliest sources for Jesus' teaching. In Q (the sayings material common to Matthew and Luke), the only example is Luke 7:35: "Wisdom is justified [*edikaiōthē*] by all her children" (// Matt. 11:19, "by her works"). Mark employs *dikaios* once to report Herod's view of John the Baptist as "just and holy" (6:20), but from Jesus' lips only in this triple tradition saying:

> "I did not come to call the *dikaious* [just/righteous, pl.], but sinners." (2:17b // Matt 9:13 // Luke 5:32, where Luke adds "to repentance")

In this text we may sense why Jesus himself (like the pristine Paul) tended to avoid *dik-* words: such terms had become victims of a kind of linguistic coup and had been taken over by arrogant, self-righteous hypocrites as a kind of badge of respectability, in contrast to others labeled "sinners" (cf. those today who flaunt exclusionary claims to being "conservative," "evangelical," or "Catholic"). So Jesus, realistically recognizing the linguistic situation, uses the *dik-* word ironically, replying to his critics that he had not come to call the "righteous" (the comfortable in-group) but sinners (the marginalized out-group: toll collectors, prostitutes, etc.).

The fact that *dik-* words are found on Jesus' lips only once in our earliest sayings source Q and but once in Mark, our earliest Gospel, is strong evidence that the historical Jesus recognized the linguistic situation (the appropriation of justice language in the majority propaganda of the oppressors), and either avoided such terms or used them ironically to mock the arrogance of the self-righteous, who opposed his inclusive approach to community formation. However, in the light of previous denunciations, readers would understand that Jesus' apocalyptic discourse (Mark 13) portrayed God's decisive liberating justice by announcing the imminent destruction of the luxurious temple and the coming final cosmic judgment (technical justice terms are absent here, but see oppression in 13:9, 19, 24; and "liberated/saved" in 13:13, 20 →James 5:1–6).

2. *Women*

Mark ends his Gospel with a narrative about the three faithful women who went to Jesus' tomb, prepared to make themselves unclean (according to Jewish law) in order to serve him by preparing his body (15:40–47). When they saw a young man (an angel?), they fled in terror and amazement (16:1–8, recalling Mark's own flight, 14:51–52). Jesus had called all his disciples to lowly "service" (10:35–45), and in Mark, women disciples best exemplify such service (8:34–9:1; 9:33–50). Significantly, the Gospel begins with angels "serving" Jesus in his temptation (1:12–13), and the first human being Mark mentions as "serving" Jesus is Peter's mother-in-law (healed of her fever, 1:29–31). However, in 16:7–8 (probably Mark's original ending), the women receive a promise, but also falter in fear (only God is faithful!).

The four miracles related in 4:35–5:43 end with a double narrative of (1) a woman, unclean for twelve years as a result of hemorrhages (5:24b–34; cf. Lev. 15:25–30), whom Jesus healed; and (2) the deceased daughter of Jairus, whom Jesus raised (5:21–24a, 35–43). Two chapters later a Syrophoenician woman takes the initiative, like Jairus, to get Jesus to heal her daughter (7:24–30). This foreign woman is the only person in the Gospel who wins an argument with Jesus! "Yes, Lord, but the dogs under the table eat from the children's crumbs!" (7:28).[4] In notable contrast are all the failed arguments by males (supposedly the "rational animal," according to Aristotle) during the day of questions during Passion Week (11:27–12:40).

During his last week in Jerusalem Jesus provoked his crucifixion when he drove out those who were selling and buying in the temple (11:15–19). Mark contrasts this scene with the poor widow and her offering in the temple (12:41–44). In contrast with the apostles, Jewish religious leaders, and Roman politicians—all males who failed during Jesus' passion—Mark introduces the

4. Mary Ann Tolbert, "Mark," in *The Women's Bible Commentary*, ed. Carol A. Newsom and Sharon H. Ringe (Louisville: Westminster John Knox, 1992), 356.

woman in Bethany, who poured her expensive perfume over Jesus, an act that he praises but that is criticized by all the other males present (14:3–8; see Matt. 26:6–13; John 12:1–8). Nevertheless, Mark does not present a romantic notion of women as incorruptible, since he also describes a few in a negative light, such as Herodias and her daughter (6:14–29), and even Mary, the mother of Jesus (3:20–21, 31–35; 6:1–6; [15:40–41, 47; 16:1–8?]). Mark's perspectives concerning women make it difficult to decide if his Gospel ended originally with 16:1–8, or if the final part of the scroll (not a book) somehow was lost. Such an ending might have described Jesus' resurrection appearances to the women and their obedience in going to invite the (other) apostles (males) to repentance. If we take as a key Mark's personal flight (14:51–52), perhaps he wanted to say that Jesus calls us all to take up our cross and to serve but that we all fail, women included. However, God forgives and restores to leadership all who repent, as Peter, the three women, and Mark himself experienced. Although such a reading is meaningful and possible, Mark also might have concluded by telling of the women's recovery and Jesus' appearances to them, as described in the other Gospels. What we can know is that such a conclusion no longer exists and that the preserved alternate conclusions do not textually represent Mark's conclusion, although it might have been similar.

With Judas's betrayal and the cowardly flight of the other male apostles, the "experiment" with a patriarchal approach to community formation had failed. The good news of Jesus' resurrection is thus first revealed to three faithful women disciples sent as God's messengers to summon the male apostles (failed messengers) to a regrouping in Galilee (16:1–8). Mark (followed by Luke and Matthew) makes clear the priority and leadership of Mary Magdalene (a prostitute, according to much later tradition) after the resurrection (Mark 15:47; 16:1; John 20:1–18; Luke 24:10; Matt. 27:56, 61; 28:1; cf. Paul's omission of Mary, →1 Cor. 15:3–8).

3. Anti-Judaism? Moses' Law (Torah) in Mark

The responsibility of certain Jewish leaders for Jesus' crucifixion receives less emphasis in Mark than in the other Gospels. On the other hand, Mark is the most radical Synoptic Gospel in terms of criticism of the law of Moses. Only Mark (7:19) explicitly says that Jesus declared all food clean (see Acts 15, Leviticus, and Deuteronomy). According to Mark, Jesus continually broke the traditions of the law: he touched lepers and cadavers, healed a woman who was unclean because of hemorrhaging, and broke Sabbath traditions (see Galatians and Ephesians).

Other texts, however, indicate respect for the law. Jesus sent the healed leper to the priest to offer the sacrifices required for healing in Leviticus (Mark 1:44, as a testimony to the priests); he interpreted the Deuteronomic law concerning divorce in the light of the preceding Torah creation stories (Mark 10:2–9; cf. Gen. 1:27; 2:24); to the Pharisees he cites the fifth commandment, about the honor due to parents (Mark 7:10); to the young rich man Jesus cites the sixth through the ninth and also the fifth commandments (with the addition of a prohibition of fraud, Mark 10:19); in 7:21–23 we have a list of twelve vices that are an adaptation of the Ten Commandments (cf. Matt. 15:19, where the list of seven vices more closely follows Moses' Ten Commandments); the love of God and the love of neighbor are the two principal commandments (12:28–34; Deut. 6:4–5; Lev. 19:18). In addition, Mark tells how John the Baptist condemned Herod for his marriage, not only as adulterous but also because Herodias had been the wife of his brother Philip (6:17–18; cf. the prohibitions in Lev. 18:16 and 20:21 of what we generally term "incestuous" relations; 1 Cor. 5:1–11).

Jesus' teachings that Mark includes, while not many, are worthy of attention because many times they represent the original and most radical form. For Mark, being Jesus' disciple is not a matter of obeying many commandments (Matt. 28:16–20), but rather to follow Jesus' footsteps of sacrificial service in the way of the cross (8:31–9:1; 9:30–37; 10:32–45). The context of this discipleship is the arrival and presence of God's rule in Jesus' ministry (1:15; cf. 1:10 and 15:38 with Isa. 64:1) and the imminent consummation of this dominion (9:1; 13:24–27, 30–32). The arrival of this new reality of God's rule in the person of Jesus makes the rigid laws based on Moses' laws and Jewish traditions lose their dogmatic character (2:21–22, 28; 3:4–6). In this context of the imminent consummation of God's rule (with the second coming of Jesus), Jesus' words "Beware, keep alert. . . . Keep awake" (13:33–37; 14:32–42) are a primary responsibility of every disciple. In the New Testament such hope and vigilance is not escapism that contradicts the praxis of service to the poor and sick; rather, it serves to motivate and intensify such solidarity (1 Thess. 1:9–10; 1 John 3:2–3; James 5:7–8).

4. Sexual Minorities

The almost total absence of legitimate married couples in Mark is noteworthy. Almost all of the women are presented as individuals free of patriarchal control (single, divorced, widowed, etc.):

1. Peter's mother-in-law, the first person who serves Jesus (1:29–31)
2. the prostitutes who accompanied the toll collectors (2:15–17)
3. Mary with her "illegitimate" son Jesus (3:20–21, 31–35; 6:3; [15:40–41, 47; 16:1–8, apparently here identified as the mother of James and Joses; cf. 6:3])

4–5. Jairus's daughter; the woman with hemorrhages (5:21–43)

6–7. Herodias and her daughter (6:17, 19, 22–28; cf. Herod; both Herod and Herodias were divorced and remarried)

8–9. the Syrophoenician woman and her daughter (7:24–30)

10. women who take the initiative in divorce in order to remarry (10:12)
11. widows who lost their houses to unscrupulous scribes (12:40)
12. the poor widow with her offering (12:41–44)

13. the woman who anointed Jesus (14:3–9)
14. the high priest's servant girl who challenged Peter (14:66–72);

15–16. Mary Magdalene, Mary (= no. 3, the mother of James and Joses? [and of Jesus, 6:3?]), and Salome, present at the crucifixion and the empty tomb (15:40–41, 47; 16:1–8)

Of the sixteen cases of women mentioned in Mark (twelve favorably), Jairus and his wife (5:40) represent the only legitimately married couple in the entire Gospel! Mark's focus is on the poor and the weak, women without legitimate husbands (sexual minority representatives). Only Mark preserves the detail that, on inviting the rich young man to follow him, "Jesus, looking at him, *loved him*" (10:21; cf. the love of Jesus for Lazarus, Mary, and Martha [John 11:1–5, 35–36], and for his Beloved Disciple [John 13:23; 21:20]). The rending of the temple veil during Jesus' crucifixion (Mark 15:38) signifies that God has eliminated the traditional separation between insiders and the marginalized, unclean outsiders—and between sacred and profane. Jesus himself has become the mysterious place where the holy is revealed.

In Acts, Luke tells us that Mark came from a well-to-do family and that the first Christian community of Jerusalem met to pray in the house of Mary, his mother (→Acts 12:12). Mark's cousin Barnabas (Col. 4:10) and Paul took Mark along as an assistant when they launched their first missionary journey (Acts 12:25; 13:5). However, Mark's instinct, to set out with exemplary courage but end up fleeing, manifested itself again. When Barnabas wanted to give his cousin another opportunity, Paul indignantly refused. As a result, he and Barnabas separated for the second missionary journey, and Paul chose Silas as his new companion (Acts 15:36–41).

Paul later recognized that Mark became "useful in my ministry" (Philem. 24; cf. Col. 4:10; 2 Tim. 4:11). Mark last appears in Rome as Peter's companion (1 Pet. 5:13), which would explain why Mark's Gospel reflects Peter's perspective and testimony. This Gospel begins with John the Baptist's ministry (1:1–11) and Jesus' ministry in Galilee (1:14–39), but omits all information concerning Jesus' birth (cf. Matthew 1–2; Luke 1–2) and his thirty years of life prior to his encounter with John the Baptist (whom Peter had followed as a disciple).

5. "The Messianic Secret": Respecting the Privacy of a Closeted Messiah

Mark wrote for persecuted house-churches in Syria when undoubtedly many had to use subterfuge to protect innocent lives. Appropriately, then, Mark also presents Jesus with his own "messianic secret," a notable characteristic of this Gospel (first recognized by Wilhelm Wrede, 1901): 1:24–25, 34, demons; 1:44, leper; 3:11–12, demons; 4:11–12, parables; 5:43, Jairus's daughter; 7:36, deaf man; 6:51–52 and 8:17–21, disciples with hardened hearts; 8:26, blind man; 8:29–30 and 9:9, disciples; cf. 11:27–33; 9:13, John the Baptist and Elijah; 10:46–50, blind Bartimaeus.

Why Jesus' continual and emphatic demand for silence concerning his true identity and mission? In his baptism (1:8–9) he demonstrated solidarity with human beings in their sin, a solidarity that culminated in the cross. Wisdom in the Bible commonly involves knowing when to keep quiet and when to speak—a trait of special importance for the persecuted and oppressed (Eccl. 3:7b). After maintaining (and insisting that others maintain) his secret for three years, Jesus appears to have repressed a lot of anger. Consequently, after entering Jerusalem, Jesus expressed his indignation by forcefully expelling the traders from the temple (11:15–19). Then, facing the high priest, Jesus "came out of the closet" and openly declared himself to be the Messiah and Son of God (14:61–64). The situation of Jews and homosexuals during the Nazi Holocaust[5] enables us to recognize that to "always tell the whole truth" is a luxury that the oppressed, persecuted, and marginalized cannot always enjoy. Confronted with a tyrannical state that invades privacy with harmful and violent intent, a lie may be neither an "obstruction of justice" nor sin, but an expression of courage and solidarity with the oppressed. In such contexts, legalistic accuracy that harms and kills the neighbor, but that parades as "speaking the truth," may be the coward's flight from solidarity. However, today churches themselves often tyrannize human consciences, obligating people to live by subterfuge and maintain their secrets instead of being able to reveal their own character and be accepted in their diversity with dignity.

6. The Physically Challenged and Ill: Multiple Identities

- the demon-afflicted (a total of four, three men and one woman—and Jesus accused of being so; plus groups):

  1. a man, 1:21–28

     Jesus! 3:22–30

  2. a man, 5:1–20
  3. daughter of the Syrophoenician woman, 7:24–30
  4. a boy (epileptic?), 9:14–29

  several, 1:32–34; 3:7–12; others healed through the name of Jesus, 9:38–40

- the sick (a total of nine, three women and six men; plus groups):

  1. fever, Peter's mother-in-law, 1:29–31 (widow, divorced?)
  2. man with leprosy, 1:40–45
  3. paralytic man, 2:1–12
  4. man with withered hand, 3:1–6

5. Many contemporary Jews prefer "Shoah" to "Holocaust," since the latter term has overtones of a divinely ordained sacrifice (Leviticus 1). However, for ordinary readers of Bible reference works, Shoah would be one more puzzling term (which they would not yet find in most dictionaries), so it seemed wiser in most contexts to continue speak of the "Holocaust," as is still most common in the media and books not specializing in Jewish studies.

5. woman with hemorrhages, 5:25–34

6. daughter of Jairus (both parents are mentioned), 5:21–24, 35–43;

7. deaf man, 7:31–37

8–9. blind men: at Bethsaida, 8:22–26; at Jericho, 10:46–52

several, 1:32–34; 3:7–12; 6:53–56; 6:5 (only a few in Nazareth)

Total: thirteen cases (nine men, four women)

Except for Jairus and his wife, all appear as sexual minorities (widows, single people, divorced).

7. Divorce to Remarry as Adultery: Mark in Canonical Context

Jesus condemned men who had sent their wives away in order to marry a more attractive spouse. However, it proves to be impossible to extract an "absolute ethic" (a Greek philosophical concept) against all divorce from his words, since (1) important variations exist (diversity) in the preserved teachings in the Gospels (Luke 16:18 [Q?]; Mark 10:1–12; Matt. 5:31–32; 19:1–12); (2) Paul adds another important variant (1 Cor. 7:10–16); and (3) the Hebrew scriptures contain other, more radical differences: not only the Deuteronomic law (which permitted males to divorce), but also the divorce of Abraham (paradigm of faith and father of all believers), the divorces mandated by Ezra, and the teachings of Isaiah, Hosea, and Jeremiah that even God had to "divorce" Israel!

Although the traditional teachings of the churches (dominated by Greek philosophical concepts) seek to establish an ethic and a legal code (not only for the churches but for all of society), if we take the Bible seriously, the texts should teach us to think and pray, asking for *discernment* to be sensitive to each person and relationship in its individuality. Perhaps it is for this purpose that the greatest variant among the Gospels concerning this theme is the Gospel of John, which omits all prohibition against divorce and limits Jesus' teaching about the conduct of his followers to the new commandment of mutual love (John 13:34–35).

7.1. Luke (16:18; Q?). Luke's Sermon on the Plain (6:17–49; cf. the Sermon on the Mount, Matthew 5–7) does not include Jesus' teaching about divorce, and his Gospel has only this isolated verse on the subject. In this context, Jesus teaches against economic oppression and points out the dangers of riches (16:10–15, 19–31). Although the attribution to Q is still debated, Luke 16:18 may represent the most original version: "Anyone divorcing his wife and marrying another commits adultery, and the man who marries a divorced woman commits adultery." Thus, in Luke:

- only the man has the right to divorce (cf. Mark);
- what Jesus condemns as "adultery" is not the divorce itself but the act of remarrying (cf. Mark);

- there are no exceptions (see Mark; but also cf. Matt. 5:32; 19:9, and 1 Cor. 7:15);
- Jesus adds that even a man not divorced who marries a divorced woman also commits adultery (without parallel in Mark and Matthew).

7.2. Mark (10:1–12). "Whoever divorces his wife and marries another commits adultery *against her;* and if she divorces her husband and marries another, she commits adultery" (10:11–12). Because they are stricter versions, Luke and Mark appear to be the earliest. In Mark, however:

- the woman also has the right to divorce (in accord with Roman law but not with Jewish law in Palestine); with this right the woman also shares the responsibility and becomes guilty of adultery if she remarries;
- the man who divorces a woman and marries another commits adultery *against her* (the first wife), not against the man of the other woman, which was common in patriarchal societies, including in Hebrew scriptures;
- the sin of "adultery" is committed only by remarrying, not by the act of divorce alone. Only in Mark and Luke does Jesus appear to condemn all divorce accompanied by a new marriage as "adultery" without exception. Consequently, many understand this as hyperbole, such as "cut off your hand" (Matt. 5:30), "sell what you own" (Mark 10:21), and so forth.

7.3. Matthew (5:31–32; 19:1–9). In each of Matthew's two versions Jesus includes an exception that deals with a case or situation where the act of divorce and remarriage is not considered "adultery," but a case of *porneia,* originally meaning simply "prostitution" but later extended to cover other sexual misconduct: relations with unmarried persons or "incestuous," illicit relations (Lev. 18:6–18), or even as a synonym for adultery.[6]

Interpreters commonly conclude that Matthew's exception (in any sense) represents his adaptation of Jesus' teaching. The ambiguity of *porneia* is notable, since the law concerning divorce in Deuteronomy (24:1–4) also includes an ambiguous word ("something objectionable/ indecent"). If God inspired the Bible to give us raw material with which to construct a coherent legal code or an absolute ethic for the church and for society, how can we explain the use at key points of such ambiguous terms and the great diversity (each text says something different)?

7.4. 1 Corinthians 7:10–16. Paul endeavors to transmit the teaching of Jesus ("not I but the Lord"), but he ends up adding another exceptional case where the act of divorce and remarriage is not considered adultery: when a believer is abandoned by an unbeliever, he or she is free (to remarry). In his context outside of Palestine, Paul follows Mark, and recognizes the right of a woman to seek a divorce. And perhaps most significantly, Paul proposes another fundamental norm to take into account in such decisions: the "peace/total well-being" of the home (a norm that may reflect a personal experience of abandonment?).

6. Richard B. Hays, *The Moral Vision of the New Testament* (San Francisco: HarperCollins, 1996), 354–56; cf. the common mistranslation "fornication."

7.5. Deuteronomy 24:1–4. To protect women from the arbitrary abuses of men in their patriarchal society, Moses' law includes the measure of giving a legal document to a woman who is sent away because of "something objectionable/indecent about her" to her husband. This ambiguity provoked the question to Jesus in Mark 10:2 and Matt. 19:3. Notably, Jesus insisted on discernment for the interpretation and application of the scriptures, since he appealed to Gen. 1:27 and 2:24 (canonical context: the purpose of marriage) to indicate the correct interpretation of Deut. 24:1–4. Deuteronomy 22:13–19 and 28–29 point out two other cases in which males had the right of divorce.

7.6. Even God Commands Divorce in Certain Cases. In Gen. 21:8–14 God commands that Abraham divorce Hagar, his slave-spouse and mother of his firstborn son, Ishmael, when the home's peace is destroyed because of rivalries between Hagar and her mistress, Sarai (see also Exod. 21:10–11).

7.7. Ezra (458 B.C.E.) ordered that the male Jews divorce their Canaanite wives (Ezra 9:1–10:17; cf. Neh. 13:23–31; Exod. 34:11–16; Deut. 20:10–18; 23:3; 7:1–6).

7.8. Malachi 2:10–16 (460 B.C.E.) may interpret marriage as a covenant between a couple, rather than as an arrangement between the man and the father of the bride, as was the previous custom. Malachi declares that "God hates divorce" (although the original Hebrew text in 2:16 is unclear). However, the prophet Jeremiah (3:1–8) taught that even God had to divorce God's unfaithful, idolatrous people (see Isa. 50:1; Hos. 2:2). This original Hebrew text in Malachi is quite obscure, and the interpretation of marriage as a covenant between the couple is very controversial. (Nowhere does the New Testament suggest that marriage is a covenant.)

Conclusions Concerning Divorce. When we carefully compare the variations in Jesus' teaching, and that of the entire Bible, we note that the texts always reflect concrete historical and cultural contexts, and hence never designated "ethics" or "morals" (Greek philosophical categories totally absent from the Bible). A similar diversity of teaching occurs in Jesus' commissioning of the Twelve, where Mark's version *permits* taking a staff and wearing sandals (6:8–9), while Matthew's version *forbids* them (10:10; cf. Luke 9:3). Although scholars offer different explanations for this diversity (Mark's long international journeys but on paved Roman roads versus Matthew's mission within Palestine but on rocky local paths), they agree that local conditions led to the adaptation of Jesus' instructions to specific historical contexts.

Similarly, Mark's divorce text may reflect his eventual location in Rome, where women were more liberated than in Palestine. The Bible thus portrays God as Sovereign of history, who knows how to wisely adjust guidelines for praxis in accord with varying historical contexts and different human situations. To take an extreme case, it is difficult to imagine that Jesus would have wanted to condemn a woman as an "adulteress" who initiates a divorce to protect her life against her husband's violence or to rescue her daughters from their father's sexual abuse. In such a case, divorce would rather be an act of courage and solidarity with the weak (the daughters)—divine liberation, not sin. Some churches thus now include liturgies of blessing for divorced persons, seeking to minister positively in times of personal crisis and need, instead of heaping up false guilt with unjustifiable and cruel condemnations. However, Jesus' explicit words about divorce make it difficult to understand how so many churches now often accept divorced persons without condemnation (including their divorced pastors) but continue condemning other sexual minorities, citing only texts by Paul and the Hebrew scriptures (misinterpreted) but without any basis in Jesus' own teaching. In addition, many of these same churches accept the equality and ordination of women, even though two patriarchal Pauline texts appear much clearer than the texts cited against sexual minorities. Such churches obviously misinterpret the Bible with a selective literalism (common in fundamentalisms of all sorts) to support an ideology predetermined on other grounds.

Note: "The Secret Gospel of Mark"

> The youth, looking upon [Jesus] loved him and began to beseech him that he might be with him. And going out of the tomb they came into the house of the youth, for he was rich. After six days Jesus told him what to do and in the evening the youth comes to him wearing a linen cloth over his naked body. And he remained with him that night, for Jesus taught him the mystery of the kingdom of God.[7]

In 1958, working in the Greek Orthodox monastery of Mar Saba in the Judean desert, Morton Smith discovered an incomplete letter of Clement of Alexandria (180–200 C.E.) to Theodore, referring to a "Secret Gospel of Mark," which some scholars hold to predate our canonical Gospel. According to Clement, in his day the Carpocratians (libertine Gnostics) were misinterpreting this Secret Gospel by ascribing sexual overtones to Jesus' encounter with the youth. Clement denies the Carpocratians' claim that the Secret Gospel included the phrase "naked man on naked man." Some scholars see in Clement's letter a reference to nude nocturnal baptism, since baptism originally involved disrobing (Gal. 3:27; Eph. 4:20–24; Col. 3:9–14) and was commonly performed by immersion at night or dawn (Acts 16:33; Hippolytus, *Trad. ap.* 21).

---

7. H. Merkel, "The Secret Gospel of Mark," in *Gospels and Related Writings,* vol. 1 of *The New Testament Apocrypha,* ed. Wilhelm Schneemelcher, rev. ed. (Louisville: Westminster John Knox, 1991), 108 (see 106–9); cf. F. F. Bruce, *The Secret Gospel of Mark,* Ethel M. Wood Lecture (London: Athlone, 1974); Robert H. Gundry, *Mark: A Commentary on His Apology for the Cross* (Grand Rapids: Eerdmans, 1993), 603–23; Marvin W. Meyer, "Mark, Secret Gospel of," *ABD,* 4:558–59.

Bibliography

Achtemeier, Paul J. "Mark, Gospel of." *ABD,* 4:541–47.

Barton, Stephen C. *Discipleship and Family Ties in Mark and Matthew.* Society for New Testament Studies Monograph Series 80. Cambridge: Cambridge University Press, 1994.

Blount, Brian K. *Go Preach! Mark's Kingdom Message and the Black Church Today.* Maryknoll, N.Y.: Orbis, 1998.

Booth, R. P. *Jesus and the Laws of Purity: Tradition History and Legal History in Mark 7.* JSNTSup 13. Sheffield: JSOT Press, 1986.

Cárdenas Pallares, José. *Un pobre llamado Jesús: Relectura del Evangelio de Marcos.* Mexico, D.F.: Casa Unida, 1982.

Delorme, Jean. *El Evangelio según San Marcos.* Estella, Navarra, Spain: Editorial Verbo Divino, 1988.

Dewey, Joanna. "The Gospel of Mark." In *Searching the Scriptures,* vol. 2, *A Feminist Commentary,* ed. Elisabeth Schüssler Fiorenza, 470–509. New York: Crossroad, 1994.

Guelich, Robert A. *Mark 1–8:26.* WBC 34A. Dallas: Word, 1989.

Gundry, Robert H. *Mark: A Commentary on His Apology for the Cross.* Grand Rapids: Eerdmans, 1993.

Kinukawa, Hisako. *Women and Jesus in Mark: A Japanese Feminist Perspective.* Maryknoll, N.Y.: Orbis, 1994.

Marcus, J. *The Way of the Lord: Christological Exegesis of the Old Testament in the Gospel of Mark.* Louisville: Westminster John Knox, 1992.

Myers, Ched. *Binding the Strong Man: A Political Reading of Mark's Story of Jesus.* Maryknoll, N.Y.: Orbis, 1988.

———, et al. *"Say to This Mountain": Mark's Story of Discipleship.* Ed. Karen Latea. Maryknoll, N.Y.: Orbis, 1996.

Perkins, Pheme. "The Gospel of Mark." In *The New Interpreter's Bible,* ed. Leander E. Keck, 8:507–733. Nashville: Abingdon, 1995.

Stegemann, Wolfgang. *The Gospel and the Poor.* Philadelphia: Fortress, 1984.

Tolbert, Mary Ann. "Mark." In *The Women's Bible Commentary,* ed. Carol A. Newsom and Sharon H. Ringe, 250–62. Louisville: Westminster John Knox, 1992.

———. "Asceticism in Mark's Gospel." In *Asceticism and the New Testament,* ed. Leif E. Vaage and Vincent L. Wimbush, 29–48. New York: Routledge, 1999.

Chapter 3

LUKE

Good News for the Poor and for Women

Outline

Note: "Mark } Luke" indicates that Luke's source is a parallel text from Mark

Prologue: most excellent Theophilus, 1:1–4

1. Birth and Hidden Life of John the Baptist and of Jesus, 1:5–2:52

   Announcement of John the Baptist's birth, 1:5–25

   Annunciation of Jesus' conception, 1:26–38

   Visitation and Magnificat of Mary, 1:39–56

   Birth and circumcision of John the Baptist, 1:57–66

   Benedictus; unknown life of John, 1:67–80

   Birth of Jesus, 2:1–21

   Presentation and circumcision of Jesus in the temple, 2:22–28

   Prophecies of Simeon (Nunc Dimittis) and of Anna, 2:29–38

   Jesus: unknown life (Nazareth); among the doctors, 2:39–52

2. Preparation for Jesus' Ministry, 3:1–4:13

   John the Baptist's preaching and imprisonment, 3:1–20

   Mark 1:2–6, 7–8 } Luke 3:2–4, 15–16; [*Luke 3:7–9, 16–17 = Q*]

   Jesus: baptism, Mark 1:9–11; Luke 3:21–22

   Jesus' genealogy, Luke 3:23–28

   Jesus' three temptations, 4:2–13 = Q, Mark 1:12–13 } Luke 4:1–2

3. Jesus' Ministry in Galilee, 4:14–9:50

   Jesus in Galilee and preaches in Nazareth, Mark 6:1–6a } Luke 4:14–30

   A busy Sabbath in Capernaum, Mark 1:21–34 } Luke 4:31–41

   Departure from Capernaum, Mark 1:35–39 } Luke 4:42–44

   Calling of four disciples, Mark 1:16–20 } Luke 5:1–11

Healings: leper, paralytic, Mark 1:45–2:12 } Luke 5:12–26

FOUR DISPUTES WITH THE PHARISEES AND SCRIBES:

Calling of Levi, meal with his sinner friends, Mark 2:13–17 } Luke 5:27–32

Dispute with Pharisees and scribes over fasting, Mark 2:18–22 } Luke 5:33–39

The wheat plucked on the Sabbath, Mark 2:23–28 } Luke 6:1–5

Healing of the man with the withered hand, Mark 3:1–6 } Luke 6:6–11

Election of twelve men as apostles, Mark 3:13–19 } Luke 6:12–16

The multitudes follow Jesus, 6:17–19

The Sermon "of the Mount" on the plain, 6:20b–49 = Q } Matthew 5–7

Healing of the centurion's beloved slave, 7:1–10 = Q

Resurrection of the widow's son in Nain, 7:11–17

The Baptist's question and Jesus' testimony, 7:18–35 = Q

Prostitute pardoned in Pharisee's house, 7:36–50

Women who aided Jesus' ministry, 8:1–3

Two parables: the sower and the lamp, Mark 4:1–25 } Luke 8:4–18

De/Reconstruction of the concept of family, 8:19–21

Four miracles: a storm, a demoniac, Jairus, a woman, Mark 4:35–43 } Luke 8:22–56

The sending of the twelve, Herod's reaction, Mark 6:7–11 } Luke 9:1–9

Food for five thousand, Mark 6:35–44 } Luke 9:10–17

Peter's confession, first announcement of the Passion, Mark 8:27–30 } Luke 9:18–27

The transfiguration, healing of an epileptic, Mark 8:38–9:8 } Luke 9:28–43a

Second announcement of the passion, Mark 9:30–32 } Luke 9:43b–45

On who is the greatest, use of Jesus' name, Mark 9:33–39 } Luke 9:46–50

4. Trip En Route to Jerusalem: Teachings and Miracles, 9:51–19:27

Bad reception in a Samaritan village, 9:51–56

Three requirements of the authentic disciple, 9:57–62 = Q

The mission of the seventy-two, redefinition of "sodomy," 10:1–16 [2–16 = Q]

Return of the seventy-two, privilege of the humble, 10:17–24 = Q

Parable of the good Samaritan, 10:25–37

Jesus in his favorite home (Martha and Mary), 10:38–42

Prayer: the Lord's Prayer (original version), 11:1–13 [*11:2–4, 9–13* = Q]

Jesus, Beelzebul, mute demon, 11:14–26 = Q

Three teachings: new family, Jonah, lamp, 11:27–36 [*11:29–36* = Q]

Six severe warnings, 11:37–13:9

Against the Pharisees and scribes, 11:37–54 [*11:39–52* = Q]

Confessing or denying Jesus, 12:2–12 [2–12 = Q]

Against the accumulation of riches, 12:13–34

Parable of the rich fool, 12:13–21

Freed to seek the just new order, 12:22–34 = Q

The urgency of the times, 12:35–48 [*12:39–48* = Q]

Conflicts and dissensions, 12:49–59 = Q

Call to repentance (sterile fig tree), 13:1–9

God's new order: freedom, justice, 13:10–17:37

Freedom of a physically challenged woman, 13:10–17

Two new order parables, 13:18–21 = Q

The mustard seed: tiny beginnings, 13:18–19

Yeast: universal purpose, 13:20–21

Two doors: one narrow, the other closed, 13:22–30 = Q

Two prophetic accusations, 13:31–35

That fox Herod, 13:31–33

Rebellious Jerusalem, 13:34–35 = Q

A banquet on the Sabbath in a Pharisee's home, 14:1–24

A breach of etiquette: healing of a man with dropsy, 14:1–6

How guests should choose their seats, 14:7–11

How hosts should select their guests (the poor), 14:12–14

Parable: the rich and the newlyweds excuse themselves, 14:16–24 [*16–24* = Q]

Two renunciations, requirements for the just new order, 14:25–35

Break ties with patriarchal families, 14:26–27 = Q

Renounce possessions (a tower, a war), 14:28–33

The danger of losing effectiveness: salt, 14:34–35 [*14:33–34* = Q]

Three parables: about the "lost" (marginalized), 15:1–32

The audience: the Pharisees and the scribes, 15:1–3

(1) *A man searches for his lost sheep, 15:4–7 = Q*

(2) A woman searches for her lost coin, 15:8–10

(3) A father waits for the return of his lost son, 15:11–32

Divine justice and human greed, 16:1–31

Parable of the shrewd manager, 16:1–8

Good use and abuse of riches, 16:9–13 [*16:13 = Q*]

Against the Pharisees, lovers of money, 16:14–15

Against the zealots and the abuse of force, 16:16 = Q

Wisdom of the Torah: God is in the details, 16:17 = Q

Defense of oppressed women (against divorce), 16:18 = Q

Parable of the unjust rich man and poor Lazarus, 16:19–31

Six instructions for the disciples, 17:1–37

Against scandals, loving correction, 17:1–4 = Q

The increase and power of faith, 17:5–6 = Q

Lesson of the poor slave: humility, 17:7–10

Lesson of ten marginalized lepers: gratitude, 17:11–19

The new order is already present among oppressors, 17:20–21

Culmination: the day of the Human One, 17:22–37 = Q

God's new order: justice and freedom, 18:1–19:27

Two parables of the new order, 18:1–14

An unjust judge and a poor widow, 18:1–8

A Pharisee and a marginalized publican, 18:9–14

Marginalized children, paradigms of the new order, Mark 10:13–16 } Luke 18:15–17

Original paradigm (Mark): the young rich man, Mark 10:17–31 } Luke 18:18–30

Approaching Jericho: third announcement of the passion, Mark 10:32–34 } Luke 18:31–34

Sign of the new order: a blind man healed, Mark 10:46–52 } Luke 18:35–43

New paradigm for the rich (Luke): Zacchaeus, Luke 19:1–10

Parable, money: investment, responsibility, 19:12–27 [*12–27 = Q*]

5. Ministry of Prophetic Denunciations in Jerusalem, 19:28–21:38

    Entry: peaceful procession of protest, Mark 11:1–11 } Luke 19:29–44

    Temple: nonviolent expulsion of exploiters, Mark 11:15–18 } Luke 19:45–48

    Three questions by Jesus' oppressors, 20:1–40

        Challenge to Jesus' subversive authority, Mark 11:27–33 } Luke 20:1–8

        Parable of the vineyard homicides, Mark 12:1–12 } Luke 20:9–19

        Dishonest political question: tribute to Caesar, Mark 12:13–17 } Luke 20:20–26

        Levirate law, a theological trap, Mark 12:18–27 } Luke 20:27–40

    Proactive strategy: Jesus asks about David, Mark 12:35–37 } Luke 20:41–44

    Two teachings about widows (poor and oppressed), Mark 12:38–44 } Luke 20:45–21:4

        Scribes who oppress widows, Luke 20:45–47

        The poor widow's offering (two small copper coins), 21:1–4

    The coming ruin of the oppressive city (70 C.E.), Mark 13:1–23 } Luke 21:5–24

    The coming of the Human One, Mark 13:24–37 } 21:25–38

6. Conspiracy, Judicial Trials, and Jesus' Death, Luke 22:1–23:56

    Conspiracy of the authorities with Judas, Mark 14:1–2, 10–11 } Luke 22:1–6

    The Passover meal, Mark 14:12–17, 22–25 } Luke 22:7–23 (24–30)

    Final teachings, 22:21–38

        Announcement of Judas's treason, Mark 14:18–21 } Luke 22:21–23

        Dispute among the apostles, Luke 22:24–30 [*22:28–30 = Q*]

        Announcement of Peter's denial, Mark 14:27–31 } Luke 22:31–34
        New orders: take money and buy a sword, 22:35–38

    Jesus' agony and arrest, Mark 14:32–52 } Luke 22:39–53

    Peter's three denials, Mark 14:54, 66–72 } Luke 22:54–62

    First trial: Jesus before the Sanhedrin, Mark 14:53–72 } Luke 22:63–71

    Second trial: Jesus before Pilate, Mark 15:1–5 } Luke 23:1–5

    Third trial: Jesus before Herod, Luke 23:6–12

    Final action: again before Pilate, Mark 15:6–15 } Luke 23:13–25

    Death penalty: the way to the cross, Mark 15:20–23 } Luke 23:26–32

    Crucifixion and death, Mark 15:24–38 } Luke 23:33–38, 44–46

    Gestures of solidarity, the good thief, 23:39–43

    Centurion, women, Joseph (burial), Mark 15:39–47 } Luke 23:47–56

7. After the Resurrection, 24:1–53

    Women find the tomb empty, Mark 16:1–8 } Luke 24:1–8

    Male apostles do not believe the women, Luke 24:9–11

    Peter in the tomb, 24:12

    Jesus appears to two disciples on the road to Emmaus, 24:13–35

    Appearance to the disciples, 24:36–43

    Last instructions, 24:44–49

    The ascension, 24:50–53

Commentary

Luke, one of Paul's companions (Philem. 24), is called "the beloved physician" in the deutero-Pauline letter to the Colossians (4:14; cf. 2 Tim. 4:11). His two-volume work comprises almost one-fourth of our New Testament (nearly one hundred of four hundred pages in some editions). Writing ca. 80 C.E., Luke utilized Mark as a source but also incorporated much of Jesus' teaching that came from an earlier source (ca. 60 C.E.) now known as Q, material common to Luke and Matthew but not included in Mark. As the only Gentile among the New Testament authors, Luke addresses his work especially toward the more educated sector of the Greco-Roman culture (1:1–4), demonstrating Jesus' significance for all of humanity and especially his solidarity with the poor and oppressed, the vulnerable and physically challenged, women, sexual minorities, and the socially despised. Luke emphasizes the place of prayer in Jesus' life, showing how, in answer to prayer, the Holy Spirit empowers and equips the weak and oppressed to fulfill God's liberating purposes in human history.

1. The Oppressed Poor and Liberating Justice

Lexicological studies easily established Luke's special focus on the beggarly poor (*ptōchos,* ten times, plus *penichros,* 21:2; but cf. *ptōchos* only five times each in Mark and Matthew; however, the total absence of these words in Acts has raised questions). Of the six uses of *ptōchos* in Luke that do not depend on Mark or Q, five are found in the narrative of the journey to Jerusalem (9:51–19:27; specifically, 14:13, 21; 16:20, 22; 19:8). In addition, 4:18–19 is particular to Luke. After Jesus' baptism Luke gives us this programmatic introduction to Jesus' ministry of liberating justice for the poor and oppressed:[1]

---

1. Thomas D. Hanks, *God So Loved the Third World: The Biblical Vocabulary of Oppression,* trans. James C. Dekker (Maryknoll, N.Y.: Orbis, 1983), 50–53; "Poor/Poverty (New Testament)," *ABD,* 5:417; Sharon H. Ringe, *Jesus, Liberation, and the Biblical Jubilee* (Philadelphia: Fortress, 1985).

"The Spirit of the Liberator is upon me,
because he has anointed me to bring good news to the *poor.*
He has sent me to proclaim *release* to the captives and recovery of sight to the blind,
to let the *oppressed go free,* to proclaim the year of the Liberator's favor" [i.e., the Jubilee Year, Leviticus 25].

Traditional studies presented Luke as the "radical" among the Gospel writers. More recent studies, however, conclude that the source Q and Mark reflect the more radical perspective concerning the poor and the oppressed. Few scholars have done justice to Luke's concern for the "immoral minorities" commonly marginalized by society: prostitutes, toll collectors, and so forth (Luke 7:34, 37, 39; cf. 7:1–10 discussed on p. 47 below).

Luke's strong concentration on the economic dimensions of the gospel is only partly reflected in the results of the lexicological studies of the vocabulary explicitly referring to the poor (cf. Luke 1:51–53; 3:10–14; 6:34–36; 9:58; 11:41; 12:33; 14:12–14, 33). Today this concentration is commonly understood as a response to the situation (in Caesarea/Antioch?) ca. 80 C.E. of a church relatively poor but faced with an unprecedented influx of more prosperous members and suddenly in danger of succumbing to the "love of money" characteristic of certain Pharisees (16:14).[2]

Luke addresses a Christian community that is economically upwardly mobile, presenting an extensive account of Jesus' teachings appropriate for their crisis. Walter Pilgrim analyzed Luke's teachings concerning riches and poverty, reducing them to three basic categories: (1) total renunciation of riches; (2) warnings against the dangers of riches; and (3) correct use of wealth.[3] The example of Zacchaeus ("*half* of my possessions, Lord, I will give to the poor," 19:8; cf. 3:10–14) is commonly seen now as Luke's preferred paradigm for recently converted wealthy disciples. From Mark's point of view (Mark 10:21, the rich young man of whom Jesus demanded *everything*) or the perspective of the Q source (from itinerant prophets who had left wives, houses, everything), the Zacchaeus paradigm may seem rather lukewarm and shockingly "conservative."

Luke T. Johnson shows how money in Luke frequently has a symbolic function connected with the acceptance or rejection of Jesus himself.[4] This is logical, since a commitment with Jesus and the poor communities of persecuted disciples many times put all possessions, positions, and human relations at risk. As in the cases of Jews and homosexuals faced with Nazi violence, and that of sexual minorities in many countries today, to publicly reveal yourself can involve risking all that you are and possess.

---

2. Halvor Moxnes, *The Economy of the Kingdom: Social Conflict and Economic Relations in Luke's Gospel* (Philadelphia: Fortress, 1988), 1–21.

3. Walter Pilgrim, *Good News to the Poor: Wealth and Poverty in Luke-Acts* (Minneapolis: Augsburg, 1981).

4. Luke T. Johnson, *The Literary Function of Possessions in Luke-Acts* (Missoula, Mont.: Scholars Press, 1977).

Luke's Gospel proves particularly helpful in enabling us to discern the relationship between poverty, oppression, and God's promised liberating justice. Most recent studies continue to reflect a kind of bondage to elitist Greco-Roman philosophical perspectives and linguistic usage in their efforts to delineate the meaning of "justice/righteousness" in the New Testament.[5] This classical approach commonly produces only majority propaganda for the "law and order" notion of "righteousness/justice" that seeks to maintain an unjust status quo. However, although the New Testament was written in Greek, the dominant biblical paradigm of the Exodus suggests that we had best *begin with the experience of the oppressed* and understand justice as the justice that liberates them from that oppression.

Jesus' parable of the "importunate widow" (Luke 18:1–8) gives us a helpful example of this alternative approach. The judge is described subversively as an oppressor (v. 6, *adikias,* "unjust"), although society would consider his function as part of the "system of justice." The widow, who may have lost her house through common mechanisms of oppression (20:47), repeatedly presents her demand for liberating justice ("vindicate me," *ekdikēson me*) from her oppressor ("my adversary," *antidikou mou*) (v. 3; cf. vv. 5, 7–8). As in James 5:1–6, the return of the Human One is understood as the decisive expression of God's liberating justice (Luke 18:7–8). God's liberating justice responds to the need and cries of the oppressed and involves social vindication from the shame of oppression and poverty.

Jesus' following parable in Luke then contrasts the prayer of the self-righteous Pharisee with that of the despised and marginalized toll collector (18:9–14). Shockingly, the "just" Pharisee returns to his home marginalized by the Liberator God, while the "unjust" toll collector returns to his household "justified" (18:14)—reminding us that justification in the New Testament commonly implies acceptance of the marginalized in the new inclusive community of Jesus' followers (→James, Galatians, Romans).

Luke contains the same number of *dik-* words as Matthew (twenty-eight) but the additional twenty-five uses in Acts make Luke the New Testament author second only to Paul (114 uses + twenty-five in the deutero-Pauline and pastoral letters). In Luke-Acts, nineteen of the fifty-three uses involve words with the alpha privative, signifying oppression/injustice. However, in Jesus' programmatic statement of his liberating ministry (Luke 4:18–19), "oppression" is signified by another term: "having been crushed" (*tethrausmenous*). In Acts, particularly, the verb *dikaioō* is employed to signify "liberation": "by [Jesus] everyone who believes is freed from everything from which you could not be freed by the law of Moses" (Acts 13:39). When we take our methodological linguistic clues from the Exodus paradigm and begin with the experience of the oppressed, we can see that justice properly understood

5. See the very erudite but ideologically skewed article by John Reumann, "Righteousness (NT)," *ABD,* 5:745–73. Commonly overlooked in such works of privileged white male scholarship are basic contributions from Latin America and feminist-womanist studies (see the works of José P. Miranda and Karen Lebacqz in the general bibliography).

in the Bible is normally "liberating justice," and justification signifies social vindication for the marginalized and their inclusion in the new community.

2. *Women*

Luke contains much more material concerning women than the other Gospels: forty-two passages, of which twenty-three are unique to Luke. The rest are taken from Mark or Q, the latter in common with Matthew. Consequently, Luke is traditionally considered the Gospel that supports women in their struggle for liberation and justice. Nevertheless, some now question whether Luke's intentions are so honorable. Jane Schaberg concludes that Luke seeks to portray passive women as models of submission, women who are thankful, dedicated to prayer, and supporting male leadership.[6] Many of the women in Luke are poor, and he includes more references to widows than the other Gospels (2:37; 4:25–26; 7:12; 18:3, 5; 20:47; 21:2–3; see chapter on 1 Timothy).[7]

Jane Schaberg points out that Luke omits the account in Mark (7:24–30) where a Gentile woman wins an argument with Jesus, nor does he include a narrative like John 4, where the Samaritan woman begins a ministry with Gentiles. Additionally, Jesus' genealogy in Luke (3:23–38) stretches back to Adam, taking in all of humanity, but it does not include women as does the genealogy in Matthew (1:1–16). Luke never refers to women as "disciples" and in fact speaks of "disciples" as those who abandon their wives to proclaim the Gospel (Luke 14:26; 18:29). In the parable of the great feast, only in Luke's version do we read that a man gives the excuse "I have just been married, and therefore I cannot come" (14:20). The prosperous women who accompany Jesus help cover the expenses of the male disciples but do not exercise a ministry of their own (8:1–3). And in Acts (see below), where Luke's own perspective is clearer, the amount of material on women is much less than in the Gospel.

On the other hand, Luke frequently manifests a certain justice in favor of women with his literary technique of presenting matched narratives that speak of men, followed by accounts that speak of women: a man sows a mustard seed, and a woman uses yeast (13:18–21, source Q); a man looks for the lost sheep, and a woman searches for a lost coin (15:4–10; also see 7:12 with 8:42, 13:10–17 with 14:1–6, 6:12–19 with 8:1–3). Although John describes a less passive Mary and Martha (John 11:1–45; 12:1–8), many have seen in Luke's presentation (Luke 10:38–42) a Mary, seated and listening at the feet of Jesus, who claims the male privilege of a theological education instead of remaining marginalized with oppressive domestic duties.

---

6. Jane Schaberg, "Luke," in *The Women's Bible Commentary,* ed. Carol A. Newsom and Sharon H. Ringe (Louisville: Westminster John Knox, 1992), 363.

7. Bonnie Bowman Thurston, *The Widows: A Women's Ministry in the Early Church* (Minneapolis: Fortress, 1989).

3. The Marginalized and Sexual Minorities

In fact, our interpretation of Luke's perspective on women must depend largely on texts where the woman represents some sexual minority. Traditional patriarchal "families" are conspicuous by their absence in Luke's Gospel. And even if we accept the traditional interpretation of Jesus' birth as virginal, Mary stands out as a sexual minority, an unwed mother threatened with the death penalty according to Mosaic law for having a child that did not belong to Joseph.

Only Luke and Matthew narrate Jesus' birth, and traditionally Luke has been read as agreeing with Matthew as affirming Jesus' conception and birth by a Mary who is virgin. Luke's words in 1:35–37, however, are not explicit, and the future verbs leave open the possibility that Joseph was the father.[8] Nevertheless, the exclusion of Joseph as father in 3:23 would seem to confirm Mary's sexual minority status, but without explicitly ruling out other paternity. Even with the traditional doctrine of the virgin birth, we are left with a Mary who ends up a kind of "single mom" and a Jesus who is legally illegitimate, a "bastard" in the discriminatory legal categories of the Hebrew scriptures.

Jane Schaberg has argued that Mary was not so much "humble," but "humiliated" (Greek *tapeinōsis,* Luke 1:48), sexually assaulted (raped), perhaps by a solider in the occupying Roman army.[9] If Mary had been raped by a Roman soldier, that would better explain her militant and prophetic words against the oppressors of her people (Luke 1:51–53). The other women in Luke 1–2 may be more traditional and somewhat passive (Elizabeth, John's mother [1:24–25, 39–45]; Anna, the widow prophet in the temple [2:36–38]), but not Mary, the indignant militant! Such an interpretation also would fit well with Luke's words about the sword that would penetrate Mary's heart (2:35) and with the bloody account in Matthew of the slaughter of the children by Herod's troops (Matt. 2:16–18).

Churches traditionally have interpreted the virginal womb as a parallel with the resurrected Jesus' empty tomb. But a triumph of God's Spirit, extracting a "holy" child rather than an "illegitimate" child, from the experience of rape could be more appropriate in a Gospel that shows us how Jesus' crucifixion ended in his resurrection. One might even argue that an incarnation redemptive for the cosmos, beginning with an imperialist soldier's rape of an innocent virgin, is a greater miracle than the traditional notion of a virgin birth (and more appropriate in a Gospel that concludes with a resurrection preceded by a crucifixion). Such an interpretation would leave only Matthew (1:20–23) narrating a virginal birth. But Matthew especially may include various elements of midrash (edifying, but nonhistorical homiletical elaborations [→Matthew]).

Luise Schottroff, however, although acknowledging significant insights from Schaberg's studies (for instance, that the Greek term for "humiliation"

---

8. Sharon H. Ringe, *Luke* (Louisville: Westminster John Knox, 1995), 32.

9. Schaberg, "Luke," 373; cf. her more detailed study, *The Illegitimacy of Jesus: A Feminist Theological Interpretation of the Infancy Narratives* (New York: Crossroad, 1987).

in Luke 1:48 may refer to sexual humiliation such as rape), insists that Mary's humiliation rather involves the oppression and poverty of Palestinian Jews under the Roman Empire and her oppression as a woman in a patriarchal culture: "Mary trusted that she would bring a child into this [patriarchal] world without the involvement of a man and that this child was to bring God's indestructible reign to the people of Israel (1:33).... [Mary and Elizabeth] beat the drum of God's world revolution.... The two women prophetically herald God's world revolution, God's option for the poor, which begins as an option for Mary and for women (1:42, 48)."[10]

Understandably, traditional white male scholarship, whether defending or critiquing the traditional doctrine of the virgin birth, continues to ignore the significant insights generated in the feminist debate.[11] Even evangelical scholars, however, increasingly acknowledge that the virgin birth "probably does not deserve to rank among the top five fundamentals of the faith."[12] Whether she was a prostitute is now seriously questioned, but Luke names Mary Magdalene as the first evangelist, who communicates the good news of Jesus' resurrection to the unfaithful male apostles (24:10). Luke then continues to narrate how Jesus appeared, not to a heterosexual couple, but to a pair of men traveling together to their village of Emmaus (24:13–35). The account of Jesus' anointing is very explicit. This is carried out by Mary (of Bethany) in the other three Gospels and takes place shortly before the crucifixion (Mark 14:3–9; Matt. 26:6–13; John 12:1–8). However, in Luke (7:36–50) Jesus' anointing occurs much earlier in the house of Simon, a Pharisee, and it is done by a prostitute ("sinner"). Luke presents this story as an illustration of Jesus' practice of being "a friend of toll collectors and sinners" (7:34), and then immediately names Mary Magdalene among the wealthy women who helped the ministry economically (8:1–3). Women biblicists, especially, now commonly indignantly reject the traditional identification of Mary Magdalene (8:2) with the prostitute of 7:36–50. However, we must question whether this dogmatic rejection may not reflect a certain prejudice against sexual minorities.[13]

Luke 7:1–10 gives us Luke's version (// Matt. 8:5–13 [// John 5:46–54?]) of the story about a Roman centurion who asked Jesus to heal his "beloved slave" (7:2). In the light of the common practices of Roman soldiers with their

10. Luise Schottroff, *Lydia's Impatient Sisters: A Feminist Social History of Early Christianity,* trans. Barbara and Martin Rumscheidt (Louisville: Westminster John Knox, 1995).

11. Raymond E. Brown, *An Introduction to the New Testament* (New York: Doubleday, 1997), 219–20; Darrell L. Bock, *Luke* (Grand Rapids: Baker, 1994), 102–31.

12. Craig L. Blomberg, *Jesus and the Gospels* (Nashville: Broadman & Holman, 1997), 209–10.

13. Richard Atwood, *Mary Magdalene in the New Testament and Early Tradition* (Bern, Germany: Lang, 1993); Esther de Boer, *Mary Magdalene: Beyond the Myth,* trans. John Bowden (Harrisburg, Pa.: Trinity, 1997); Susan Haskins, *Mary Magdalen: Myth and Metaphor* (New York: Harcourt, Brace, 1993); Carla Ricci, *Mary Magdalene and Many Others: Women Who Followed Jesus,* trans. Paul Burns (Minneapolis: Fortress, 1994); Jane Schaberg, "How Mary Magdalene Became a Whore," *Bible Review* 8, no. 5 (October 1992): 30–37; Mary R. Thompson, *Mary of Magdala: Apostle and Leader* (New York: Paulist Press, 1995). For detailed discussion, see under Matthew.

slaves, it is best understood as a sexual relationship. Respecting the couple's privacy, Jesus heals the slave at a distance without inquiring into the relationship or seeking to break it up. The probability that the centurion's relationship with his slave included a sexual dimension has been pointed out by various scholars, but this probability has been systematically ignored by heterosexist male advocacy scholarship.[14]

Archaeologists conclude that Peter's spacious house in Capernaum stood under the very balcony of the synagogue built by this centurion. If this is true, the presence of gay men on the threshold of the Vatican has an even longer history than previously supposed! The centurion's story also is one of but two miracle stories where Jesus heals from a distance. The "unclean" Gentile centurion's insistence that he is not worthy to have a famous Jewish rabbi enter his home might well remind us of common humorous efforts to "dedyke the house," classically portrayed in both the original French and later Hollywood versions of *La Cage aux Folles*. Finally, the importance of the story to early followers of Jesus is indicated by the fact that Luke places it immediately after his version of the Sermon on the Mount, perhaps a counterpoint to Moses' ten plagues leading to the Exodus and the Ten Commandments (→Matthew).

4. Solidarity with the Sick and Physically Challenged

By linking physical affliction with poverty, Luke reminds us how often such factors cause poverty (4:18–19; 7:21–22; 14:12–14, 21). For example, Luke refers most often to the visually challenged, and the six references to blind persons link their blindness to their poverty (4:18; 7:21–22; 14:12–14, 21; 18:35–43). Thus, approaching Jericho, Jesus encountered "a blind man seated by the road begging" (18:35). If the author of Luke is the "beloved physician" (Col. 4:14), sometime traveling companion of Paul (Philem. 24; 2 Tim. 4:11), the Gospel could be expected to demonstrate special interest in Jesus' solidarity with the sick and healing ministry (Mark). This would explain why Luke 8:43 omits Mark's implicit criticism of the failed physicians of the woman thus left impoverished (5:26), as well as the fact that only Luke cites the proverb "Physician, cure yourself" (4:23). In the nineteenth century scholars commonly concluded that Luke's medical profession was indicated in his Gospel by his use of technical medical terms, but in recent decades the consensus is that Luke's medical vocabulary represents only what might be expected of an educated Greek author. In Luke unbelief may produce physical impairment (1:20), and healing constitutes one basic dimension of the "salvation" that comes by faith (6:9; 7:50; 8:12, 48, 50; 17:19; 18:42). The following three categories help clarify Luke's own perspective on illness and healing:

14. Donald Mader, "The *Entimos Pais* [Beloved Slave] of Matthew 8:5–13 and Luke 7:1–10," in *Homosexuality and Religion and Philosophy*, ed. Wayne R. Dynes and Stephen Donaldson, Studies in Homosexuality 12 (New York: Garland, 1992), 223–35; Gerd Theissen, *In the Shadow of the Galilean: The Quest of the Historical Jesus in Narrative Form* (London: SCM, 1987), 106; Michael Gray-Fow, "Pederasty, the Scantian Law and the Roman Army," *Journal of Psychohistory* 13 (1986): 449–60; James E. Miller, "The Centurion and His Slave Boy," in the journal *Theology and Sexuality*, forthcoming in 2001.

4.1. Q. The only healing narrative in Luke proceeding from our earliest source (Q, in common with Matthew) is the story of the centurion and his beloved slave (7:1–10 // Matt. 8:5–13 [see above]). The great significance of this story for Luke is indicated by its placement immediately after the Sermon on the Plain ("Mount" in Matthew 5–7). In addition to this healing story and the teaching about the splinter in the eye (6:41–42 // Matt. 7:3–5), also from Q, other references to illness in our earliest source are:

- the summary of the manifestations of God's just new order (7:18–23 // Matt. 11:2–6)
- the sending of the seventy to heal (10:9, 17–20 // Matt. 10:7–8)
- the parable of the demon who returns with seven others (11:24–26 // Matt. 12:43–45)
- the marginalized invited in the parable of the great feast (14:15–24 // Matt. 22:1–14)
- the great effect of a good or evil eye (11:34–36 // Matt. 6:22–23)

4.2. L. For delineating Luke's theology, of course, the references to the sick and stories of healing that occur only in Luke ("L," especially in Luke 9:51–21:38) are particularly significant. Already in the introductory chapters (1:1–4:30) we may observe that only Luke tells us about Elizabeth, who was "sterile" (1:7), and about Zechariah, who, due to his unbelief, was struck dumb (1:20, 22) but at the birth of John the Baptist was enabled to speak again (1:64); and that only Luke narrates Jesus' Jubilee project to proclaim good news to the poor and restore sight to the blind (4:18–19, citing Isa. 61:1–2 and 58:6; cf. Naaman the leper [4:27] and the hungry widow of Zarephath [4:26]). For Jesus' early ministry (4:31–9:50) Luke mainly adapts healing stories from Mark; only the resurrection of the widow of Nain's son (7:11–17) is uniquely Luke's (cf. the exorcism of Mary Magdalene, 8:1–3). In the travel narrative (9:51–21:38), however, Luke includes three healings unique to his Gospel:

- the woman bent double (13:10–17)
- the man suffering from dropsy (14:1–6)
- the ten lepers, with only the Samaritan expressing thanks (17:11–19)

Also unique to Luke is the parable of the good Samaritan (10:29–37), who managed to restore the victim of violence by paradigmatic solidarity and common home remedies (oil, wine, rest, but with no mention of prayer; cf. the blind person seeking to guide another who is visually challenged [6:39], the marginalized invited to the dinner party [14:12–14], and poor Lazarus's wounds [16:20–22]). Only Luke tells us that Jesus restored the ear of the high priest's slave, which Peter had cut off during Jesus' arrest (22:51), and that Jesus, after his resurrection, opened the eyes of his two male disciples from Emmaus (24:16, 31).

4.3. From Mark. Especially in 4:14–9:50 almost all of Luke's healing stories are adapted from Mark, and the fact that Luke scrupulously includes ten healing narratives from Mark makes clear that Luke shares Mark's appreciation for Jesus' solidarity with the sick and physically challenged:

4:33–37 // Mark 1:23–28	exorcism of a man in the Capernaum synagogue
4:38–39 // Mark 1:29–31	Jesus heals Simon Peter's mother-in-law ("rebuked the fever")
5:12–16 // Mark 1:40–45	leper cleansed
5:17–26 // Mark 2:1–12	paralytic healed
6:6–11 // Mark 3:1–6	man with withered hand healed
8:26–39 // Mark 5:1–20	exorcism of a Gerasene man
8:40–56 // Mark 5:21–43	woman with hemorrhages healed and Jairus's daughter raised
9:37–43 // Mark 9:14–27	exorcism of a son (epileptic)
18:35–43 // Mark 10:46–52	blind beggar healed

Of Mark's healing narratives Luke takes over and adapts all but three:

Mark 7:24–30 (// Matt. 15:21–28)	daughter of the Syrophoenician woman
Mark 7:31–37 (cf. Matt. 15:29–31)	healing of a deaf mute person
Mark 8:22–26	healing (with saliva), by stages, of a blind man from Bethsaida

In addition to healing stories, Luke adapts from Mark other references to the sick and physically challenged: numerous healings (4:40–41 // Mark 1:32–34), multitudes (6:17–19 // Mark 3:7–12), the commission of the twelve (9:1–2 // Mark 3:13–15; 6:7); hearing or seeing impaired (8:8, 10, 18 // Mark 4:9, 13, 24–25); and the isolated exorcist (9:49–50 // Mark 9:38–41). Compare the other general lists (Luke 5:15; 6:17–19; 9:1, 6, 11).

4.4. Summary. Texts about the sick, the physically handicapped, and multiple identities in Luke are summarized as follows:

- Demoniacs: nine times (4:31–37, 40–41; 6:17–19; 7:21; 8:1–3, 26–39; 9:37–43, 49–50; 13:32). In the case of the boy whom the disciples could not exorcise (9:37–43), commentators point out that he had symptoms of epilepsy. As in the case of Elizabeth, considered "sterile" (1:7), to the modern reader the biblical perspective appears prescientific.

- Blind: five times, always with indication of resulting poverty (4:18; 7:21–22; 14:12–14, 21: 18:35–43; cf. metaphors and visual problems with no indication of poverty in 6:39–42; 8:10; 24:16, 31).

- Lepers: four times (4:27; 5:12–16; 7:21–22; 17:11–19). "Unclean" and marginalized, according to Moses' law (their healing always is described as "purification," not exorcism).

- Lame: three times (only in lists: 7:22; 14:13, 21).

- Deaf, or ear cut off: two times (7:21–22; 22:49–51, the slave's ear; cf. 8:8; 14:35).

- Crippled: two times (only in lists: 14:13, 21).

- Dead restored to life: two times (7:11–17; the list in 7:22; cf. Jesus' resurrection, chap. 24).

For seven other categories Luke provides only one example: a mute person (1:20, 22, 64); with fever (4:38–39); paralytic (5:17–26); shriveled hand (6:6–11); the centurion's slave at death's door (7:1–10; cf. // Matt. 8:6, "paralyzed"); a woman bent over (13:10–17); a man suffering from dropsy (14:1–6).

Multiple identities. Multiple identities (references in Luke to persons in need of healing; *=individuals):

5 Poor (illness/handicap as cause of poverty):

- 4:18–19, poor, captives, blind, oppressed
- *7:1–10, centurion's beloved slave
- *7:11–17, son of the widow of Nain
- 7:21–22, blind, lame, lepers, deaf, dead, poor
- *8:43–48, woman with hemorrhages (her poverty indicated only in Mark 5:26)
- 14:12–14, poor, crippled, lame, blind
- 14:15–24, poor, crippled, blind, lame
- *18:35–43, a blind beggar
- *22:51, high priest's slave (L; cf. Mark 14:47)

4 Women (all sexual minorities):

- *4:38–39, Simon Peter's mother-in-law (widowed/divorced? lives with Peter)
- *8:1–3, Mary Magdalene
- *8:43–48, woman with hemorrhages (see under poor)
- *13:10–17, woman bent double

  cf. 7:11–17, widow of Nain, whose son died

3 Children, Youths:

- *7:11–17, son of the widow of Nain (see under poor and women)
- *8:40–42, 49–56, daughter of Jairus (see 8:51, his wife)
- *9:37–43a, epileptic son exorcised

16 Sexual Minorities:

3 Women

- *8:1–3, Mary Magdalene
- *8:43–48, woman with hemorrhages (see under poor)
- *13:10–17, woman bent double
- cf. 7:11–17, widow of Nain's son (see under poor)

13 Men (3 poor, see above)

- *4:27 (L), Naaman, the Syrian leper (purified by the prophet Elisha)
- *4:33–37 // Mark 1:23–28, demoniac in the synagogue of Capernaum
- *5:12–16 // Mark 1:40–45 // Matt. 8:1–4, leper purified
- *5:17–26 // Mark 2:1–12 // Matt. 9:1–8, a paralytic (carried by four friends)
- *6:6–11 // Mark 3:1–6 // Matt. 12:9–14, man with a withered hand
- *7:1–10 (Q; // Matt. 8:5–13), centurion's beloved slave (see under poor)
- *8:26–39 // Mark 5:1–20 // Matt. 8:28–34, the Gerasene demoniac(s)
- *11:14–23 // Matt. 12:22–30; cf. Mark 3:22–27, exorcism of a mute man
- *14:1–6 (L), man with dropsy
- *17:11–19 (L), ten lepers, with only the Samaritan expressing gratitude
- *18:35–43 // Mark 10:46–52 (// Matt. 9:27–31 and 20:29–34), blind person(s) (see under poor)
- *22:51 (L; cf. Mark 14:47), the high priests's slave (see under poor)
- *24:16, 31 (L), two male disciples from Emmaus.

Remarkably, certain individual men in Mark and Luke appear in Matthew as male pairs (the two demoniacs, Matt. 8:28–34; two blind men two times (!), 9:27–31 // 20:29–34). Moreover, only Matthew names the twelve apostles in pairs (10:2–4), only Mark indicates that Jesus sent out the twelve two by two (6:7), and only Luke adds that the seventy also were sent out in pairs (10:1; possibly including a few women and childless couples). As would be expected in the only Gospel where Jesus indicates that his disciples commonly abandoned their wives (Luke 14:26; 18:29), Luke's healing stories rarely refer to married couples: only the parents of John the Baptist (1:5–25), and Jairus with his wife (8:40–42, 49–56).

5. Anti-Semitism in Luke?

Because Luke was the only non-Jewish author in the New Testament, modern studies after the Nazi Holocaust concern themselves a great deal with those texts that through the centuries have lent themselves to encourage violence against Jews. Luke appears to attribute more guilt for the crucifixion to certain Jews and less to Roman authorities (22:54; 23:23–25; 24:20; cf. 11:47–51; 13:34; 19:39–44). At any rate, today it is essential that we keep in mind the danger that such texts represent in powerful churches and in cultures with a history of much violence against Jews. Such dangers concern Jane Schaberg so much that she suggests we read Luke as a "formidable opponent" and not as an ally.[15] David Tiede, however, points out how Luke maintains a future

15. Schaberg, "Luke," 291.

hope for Israel when the "times of the Gentiles are fulfilled" (21:24).[16] At least a less simplistic and more dialectic reading of Luke is appropriate, since the Jesus portrayed by Paul's "beloved physician" did not come to seal our minds with narrow dogmas but to open them (24:45).

Bibliography

Atwood, Richard. *Mary Magdalene in the New Testament and Early Tradition.* Bern, Germany: Lang, 1993.

Bock, Darrell L. *Luke.* 2 vols. Baker Exegetical Commentary on the New Testament. Grand Rapids: Baker, 1994–96.

Boer, Esther de. *Mary Magdalene: Beyond the Myth.* Trans. John Bowden. Harrisburg, Pa.: Trinity, 1997.

Cassidy, Richard J. *Jesus, Politics and Society: A Study of Luke's Gospel.* Maryknoll, N.Y.: Orbis, 1978.

———. *Society and Politics in the Acts of the Apostles.* Maryknoll, N.Y.: Orbis, 1987.

Garrett, Susan R. "Beloved Physician of the Soul? Luke as Advocate for Ascetic Practice." In *Asceticism and the New Testament,* ed. Leif E. Vaage and Vincent L. Wimbush, 71–95. New York: Routledge, 1999.

Haskins, Susan. *Mary Magdalen: Myth and Metaphor.* New York: Harcourt, Brace, 1993.

Johnson, Luke Timothy. "Luke-Acts, Book of." *ABD,* 4:403–20.

———. *The Literary Function of Possessions in Luke-Acts.* Missoula, Mont.: Scholars Press, 1977.

Mader, Donald. "The *Entimos Pais* [Beloved Slave] of Matthew 8:5–13 and Luke 7:1–10." In *Homosexuality and Religion and Philosophy,* ed. Wayne R. Dynes and Stephen Donaldson, 223–35. Studies in Homosexuality 12. New York: Garland, 1992.

Miller, James E. "The Centurion and His Slave Boy," in the journal *Theology and Sexuality,* forthcoming in 2001.

Moxnes, Halvor. *The Economy of the Kingdom: Social Conflict and Economic Relations in Luke's Gospel.* Philadelphia: Fortress, 1988.

Pilgrim, Walter. *Good News to the Poor: Wealth and Poverty in Luke-Acts.* Minneapolis: Augsburg, 1981.

Reid, Barbara E. *Choosing the Better Part? Women in the Gospel of Luke.* Collegeville, Minn.: Liturgical Press, 1996.

Ricci, Carla. *Mary Magdalene and Many Others: Women Who Followed Jesus.* Trans. Paul Burns. Minneapolis: Fortress, 1994.

Ringe, Sharon H. *Luke.* Louisville: Westminster John Knox, 1995.

———. *Jesus, Liberation, and the Biblical Jubilee.* Philadelphia: Fortress, 1985.

Roth, S. John. *The Blind, the Lame, and the Poor: Character Types in Luke-Acts.* JSNTSup 144. Sheffield: Sheffield Academic Press, 1997.

Schaberg, Jane. "Luke." In *The Women's Bible Commentary,* ed. Carol A. Newsom and Sharon H. Ringe, 363–80. Louisville: Westminster John Knox, 1998.

---

16. David L. Tiede, "Fighting against God: Luke's Interpretation of Jewish Rejection of the Messiah Jesus," in *Anti-Semitism and Early Christianity,* ed. Craig A. Evans and Donald A Hagner (Minneapolis: Fortress, 1993), 102–12; see further under Acts.

———. *The Illegitimacy of Jesus: A Feminist Theological Interpretation of the Infancy Narratives*. New York: Crossroad, 1987.

Schottroff, Luise. *Lydia's Impatient Sisters: A Feminist Social History of Early Christianity*. Trans. Barbara and Martin Rumscheidt. Louisville: Westminster John Knox, 1995.

Seim, Turid Karlsen. "The Gospel of Luke." In *Searching the Scriptures*, vol. 2, *A Feminist Commentary*, ed. Elisabeth Schüssler Fiorenza, 728–62. New York: Crossroad, 1994.

———. *The Double Message: Patterns of Gender in Luke-Acts*. Nashville: Abingdon, 1994.

Thompson, Mary R. *Mary of Magdala: Apostle and Leader*. New York: Paulist Press, 1995.

Thurston, Bonnie Bowman. *The Widows: A Women's Ministry in the Early Church*. Minneapolis: Fortress, 1989.

Wenk, Matthias. *Community Forming Power: The Socio-Ethical Role of the Spirit in Luke-Acts*. Sheffield: Sheffield Academic Press, 2000.

Chapter 4

JOHN

Jesus' Beloved Disciple Subverts Literalism and the Law

Outline

Prologue: "The Word became flesh"	1:1–18
1. The Book of Signs: Empowerment for the Weak and Marginalized	1:19–12:50
Jesus' forerunner: John the Baptist	1:19–34
Counterculture community in formation: first disciples	1:35–51
Sign #1: a poor patriarchal family and Jesus' new wine	2:1–12
A second oppressive institution: Jesus purifies the temple	2:13–22
How to enter Jesus' fictive kinship community: spiritual birth	2:23–3:21
"Bridegroom" Jesus' best man: John the Baptist	3:22–36
Leadership in Jesus' new community: a Samaritan divorcée	4:1–42
Sign #2: An official's son healed (// Luke 7:1–10; Matt. 8:5–13?)	4:43–52
Sign #3: Healing of a paralytic marginalized for thirty-eight years	5:1–47
Sign #4: Jesus feeds a poor, hungry multitude	6:1–15, 22–71
(1) I AM THE BREAD OF LIFE, 6:35	
Sign #5: Jesus strides over the sea	6:16–21
Jesus at the Feast of Booths (A): source of "living water"	7:1–52
[Later addition: Jesus liberates an adulterous woman	7:52–8:11]
Jesus at the Feast of Booths (B):	8:12–29
(2) I AM THE LIGHT OF THE WORLD, 8:12	
Sign #6: Jesus gives sight to a beggar born blind	9:1–41
Jesus, a shepherd, who has "other sheep" (unclean Gentiles)	10:1–21
(3) I AM THE DOOR, 10:7, 9	

(4) I AM THE GOOD SHEPHERD, 10:11, 14

Sign #7: Jesus raises Lazarus from the dead 11:1–54

(5) I AM THE RESURRECTION AND THE LIFE, 11:25

End of public ministry: a grain of wheat that dies... 11:55–12:50

2. Jesus Prepares His New Community for the Spirit's Coming 13:1–17:26

Exemplary leadership: Jesus washes his disciples' feet 13:1–20

Exemplary love (the Beloved Disciple) and betrayal (Judas) 13:21–30

A new commandment: "Love one another as I have loved you" 13:31–35

Jesus foretells how Peter (married) will deny him 13:36–38

Jesus will depart, to prepare the way to the Father 14:1–14

(6) I AM THE TRUE AND LIVING WAY, 14:6

Jesus promises to send the Holy Spirit to empower 14:15–31

The new community, a vine with fruitful branches 15:1–17

(7) I AM THE TRUE VINE, 15:1, 5

How the world will hate and oppress the new community 15:18–16:4a

The Holy Spirit's work: defense attorney for the oppressed 16:4b–15

Jesus promises to return quickly after his death 16:16–33

Jesus intercedes for himself and the new community 17:1–26

3. Oppressive Judgments, Violent and Shameful Death—Resurrection! 18:1–20:31

Jesus' betrayal and arrest 18:1–11

Religious-political process before the high priests 18:12–27

Peter's threefold denial that Jesus had foretold 18:15–18, 25–27

Political-religious process before Pilate 18:28–19:16a

Shame and violence of the crucifixion 19:16b–37

Burial: courageous but tardy solidarity of two rich friends 19:38–42

Divine vindication: Jesus' glorious resurrection 20:1–31

The Beloved Disciple's paradigmatic faith 20:1–10

Jesus' first appearance: to Mary of Magdala 20:11–18

Jesus' appearances to his other disciples 20:19–29

John's purpose: empowering the community for evangelism? 20:30–31

Epilogue: Peter's restoration, the Beloved Disciple's longevity 21:1–25

Commentary

The first explicit testimony concerning John's Gospel is that of St. Irenaeus, around 180 C.E.: "Then John, the Lord's disciple, the same who rested on his breast, also published the Gospel during his stay in Ephesus." If not put in final form by the Beloved Disciple himself, as the majority of experts now conclude, the Gospel may well reflect the apostle John's teachings, written by a disciple after his death (ca. 90 C.E.). The identification of the Beloved Disciple with John the son of Zebedee is often questioned in modern scholarship, but remains the preferable hypothesis regarding the authoritative source behind the Fourth Gospel.[1]

1. Life Abundant for the Poor, the Weak, and the Physically Challenged

Even more so than John's letters, the Gospel would appear to be singularly deficient in terms of a specific "ethical" content. Jesus only reveals that he is the revealer (so Rudolf Bultmann), and he demands a *love* that obeys his *commandment:* "*love* one another" (another apparent tautology). In this Gospel Jesus commands love to the brothers/sisters of the new community, not the general love of neighbor and much less of an enemy (cf. Matthew 5, Luke 6, and Romans 12). In addition to the seven signs and the crucifixion, the most concrete illustration of this love that is given in this Gospel is the washing of the feet (13:1–20).

The four references to the "always present" poor/beggars (*ptōchos,* 12:5, 6, 8; 13:29) hardly appear to demonstrate great concern for them. Consequently, the privileged Johannine researchers have concentrated their efforts in other areas and generally ignored the significant points contributed by José P. Miranda, Frederick Herzog, Hugo Zorilla, and the feminist/womanist and African American studies.[2] However, a growing minority of theologians

---

1. Raymond E. Brown, *An Introduction to the New Testament* (New York: Doubleday, 1997), 368–71. Craig Blomberg concludes that there is "strong circumstantial evidence for equating the beloved disciple with the apostle John" (*Jesus and the Gospels* [Nashville: Broadman, 1997], 170). Blomberg cites the classic statement of the case for John as Beloved Disciple and Gospel author by B. F. Westcott, *The Gospel According to St. John* (London: John Murray), 1908, x–lii, with important updating by Leon Morris, *Studies in the Fourth Gospel* (Grand Rapids: Eerdmans, 1969), 139–292. Those who argue for alternative identifications of the Beloved Disciple include R. Alan Culpepper, *John, the Son of Zebedee: The Life of a Legend* (Columbia: University of South Carolina Press, 1994); Joseph A. Grassi, *The Secret Identity of the Beloved Disciple* (New York: Paulist Press, 1992), 117–18 ("A Note on This Close and Affectionate Male Relationship"). Vernard Eller (*The Beloved Disciple—His Name, His Story, His Thought: Two Studies from the Gospel of John* [Grand Rapids: Eerdmans, 1987]) concludes that the Beloved Disciple was Lazarus. Only in the latter half of John do we find explicit references to the Beloved Disciple (13:23; 19:26; 20:2; 21:7, 20), but cf. Lazarus in 11:3. See also Richard J. Bauckham, "The Beloved Disciple as Ideal Author," *Journal for the Study of the New Testament* 49 (1993): 21–44; J. H. Charlesworth, *The Beloved Disciple: Whose Witness Validates the Gospel of John?* (Valley Forge, Pa.: Trinity, 1995), argues that the Beloved Disciple was Thomas.

2. José P. Miranda, *Being and the Messiah: The Message of St. John,* trans. John Eagleson (Maryknoll, N.Y.: Orbis, 1977); Frederick Herzog, *Liberation Theology: Liberation in the Light of the Fourth Gospel* (New York: Seabury, 1972); Hugo C. Zorrilla, *La fiesta de*

interpret the Johannine writings as representative of a unique and radical perspective. On opposing the traditional "feudalization" of God's realm in the Synoptic Gospels, they also reject the "Platonization" of eternal and abundant life in the Johannine writings.

In the prologue of his Gospel, John states that the Word became *flesh* (1:14), that is humanity in the generic sense, not explicitly male. Furthermore, if John 1:14 is not an explicit designation of the option for a humanity that is intrinsically poor, at least it aims to characterize human *weakness* ("the flesh is weak," 6:63), whose major expression is weakness in the economic sphere, that is, poverty. The abandonment and marginalization of the incarnate Word ("his own people did not accept him," 1:11; cf. 1:46; a lack of hospitality; see Sodom, Genesis 19) is another Johannine topic that expresses the painful dimension of poverty. It is now common to place emphasis on persecution and excommunication as dominant formative experiences in the history of the Johannine communities. However, many seem not to take into account the mortal economic deprivations and the violence that commonly accompany such persecution.

As in the Synoptic Gospels, Jesus' miraculous healings generally are directed toward the poor and physically challenged (blind beggar, 9:1–12; paralytic, 5:1–9) and the weak (son, 4:46–54). John 5:3 mentions not only paralyzed but also weak, sick, blind, and lame. See the needy in the miracles of provision (2:1–12, wine; 6:1–15, bread). In John the early placement of the purification of the temple (at the beginning, 2:13–22, following the provision of wine for an obviously poor family) demonstrates the prominence of John's criticism of the oppressive Jewish oligarchy: "It is precisely in the temple where Jesus opts for the marginalized: the sick, the poor, the toll collectors, women, children, foreigners."[3]

While the Synoptics refer to the *realm of God,* John prefers to speak of (eternal) *life.* This change should be understood above all as a dialectical and political mode[4] in a context of excommunication, persecution, and violence. The traditional (Platonizing) interpretations of John radically distort its original meaning and try to elude the sharpness of its polemics. The "abundant life" offered in John (10:10) invalidates the extremes of "prosperity theology" (Pentecostal-Charismatic, not dialectical), but neither is it limited to a Platonically spiritualized, or immaterial, sphere (cf. 3 John 2). Miranda may have been mistaken when he gave in to the elimination of a futuristic eschatology (following Rudolf Bultmann).[5] But he was not mistaken when he delineated the radical character of the Johannine perspective concerning the poor, jus-

---

liberación de los oprimidos: Relectura de Juan 7:1–10:21 (San José, Costa Rica: Seminario Bíblico Latinoamericano, 1980); idem, *Las fiestas de Yavé* (Buenos Aires: Aurora, 1988).

3. Zorrilla, *Las fiestas de Yavé,* 71.

4. C. K. Barrett, "The Dialectical Theology of St. John," in *New Testament Essays* (London: SPCK, 1972), 49–69.

5. Miranda, *Being and the Messiah,* 172–92.

tice, injustice/oppression (*adikia,* 7:18; cf. 1 John 1:9; 5:17), sacrificial love (solidarity), and life.

John's Gospel indicates causes for poverty when it points out the persecution, oppression, and violence suffered by the communities. The first letter of John explicitly points to the commonly resulting poverty (1 John 3:17, "in need"; cf. 3 John 5–8) and the appropriate response of *agape*-love in the context of the Christian communities characterized by sharing-*koinōnia.* Love in John is for the dispossessed, the poor, the needy.[6] Thus, as in Matthew (27:57–60), the rich Joseph of Arimathea (together with Nicodemus) is presented at the end of the Gospel as a paradigm of the "poor in spirit" who express solidarity with the oppressed and persecuted (John 19:38–42).

Like our earliest traditions of Jesus' teaching (→Mark and Q; see also Paul, →1 Thessalonians), justice (*dik-*) terms are remarkably rare in John (six times). "Justice" (*dikaiosunē*) occurs but twice in one context (16:8, 10), where some conclude that the sense is ironic (see Mark 2:17, "I have not come to call the [self-]righteous, but sinners"). Probably, however, Jesus' vindication (God's liberating justice manifest in the resurrection and ascension) is meant, in contrast to the world's sin and violence. Oppression (*adikia*) is used but once (7:18, with reference to Jesus' innocence of fraud or dishonesty; cf. 1 John 1:9; 5:17; →Revelation). Jesus exhorts the crowd to "Stop judging by mere appearances but express liberating justice [for the oppressed] in your judgments" (John 7:24, *dikaian krisin,* "just judgment"). He insists that his judgments exemplify such justice (5:30). And in his prayer Jesus addresses God as characterized by liberating justice, in contrast to the world that does not know God (17:25; to know God is to practice liberating justice [Jer. 22:16]).

The sparsity of references to oppression and liberating justice in John in comparison to →Revelation may be due to the latter's apocalyptic genre rather than to different authors or widely varying dates. In the context of an excommunicated, persecuted community, John's Gospel focuses more on threats of marginalization, persecution, and violence than on economic poverty as such. His theology, rooted in the Exodus paradigm of the Hebrew Bible, develops more the abundant life offered and experienced in the new, inclusive community of Jesus' disciples and friends (→3 John; cf. "realm of God" in the Synoptic Gospels).

2. *For Women and Sexual Minorities: A Community of Friends*

Also oppressed, persecuted, and marginalized, sexual minorities and marginalized women are treated with concern and special honor in John. He portrays five women: Jesus' mother (Mary, widowed?), the Samaritan, the sisters Mary and Martha, and Mary Magdalene, each representing some type of sexual minority. Mary the wife of Clopas (19:25) is listed as present at the cross but is

6. "John's love is love of the deprived, the poor, the needy. Therefore it is identified with justice" (Miranda, *Being and the Messiah,* 95). Note Raymond Brown's conclusion: "For John there are no second-class citizens among true believers; all of them are God's own children" (*Introduction to the New Testament,* 378).

otherwise unknown (cf. Pilate's wife in Matt. 27:19, and Jairus and his wife in Mark 5:40; on the adulteress in 7:53–8:11, see section 5 and the outline above). Mark's "messianic secret" is detonated quite early in John's Gospel when Jesus reveals himself fully and explicitly as Messiah to the Samaritan woman who has had multiple husbands and sexual companions (4:1–42). Jesus then repeatedly declares "I am. . . . " (6:35; see the outline above).

The place of sexual minorities in John's theology and the structure of his book is impressive. In John 2 we have the wedding at Cana with the Gospel's first miracle (sign), the water made wine, followed surprisingly by the purification of the temple, an event the Synoptic Gospels place in the last week (passion) as the occasion of Jesus' crucifixion. Specialists in John remain perplexed concerning the radical change in order. However, if we understand the situation and attitude of the Beloved Disciple (unmarried), we can understand how this order is key to understanding his theology.

For John the wedding at Cana (2:1–12) does not constitute a motive to celebrate the continuity of the traditional patriarchal family but a point of departure with the counterculture network of Jesus' disciples (2:11–12). In John 1 we have the formation of the new community of Jesus' disciples (1:35–51), and in John 2 a presentation of the two traditional institutions that will be replaced by this new community: the traditional patriarchal household (2:1–12), and the temple and feasts in Jerusalem (2:13–22). The eucharistic wine that the disciples enjoy in the new community is superior to the wine (depleted) of the traditional patriarchal household, just as the new community of disciples (primarily unmarried) that surround Jesus also is superior to that institution.

John's account of the wedding at Cana (2:1–12) is consistently misinterpreted because of idolatrous family ideologies. Fundamental to proper interpretation of this passage—much abused in weddings—is the preceding context, where Jesus contacts a "network of marginalized acquaintances" to form a fictive kinship, countercultural "antisociety."[7] Then at Cana, with his presence and first miraculous sign, Jesus (now over thirty but still single) first blesses the patriarchal wedding, but then proceeds to deconstruct patriarchy by insisting on his freedom from family demands—from his mother, who in this narrative evidences all the nervous symptoms of a new member of PFLAG (Parents and Friends of Lesbians and Gays). Bruce Malina and Richard Rohrbaugh point out, "In 'straight' society, as opposed to antisociety, [such] in-group persons all deserve and receive immediate compliance. . . . Perhaps John uses this pattern to inform members of his group about how to deal with their relatives and other natural in-group persons."[8] With his newly formed (1:35–51) nucleus of disciples (also almost all unmarried), Jesus demonstrates that his new counterculture community exemplifies authentic freedom and enjoys a lifestyle superior to that of the traditional patriarchal family represented

7. Bruce J. Malina and Richard L. Rohrbaugh, *Social-Science Commentary on the Gospel of John* (Minneapolis: Fortress, 1998), 60–61.

8. Ibid., 68.

by the wedding. The shortage of wine signals a lack of friends. Afterwards, "Jesus' biological and fictive families are . . . portrayed as traveling together,"[9] but John's succeeding narrative makes clear that the new network of "friends" (15:9–15), not the patriarchal household, is fundamental and normative for society in God's new order.[10]

John's early placement of Jesus' temple cleansing also may reflect the repressed anger of the unmarried John faced with two oppressive institutions: the patriarchal family (2:1–12) and the temple (2:13–22). Jesus called John and his brother James—irate youths—"sons of thunder" (Mark 3:17; see "thunder" in the Johannine Revelation, 4:5, plus nine other occurrences). John's anger, then, not only is directed against religious leaders and the temple, but also focuses on the patriarchal institution of the heterosexual, procreative household (the wedding at Cana). Such anger (commonly unconscious and repressed) has been characteristic of sexual minorities, who commonly have had to spend their lives repressing and hiding their true feelings of love. Both the wedding at Cana and the Jerusalem temple represent targets for John's anger, and the entire book carries out a deconstruction of the oppressive institutions of the patriarchal household and patriarchal religion. Jesus' new community of disciples replaces both the patriarchal household and patriarchal religion and thus manifests the truth that liberates from oppression (8:32).

The displacement of the patriarchal household by the new community of disciples is seen immediately following in the dialogue with Nicodemus (3:1–21). Jesus with his teaching replaces "the teacher" of Israel, and people (mainly marginalized) enter into the new community by a new spiritual birth instead of inheriting such a status through natural birth. The Johannine process of displacement continues in the account concerning the Samaritan woman (4:1–42), where a non-Israelite—moreover, someone of a sexual minority, a woman of bad repute—receives the first explicit revelation concerning the messianic identity of Jesus and then shares it, as an evangelist, with her village. In the dialogue Jesus emphasizes that worship of God in spirit and truth (the practice of the Johannine communities excluded by the synagogues) replaces any temple as the center of divine revelation and source of life.

In the second sign, which then follows (John 4:43–52), John transforms the Q account (Luke 7:1–11 // Matt. 8:5–13) concerning the centurion and his beloved slave who was healed (or perhaps John follows an independent tradition). Remarkably, John appears to "clean up" both portrayals of sexual minorities described in Luke 7. First, although in Luke 7:1–10 Jesus heals the Roman centurion's slave, in John 4:43–54 the much beloved slave becomes a "son" (adopted slave?). Second, in Luke 7:36–50 a prostitute ("sinner" par excellence) anoints Jesus' feet, but in John 12:1–8 it is the pious Mary, who had sat at Jesus' feet to listen to his teachings (Luke 10:39), who anoints

9. Ibid., 69.

10. Ibid., 66. For friendship, not the family, as society's fundamental institution, see Mary E. Hunt, *Fierce Tenderness: A Feminist Theology of Friendship* (New York: Crossroad, 1991).

Jesus' feet. Matthew and Mark describe the anointing in Bethany as taking place in the house of Simon "the leper" (perhaps Mary, Martha, and Lazarus had separated from their father and owner of the house, since he would be "unclean" according to Moses' law; Mark 14:3–9; Matt. 26:6–13).

In John 5:1–47 Jesus goes up again to Jerusalem during a Jewish feast, but instead of going to the temple for the feast, he goes straight to the "hospital" for the marginalized sick and physically challenged, the pool of Bethesda, where he heals a paralyzed man. A sharp conflict results with the religious authorities concerning the Sabbath and the law. Jesus causes even greater opposition when he insists that he—not the temple with its feasts—represents the new center for God's liberating, life-giving work.

John 6 includes the narrative of Jesus feeding five thousand poor followers (as in the Synoptics), but he then declares, "I am the bread of life" (6:35), displacing Moses (cf. the manna of the Exodus) as the father of the patriarchal household. In John 7 the conflict with the Jewish authorities becomes more serious, and the last day of the Feast of Booths Jesus presents himself as the water of life, again displacing the temple (see Ezekiel 47).

In John 8 Jesus declares himself the light of the world that liberates the new community of his followers from two oppressive institutions: the patriarchal household (descendants of Abraham, 8:3, 7) and the temple authorities. This subversive teaching is followed by the narrative of the healing of a man blind from birth (9:1–41), a single man dependent on his parents who, after being driven out of the synagogue, became a part of Jesus' new community. John 10 includes Jesus' proclamation, "I am the good shepherd," the leader who replaces oppressive temple authorities and whose "sheep" (disciples) replace the oppressive patriarchal household. During the Feast of Dedication in Jerusalem (10:22–42) the conflict with authorities increases again, and they resort to violence and try to stone Jesus.

With Lazarus's resurrection (11:1–54) John's purpose and theology are clearly revealed. Jesus had participated in the traditional patriarchal wedding in Cana under pressure from his mother. However, John clearly demonstrates that Jesus' favorite home was not that of his own mother and brothers, nor that of a traditional married couple, but that of Mary, Martha, and their brother, Lazarus, all unmarried. Just as Mark points out that Jesus loved the rich young man, John emphasizes the special love that Jesus had for Lazarus, Mary, and Martha (11:3, 5, 11). And just as Paul greets primarily households of sexual minorities in Romans 16, John makes it clear that the place where Jesus felt most "at home" was a household of sexual minorities, persons who broke with the patriarchal expectation of marriage and having children. According to John, this is the Mary who anointed Jesus' feet with perfume in Bethany (12:1–8).

Lazarus's resurrection makes clear that God's power in Jesus now operates outside the environment of the temple and the religious authorities and also outside the control of the traditional patriarchal families. The conclusion of the first half of John continues demonstrating how the nontraditional home of Mary, Martha, and Lazarus displaces the traditional patriarchal household and the temple as the center of divine action. John 12 culminates the Book of Signs by announcing the arrival of some Greeks ("other sheep") who seek to join the new community of Jesus' followers (displacing the incredulous Jews; 11:55–12:50).

In the second part of the Gospel (chaps. 13–21), John first gives us Jesus' teaching that seeks to empower the disciples and prepare them for the crucifixion. In John 13–17 Jesus speaks of the presence of God's Spirit with his new community (not in the temple). With his radical perspective, John focuses on the simple command of mutual love in the new community (13:34–35) instead of the multiple legal codes of the Pentateuch (see Paul, with his similar advocacy of freedom from the law, especially in Galatians and Romans). As John insists in his prologue, "The law indeed was given through Moses; but grace and truth came through Jesus Christ" (1:17). John's radical elimination of the multiple marginalizations prescribed in the Pentateuch codes with reference to sexual minorities (Deut. 23:1–2, Lev. 21:18–20; especially "eunuchs") makes the Gospel of the Beloved Disciple quite explicitly "good news" for sexual minorities. As spiritual birth (3:1–9) is distinct, so also the "fruit" of the new community is not natural children but the multiplication of disciples (15:1–17).

In his narrative of Jesus' death, John stresses the conflict with the temple's religious leaders. Shortly before dying on the cross, Jesus entrusts his mother not to Peter, with his traditional "straight" family, but to the unmarried Beloved Disciple, who in this way formed another nontraditional home (19:26–27). It is this Beloved Disciple who had "leaned on Jesus' chest" during the Last Supper (13:23, 25; modern translations create more space between Jesus and the Beloved Disciple than indicated by the Greek text) and was, according to tradition, the author of the Gospel (see 1:35–40; 18:15–16; 19:26–27; 20:1–10; 21:7, 20–24). As an example of literary inclusion, Jesus' mother appears in John only in the narrative of the wedding at Cana (2:1–12) and then at the end when Jesus sends her to form part of the new community in connection with his unmarried Beloved Disciple (19:26–27).

Mark had told how the faithful women arrived first at the empty tomb, and Luke and Matthew added how the resurrected Jesus appeared first to these women, and not to the failed male apostles. John, however, insists that, even before the appearances to the women, the Beloved Disciple, having run to the tomb faster than Peter, was the first to believe in the resurrection, even without having seen Jesus. It is the unmarried Beloved Disciple, then, who serves as the fundamental paradigm for future generations who believed without seeing the resurrected Jesus. In the Gospel it is this unmarried Beloved Disciple (not a "family") who symbolizes the Christian community.

Moreover, the first appearance of the resurrected Jesus is not to the faithful women as a group but to Mary Magdalene, traditionally identified as a prostitute (20:1–18; see under Luke and Matthew). Adeline Fehribach sensitively portrays Mary's determined search for Jesus' body, comparing her to the woman in Song of Songs and to Greek love novels where wives search for the bodies of dead husbands. Jesus is seen as the "messianic bridegroom." Fehribach is bothered by Jesus' refusal to reciprocate Mary's embrace and observes that Jesus "remains aloof from the earthly concerns of others, especially the women in his life,"[11] but limits imposed by her heterosexist ideology keep her from detecting more radical possibilities.

John's subsequent epilogue (21:1–25), however, stubbornly insists that the unmarried John, Jesus' Beloved Disciple, maintains a certain priority over Peter and will outlive him (just as he outran him in the race to the tomb). Most significantly, however, both the married disciple and Jesus' Beloved Disciple became a leadership team (see Acts 1–5) for Jesus' new community that displaces the traditional oppressive patriarchal household and the temple with its priests.

From St. Irenaeus we have another tradition (now commonly suppressed):

> There are also those who heard from [Polycarp] that John, the disciple of the Lord, going to the baths at Ephesus, and perceiving Cerinthus within, rushed out of the bath-house without bathing, exclaiming, "Let us fly, lest even the bath-house fall down, because Cerinthus, the enemy of the truth, is within."[12]

Cerinthus was a Gnostic heretic (ca. 100 C.E.). This St. Irenaeus tradition used to be cited frequently by traditional authors eager to defend Johannine authorship—before Kinsey (1948) and Stonewall (1968) led to more public diffusion of information concerning homoerotic practices in the Greco-Roman societies. Until then, nobody used to ask why a Jewish-Christian like John would be found frequenting the public baths, a Greco-Roman institution of bad repute among the Jews.

3. *Anti-Judaism/Anti-Semitism in John?*

Although Jesus was always a Jew (John 4:9, 22), as was John himself, of all the New Testament books, John's Gospel appears to contain the most negative and numerous expressions (seventy-one times) against "the Jews" (see 5:16–18, 39–40, 45–47; 9:22; 12:42; 15:18–21, 24b–25; 16:2–3; and especially 8:39b–47, containing "You are from your father the devil"). However, the expression "the Jews" in John almost always appears to refer only to certain hostile leaders or their followers, and nothing in the New Testament reflects the type of racist anti-Judaism of the modern era. John's negative rhetoric now commonly is understood to reflect the painful experiences of the Johannine communities on being excluded from the synagogues (9:22; 12:42; 16:2). These communities saw themselves as living separated from "the world" (Jewish society).

The word "covenant" never occurs in John, and Jesus' teaching about the new love commandment and, for the new community, the Holy Spirit's guid-

---

11. Adeline Fehribach, *The Women in the Life of the Bridegroom: A Feminist Historical-Literary Analysis of the Female Characters in the Fourth Gospel* (Collegeville, Minn.: Liturgical Press, 1998), 165.

12. Irenaeus *Adv. haer.* 3.3.4; Eusebius, *Hist. eccl.* 5.8.4.

ance (13:1–17:26) take the place of Moses' Torah (1:17; see "your law" in 8:17 and 10:34; "their law" in 15:25; cf. Matt. 5:17–20!). According to John's theology, Jesus himself takes the place of the temple, and the new community of his disciples takes the place of the oppressive patriarchal family (see above on John 2). When the decisive breach occurred between Judaism and the followers of Jesus' "Way" (perhaps as late as 130 C.E.), the cause was not so much John's high Christology but differences regarding Torah. Richard B. Hays concludes that although in the light of the original historical context we may understand John's recourse to negative rhetoric, the church today (post-Holocaust) should never imitate such rhetoric. Rather, for dialogue with the synagogue, we do better to work from more positive texts such as Romans 9–11.[13]

4. *Literalistic Hermeneutics as an Instrument of Oppression*

Faced with the literalism common in the fundamentalisms of every age, John points out how Jesus corrected the literalist interpretations: not the literal temple but his body as the temple (2:19–22); not returning literally to one's mother's womb but being born of the Spirit (3:4–5); not the water from patriarch Jacob's well but the water that Jesus gives (4:10–14; 7:37–39); not Moses' manna but the bread of life that Jesus provides (6:31–35, 48–51).[14] Against the common literalisms of his culture, Jesus presents himself in seven transcendent metaphors ("I am. . . . "): the definitive revelation of God the Liberator and the answer to the eternal human quest (see the outline above).

5. *John 7:53–8:11. Jesus Liberates a Woman Accused of Adultery from the Death Penalty*

This story probably was not originally part of John's Gospel, since it does not appear at this point in the best textual evidence (older manuscripts, versions, and church fathers). In a few manuscripts the story is found at the end of John, or after Luke 21:38. Nevertheless, scholars commonly conclude that the narrative does preserve an authentic tradition about Jesus. Moreover, it is consistent with John's emphasis on Jesus' authority, which replaces patriarchal authority and its death penalty for adultery (Moses), and substitutes the requirement of love that forgives among the disciples in the new community. Some church fathers feared that the story might motivate wives to commit adultery (Augustine); later, Calvin feared that the text might discredit the death penalty law for adultery (Lev. 20:10; Deut. 22:22–24). Nevertheless, the text's theme is not so much "the adulteress woman" (the traditional title) but the double standard and hypocrisy of the patriarchal males whom Jesus unmasked when he liberated the woman from the death penalty (cf. 3:17).[15]

---

13. Richard B. Hays, *The Moral Vision of the New Testament* (San Francisco: HarperCollins, 1996), 434; cf. Robert Kysar, "Anti-Semitism and the Gospel of John," in *Anti-Semitism and Early Christianity*, ed. Craig A. Evans and Donald A. Hagner (Minneapolis: Fortress, 1993), 113–27.

14. D. A. Carson, *The Gospel According to John* (Grand Rapids: Eerdmans, 1991), 98–99.

15. Gail R. O'Day, "John 7:53–8:11: A Study in Misreading," *Journal of Biblical Literature* 111, no. 4 (1992): 631–40. Cf. the other principal textual problems in the New Testament (Mark 16:9–20 and 1 John 5:7).

Bibliography

Barrett, C. K. "The Dialectical Theology of St. John." In *New Testament Essays,* 49–69. London: SPCK, 1972.

Cassidy, Richard J. *John's Gospel in New Perspective: Christology and the Realities of Roman Power.* Maryknoll, N.Y.: Orbis, 1992.

Carson, D. A. *The Gospel According to John.* Grand Rapids: Eerdmans, 1991.

Fehribach, Adeline. *The Women in the Life of the Bridegroom: A Feminist Historical-Literary Analysis of the Female Characters in the Fourth Gospel.* Collegeville, Minn.: Liturgical Press, 1998.

Herzog, Frederick. *Liberation Theology: Liberation in the Light of the Fourth Gospel.* New York: Seabury, 1972.

Howard-Brook, Wes. *Becoming Children of God: John's Gospel and Radical Discipleship.* Maryknoll, N.Y.: Orbis, 1994.

Karris, Robert J. *Jesus and the Marginalized in John's Gospel.* Collegeville, Minn.: Liturgical Press, 1990.

Kysar, Robert. "John, The Gospel of." *ABD,* 3:912–31.

———. "Anti-Semitism and the Gospel of John." In *Anti-Semitism and Early Christianity,* ed. Craig A. Evans and Donald A. Hagner, 113–27. Minneapolis: Fortress, 1993.

Maccini, Robert Gordon. *Her Testimony Is True: Women as Witnesses According to John.* JSNTSup 125. Sheffield: Sheffield Academic Press, 1996.

Malina, Bruce J., and Richard L. Rohrbaugh. *Social-Science Commentary on the Gospel of John.* Minneapolis: Fortress, 1998.

Miranda, José P. *Being and the Messiah: The Message of St. John.* Trans. John Eagleson. Maryknoll, N.Y.: Orbis, 1977.

Morris, Leon. *The Gospel According to John.* Rev. ed. NICNT. Grand Rapids: Eerdmans, 1995.

Neyrey, Jerome H. *An Ideology of Revolt: John's Christology in Social Science Perspective.* Philadelphia: Fortress, 1988.

O'Day, Gail R. "John." In *The Women's Bible Commentary,* ed. Carol A. Newsom and Sharon H. Ringe, 381–93. Louisville: Westminster John Knox, 1998.

Reinhartz, Adele. "The Gospel of John." In *Searching the Scriptures,* vol. 2, *A Feminist Commentary,* ed. E. Schüssler Fiorenza, 561–600. New York: Crossroad, 1994.

Rensberger, David. *Overcoming the World: Politics and Community in the Gospel of John.* London: SPCK, 1988.

———. *Johannine Faith and Liberating Community.* Philadelphia: Westminster, 1988.

———. "Oppression and Identity in the Gospel of John." In *The Recovery of Black Presence,* ed. Randall C. Bailey and Jacquelyn Grant, 77–94. Nashville: Abingdon, 1995.

Rubeaux, Francisco. *Mostra-nos o Pai: Uma leitura do quarto evangelho.* Belo Horizonte, Brazil: Centro de Estudos Biblicos, 1989.

Slade, Stan. *Evangelio de Juan.* Buenos Aires: Kairos, 1998.

van Tilborg, Sjef. *Imaginative Love in John.* Leiden: Brill, 1993.

Witherington, Ben, III. *John's Wisdom: A Commentary on the Fourth Gospel.* Louisville: Westminster John Knox, 1995.

Zorrilla, C. Hugo. *La fiesta de liberación de los oprimidos: Relectura de Juan 7:1–10:21.* San José, Costa Rica: Seminario Bíblico Latinoamericano, 1980.

———. *Las fiestas de Yavé.* Buenos Aires: Aurora, 1988.

Chapter 5

PRAXIS OF THE APOSTLES (ACTS)

Queer Couples Collaborate in Mission to the Unclean

Outline

Outline keys: *women* (italics); PETER etc. (married, first use all capitals).

Nothing in the text indicates that Cornelius and the Philippian jailer were married (despite common recourse to the baptisms of their "households" ["families"] to justify infant baptism). Luke presents Cornelius as a case like the centurion of his Gospel (7:1–10); similarly, the single jailer, not someone's wife, washes their wounds and prepares the meal for Paul and Silas (16:33–34; cf. Lydia, 16:13–15).

> *"When the Holy Spirit comes upon you, you will be empowered*
> *to become my witnesses*
> *both in Jerusalem [chapters 1–5],*
> *and in all Judea and Samaria [chapters 6–12],*
> *and even to the extremity of the earth [chapters 13–28]."*
> (Jesus, Acts 1:8)

1. Jerusalem, Judea, and Samaria (PETER), Chapters 1–12

Prologue: Luke to Theophilus (→Luke 1:1–4)	1:1–3
Commission and ascension (→Luke 24:51)	1:4–11
Matthias elected to replace Judas	1:12–26
(*women* + *Mary, widowed* + Jesus' brothers, 1:14)	
Feast of Pentecost and the coming of the Holy Spirit	2:1–13
(*"your daughters will prophesy . . . my female slaves . . . will prophesy,"* 2:17–18)	
Peter proclaims Jesus' resurrection, three thousand baptized	2:14–41

The first community (1): in house-churches and in the temple	2:42–47
Peter (with John) heals a paralytic	3:1–10
Peter in the temple proclaims Jesus' resurrection	3:11–26
Peter and John arrested; taken before the supreme court	4:1–20
Peter and John liberated, pray with their friends	4:21–31
The first community (2): primitive commun-ism	4:32–37
Co-conspirators in fraud and death: ANANIAS AND SAPPHIRA	5:1–11
The apostles heal many (Peter's shadow)	5:12–16
(*"multitudes of... women"* believe, 5:14)	
Arrest and miraculous liberation of the apostles	5:17–21
Peter and the apostles before the supreme court (Sanhedrin)	5:21–33
Intervention of Gamaliel, a wise Pharisee	5:34–42
Hellenist widows and the naming of seven deacons	6:1–7
Deacon Stephen arrested: before the supreme court	6:8–15
Stephen's defense: a rereading of Israel's history	7:1–53
Stoning of the first martyr (Saul collaborates)	7:54–60
Saul seeks to destroy the church in Jerusalem	8:1–4
(*persecution, baptism of women,* 8:3, 12; →9:2; 22:4)	
Refugees spread the good news: Philip in Samaria	8:5–25
Philip baptizes an Ethiopian eunuch (African Black)	8:26–40
("*Candace, Ethiopian queen,*" 8:27)	
Saul's vocation (not "conversion") as apostle to the Gentiles ("*...women,*" 9:2)	9:1–18
Saul testifies in Damascus and Jerusalem	9:19–31
Peter in →Lydda, Joppa: heals Aeneas, raises *Dorcas*	9:32–43
Peter baptizes the Roman centurion Cornelius (household)	10:1–48
Peter in Jerusalem reports the baptism of Gentile believers	11:1–18
Barnabas and Saul visit the new church in Antioch	11:19–30
Herod executes John's brother James and arrests Peter	12:1–5
An angel liberates Peter (John Mark's mother *Mary* + *maidservant Rhoda*)	*12:6–19*
Another angel strikes down Herod, who then dies	12:20–25

2. The Other Nations, Gentiles (Paul), Chapters 13–28

First missionary journey: Saul/Paul with Barnabas (13:1–14:28)

The Antioch church commissions Barnabas and Saul	13:1–3
Barnabas and Saul evangelize in Cyprus: denounce the sorcerer Elymas	13:4–12
Paul speaks in the synagogue in Pisidian Antioch	13:13–43
The entire city hears Paul and Barnabas (→13:50)	13:44–52
Paul and Barnabas in Iconium, barely escape stoning	14:1–7
Paul heals a paralytic in Lystra	14:8–18
Paul, stoned in Lystra, arrives with Barnabas in Derbe	14:19–20
Return to Lystra, Iconium and Pisidian Antioch	14:21–23
Return to Syrian Antioch, report to the church	14:24–28
Controversy arises in Antioch: Gentiles and the law	15:1–4
Conference in Jerusalem: speeches of Peter and JAMES (Jesus' brother)	15:5–21
Letter from Jerusalem to Gentile believers	15:22–35
Paul's second missionary journey (15:36–18:22)	
Paul separates from Barnabas, goes with Silas to Cilicia	15:36–41
Paul chooses Timothy (→*believing mother*) and circumcises him	16:1–4
Paul's vision about Macedonia: travels with Luke to "Europe"	16:5–10
Paul and Luke in Philippi, evangelize *Lydia* (baptized with her household)	16:11–15
Paul liberates a *slave girl* who had a spirit of divination	16:16–18
Paul and Silas captured, beaten, and jailed	16:19–24
Earthquake and baptism of Philippian jailer + household	16:25–34
Paul and Silas liberated, sail from Philippi (see Philippians)	16:35–40
Paul and Silas and a riot in Thessalonica (see 1–2 Thessalonians) (*"not a few prominent women,"* 17:4)	17:1–9
Paul and Silas (+ Timothy) and another riot in Berea (*"a number of prominent Greek women,"* 17:12)	17:10–15
Paul evangelizes in Athens (Silas and Timothy in Berea) (*"a woman named Damaris,"* 17:34)	17:16–34
Paul meets AQUILA AND *PRISCILLA* in Corinth (see 1–2 Corinthians)	18:1–11
Paul, *Priscilla* and Aquila to →Ephesus; Paul to →Antioch	18:12–22

Paul's third missionary journey (18:23–20:38)

Priscilla and Aquila correct the theology of erudite Apollos	18:23–28
Paul in Ephesus for three years (disciples of John the Baptist)	19:1–20
Paul plans to visit Rome	19:21–22
Riot of silversmiths in Ephesus (*the goddess Artemis*)	19:23–40
Paul travels to Macedonia, Greece, Troas, Miletus	20:1–16
Paul's farewell to the Ephesian elders/presbyters	20:17–38

Paul travels to Jerusalem, imprisoned, sent to Rome (21:1–28:31)

Paul (+ Luke) travels to Jerusalem (“*women*” [not “wives,” contrary to NRSV and NIV], 21:5–6) (deacon-evangelist Philip's “*four virgin daughters . . . prophesied,*” 21:9)	21:1–16
Paul with JAMES and elders in Jerusalem	21:17–25
Riot in the Temple, Paul's arrest	21:26–40
Paul defends himself before his compatriots (“ . . . *women,*” 22:4)	21:37–22:21
Paul, a Roman citizen, negotiates with the chiliarch and centurion	22:22–29
Paul defends himself before the supreme court	22:30–23:11
Paul's nephew uncovers a plot to kill the apostle (“son of Paul's *sister,*” 23:16)	23:12–22
Paul sent to Caesarea with a letter for *GOVERNOR FELIX*	23:23–35
Before Felix (+ *DRUSILLA*, 24:24) Paul refutes a lawyer	24:1–27
Paul defends himself before Festus and appeals to the emperor	25:1–12
Festus discusses the case with *KING AGRIPPA AND BERNICE* (incestuous)	*25:13–26*
Paul defends himself before King Agrippa and Bernice	26:1–32
Festus sends Paul to Rome	27:1–8
Storm and shipwreck: Paul prophesies salvation	27:9–44
Paul in Malta: saved from a viper, heals the sick	28:1–10
“And thus we arrived in Rome” (Luke), under house arrest	28:11–16
Paul's two interviews with other Jews in Rome	28:17–28
Two years under house arrest, evangelizing *without hindrance*	28:29–31

Note also the “we” sections in Acts 16:10–17; 20:5–15; 21:1–18; 27:1–28 (probably indicating times when Paul was accompanied by Luke, the author).

Commentary

In volume two of his work, Luke, the unmarried doctor and only non-Jew among the New Testament authors, tells how, by means of Peter and Paul's ministry (especially the latter), "unclean" Gentiles like himself became accepted as full members of the early churches. Contemporary studies point out that in volume two, Acts (*praxeis*), there is less focus on the poor and on women than in volume one (see the Gospel of Luke). However, the focus on the marginalized continues, since Luke and the other Gentiles were "unclean" and marginalized by traditional Judaism. In his second volume Luke, Paul's sometime companion, shows how people like him came to be included in the people of God. The basic literary technique Luke uses to underscore the importance of the inclusion of "unclean" Gentiles is that of narrative repetition. Consequently, in Acts 10 and 11:1–18, Luke gives us duplicate accounts of Peter's experience and vision, which resulted in Cornelius's baptism and the fundamental policy change in the early churches (which still constituted a sect within Judaism).

Peter is the central character of Acts 1–12, but in Acts 13–28 the dominant personage is Paul, obviously Luke's hero. The traditional Greek title of this book is "Praxis of the Apostles," but in Luke's terminology "apostle" refers only to the original twelve (see Acts 1:12–26), so Paul is not such an apostle. Consequently, even Paul suffers a certain marginalization by "the establishment" in Jerusalem (see Galatians 2). Because of his emphasis on the Holy Spirit, Luke might well have preferred to call his volume two "Jesus' Continuing Praxis through the Holy Spirit" (1:1–4; 4:31; 8:29; 15:8; 19:21, etc.; see the outline above).

1. The Oppressed Poor and Liberating Justice

In the first half of Acts we find a relative concentration on the needs of the poor. After Pentecost the first disciples possessed everything in common (Acts 2:42–47; 4:32–37), and the poor, those with "need" (*chreia,* 2:45; 4:35), had their basic needs met, resulting temporarily in a community where no one was "poor" anymore (*endeēs,* "needy," 4:34). Soon, however seven deacons had to be appointed to correct injustices in the church's ministry to Hellenist Jewish widows (6:1–7). Later we read of Dorcas's exemplary ministries (9:36–43) and of Cornelius giving alms (10:2, 4, 31).

Nevertheless, such explicit concern for the poor is almost totally absent from the second half of Acts (chaps. 13–28), which relate Paul's three missionary journeys. Paul is characterized personally as an example of freedom in terms of the love of money (20:33–34). However, Paul's strategic offering for the poor in Jerusalem (a project Luke may have viewed as a failure) receives only a brief mention in Acts (24:17; cf. the emphasis in Paul's own writings: 1 Cor. 16:1–4; →2 Corinthians 8–9; Rom. 15:25, 29; Gal. 2:10). In accordance with the anthropological perspective of certain recent studies, the Gentiles in Acts 13–28, because of their "impurity," were despised and marginalized from Jewish life and worship. However, with Paul's ministry these uncircumcised, unclean Gentiles (Israel's traditional oppressors) were baptized and became part of God's people, without submitting to the "yoke" of Moses' law (see Acts 15:10). Acts 13–28 has been criticized for concentrating on the "quantitative aspects of church growth" (statistics). The type and quality of community life, however, had already been amply established in Luke and Acts 1–12. Acts 13–28 then shows how Paul planted the radical subversive paradigm of the early Jerusalem community throughout an oppressive empire.

Vocabulary for oppression is particularly common in Acts, and descriptions of experiences of oppression are even more common. Acts includes more than a hundred references to experiences of oppression and injustice suffered![1] Experiencing oppression and facing a mob bent on violence, deacon Stephen, the church's first martyr, speaks with acute awareness of the Exodus paradigm (oppression experiences and vocabulary in 7:6, 9–11, 19, 21, 24–27, 34, 52, 58–59; liberating justice in 7:7, 10, 24–25, 27, 34–35, 52, 55–56, 59). Throughout Acts, terms related to the *adik-* root ("injustice, oppression") occur: in 1:18; 7:24 (*// kataponoumenō*), 26–27; 8:23; 18:14; 24:15, 20; 25:10–11; terms related to the verb *thlibō* ("oppress, afflict") occur in 7:10–11; 11:19; 14:22; 20:23 (cf. also 10:38, "oppressed [*katadynasteuomenous*] by the devil)."

Not surprisingly, for persons experiencing so much injustice, oppression, and violence, echoing the Exodus paradigm of the Hebrew Bible, God's justice and the justice expected in human behavior was understood above all as liberating justice. For such justice vocabulary in Acts (*dik-* words), see 3:14; 4:19; 7:24, 27 (cf. "redeemer" in v. 35), 52; 10:22, 35; 13:10, 38–39 ("justified = freed" from Moses' law; →Romans); 17:31; 22:14; 24:15, 25; (note 26:17, God liberates Paul from oppression); 28:4. Acts ends, significantly, with Paul under house arrest in Rome, but at the end able to proclaim Jesus' good news to the poor "freely" (28:31), with no mob violence or political interference.

2. *The Praxis of Women*

Although women receive much less attention in Acts than in his Gospel, Luke signals Mary's presence at the birth of the church (Acts 1:14) as in Jesus' birth (Luke 1–2). Moreover, in Peter's Pentecost sermon, Luke includes the citation from Joel that specifies "daughters" that prophesy and "women slaves" empowered by the Spirit (2:17–18; Joel 2:28–29; see also deacon-evangelist Philip's four virgin daughters who prophesy, Acts 21:9). Like an experienced, subversive feminist, Luke "chooses his battles," and in Acts his battle concerns

1. On the explicit vocabulary, see Thomas D. Hanks, *God So Loved the Third World: The Biblical Vocabulary of Oppression,* trans. James C. Dekker (Maryknoll, N.Y.: Orbis, 1983), 47–60. For the references to experiences of oppression and violence, see Acts 1:3, 16, 18; 2:22–23, 35–36, 40; 3:13–15, 17, 19, 26; 4:1–3, 5–11, 17, 21, 27–28, 29; 5:17–18, 25, 30, 33, 40–41; 6:11–13; 7:6–7, 9–10, 18–21, 34, 52, 58–59, 60–8:1a; 8:1b–3, 23; 9:1–5, 13–14, 16, 21, 24, 29; 10:38, 39; 11:19; 12:1–7, 11, 19; 13:10, 27–28, 50; 14:2–5, 19, 22; 15:10 (cf. v. 28); 16:19, 22–24, 37; 17:3, 5–6; 18:2, 10–12, 17; 19:29, 37; 20:3, 19, 23; 21:11, 13, 27–36; 22:4–5, 7–8, 19–20, 24–25, 29; 23:2, 12–14, 21, 27; 24:6, 15, 20; 25:3, 8–11, 15, 24; 26:10–12, 14–15, 21, 29, 31; 27:1, 6, 11, 24, 31–32, 42–43; 28:17, 20 (cf. v. 30).

the inclusion of Gentiles (both women and men), unclean and uncircumcised, as he himself, and a sexual minority (unmarried). The needs of all marginalized or oppressed groups are related to this main concern.

Luke's political dimension stems from his hope of seeing even rulers (Theophilus?) accept Jesus' good news to the poor. Consequently, Luke emphasizes Paul's speeches to rulers (ch. 24, Felix; 25:6–12, Festus; 26:1–32, Agrippa), and ends his book with Paul in Rome, with an appointment to appear before the emperor Nero (27:24), and with the suggestion that the just and appropriate political response in terms of the Gospel is not continued persecution but freedom: "[Paul] proclaimed God's just new order and taught about the Liberator Jesus Christ boldly and *without hindrance*" (Acts 28:31).

The fact that Luke dedicated his two volumes to Theophilus (apparently politically influential) makes it likely that freedom and justice for women are included in the author's agenda only indirectly, in order to more effectively influence the subconscious. Undoubtedly, Luke himself shared something of his patriarchal culture's prejudice against women, and in his volumes only unintentionally communicated the more radical traditions concerning women. At any rate, contemporary feminist studies focus especially on five instructive narratives concerning women in Acts.

2.1. Ananias and Sapphira, Co-conspirators in Fraud, 5:1–11. Considered difficult and scandalous, this account prevents any tendency to romanticize women as ever innocent victims of oppression. Nevertheless, as Gail O'Day points out, Luke reveals an important detail, probably unintentionally, concerning Ananias and Sapphira's marriage: Ananias does not make decisions unilaterally in his household, but consults with his wife concerning the sale of a property.[2] The couple suffer an excessively harsh punishment, according to many modern commentators, but we should note that it is a judgment against the hypocrisy of having pretended solidarity with the poor (cf. 4:32–37), while actually collaborating in economic fraud.

2.2. Hellenist Widows and the Ministry of Seven Deacons, 6:1–7. Hellenist (Grecian Jewish) widows were among those who struggled against marginalization and for justice and inclusion in the early church, and the Hellenists were also those who promoted the multiplication of the church in Jerusalem. By pointing out the poverty of these widows, Luke demonstrates the continuity of the church with the people of God in the Hebrew scriptures, where we find many exhortations to care for the widows, children, and immigrants. The immediate solution was the establishment of the seven deacons (men) to serve the needy widows. Stephen, the first martyr (6:8–7:60), whose testimony led to the calling of Saul/Paul (8:1; 9:1–19), was among the seven. Although none of the seven deacons were women, it is notable that their function was to serve the widows. Later the churches also designated women as deacons, and when the ecclesiastical bureaucracy grew overly cumbersome, 1 Timothy

2. Gail R. O'Day, "Acts," in *The Women's Bible Commentary*, ed. Carol A. Newsom and Sharon H. Ringe (Louisville: Westminster John Knox, 1992), 309.

5 (deutero-Pauline) sought to limit the kinds of widows who could expect economic assistance from the churches.

2.3. In Joppa Peter Raises Dorcas/Tabitha, 9:36–43. Although Luke does not designate Dorcas as a deacon, she appears to have been an important and well-to-do widow in the church in Joppa, since when she died, the disciples sent two men to bring Peter from Lydda, a neighboring village. Dorcas is identified as a "disciple" (9:36, *mathētria*), the only time in the New Testament that we find the feminine form. With this narrative, Luke continues his practice in his Gospel of presenting texts in pairs, focusing first on a man, in this case the paralyzed Aeneas in Lydda (9:32–35), and then on a woman (a type of balanced justice that anticipates modern inclusive language). Dorcas's work is characterized as "always doing good and helping the poor" (NIV), manifestations of her compassion and solidarity with the poor widows. Some critique Luke for designating male deacons' work with widows as "ministry" (6:1–2, 4), but describing Dorcas's care for other widows merely as "good works and acts of charity" (NRSV).[3] However, the Greek word for "ministry" simply means "service" and may indicate inferior slave duties. More significantly, however, while Ananias and Sapphira died for their greed, fraud, and lack of solidarity with the poor, Dorcas, a paradigm of solidarity with the poor widows, was raised from the dead!

2.4. The Church in Mary's Home and Her Maidservant Rhoda, 12:1–17. With a touch of humor, Luke narrates how Rhoda leaves Peter, miraculously liberated from prison, knocking at the door (risking that Peter be recaptured) and runs to announce his arrival to the fervently praying disciples. The men refused to believe that God had answered their prayers and proposed two typically male chauvinist hypotheses: that Rhoda was crazy, or, that she had experienced an illusion, seeing only Peter's angel. Of course, as in the parallel experience of the women who first reported Jesus' resurrection (Luke 24:11), the humor of the situation was at the unbelieving men's expense. In addition to honoring the veracity of a maidservant's testimony, the account reveals significant aspects about the economic status of Mary, who was John Mark's mother and the owner of the spacious house. The house was sufficiently large for church meetings and had a patio in front with an outer gate. Perhaps for Luke, an unmarried Gentile, part of the humor in this account was in portraying Peter himself, a married Jew, but foolishly excluded by his community, struggling with a maidservant against unbelief to achieve his inclusion.

2.5. Lydia and Other Women in Philippi, 16:11–40. For Luke, perhaps the tension and the humor of Acts 12 prepares readers to accept the more subversive narrative in Acts 16. On a Sabbath by the riverside Paul found the door wide open for the gospel with a group of women, among whom was Lydia, a dealer in purple cloth. Lydia opened her heart to the good news and her home for the new church and together with her household was baptized. Cornelius

3. Ibid., 310.

was the first Gentile to be baptized, but Lydia became the first "European" Gentile to be baptized.

Lydia, an independent professional woman, managed a business that gave her contacts with the elite of Philippi (purple cloth was a luxury item, Luke 16:19). For patriarchal societies, a prosperous woman like Lydia, economically independent, who made the decisions for her household without consulting any male as head, represented a subversive threat (sexual minority) to the dominant system. Luke does not specify any verbal role for Lydia (as a prophet or teacher), but inevitably the church that met in her home, in order not to lose their space, would have to respect any limits that she as owner of the house might set. Later, Paul's letter to the Philippians (56 C.E.) shows us a church with women still among the most prominent leaders.

As a social counterpoint in contrast with Lydia, Luke also tells of a slave girl whose owners exploited her spirit of divination (16:16–17). Some interpret Paul's effort to impose silence on the slave as an oppressive act, but this can also be seen as an act of solidarity to free the slave girl from the exploitation by her owners (cf. Jesus' subversive silence before Pilate). At any rate, the owners, deprived of their income from exploitation, had Paul and Silas jailed. Luke narrates Paul and Silas's miraculous liberation from jail by means of an earthquake, but says nothing more about the slave girl. Some criticize Luke's apparent indifference to her fate, but he may have preferred simply to leave us with the subversive image of the liberated slave girl.

2.6. Priscilla and Aquila, 18:1–4, 18–28. Although Luke mentions Aquila first (18:2), the fact that later Priscilla is named first by both Luke (Acts 18:18, 26) and Paul (Rom. 16:3–4; cf. 1 Cor. 16:19) seems to indicate that in the churches it was she who exercised leadership. Aquila probably dedicated more of his time to his secular work as a tentmaker, a profession highly desired because of the economic privileges it offered. Luke presents Priscilla explicitly as a teacher in the church, who even corrected the theology of Apollos (18:26), a learned orator and perhaps the author of Hebrews.

In Rom. 16:3–4 Paul praises both Priscilla and Aquila for having exhibited the male virtue of courage (in the Greek of 1 Cor. 16:13, "act like a man," *andrizesthe,* but not specifically so here). The Hebrew scriptures give us other examples of women, such as Deborah and Esther, who broke with the stereotypes of their gender and "acted like men." (Even languages themselves in their very vocabulary and structures reflect the power of the oppressors.) Possibly it was Priscilla's preaching, not Peter's, which led to the establishment of the first house-churches in Rome. At any rate, Priscilla and Aquila were expelled from Rome by the edict of the emperor Claudius and later worked in the churches in Ephesus (18:18–21).

Some biblicists criticize Luke for not detailing Priscilla's leadership, but possibly in the art of narration for a patriarchal society, Luke's technique is more subversive and thus more effective. We may trace a certain development in the women Luke presents. The contrast between Dorcas, a well-to-do widow dedicated to charitable tasks with poor widows, and the secular leadership of

Lydia and the church leadership of Priscilla is very pronounced. By presenting only a few women, but well chosen and with a certain progression in prominence of roles, Luke's method may be more effective for changing prejudices than blunt narratives that scandalize and produce negative reactions.

3. Sexual Minorities

Among the excellent studies concerning the poor and women in Luke-Acts, the lack of complementary concerns for sexual minorities is notable. The physician Luke, an unmarried Gentile, was marginalized from Jewish life. He was a companion of his hero, Paul, also unmarried. Only Luke preserves Jesus' statement concerning leaving one's wife in order to become his disciple (Luke 14:26; 18:29).

Significantly, of all the women in the churches, Acts presents only two married couples: first, the negative example of Ananias and Sapphira; and second, the positive (nonpatriarchal) example of Priscilla and Aquila. Ananias and Sapphira are co-conspirators in fraud, hypocrisy, lacking solidarity with the poor. Priscilla and Aquila represent a less traditional couple, where the woman exercises more leadership in the church, dares to correct the theology of a scholarly man, and manifests the "masculine" virtue of courage to save Paul's life. All the other church women named in Acts (Mary, Dorcas, Rhoda, Lydia) represent sexual minorities not subject to male authority of men; they are widows, unmarried, or perhaps divorced.

Luke's hero, Paul, is not only unmarried (possibly a widower or divorced), but always seeks the companionship of another man in his journeys (Barnabas, Silas, Timothy). Even Peter, the principal figure of Acts 1–12, although married (Mark 1:29–31), in Acts goes about accompanied by Jesus' unmarried beloved disciple John (Acts 3–4; cf. 1 Cor. 9:5). And when Luke names the other apostles, he presents them in male pairs (Acts 1:13–14, according to the Greek). Modern translations speak much of "families," when the original Greek refers only to "households": all who live under the same roof, which in Acts usually are not traditional "families." The Bible never speaks of "families," only of households, clans, tribes, and so forth. The salvation and liberation offered by Jesus at times extends to the "household" and is not limited to the "family" in the sense of the modern nuclear family (Acts 16:31).

In a book dominated by sexual minorities, the most explicit and memorable example is that of the Ethiopian eunuch (also black, Acts 8:26–40). Although Moses' law discriminated against eunuchs, prohibiting them from becoming priests (Lev. 21:20) and excluding them from all participation in the worship community (Deut. 23:1), in Isaiah we find a change in attitude that invites eunuchs to approach God (56:3–5). The science of "eunuchology" advances even more with Jesus' analysis of three types of eunuchs (→Matt. 19:12), while Jesus (like Paul) exemplifies the "single" type who voluntarily avoids having a wife and children in order to give priority to the proclamation of Jesus' good news.

Also of great significance for sexual minorities are the conclusions of the council at Jerusalem (Acts 15), so central to Luke's theological perspective. Faced with the crisis provoked by the inclusion of unclean Gentiles in the churches, which were originally entirely Jewish, the council sought an agreement that would respect Jewish sensitivities but also preserve the Gentiles' freedom (15:20, 29). Peter describes Moses' law as "a yoke that neither we nor our ancestors have been able to bear" (15:10). The council "settles the debate over a Torah-observant form of Christianity by opting for freedom from the Law.... Scripture is important not as Law to be obeyed but as God's Word which is fulfilled in Christ."[4] The only sexual prohibition is to abstain from "*porneia*" (Acts 15:20, 29), originally "prostitution" but perhaps better translated in this context as "irresponsible/unjust sexuality" (remembering that in ancient times heterosexual relations resulted in children more commonly than today). Notably, even this quite simple prohibition (cf. the detailed codes of the Pentateuch) places the prohibition against *porneia* in between three prohibitions concerning food, related to idolatry. We find no further reference to the decision of the council in the New Testament, and soon Paul introduces significant modifications (Romans 14; 1 Corinthians 8–10; see the chapter on Galatians). Once again we note that the Bible never speaks of "morals" or "ethics" in the sense of universal absolutes (as in Greek philosophy) but of instructions for a "walk" in "the way." Such instructions reflect concrete historical contexts of communities and individuals, and lead to adjustments in the light of changed historical contexts. Above all in Acts, the acceptance of Gentiles like Cornelius is also pertinent for women and sexual minorities. Before (Leviticus 15), the discharge of blood (women) or discharge of semen (men) left the Jewish person "unclean," like the Gentiles. But a voice from heaven declared, "What God has made clean, you must not call profane" (10:15; 11:9; →Rom. 1:24–27; 14:14–20; Titus 1:15).

4. Solidarity with the Sick and Physically Challenged

In general, like Jesus, the apostles demonstrate solidarity with the sick and physically challenged, freeing them of their afflictions and dependence (poverty). Physical healing represents a fundamental dimension of "salvation" (better, "integral liberation") for Luke, and Peter's sermon even describes Jesus as "healing all who were *oppressed* by the devil" (Acts 10:38).[5] We may note also in Acts:

- signs and miracles performed by the apostles (2:43; cf. 2:19) and Stephen (6:8)
- a man crippled from birth, begging at the temple gate, healed by Peter and John (3:1–16; 4:5–17, 30)

---

4. Craig L. Blomberg, "The Christian and the Law of Moses," in *Witness to the Gospel: The Theology of Acts,* ed. I. Howard Marshall and David Peterson (Grand Rapids: Eerdmans, 1998), 410, 397.

5. Ben Witherington III, "Salvation and Health in Christian Antiquity: the Soteriology of Luke-Acts in Its First Century Setting," in Marshall and Peterson, eds., *Witness to the Gospel,* 145–66; Hanks, *God So Loved the Third World,* 53–54.

- the sick, the physically challenged, and those tormented by unclean spirits healed by the hands of the apostles, especially Peter and even his shadow (5:12–16)
- many possessed of unclean spirits, many who were paralyzed and lame cured by Philip in Samaria (8:4–8)
- Aeneas, a paralyzed man in Lydia, cured by Peter (9:32–35), and Dorcas in Joppa raised from the dead by Peter (9:36–43)
- in Lystra, a man crippled in the feet from birth, healed by Paul (14:8–10)
- in Troas, Eutychus (who went to sleep in a window during a long sermon and fell three floors to the ground) raised from the dead by Paul (20:7–12; cf. v. 35, "support the weak")
- in Malta, Paul saved from a viper (28:1–6; cf. Luke 10:19; Mark 16:18); father of the ruler Publius, in bed with fever and dysentery, healed by Paul, and later Paul heals others on the island who are sick (28:7–10)

These accounts of healings are mixed in with accounts concerning solidarity with the poor (2:42–47; 4:32–37), especially widows (6:1–7), and accounts of persecution and oppression (4:1–22; 5:17–42; 6:8–8:3; 9:1–19a). In contrast with divine healings, Acts also refers to Moses' miraculous plagues (7:36), Ananias and Sapphira being struck dead (5:1–11), Paul being blinded (9:1–19a; 22:11; cf. the metaphors in 26:18; 28:27), and Paul's curse that blinds the magician Elymas (13:4–12). Jesus cursed no one (but cf. the fig tree, Mark 11:12–14, 20–24 // Matt. 21:18–22; also Luke 13:6–9, and the seven "woes" in Matthew 23).

5. *Anti-Judaism in Acts?*

Anti-Judaic misinterpretations of Acts have developed principally from misinterpreting the *call* of the Jew Paul as a "conversion" from Jew to Christian and from misinterpreting Paul's words at the end of the book (28:25–28) as a general divine rejection of the Jews. The literary technique of repetition (for emphasis, signifying importance) is exemplified when Luke in three texts refers to Paul's *call* as a missionary to the Gentiles (9:1–18 // 22:4–16 // 26:9–18; see also Gal. 1:12–17; cf. the women persecuted by Saul/Paul, 8:3; 9:2; 22:4). We are not dealing with Paul's "conversion," the anti-Jewish misinterpretation in the church that suggests that Paul had to stop being a Jew in order to become a Christian. Paul, who was born a Jew and died a Jew, received a special *call* (Gal. 1:15) from the resurrected Jesus to become a Jewish missionary to the Gentiles and invited them to become part of the People of God, but without submitting to circumcision and Moses' law. Moreover, Paul's concluding words in 28:25–28 do not signify his general rejection of Jews, since the immediate context indicates that some Jews accepted his message (28:23–24), and this is the third time in Acts that Paul makes such an affirmation (13:46–48; 18:5–6)—but each time he continued his ministry with his fellow Jews!

(see Rom. 1:16; 9–11).[6] True, "It was in Antioch that the disciples were first called 'Christians'" (11:26), but always such disciples constituted a Jewish sect (24:5, 14; 28:22), commonly called "the Way" (9:2; 18:25–26; 19:9, 23; 22:4; 24:14, 22). The "way" (more than a creed) refers to a praxis always in a series of concrete historical contexts, never to the abstract and universal "ethics" or "morals" of Greek philosophy.

For Luke the church never takes the place of Judaism but anticipates Israel's renewal and restoration (Acts 3:19–21) when "the times of the Gentiles will reach their divinely appointed goal" (Luke 21:24) and the realm be restored to Israel (Acts 1:6–7).[7]

Bibliography

Arlandson, James M. *Women, Class and Society in Early Christianity: Models from Luke-Acts*. Peabody, Mass.: Hendrickson, 1997.

Barrett, C. K. *A Critical and Exegetical Commentary on the Acts of the Apostles*. 2 vols. ICC. Edinburgh: T. & T. Clark, 1994–98.

Bruce, F. F. *The Book of Acts*. Rev. ed. Grand Rapids: Eerdmans, 1988.

Dunn, James D. G. *The Acts of the Apostles*. London: Epworth, 1996.

Johnson, Luke Timothy. "Luke-Acts, Book of." *ABD*, 4:403–20.

Marshall, I. Howard, and David Peterson, eds. *Witness to the Gospel: The Theology of Acts*. Grand Rapids: Eerdmans, 1998.

Martin, Clarice J. "The Acts of the Apostles." In *Searching the Scriptures*, vol. 2, *A Feminist Commentary*, ed. Elisabeth Schüssler Fiorenza, 763–99. New York: Crossroad, 1994.

O'Day, Gail R. "Acts." In *The Women's Bible Commentary*, ed. Carol A. Newsom and Sharon H. Ringe, 394–402. Louisville: Westminster John Knox, 1998.

Reimer, Ivoni Richter. *Women in the Acts of the Apostles: A Feminist Liberation Perspective*. Trans. Linda M. Maloney. Minneapolis: Fortress, 1995.

Seim, Turid Karlsen. *The Double Message: Patterns of Gender in Luke-Acts*. Nashville: Abingdon, 1994.

Smith, Abraham. "'Full of Spirit and Wisdom': Luke's Portrait of Stephen (Acts 6:1–8:1) as a Man of Self-Mastery." In *Asceticism and the New Testament*, ed. Leif E. Vaage and Vincent L. Wimbush, 71–95. New York: Routledge, 1999.

---

6. Richard B. Hays, *The Moral Vision of the New Testament* (San Francisco: HarperCollins, 1996), 417–21.

7. David L. Tiede, "Fighting against God: Luke's Interpretation of Jewish Rejection of the Messiah Jesus," in *Anti-Semitism and Early Christianity*, ed. Craig A. Evans and Donald A. Hagner (Minneapolis: Fortress), 102–12.

Chapter 6

ROMANS

Anti-Judaism and Homophobia Deconstructed

Outline

For an initial approach to the letter, contemporary readers may best grasp Paul's liberating message and avoid traditional misinterpretations by following a different reading order.

1. Historical context: sexual minority recipients and author	1:1–15; 15:14–16:27
Five sexual minority house-churches in Rome	1:1–7; 16:1–27
Crucial transition in Paul's ministry to the oppressed	1:8–15; 15:14–33
2. Paul's pastoral goal: viable, inclusive (tolerant) churches	15:7–13
Conflict resolution: the weak and the strong	14:1–15:6
The countercultural community: leaders and oppressors	12:1–21
Select, subversive submission to imperial authorities	13:1–14
3. God's project in human history: universal liberation	9:1–11:33
The final goal: covenant mercy for all	11:1–35
Intransigent obstacle: human unbelief	9:30–10:21
God's goodness, faithfulness, patience, liberating justice	9:1–29
4. Four fundamental dimensions of authentic Christian freedom	5:1–8:39
Liberation from death by the Spirit of life	8:1–39
Liberation from the law, guided by the Spirit	7:1–25
Liberation from sin, slaves of God's liberating justice	6:1–23
Liberation from divine wrath through Jesus' sacrifice	5:1–21
5. Amnesty for the marginalized: incorporation of the excluded	3:21–4:25
Abraham, sexual minority, justified by his trust	4:1–25
The redemption accomplished by Jesus Christ	3:21–31

6. All humanity under sin's tyrannical power	3:9–20
All who condemn others: themselves subject to God's wrath	2:1–16
God's people under God's wrath, in spite of their law	2:17–24
In spite of their circumcision	2:25–29
In spite of God's promises of blessing to them	3:1–8
Gentiles under God's wrath	1:18–32
Because of their idolatry	1:18–23
Handed over to their sexual uncleanness	1:24–27
Handed over to their sin (oppression and violence)	1:28–32
7. Paul's powerful good news for oppressed sexual minorities	1:16–17

Commentary

Introduction

The apostle Paul's letter to the Romans (some five house-churches in Rome) is without doubt

1. the biblical book with the greatest impact in world history, instrumental in the conversions of St. Augustine, Martin Luther, and John Wesley, and in the early twentieth century detonating the explosion of Karl Barth's theology that signaled the collapse of nineteenth-century optimistic liberalism;
2. the focus of the most scholarly study, especially from the Reformation to the present;
3. of greatest theological controversy in terms of its interpretation and its significance as a guide for life in the modern world.

In the last century, for instance, note the following:

1. Rom. 13:1–17 was the favorite text of Nazi theologians and religious leaders seeking to promote submission to authorities and collaboration with Hitler's extermination of Jews.
2. Rom. 1:26–27, as misinterpreted by Thomas Aquinas, provided the principal biblical justification for Nazi persecution of homosexuals (for their "unnatural acts"), leading to their inclusion in the Holocaust violence.
3. More recently, however, Romans 16 has played a key positive role in feminist and Latin American theologies, transforming the interpretation of Paul concerning both women and the poor.

Of the seven New Testament letters undoubtedly written by Paul himself, Romans is the last (58 C.E.). Dictated to Tertius (16:22–23) in Corinth (cf. 1 Cor. 1:14) prior to the apostle's trip to Jerusalem, imprisonment, and journey to Rome as Nero's prisoner, Romans represents the classic and mature expression of the apostle to whom we mainly owe the diffusion of the Christian faith to Gentiles and the Western world.

How the first house-churches in Rome were originally established we cannot be sure. Prisca/Priscilla possibly was the pioneer evangelist in Rome (ca. 48–49), since she is the first person mentioned in the letter as a leader, and one of the churches met in her house (16:3–5a; →Mary Magdalene, the first witness of the resurrection in all four Gospels). Both Paul and Peter arrived in Rome many years later, Paul as a prisoner ca. 59–61 C.E. and Peter ca. 63–65 C.E.

Priscilla's preaching may have occasioned the uprisings among the Jews of Rome that caused Emperor Claudius's decree expelling the Jews—including Priscilla and Aquila—from the city in 49 C.E. The couple then took up residence in Corinth and later moved to Ephesus, where they instructed Apollos (Acts 18:26). Following Claudius's death Priscilla and Aquila returned to Rome (ca. 55–56 C.E.). When Paul greeted them at the close of the letter (16:3–5b), they had resumed their work and ministry in the capital, and one of the five churches met in their house. During their absence from Rome, however, the membership of the churches had changed. When Claudius decreed the expulsion of the Jews from Rome—including the small Jewish sect of believers in Jesus as Messiah—Gentiles were a tiny minority in the churches. But after Claudius's death only a few Jews managed to return to the capital, and when Paul wrote Romans, the great majority in the five house-churches were Gentiles.

Consequently, Romans mainly addresses these Gentiles. In Jerusalem Paul had defended the freedom of the Gentiles to join the churches without submitting to Moses' law (→Galatians). In Romans, however, confronting the contempt of "the strong" (mainly Gentiles), the apostle finds it necessary to defend Israel's permanent place in God's project of universal liberation (chaps. 9–11; 14). Paul's goal in Romans is a network of house-churches characterized by inclusivity and mutual acceptance (15:7–13), which could then serve as a base for his projected mission to Spain (15:14–33).

1. God's Wrath against Those Who Oppress the Weak and the Poor (Romans 1:18–3:20)

Is the gospel that Paul proclaims (1:16–17) "good news to the poor and oppressed," as was Jesus' message? Or has it been transformed into "another gospel" (→Gal. 1:6–9; 2:10) that supports the unjust and oppressive status quo of the Roman Empire (13:1–7)? This is a question highly significant for us, as well as for the original readers. Of the twenty-eight persons Paul greets in the five house-churches in Rome (16:3–16), twelve had names that were common among slaves (25 to 33 percent of the city's population were slaves). Many probably sold themselves into slavery due to debt problems, to which Paul may allude in 13:7–8 ("owe no one anything"; but cf. 1:14; 15:25–29). In 12:8 Paul exhorts the house-churches to contribute generously to meet the needs of others (cf. Gal. 6:10)—even hungry enemies are to be fed (12:20, citing Prov. 25:21). Phoebe (16:1–2) is called a *prostatis,* most likely a "patron," who had generously contributed to Paul's ministry (cf. the possible allusions to civic benefactors in 13:3, 12:8). In Romans we also find Paul's final reference to his great project of an offering for the poor saints of Jerusalem, which he now prepares to deliver (15:25–28; cf. Gal. 2:10; 1 Cor. 16:1–4; →2 Corinthians 8–9; cf. Acts 24:17). Elsa Tamez has shown that Paul's teaching concerning God's free grace and justification by faith was of special significance for the poor, oppressed, and marginalized (Romans 1–4; Galatians), as was also his concern for those weak in the faith (Romans 14).[1]

Even more evident than his concern for the poor, however, is Paul's explicit emphasis in Romans on oppression as the dominant characteristic of human life under the empire:

- he begins his proclamation in prophetic tones declaring God's wrath revealed against all impiety/idolatry and "oppression," *adikia,* twice in 1:18; cf. liberation/salvation, 1:16; see similarly Yahweh's wrath against those who oppress the poor, (Exod. 22:21–24); in 1:29 "oppression/injustice" (*adikia*) heads the vice list (contrasted with God's just ordinances), and brings death (1:32);
- in 2:8 and 3:5, oppression again is said to provoke divine wrath;
- in 6:13 Christians are to stop collaborating with the oppressive world system and present their bodies to God as instruments of divine liberating justice;
- in 9:13 in a context referring to the Exodus, Paul energetically renounces the notion (rhetorical question) that God should be an oppressor (cf. 3:5b).

In addition to these eight references to oppression/injustice (*adikia*) in Romans, Paul also employs the other common New Testament term for oppression/affliction (*thlipsis)* five times:

- "we boast in our oppressions" (5:3, twice);
- oppression, paralleling persecution and followed by three expressions for poverty, (scarcity, famine, nakedness), none of which can separate us from God's love (8:35);
- oppression produces endurance (12:12) and is related to "solidarity" with the needs of the saints in time of persecution (12:13–14).

Thus, while Paul in Romans does not set out to analyze poverty or to demonstrate that oppression is its most common cause, the apostle's linguistic habits and associations (oppression, poverty, and divine wrath against oppressors) clearly reflect the Exodus paradigm (22:21–24) so fundamental to Israel's historical consciousness and relived by the oppressed in every epoch.

---

1. Elsa Tamez, *Contra toda condena: La justificación por la fe desde los excluidos* (San José, Costa Rica: DEI/SEBILA, 1991); *Justicia de Dios: Vida para todos: La justificación por la fe en Pablo* (San José, Costa Rica: SEBILA, 1991).

2. God's Liberating Justice for the Weak and Oppressed (Romans 3:21–11:33)

Starting thus, with the experience of the oppressed and poor—not with elitist Greco-Roman concepts and linguistic usage—enables us to understand Paul's enormous emphasis in Romans on God's justice as liberating justice. According to Paul's understanding of Jesus' good news, therein is *God's liberating justice*—especially for the weak, oppressed, and poor—*revealed* (1:17–18; cf. the oppressed weak, 5:3, 6). In Paul's dazzling rhetoric in Romans, favorite terms ("law," "justice") are tossed about, co-opted from the opposition, cunningly returned, and then snatched back "for keeps" (→Galatians)—a kind of "Star Wars" performance that has kept theologians battling and commentators working overtime virtually since Tertius in Corinth plopped down his pen in exhaustion (→bibliography below).

2.1. Romans 3:21–26. In this nuclear center of Paul's gospel dynamite, Jesus—faithful unto death—is the new Moses, who accomplishes "redemption" (slave market metaphor) by his sacrifice ("atoning death . . . blood," temple metaphors), resulting in liberating justice/vindication (courtroom metaphor). Continuity with the classic Exodus paradigm is clear (a redemption attested by the Law and the Prophets, and a Passing Over), but the traditional "we-they" dichotomy between Israel and Gentiles, oppressed and oppressors, has vanished: since "all have sinned," Christ died for idolatrous enemies/oppressors as well as ordinary weak sinners (5:6–8).

2.2. Romans 3:27–4:25. Participation in God's just new order of the world (4:13) begins when anyone forsakes habitual oppressive ways and takes the stance of the beggarly poor, extending the empty hands of faith. Our common translations here easily give the impression of a "sloppy accountant" God (ever "reckoning" things that aren't so)—or worse, a bribed judge who punishes the innocent and rewards a violent oppressor. For Paul, however, the creator God who—with performative language—"gives life to the dead and calls into existence things that are not so that they come to exist" (4:17) rehabilitates those who begin to "walk in the footsteps of the faith" of father Abraham (4:11).

2.3. Romans 5–8. Four fundamental facets of Christian liberation and freedom can be sketched:

- This divine liberation accomplished by Jesus is above all liberation from the wrath that God historically manifests against oppressors of the weak and poor (Rom. 5:9; cf. 1 Thess. 5:9).

- Then, just as Exodus made clear that Israelite slaves also were prone to oppression and violence (Exod. 2:13–14), so Paul in Romans 6 emphasizes how Jesus' followers need to be liberated from their own oppressive and violent tendencies ("justified/liberated from sin," 6:7; "instruments of liberating justice," 6:13).

- In Romans 7 Paul does not "demonize" or relativize the law to the extent we may observe in →Galatians, but, though "holy and just and good" (7:12), the law still may be co-opted by the flesh for enslaving people. Therefore, as in →Galatians, believers also must be liberated by Christ from the law (7:24–25; cf. 10:4, "Christ is the end of the law").

- In Romans 8 Paul develops his vision of God's purpose as cosmic liberation from death and all the oppressive forces that impoverish (8:21–23, 33–39). He thus stands in the Exodus tradition, which culminates in Jesus' good news to the poor: Paul expounds his gospel as focusing on God's liberating justice accomplished decisively by Jesus' death and resurrection.

2.4. Romans 9–11 (no longer viewed as a parenthesis on the predestination of Presbyterians). Clearly Paul's concern here is with God's project of liberating justice in human history and how the dialectics—between the roles of Israel and the Gentiles, unbelief and faith, human freedom and the sovereignty of divine grace—all are to be affirmed. Paul refers again here to divine wrath (9:22) and frequently to salvation/liberation (9:27; 10:1, 9–10, 13; 11:11, 14, 26), and in the end makes clear that he speaks of an integral salvation that culminates in the arrival of God's promised Liberator from Zion (11:26, citing texts from Isaiah). After referring to liberation from divine wrath, Paul speaks of Israel as racing madly to establish their own "justice" (a self-righteousness that merits divine recognition, 9:31; cf. 10:3, 5), but they stumble over a crucified Messiah (9:32–33) and thus fail to reach Christ, who represents the goalpost of the law (10:4). Believing Gentiles, meanwhile, wandering aimlessly, find themselves overtaken and caught up in the powerful embrace of God's justification by grace (9:30). Such justification by faith manifests God's liberating justice (10:10 // liberation/salvation, 10:9–10, 13).

3. Romans 12–15:14. Appropriate Praxis in the Communities of the Liberator

Having established that all humanity lies prostrate under the power of sin (characterized by oppression and violence that provoke God's just indignation, 1:18–3:20), Paul concludes his letter beginning with exhortations regarding appropriate "praxis" (12:4), insisting first of all that the house-churches not be squeezed into the mold of the oppressive and violent Roman society surrounding them (12:1–2). In contrast to his previous polemical discourse, Paul's pastoral exhortations here avoid heavy use of conflictive justice terminology, preferring other concepts (grace, mercy, the good, solidarity with the weak, and a love that fulfills the just requirements of the law (13:8–10; cf. 8:4; 3:31). Nevertheless, he does refer to God's wrath manifest in vengeance (punitive justice "repaying" enemies/oppressors, 12:19; cf. the wrath and vengeance of rulers, 13:4–5). Finally, in one of his rare references to God's "realm/rule," Paul describes it as signifying "liberating justice, peace, and joy in the Holy Spirit" (14:17; cf. Isa. 32:15–18), in a context that radically emends Torah's cultic provisions and declares "all things [not just foods]" clean (14:14, 20; →Mark 7:19; →Titus 1:15).

4. Anti-Semitism and "the Weak"

Traditionally, the "weak" in Rom. 14:1–15:13 has been assumed to refer to Jews who accepted Jesus as Messiah but continued to live under the yoke of the law (together with any Gentiles who shared this lifestyle). Mark Nanos, however, assuming a still close relationship between house-churches and synagogues, proposes that the "weak" in Romans are *non-Christian* Jews associated with the churches.[2] Nanos also proposes that in Rom. 13:1–7 the "authorities" are synagogue authorities, not those of the Roman Empire (see "Moses' seat" in Matt. 23:1–3).[3] The more common current interpretation of Rom. 13:1–7 is based on studies of tax revolts in Rome in 55–58 C.E. Public protests against abuses by authorities who collected the taxes culminated in 58, the very year Paul wrote Romans. In that very specific historical context Paul clearly exhorted Christians to pay both "tax" and "tribute" to avoid the strong penalties for tax evasion (13:6–7).[4]

Nanos's interpretations, nevertheless, bolster the conclusion that Paul's argument in Romans reaches its goal only with the exhortation for mutual and inclusive acceptance in 15:7–13.[5] Furthermore, whether the "weak" be Jews who believed in Jesus or non-Christian Jews, Paul insists that the gospel is first for the Jews (1:16), a weak minority in the pagan Roman Empire (some 10 percent).

Although Romans does not refer explicitly to physical weaknesses, illnesses, or handicaps, such sufferings are included implicitly in Paul's list of oppressions and afflictions that cannot separate us from the love of God in Christ Jesus (8:35–39). In addition, in 2:19 we have the metaphor by which Paul refers to the pride of certain other Jews who offered to serve as "guides for the blind" (Gentiles).

On the question of anti-Judaism in the New Testament, in Paul's letters Romans 9–11 ("all Israel will be saved," 11:25–26) is commonly recognized as unique in holding forth a radically optimistic hope for Jews (cf. 1 Thess. 2:14–16!).[6] The letter shares with Galatians the emphasis on Christians as "free from the law" and still insists that Christ represents the "goal of the law and end of its authority" (10:4). However, Romans also insists on certain abiding norms for the churches: God's liberating justice—paradigmatically exemplified in the Exodus and inculcated as praxis in the pentateuchal laws—as well as love

---

2. Mark D. Nanos, *The Mystery of Romans: the Jewish Context of Paul's Letter* (Minneapolis: Fortress, 1996), 85–165.

3. Ibid., 289–336.

4. Charles D. Myers, "Romans, Epistle to the," *ABD,* 5:816–30. For alternative New Testament perspectives on the state, see our chapters on 1 Peter (a human institution, not divinely instituted) and Revelation ("the great harlot" to be resisted by martyrs).

5. N. T. Wright, *The Climax of the Covenant: Christ and the Law in Pauline Theology* (Minneapolis: Fortress, 1992), 234–35; Thomas R. Schreiner, *Romans* (Grand Rapids: Baker, 1998), 15–23.

6. Donald A. Hagner, "Paul's Quarrel with Judaism," in *Anti-Semitism and Early Christianity,* ed. Craig A. Evans and Donald A. Hagner (Minneapolis: Fortress, 1993), 128–50; cf. J. Lanier Burns, "The Future of Ethnic Israel in Romans 11," in *Dispensationalism and the Church,* ed. Craig A. Blaising and Darrell L. Bock (Grand Rapids: Zondervan, 1992), 188–229.

for neighbor and enemy/oppressor (8:1–4; 13:8–10; 12:14–21; see 2 Tim. 3:14–17).

5. *Women Apostles?*

In Rom. 16:1–16, where Paul names twenty-nine persons (greeting twenty-eight of them), ten of the persons named are women. Nine women are greeted (+ Phoebe named, 16:1–2), while nineteen men are greeted. Among those greeted we find Junia and her husband, Andronicus, both called "apostles" (16:7)—a strong confirmation of the leadership of women in the early churches. In the later Greek manuscripts scribes changed Junia's name to the masculine form (Junias). If Junia had been male, co-apostle with Andronicus, we would have one more example of same-sex apostolic pairs (like the six pairs among Jesus' chosen twelve; Matt. 10:1–4, Greek).

In Romans 16 Paul greets Prisca and Aquila (vv. 3–5), his "co-workers," naming Prisca/Priscilla first, as was most common (except in →1 Cor. 16:19 and Acts 18:2), and praising both of them for their courage (a "masculine" virtue commonly expressed in Greek by a verb "act manly, play the man," 1 Cor. 16:13). Notably, of the ten women Paul names in Romans 16, he specifies that eight are his "co-workers" in the work of the churches, while only one of the single men is called a "co-worker" (16:9; see also Aquila and Andronicus with their wives). The church work thus was done mostly by women, perhaps partly because the men had to dedicate themselves to their secular work. Paul, nevertheless, expressed most affection for the men, since rather than call them his "co-workers" he called them "beloved" (vv. 5, 8, 9). Among the women only his "co-worker" Persis is also termed "beloved" (v. 12).

In addition to the women who are leaders in the five house-churches in Rome, Paul commends Phoebe (16:1–2), to whom the apostle had entrusted his letter from Corinth for the five house-churches of Rome. Paul refers to Phoebe as "minister, deacon" (*diakonos,* using the masculine form), although translations commonly obscure this fact with the rendering "servant" (NIV). The apostle indicates Phoebe's high economic status, describing her as a "benefactor" of many, including Paul himself. Phoebe probably traveled to Rome for legal reasons (concerning an inheritance?), and Paul took advantage of her trip to send his Magna Carta to the capital. When we recall the enormous impact Romans has had throughout church history (in the conversions of Augustine, Luther, and Wesley and on Karl Barth's theology), how unimaginably different this history would have been had Phoebe lost the letter!

Centuries later the church in Rome came to be characterized by an exclusively male hierarchy (pope, cardinals, archbishops, bishops), enormous and luxurious buildings, support for corrupt politicians, and with its own oppressive political power and military forces. In stark contrast, the five house-churches Paul addressed in his letter consisted largely of slaves and other marginalized people, led mainly by women, with women doing most of the work—a community of equals with no hierarchy. Yet these weak little communities soon were recognized to be a subversive threat to the empire. The same picture emerges also from the other six letters that come from Paul himself but is somewhat modified in the three deutero-Pauline letters. The pastoral letters establish male elders, but with no hierarchy, and limit the authority and ministry of women. The Protestant Reformation took a few steps to return the church to its original norms. Luther rejected the supreme authority of the pope; Calvin, in accord with the pastoral letters, eliminated hierarchy among male clergy (presbyters/elders). However, women's equality and leadership are still in the process of being restored today.

With exception of the striking testimony in chapter 16, Romans has little to say concretely concerning women. Perhaps of most theological significance is the absence of Eve when Paul deals with Adam's "fall," and compares Adam and Christ. Much later, 1 Timothy blamed the first sin on Eve as being "deceived" (1 Tim. 2:14), in a context that sought to restrict women's leadership in the churches. In Romans, however, the responsibility for introducing sin into the world is solely that of the male, Adam (Rom. 5:12–21).

In Rom. 7:1–6 Paul utilizes the woman as a means of reflection when he refers to a married woman to illustrate Christian freedom from the law.[7] Here the married woman is described as "subject to/bound to" her husband during this life, but when he dies, as "free" (so much for the glorious state of marriage in Paul's view!). Similarly, Christian men and women had been subject to the law, but now are "free" from the law (7:6). In 1 Corinthians (7:2–4, 10–16) Paul describes marriage in more positive terms as a relationship characterized by mutuality (cf. the almost sacramental view of marriage in Ephesians 5, probably deutero-Pauline).

In Rom. 2:25–29 Paul specifies that the male circumcision prescribed by the law (Genesis 17; Lev. 12:3) is not required for Christian Gentiles (cf. deutero-Pauline Col. 1:11–12, where baptism of both sexes takes the place of male circumcision as the initiation rite for entering the new Christian communities). In the law, Leviticus even spoke of trees with fruit considered as "uncircumcised" for three years, perhaps indicating circumcision as a rite to maximize fertility (Lev. 19:23–25), but the New Testament abandons circumcision and the demand for procreation and maximum fertility, insisting rather on multiplication of disciples (John 15:1–17) and the fruit of the Spirit (Gal. 5:22–23).

6. *Sexual Minorities in Inclusive House-Churches*[8]

Of the ten women named in Rom. 16:1–16, only three are married (Prisca, vv. 3–4; Junia, v. 7; also Julia, v. 15a [Greek, contrary to NIV and NRSV]), while the other seven represent sexual minorities (Phoebe, vv. 1–2; Mary,

---

7. See Elizabeth A. Castelli, "Romans," in *Searching the Scriptures,* vol. 2, *A Feminist Commentary,* ed. Elisabeth Schüssler Fiorenza (New York: Crossroad, 1994), 280–84.

8. See Thomas D. Hanks, "Paul's Letter to the Romans as a Source of Affirmation for Queers and Their Families," in *Our Families, Our Values,* ed. Robert Goss and Amy Strongheart (New York: Harrington, 1997), 137–49. The statistics here are slightly inaccurate but do not affect the argument.

v. 6; Tryphaena and Tryphosa, probably sisters, v. 12a; Persis, v. 12b; Rufus's mother, a widow or divorced, v. 13b; and Nereus's sister, v. 15b).

Of the nineteen men greeted (16:3–16), only three are married: Aquila, vv. 3–4; the co-apostle Andronicus, v. 7; and Julia's husband, Philologus, v. 15a. However, Paul greets sixteen unmarried men who represent sexual minorities (vv. 5, 8–11, 13–15). Furthermore, in the greetings he sends on behalf of his co-workers in Corinth (16:21–24), Paul names only single men, all eight living with the apostle in Gaius's house (nine unmarried men in all—a living arrangement considered "immoral" and not permitted in some parts of the world today!). Thus, of the thirty-eight persons named in Romans 16, only six are married; the other thirty-two (including Paul) were following Jesus' example and remained free of marriage ties—some perhaps may even have abandoned their spouses (Luke 14:26; 18:29).

In addition, as noted above, seven of the ten women named represent sexual minorities. Other New Testament books present a similar picture (see especially our chapters on Philemon, Colossians, and 2 Timothy). Such data make clear what little place married couples (our modern nuclear "family") had in the earlier New Testament churches (cf. the later deutero-Pauline and pastoral letters) and how great was the role of sexual minorities (single men and women, widows, separated and divorced persons, etc.) in these churches.

Nevertheless, Paul, living in Corinth in a house with eight other unmarried males and writing to Roman house-churches where the vast majority of the membership represented sexual minorities, in Rom. 1:26–27 is supposed to have bequeathed to the church the only text in the New Testament that explicitly condemns homosexuals, declaring them objects of God's wrath! In fact, according to traditional interpretation, Rom. 1:26–27 constitutes the great pretext for persecuting and even killing homosexual persons, especially from the thirteenth to twentieth centuries. In part this has been due to the enormous influence of Thomas Aquinas (1225–74) and his Aristotelian theology of "nature."

The influence of Aquinas's interpretation, followed by Luther and other Reformers, reached its culmination with the Nazi Holocaust, where some ten to fifteen thousand homosexuals were killed, along with the six million Jews and other minority groups. The Nazis actually began their persecution and violence against homosexuals immediately after assuming power in 1933, five years before the *Kristallnacht* attack against the Jews in 1938.[9] At a time when the world is beginning to recognize and respect the full human dignity of sexual minorities (South Africa even prohibits discrimination against them in its new constitution), we must ask whether support for such a terrible history of violence can really be found in Romans.

Although totally ignored by traditional apologists determined to refute details of his biblical exegesis, the main point of John Boswell's classic study was

9. Günter Grau, ed., *Hidden Holocaust? Gay and Lesbian Persecution in Germany, 1933–45*, trans. Patrick Camiller (New York: Cassell, 1995).

to show how the bitter fruits of anti-Semitism and homophobia blossomed together in the late-medieval church, probably for similar causes.[10] Proper understanding of Paul's actual teaching in Romans may enable us to counteract both tragic expressions of prejudice and bigotry. Sadly, most post-Holocaust evangelical biblical scholarship has shown itself desperate to rescue Paul from any taint of anti-Semitism, while flaunting a "zeal without knowledge" (Rom. 10:2) to convict Paul of homophobia! Evidently missing the main point of Boswell's work and not knowing that the Nazi violence, culminating in the Holocaust, began by targeting homosexuals, evangelical leaders commonly have sadly failed to distinguish between following Jesus and following Hitler.

For details and documentation on the complex and hotly debated subject of proper interpretation of Rom. 1:26–27, the inquisitive reader must be referred to the bibliography. Here we will only briefly outline the most probable interpretation, which stands in stark contrast with traditional prejudices and common popular religious-political propaganda.

1. In Rom. 1:26 Paul speaks of Gentile women who sexually offer themselves to men for anal sex, to avoid procreation:[11] "Therefore God gave them up to dishonorable desires, for even their females changed natural relations for unnatural ones." This text does not speak of "changing" male sexual companions for female (cf. 1:27), but only of acts that are termed "unnatural," that is, according to the sexual ideology of the day, acts that avoid procreation. This is the only interpretation attested in the church fathers for the first four hundred years! Clement of Alexandria (ca. 250 C.E.), the church's first significant theologian of sexuality, followed his citation of Rom. 1:26–27 with the comment, "Nature has not even permitted the most unclean animals to procreate by means of the passage of evacuation!" (*Paed.* 2.87.1). And even St. Augustine, about a century later, clearly taught that Rom. 1:26 speaks of women in relations "against nature," but in anal sex with men to avoid procreation. Not until John Chrysostom (ca. 400 C.E.) does anyone (mis)interpret Romans 1:26 as referring to relations between two women ("lesbians")! Consequently, we must conclude that the New Testament, like the Hebrew Bible and the Koran, contains no mention or prohibition of relations between women ("lesbians").[12] Furthermore, although traditional apologists tend to forget that women exist, since "homosexuals" obviously include lesbians, Rom. 1:26 (properly interpreted) by itself makes clear that the New Testament nowhere condemns "homosexuals." In the other four relevant New Testament texts, only males

---

10. John Boswell, *Christianity, Social Tolerance, and Homosexuality* (Chicago: University of Chicago Press, 1980).

11. Thomas D. Hanks, "Bernadette J. Brooten on Natural Theology and Unnatural Acts in Romans 1" (paper presented at the annual meeting of the Evangelical Theological Society, Claremont, Calif., 20–22 November 1997 [copyright, Other Sheep, St. Louis, 1997]).

12. James E. Miller, "The Practices of Romans 1:26: Homosexual or Heterosexual?," *Novum Testamentum* 35 (1995): 1–11; idem, "Romans 1 Revisited" (1997 article awaiting publication). Significantly for evangelicals, already in the 1960s the late Francis A. Schaeffer recognized that Romans 1:26 "does not speak of homosexuality"; see his published lectures, *The Finished Work of Christ: The Truth of Romans 1–8* (Wheaton, Ill.: Crossway, 1998), 42–43.

are described, and the condemnations have in view specific male sexual acts that are abusive, not persons with a certain sexual orientation.

2. Recent studies point out that in Romans 1 Paul appears to manifest a considerable indebtedness to Leviticus 18 and 20.[13] However, as Saul Olyan demonstrated, the only sexual act prohibited in the Leviticus texts is male-male anal relations, not other homoerotic expressions[14]—and that in an epoch prior to prophylactics. If we wish to express Leviticus's teaching in modern terms, therefore, we should not say that it condemns "homosexuality" (nothing here about lesbians or the sexual orientation of persons involved), but that *Leviticus teaches safer sex* (avoid male-male anal intercourse without condoms), which is wise counsel in any century. Daniel Boyarin has shown that Jewish rabbis in the early centuries C.E. properly understood that Leviticus prohibited only male-male anal sex.[15] Bernadette Brooten points out that Lev. 20:13 prescribes the death penalty for both males involved in anal sex, since both thus become contaminated and are unclean—even though one of the two might have been raped or be an abused minor.[16] Leviticus here, however, does not refer to women. Neither does Leviticus condemn other (non-anal) homoerotic expression. Nothing is said here against oral sex, mutual masturbation, and so forth. Much less does Leviticus speak of a group of persons with a definite homosexual orientation, but refers only to acts, not the modern scientific concept of sexual orientation.

Paul, having spoken in Rom. 1:26 of females who offer themselves to males for anal sex, turns to males in Rom. 1:27, and following Leviticus, refers to males who have "left" the use of females in order to engage in anal sex (without prophylactics) with other males. Hence, in Rom. 1:26–27 Paul simply extends Leviticus's prohibition of unprotected anal sex to include females with males, while repeating Leviticus's prohibition of male-male anal sex. Hence, in Paul's case also, we have no condemnation of "homosexuality" (nothing about lesbians or the sexual orientation of the males involved): like Leviticus, but extending the prohibition of anal sex to include females with males, *Paul teaches safer sex*. Before condoms became widely available, anal sex was highly dangerous to health, facilitating the transmission of many diseases (before AIDS).

3. As Paul develops his argument throughout his letter, we may observe how he impressively "deconstructs" the three key elements in his rhetoric against anal sex and other practices referred to in Rom. 1:24–27 as "unclean" (1:24, mistranslated by the NIV as "sinful").

---

13. Bernadette J. Brooten, *Love between Women: Early Christian Responses to Female Homoeroticism* (Chicago: University of Chicago Press, 1996), 282–83.

14. Saul M. Olyan, " 'And with a Male You Shall Not Lie the Lying down of a Woman': On the Meaning and Significance of Leviticus 18:22 and 20:13," in *Que(e)rying Religion: A Critical Anthology*, ed. Gary David Comstock and Susan E. Henking (New York: Continuum, 1997), 179–206.

15. Daniel Boyarin, "Are There Any Jews in 'The History of Sexuality'?" *Journal of the History of Sexuality* 5, no. 3 (1995): 333–55.

16. Brooten, *Love between Women*, 290–91.

First, although Romans 1 does not explicitly say that anal relations are "sinful" but only that they are "unclean" (1:24), Paul later insists that "everything" is clean (14:14, 20, not only "food," as in many modern translations). David Fredrickson, however, has pointed out that Paul's condemnation throughout 1:24–27 is not concerned with the gender of the sexual partner, but with the question of "coveting," or sexual lust, whereby destructive emotion overwhelms reason to the detriment of self and neighbor (Exod. 20:17; Deut. 5:21; Rom. 7:7–8; 13:8–10; 13:13).[17] Thus, in effect, Paul in Romans redefines "uncleanness" (6:19) to signify, not cultic prohibitions, but injustice, oppression, and (sexual) exploitation (6:19, 12–13). Both the "change" to anal sex (1:26) and the "change" of partners (1:27) are simply examples of the kind of actions that are "against nature," later deconstructed as characteristic of God's own actions and hence not breaking any "ethical absolutes" nor the normative elements Paul establishes in Romans (condemnations of coveting, lust, oppression, harm to neighbor).

Second, Rom. 1:26 refers to anal sex as "against nature" (with apparently negative overtones); however, in Rom. 11:24 Paul celebrates the fact that God, the great Creator of miracles, acts "against nature" by grafting believing Gentiles into the olive tree (which represents Israel, the people of God; "against nature, unnatural," *para physin,* is precisely the same phrase as in 1:26, and occurs only in these two texts in the entire Bible).

Third, Romans says that the unclean anal sex referred to results in "shame" (1:26–27). However, Paul declares himself "not ashamed" (1:16) of his gospel in which Jesus' crucifixion—the most shameful experience in antiquity—is the central element (3:21–26)! The apostle even encourages the churches in Rome to learn to "boast" of culturally shameful experiences (5:2–3, 11).

Some scholars have concluded that Paul's rhetorical strategy of deconstruction apparent in Romans is quite intentional.[18] However, as Gerd Theissen shows, as far back as 1955 German biblical and psychological studies recognized in Paul a person of homosexual orientation (albeit latent and repressed)—literature and insights still universally ignored in homophobic Anglo-American biblical studies.[19] In the light of Theissen's insights, it may be preferable to suppose that the deconstruction of his own rhetoric that Paul carries out in this letter is largely unconscious, surging forth from within, by the Spirit's inspiration, as he expounds his liberating Gospel (cf. John 7:38). This would make Romans, somewhat like Augustine's *Confessions,* a kind of latent "coming out" (to himself) manifesto. But whether intentional or

---

17. David E. Fredrickson, "Natural and Unnatural Use in Romans 1:24–27: Paul and the Philosophic Critique of Eros" in *Homosexuality, Science, and the "Plain Sense" of Scripture,* ed. David L. Balch, ed. (Grand Rapids: Eerdmans, 2000), 197-222.

18. L. William Countryman, *Dirt, Greed, and Sex: Sexual Ethics in the New Testament and Their Implications for Today* (Philadelphia: Fortress, 1988); Daniel A. Helminiak, *What the Bible Really Says about Homosexuality* (Tajique, N.Mex.: Alamo Square, 2000), 75–104.

19. Gerd Theissen, *Psychological Aspects of Pauline Theology* (Philadelphia: Fortress, 1987), 26.

unconscious, by the end of his letter Paul's call for an inclusive, tolerant community of mutual acceptance is unmistakable (15:7–13).[20] He then proceeds to show us how the five house-churches in Rome—with their sexual minority majorities—already exist as paradigms of his ideal (16:1–16).

However we interpret Rom. 1:26–27, any attempt to deduce modern sexual norms must take into account that Paul devotes half a chapter to insisting on the necessity of some kind of head coverings for women who pray or prophesy in the worship service (1 Cor. 11:2–16; see the chapter on 1 Corinthians). Modern readers may find significant divine wisdom through informed, culturally sensitive study of such texts.

Especially the great majority of heterosexual men in modern churches may find the prohibitions against abusive, unprotected, male-male anal sex in Leviticus 18 and 20 and Rom. 1:27 perfectly acceptable as a norm without exceptions to guide their own behavior. Similarly, women of whatever sexual orientation should have no problem with Paul's rejection of unprotected anal sex with males in Rom. 1:26. However, for more than a century we have realized that a minority of persons are homosexual or bisexual by orientation, and the ready availability of condoms and teaching of safer sex already has significantly altered the risks involved if male homosexuals decide to engage in anal sex. Moreover, with our modern scientific understanding of the transmission of diseases, we now realize that two gay men in an exclusive relationship may practice anal sex without any risk—and the situation is similar even if the relationship is not exclusive, if safer sex guidelines are followed carefully. If such persons prefer non-anal sexual relations, Leviticus 18 and 20 and Rom. 1:27 have nothing directly to say to them.

However, if we would have biblical norms to guide everyone's sexual behavior today, they must be constructed mainly from more fundamental biblical texts that speak of freedom and voluntary acts (with neither coercion nor rape), of justice, of love, of wisdom, and—in relationships established by promises or vows—of faithfulness. Such a creative, constructive (nonliteralistic/legalistic) approach will enable us to stop torturing the biblical texts and using them to fortify and recharge our tendencies toward hate, fear, discrimination, oppression, and violence. Instead, from Paul's letter to the Romans, we may learn to respect the limitation of biblical texts in their original cultural and historical context. Interpreted in this way, even today such texts, traditionally twisted and manipulated to promote violence, may teach us wisdom. Perhaps the wisest counsel that Paul gives us in these matters is in his letter to the Romans:

---

20. Robert Jewett, *Christian Tolerance: Paul's Message to the Modern Church* (Philadelphia: Westminster, 1982). Jewett now wisely reminds us of the large proportion of slaves and liberated ex-slaves in the house churches in Rome, and how Paul's negative rhetoric in Romans 1:24–27 would ring in their ears as a denunciation of the kind of sexual exploitation they had suffered and witnessed (in the cases of their friends, spouses, and children). See "The Social Context and Implications of Homoerotic References in Romans 1:24–27," in *Homosexuality, Science, and the "Plain Sense" of Scripture*, ed. David L. Balch (Grand Rapids: Eerdmans, 2000), 278–304.

> . . . the one who loves another has fulfilled the law. . . . Love *does no harm to a neighbor;* therefore, love is the fulfilling of the law." (13:8–10, citing Lev. 19:18)

Sexual practices that do no harm to one's neighbor are not condemned in the Bible, including Romans. To facilitate the reader's approach to this letter, so controversial in our day and so loaded with emotion and strong, cultural, traditional prejudices, we encourage that the entire book be read. And especially in the case of Romans, we recommend reading the book in reverse, beginning at the end, in order to arrive at the most controversial text only when we have observed the complete context (see the outline above).

During World War I, the homosexual military hero Lawrence of Arabia (Thomas E. Lawrence, 1888–1935) achieved his fame by a similar tactic. He observed that the cannons in the city of Aqaba were pointed toward the Red Sea and that the Turks could not alter the cannons' direction. Consequently, Lawrence decided to march with his Arab soldiers across the enormous "impassable" desert and attacked the imperial Turkish forces from behind, thus gaining a legendary triumph.

Sexual minorities—misled victims of majority propaganda—have long been convinced that Rom. 1:26 and 27 are two cannons pointed directly at them. After carefully analyzing the context of the whole book and determining what the two verses say, we have seen that Paul does not aim any cannons at persons with a homosexual orientation. He speaks only of acts of anal sex (without a prophylactic), first of women with men (v. 26) and then between two men (v. 27). Furthermore, the three elements in the context that on first impression sound like derogatory rhetoric (uncleanness, against nature, causing shame) are each carefully deconstructed in the later chapters as the argument develops, and come to be viewed as highly positive.

Consequently, we conclude that Rom. 1:26–27 offered wisdom for another epoch that did not understand sexual orientations or the ways venereal diseases are transmitted and that did not have the option of utilizing prophylactics in the acts of anal sex. To point these two verses like cannons to condemn persons with a homosexual orientation today is to do violence to the Bible and promote violence against an oppressed minority that we should support with solidarity in their search for justice.

Bibliography

Boswell, John. *Christianity, Social Tolerance, and Homosexuality.* Chicago: University of Chicago Press, 1980.

———. *Same-Sex Unions in Premodern Europe.* New York: Villard, 1994.

Brooten, Bernadette J. *Love between Women: Early Christian Responses to Female Homoeroticism.* Chicago: University of Chicago Press, 1996.

Castelli, Elizabeth A. "Romans." In *Searching the Scriptures,* vol. 2, *A Feminist Commentary,* ed. Elisabeth Schüssler Fiorenza, 272–300. New York: Crossroad, 1994.

Cranfield, C. E. B. *The Epistle to the Romans*. Grand Rapids: Eerdmans, 1985.

Dunn, James D. G. *Romans 1–8*. Word Biblical Commentary 38A. Dallas: Word, 1988.

———. *Romans 9–16*. Word Biblical Commentary 38B. Dallas: Word, 1988.

Elliott, Neil. "Asceticism among the 'Weak' and 'Strong' in Romans 14–15." In *Asceticism and the New Testament*, ed. Leif E. Vaage and Vincent L. Wimbush, 231–51. New York: Routledge, 1999.

Fitzmyer, Joseph A. *Romans*. AB 33. New York: Doubleday, 1993.

Fredrickson, David E. "Natural and Unnatural Use in Romans 1:24–27: Paul and the Philosophic Critique of Eros," in *Homosexuality, Science, and the 'Plain Sense' of Scripture*, ed. David L. Balch, 197–222. Grand Rapids: Eerdmans, 2000.

Gaventa, Beverly Roberts. "Romans." In *The Women's Bible Commentary*, ed. Carol A. Newsom and Sharon H. Ringe, 403–10. Louisville: Westminster John Knox, 1998.

Hanks, Thomas D. "Paul's Letter to the Romans as a Source of Affirmation for Queers and Their Families." In *Our Families, Our Values*, ed. Robert Goss and Amy Strongheart, 137–49. New York: Harrington, 1997.

———. "Bernadette J. Brooten on Natural Theology and Unnatural Acts in Romans 1." Paper presented at annual meeting of Evangelical Theological Society, Claremont, Calif., 20–22 November 1997. Copyright Other Sheep, St. Louis, 1997. Also published as "Sleeping with the Enemy: A Political Necessity for All of Us?" a review of *Love between Women: Early Christian Responses to Female Homoeroticism*, by Bernadette J. Brooten, *More Light Update* 17, no. 4 (March–April 1997): 13–17.

Helminiak, Daniel A. *What the Bible Really Says about Homosexuality*. Millennium edition, updated and expanded. Tajique, N.Mex.: Alamo Square, 2000.

Jewett, Robert. *Christian Tolerance: Paul's Message to the Modern Church*. Philadelphia: Westminster, 1982.

———. "The Social Context and Implications of Homoerotic References in Romans 1:24–27," in *Homosexuality, Science, and the "Plain Sense" of Scripture*, ed. David L. Balch, 278–304. Grand Rapids: Eerdmans, 2000.

———. *Romans*. Hermeneia. Minneapolis: Fortress, 2001.

Miller, James E. "The Practices of Romans 1:26: Homosexual or Heterosexual?" *Novum Testamentum* 35 (1995): 1–11.

———. "Romans 1 Revisited." 1997 article awaiting publication.

———. "Pederasty and Romans 1:27: A Response to Mark Smith." *Journal of the American Academy of Religion* 65, no. 4 (1997): 861–65.

Moo, Douglas. *The Epistle to the Romans*. NICNT. Grand Rapids: Eerdmans, 1996.

Myers, Charles D. "Romans, Epistle to the." *ABD*, 5:816–30.

Nanos, Mark D. *The Mystery of Romans: the Jewish Context of Paul's Letter*. Minneapolis: Fortress, 1996.

Reid, Marty L. "Paul's Rhetoric of Mutuality: A Rhetorical Reading of Romans." In *Society of Biblical Literature 1995 Seminar Papers*, ed. Eugene H. Lovering Jr., 117–39. Atlanta: Scholars Press, 1995.

Schreiner, Thomas R. *Romans*. Baker Exegetical Commentary on the New Testament. Grand Rapids: Baker, 1998.

Stowers, S. K. *A Re-Reading of Romans: Justice, Jews, and Gentiles*. New Haven: Yale University Press, 1994.

Tamez, Elsa. *Contra toda condena: La justificación por la fe desde los excluidos*. San José, Costa Rica: DEI/SEBILA, 1991.

———. *Justicia de Dios: Vida para todos: La justificación por la fe en Pablo*. San José, Costa Rica: SEBILA, 1991.

Williams, Craig A. *Roman Homosexuality: Ideologies of Masculinity in Classical Antiquity*. New York: Oxford University Press, 1999.

Wright, N. T. *The Climax of the Covenant: Christ and the Law in Pauline Theology*. Minneapolis: Fortress, 1992.

For updates on the Romans debates, see the papers presented each year at the Society for Biblical Literature (Atlanta, Scholars Press).

Chapter 7

1 CORINTHIANS

Use Your Gifts to Strengthen the Body

Outline

Introduction, 1:1–17

Greeting, 1:1–3

Thanksgiving: *koinōnia*-solidarity in Christ, 1:4–9

Theme/reasoning: elitist divisiveness versus unity in Christ, 1:10–17

Divisions (Causes) and Unity in Diversity (Solutions), 1:18–15:58

1. Egotism: eloquence, wisdom, knowledge, and wealth 1:18–4:21

   Elitist eloquence and wisdom, 1:18–2:16

   Elitist "knowledge," 3:1–23

   Rejection of arrogance, 1:26–31; 3:18–23

   Elitist wealth and apostolic poverty, 4:1–21

2. Specific expressions of elitist divisiveness, 5:1–11:1

   Porneia, 5:1–7:40 (prostitution, sexual exploitation; 5:1, 9–11; 6:9, 13, 15–16, 18; 7:2)

   Porneia (as incest), 5:1–13

   Resulting legal battles: divorces, inheritances, 6:1–11

   Christian husbands who exploit prostitutes, 6:12–20

   Celibacy, virginity, marriage, widows, slaves, 7:1–40

   Idolatry, meat from idol sacrifices, freedom, 8:1–11:1

   Idolatry (1): *agapē* (love-solidarity) vs. *gnōsis* (elitist "knowledge"), 8:1–13

   Paul as apostle: paradigm of authentic freedom, 9:1–27

   Idolatry (2): Exodus paradigm: slavery, liberation, Israel in the desert, (idolatry, food, *porneia*) versus the Christian Passover festival (eucharist), 10:1–22

   Conclusion: *agapē*-love, Paul and Christ, 10:23–11:1

3. Divisions arising in worship, 11:2–14:40

   Divisions resulting from two traditions (11:2, 23):

      The tradition of head coverings for women and the risk of offending or being raped by angels in worship, 11:2–16

      The eucharist tradition: the rich abuse the poor, members of the body, 11:17–34

   Gifts of the Spirit (1): the body of Christ, 12:1–31a

   The *agapē*-love that unites the diverse members of the body (12:25), 12:31b–13:13

   Gifts of the Spirit (2): tongues that divide, prophecy that edifies the body, 14:1–40

4. Elitist ideological deviations: denial of bodily resurrection, 15:1–58

Conclusion: Gestures of Solidarity, 16:1–24

   The offering for the poor saints in Jerusalem, 16:1–4

   Visits by Paul (vv. 5–9), Timothy (vv. 10–11) and Apollos (v. 12), 16:5–12

   Unifying love; submission to the household of Stephanas, 16:13–18

   Greetings and kisses (on the mouth) for all, 16:19–21

   Curse, a blessing, love for all, 16:22–24

Commentary

Introduction

Around 50–52 C.E., during his second missionary journey, Paul founded the church in Corinth, capital of the Roman province of Achaia in Greece (Acts 18:1–18; 1 Cor. 2:1–5; 2 Cor. 1:19). Then, about 56–57 C.E. the apostle wrote 1 Corinthians from Ephesus (16:8), in what is now Turkey, and probably sent it via the three men named in 16:17. Nevertheless, the book titled 1 Corinthians was not the first letter that Paul wrote to the house-churches of Corinth but the second, since 5:9 mentions an earlier letter, apparently lost or perhaps now forming part of 2 Corinthians (6:14–7:1?).

The sexually disreputable ancient Greek city of Corinth was destroyed by the Romans in 146 B.C.E., and a new Roman colony was founded by Julius Caesar a century later in 44 B.C.E. The new Roman colony was inhabited primarily by former Roman soldiers and former slaves, both coming from Italy. Therefore, when 1 Corinthians 5–7 (concerning sexuality) is interpreted, it is erroneous to cite as being directly pertinent classical authors who wrote about the sexual profligacy of the ancient destroyed Greek city.

The house-churches in Corinth consisted primarily of women and slaves, poor and marginalized people with little formal education (1:26). However, for the first time in history, the Christian community in Corinth began to attract a few more cultured and prosperous persons, principally Gentiles, which created a great *diversity.* Some sought to develop the community in conformity with Hellenistic rhetoric and religiosity, others according to the Jewish tradition of Palestine ("I belong to Cephas [Peter]," 1:12). The major problem Paul confronted in Corinth, therefore, was the proliferation of factions, with resulting elitist *tendencies to divide* the church (1:11–12). Consequently, the fundamental theme of the letter is the *unity* of the various house-churches in Corinth: all of Paul's rhetoric and reasoning aim to establish this unity in diversity (economic, social) of those "called into *koinōnia*-solidarity" in Christ (1:9–10).

To promote a unity that transcends elitist sectarianism, Paul for the first time developed his teaching on the church as the "body of Christ." This image, repeated throughout the letter (6:15–20; 10:16–17; 11:29; 12:4–27; cf. 1:13), is derived from a political analogy popular in the Greco-Roman literature to represent social cohesion. Faced with similar conflicts, Paul repeated the image in his letter to the Romans (12:3–8). The deutero-Pauline letters thirty years later picked up this body image but used it to speak of the church universal rather than local assemblies and elaborated the image to include reference to Christ as the "head" (source/authority) of this body (→Col. 1:18, 24; 2:16–19; Eph. 1:22–23; 4:4–16; 5:23, 30).

Paul's pastoral and theological methods are clearly evident in his letters to the Corinthians: these letters integrate a sequence of personal visits with oral and written interchanges based on concrete historical situations in which the apostle responds to various questions the community addressed to him (1 Cor. 7:1, 25; 8:1; 12:1; 16:1, 12). Paul's method thus is not abstract, authoritarian, or dogmatic, but dialogical in nature with the church invited to participate in a creative and flexible reflection, starting from real life and a pastoral praxis. Today the letter continues to be of maximum significance for its perspectives on (1) the poor, weak, and marginalized; (2) women; and (3) human sexuality.

1. Women Silenced? An Outcry from a Violated Text

First Corinthians 14:34–35 demonstrates the great value for Bible interpretation of scientific textual studies (textual "criticism"), the study of the Greek manuscripts to establish the preferred text. In this case the common text literally translated reads as follows:

> 32And the spirits of prophets are subject to the prophets, 33 for God is a God not of disorder but of peace. (As in all the assemblies of the saints, 34*women should be silent in the assemblies. For they are not permitted to speak, but should be subordinate, as the law also says.* 35*If there is anything they desire to know, let them ask their husbands at home. For it is shameful for a woman to speak in an assembly....*)

In the study of the original language texts, specialists commonly recommend that we not "count" the manuscripts (since the great majority are late and of little authority) but "weigh" them—that is, recognize the importance of the oldest and most accurate. Nevertheless, scholars realize that in a few cases textual errors have been introduced even in the earliest manuscripts of greatest authority, which can be corrected by comparing texts of lesser importance.

Scientific textual studies of 14:34–35, however, take us a step further, providing us with a case study that is almost unique in the Bible. These verses appear in this location in our earliest and most authoritative manuscripts (𝔓46, A, B, etc.). However, in a series of manuscripts called the Western tradition, which also are important (D, F, G, etc.), these verses appear at the end of the chapter, after 14:40. Such a shift in place suggests the possibility that a gloss (commentary written in the margin) may have been inserted into a text by a copyist who thought that the words had been omitted from the text itself by oversight.[1]

The scholar also examines the context and syntax to see whether the text is more coherent without the suspect verses. Although obscured by our translations, the context here strongly supports the introduction of a gloss, since the repetition of the word "assembly/church" in 14:33b and 34a is redundant and in poor style (in Greek as well as in English): "As in all the *churches* of the saints, women should be silent in the *churches*." To avoid this awkwardness our translations tend to vary the translation with synonyms ("congregations . . . churches," NIV).

The broader context of a document also is pertinent. In this case, significantly, 14:34–35 appears to contradict Paul's earlier comments about women prophesying and praying out loud in the church/assembly (11:2–16). In other New Testament texts, including several from Paul, women freely speak and teach (→Acts, Galatians, Philippians, Romans; cf. Colossians).

Another difficulty is that the disputed verses support their teaching with a reference to the Mosaic law, but the Torah says nothing about imposing silence on women during worship. How could Paul, one of the best-educated rabbis of his time, commit such an error regarding the Torah? Finally, the instruction to consult husbands at home overlooks cases of widows and single women, who had no such oracle to consult. How could Paul (himself unmarried and collaborating primarily with single men and women [→Romans 16]) pretend that every woman had a husband at home to consult? Thus, increasingly, modern scholars conclude that 1 Cor. 14:34–35 is a gloss (marginal comment), originally composed by a prejudiced scribe—perhaps under the influence of the deutero-Pauline text in 1 Tim. 2:9–15—and then mistakenly introduced by later copyists into the text at two different points. When we recognize that 1 Cor. 14:34–35 is a scribal addition and that 1 Tim. 2:9–15 does not come

---

1. Gordon D. Fee, *The First Epistle to the Corinthians*, NICNT (Grand Rapids: Eerdmans, 1987); Dale B. Martin, *The Corinthian Body* (New Haven: Yale University Press, 1995), 289 n. 2; Richard B. Hays, *First Corinthians* (Louisville: Westminster John Knox, 1997), 245–49; Philip Payne now has early manuscript evidence not just for the displacement but also for the absence of 14:34–35 from the text; "Fuldensis, Sigla for Variants in Vaticanus, and 1 Cor. 14:34–35," *New Testament Studies* 41 (1995): 240–62; "MS 88 as Evidence for a Text without 1 Cor 14:34–5," *New Testament Studies* 44 (1998): 152–58.

from Paul himself, our understanding of Paul's teaching concerning women changes radically!

Nevertheless, some feminist theologians do not recognize 1 Cor. 14:34–35 as a gloss, but rather emphasize the limitation (the head covering) and the inferiority attributed to women reflected in 1 Cor. 11:2–16.[2] They also correctly point out:

- Paul's omission of women as the first witnesses to Jesus' resurrection (1 Cor. 15:5–8; cf. Mark 16; Luke 24; Matthew 28);
- the naming of Aquila before Prisca (1 Cor. 16:19; also in Acts 18:2); in the four other texts Prisca/Priscilla is named first (Rom. 16:3–5; 2 Tim. 4:19; Acts 18:18, 26); and
- the elimination of the category "man and woman" in 1 Cor. 12:13 (cf. the baptismal formula in Gal. 3:28).

Given the delicate situation, Paul clearly expresses himself quite cautiously in 1 Corinthians when referring to women. Undoubtedly, we may perceive limitations in his teaching concerning women that most today do not accept (1 Cor. 11:2–16). Nevertheless, scientific scrutiny of the Bible ("textual criticism" that detects a scribal addition in 1 Cor. 14:34–35, and "higher criticism," investigating questions of authorship and date, which concludes that →1 Timothy was not composed by Paul himself) assists in perceiving greater diversity in the New Testament and permits a more positive appreciation of a Paul who often transcends his patriarchal cultural background.

In 1 Cor. 11:2–16 Paul obviously reflects concepts from his patriarchal culture (inferiority of women, with rigid roles that differentiate men from women), but also, to a certain degree, he transcends them. Certain points that remain in dispute are worth emphasizing:

- "The husband is the head of his wife" (11:3). Nevertheless, "head" often did not connote "authority" but "origin, source of life" (Col. 2:19; Eph. 4:15–16). Moreover, Paul dialectically relativizes male superiority and privilege by the lordship of Christ (11:3) and by reminding us that men are born from women and that we all come from God (11:12).
- Paul presupposes a concept of a "nature" (11:14) that determines male and female differences in modes of dressing; however, what Paul calls "nature" we would understand as "culture." Moreover, Paul elsewhere points out that even God delights to act "against nature," and such divine acts are celebrated not condemned! (→Rom. 11:24; cf. 1:26–27).
- For those of us who live in the culture of the bikini, it is difficult to understand a culture where a woman could not leave her house without a head covering. Although Paul encouraged women to break with patriarchal religions, form new

2. Antoinette Clark Wire, *The Corinthian Women Prophets: A Reconstruction through Paul's Rhetoric* (Minneapolis: Fortress, 1990); idem, "1 Corinthians," in *Searching the Scriptures*, vol. 2, *A Feminist Commentary*, ed. Elisabeth Schüssler Fiorenza (New York: Crossroad, 1994), 153–95.

Christian communities, and to participate freely in the charismatic worship services, praying out loud and boldly prophesying (which implied great authority), the apostle flexibly adapted to certain cultural concerns by insisting on long hair and head coverings for Christian women, who otherwise enjoyed remarkable freedom.

- Paul's argument concerning long hair and head coverings for women "because of the angels" (11:10) appears strange to modern readers. Angels were understood to be guardians of order in the world and in worship (1 Tim. 5:21), but they also represented a sexual threat for women (Gen. 6:1–4; Jude 6–7; cf. 1 Cor. 6:2–3; 2 Cor. 12:7; Rom. 8:38).[3]

2. Good News for the Poor

Although unprecedented socioeconomic diversity existed in the house-churches in Corinth, most members were poor with little formal education (1 Cor. 1:26, "not many wise . . . " = few). Paul called the powerful minority "the strong," in comparison with "the weak." The "strong" (house owners) particularly could threaten the unity of house-churches, so throughout the letter Paul makes clear his "option for the poor," exhorting the strong to adjust their lifestyle to take into account the needs of the poor and vulnerable.

2.1. 1 Corinthians 1–4. In ancient times the techniques of rhetoric and formal education served to maintain and strengthen the elite with their privileges. Paul himself obviously was quite gifted and well trained in rhetoric. But he employed his rhetoric to appeal to the strong to abandon their fascination for rhetoric and their excessive adulation of formal education to focus on the good news of Christ crucified and the humble community of his followers.[4]

2.2. 1 Corinthians 5–7, "Fast Sex"; 8–10, "Fast Food." The "strong" men could eat meat daily and pay prostitutes and lawyers whenever they wished. In this way they developed a casual and irresponsible sexual ideology, exploiting prostitutes and participating in idolatrous banquets (where meat previously cooked and served to idols was consumed)—a patriarchal male ideology of "fast food and fast sex," frequently interrupted by quick but costly divorces and legal battles over inheritances. Paul here responds, proposing an alternative theology, focusing on the Christian body as the temple of the Holy Spirit that should never be defiled or damaged.[5]

2.3. 1 Corinthians 11:2–16. Women, socially vulnerable, enjoyed freedom in the churches to reject the idolatrous ideologies and religions of their fathers and husbands. Further, in the worship services they prayed out loud, directly addressing the deity without male priests as intermediaries, and they spoke to the assembled church with divine authority ("prophecy," which could strongly criticize the dominant oppressive patriarchal theologies). Such unprecedented freedom brought counterattacks from the threatened patriarchal culture, which sought to deny such freedoms for women (see the "backlash" gloss, 14:34–35). Paul insisted on freedom for women in principle, but did

3. Dale B. Martin, *The Corinthian Body* (New Haven: Yale University Press, 1995), 229–49.
4. Ibid., 38–68.
5. Ibid., 69–86.

accommodate to the cultural tradition that women keep their hair long and heads covered. According to Paul's thinking, women's head covering avoided scandal and guaranteed essential freedom for Christian women. He may also have believed that women would thus be protected from possible sexual abuse by angels.[6]

2.4. 1 Corinthians 11:17–34. The Lord's Supper (eucharist) was not a ritual in a temple but a complete meal in the homes of more affluent believers, that is, in the homes of the "strong," who owned their own spacious houses. In these meals the strong, persons of leisure, arrived punctually to enjoy the food and wine of the host, to the point of drunkenness, illness, and even death in some cases (from excesses?). The majority of the members (slaves, widows, and other poor people) came later, after finishing their day's work and their household chores. When they arrived, they found only the remains of the meal and suffered hunger pains during worship. Paul fervently denounced this scandalous practice, insisting that this elitist banquet had ceased to be the Lord's Supper and that the strong, who did not discern the needs of the poor members of the Lord's body, were going to be judged: oppression, injustice, and class struggle should never come to characterize the body of Christ.[7]

2.5. 1 Corinthians 12–14. In the house-churches' worship services (charismatic and democratic) everyone participated with their spiritual gifts, but in this context the poor and vulnerable had a certain advantage. The strong (a minority), as owners of spacious houses, could seek to dominate and maintain order with their gifts of teaching and administration of funds. However, what were they to do with the motley illiterate *majority,* who sought to contribute by speaking in tongues, interpretations, prophecies, healings, and so forth? Here, as in the case of head coverings for women, Paul firmly insists on freedom and justice for the poor, but seeks a certain accommodation to the dominant culture to avoid creating unnecessary scandals. Although the poor and vulnerable could prophesy and even speak in tongues, in the worship service they should do so only with interpretation of tongues while maintaining some kind of "order" (always a concept relative to a given culture!). Above all, however, Paul exalted the sacrificial mutual love that unites the church as being more important than any charismatic gift.[8]

2.6. 1 Corinthians 15. The strong, influenced by their elitist Greco-Roman education, questioned Christian teaching concerning the resurrection of the body, the last divisive issue Paul sought to correct in this letter. The poor and weak, lacking formal education, easily accepted the idea of miraculously resuscitated bodies (with flesh and blood as before). Decades later Luke (ca. 80 C.E.) spoke of Jesus' resurrection as a resurrection of the flesh (Luke 24:39; cf. Acts 2:24), and John (ca. 90 C.E.) also stressed the death and resurrection of Jesus as tangibly physical (John 19:33–34; 20:27). Paul, however (agreeing

6. Ibid., 229–49.
7. Ibid., 190–97.
8. Fee, *First Corinthians;* cf. Martin, *Corinthian Body,* 87–103; Martin concludes that glossolalia may have been a gift more characteristic of the strong.

with the "strong" elite), conceded that "flesh [*sarx*] and blood cannot inherit the realm of God" (1 Cor. 15:50); he also insisted (with the poor) in a resurrection of the body, but a "*spiritual* body"! To us this phrase may appear to be a complete contradiction in terms, like "square circle."

Our problem with Paul's language here, however, is that we are heirs of the Catholic philosopher René Descartes (1596–1650), who established our modern meaning for the word "spiritual" as something "not material." In ancient times, nevertheless, the S/spirit, although invisible, was just as "material" as the body (like the wind, or breath of God, in the creation, Genesis 1–2). Obviously the resurrection involves issues beyond our finite comprehension. Nevertheless, Paul insisted on a resurrection of the body (both of Jesus and of humanity), but as a "spiritual body," "glorified" and "transformed." In solidarity with the poor and vulnerable in Corinth, Paul maintained the "materialist" tradition of Judaism and Jesus, insisting on the importance of the body, with its physical necessities (daily bread). However, he also accommodated to certain objections of the strong by recognizing that the fundamental teaching of bodily resurrection in the Christian gospel was not equivalent to common superstitions about resuscitated corpses. Paul thus insisted that his gospel—Christ crucified (1 Corinthians 1–4) and resurrected (1 Corinthians 15)—is always good news for the poor.[9]

2.7. 1 Corinthians 16:1–4. Paul's proclamation of Jesus' good news, with its option for the oppressed, focuses finally on common elements in Christian praxis: the apostle's "rainbow angel" dream project of the offering for the poor in Jerusalem (→2 Corinthians 8–9; Rom. 15:25–29)—an international and multicultural project that sought to bridge the growing gap between predominantly Gentile churches and the impoverished original community in Jerusalem.

2.8. The Exodus Paradigm: From Oppression to Poverty to God's Liberating Justice. Two passages in 1 Corinthians make especially clear how fundamental is the Exodus paradigm for Paul's understanding of his own and the Corinthians' experiences of oppression, poverty, and God's liberating justice. He addresses the largely Gentile church as those whose spiritual ancestors were the Israelites in the Exodus, whose liberation is the type of Christians who find a "way out" from their testings and oppressions (10:1–13). The eucharist, thus, is not viewed (as in Matthew) as a solemn reminder of sin and a call to penitence and forgiveness, but as a joyous festival celebrating the liberation of slaves from oppression with Christ the Passover lamb, whose sacrifice results in redemption (5:7–8; cf. the absence of Matthew's forgiveness motif in 1 Cor. 11:17–34 and other Gospel parallels). In such a celebration any focus on sin has in view primarily the sins of the oppressors and the liberation

9. Martin, *Corinthian Body,* 104–36; see especially Irene Foulkes, *Problemas pastorales en Corinto: Comentario exegético-pastoral a 1 Corintios* (San José, Costa Rica: DEI/SEBILA, 1996), who expounds the significance of the letter for the poor, oppressed, and marginalized.

of the oppressed, not the sins—universal though they are—of the oppressed and poor.

Speaking from his own experience (→catalogs of oppression, 2 Corinthians), Paul links his own deprivations (4:10–11a) to the oppression and violence he repeatedly suffered (4:11b–13 "buffeted... reviled... persecuted ... defamed"). Such experiences enabled him to realize (epistemological privilege of the oppressed) that human courts are characterized by injustice and oppression (*adik-* term, 6:1) and hence rarely defend the poor when they suffer oppression and violence (*adik-* terms, 6:1, 7–9). The vice list (6:9–10) then details examples of the oppression and injustice of covetous and rapacious persons, who cannot participate in God's just new order (see the inclusion and repetition of "realm," 6:9–10; cf. below under sexual minorities for homophobic mistranslations of 6:9). The "justification" celebrated in 6:11 thus refers to God's liberating justice: vindication and acceptance of the poor, weak, oppressed, and marginalized, which results in freedom from control freaks (6:12). Similarly, in 1:30 God's liberating justice (*dikaiosynē* // "redemption") vindicates and liberates precisely the poor, marginalized, and despised (1:26–29), incorporating them without discrimination into the body of the church (cf. 8:9; 9:1; 10:29; 15:34). In our earliest account of the Lord's Supper (11:17–34), the focus is not on sin in general, but only on the sins of the rich who failed to discern that the poor—perhaps mainly slaves who arrived late for the love-feast and were left hungry—also were members of Christ's body. Even this liturgical celebration scandalously becomes in effect a mechanism of oppression and marginalization that lets the poor go hungry! Authentic love, Paul thus insists, can never party over such oppression (13:6; cf. oppression in 15:9, 25, 32; 16:9).

3. Good News for Sexual Minorities (1 Corinthians 5–7; 16:5–24)

1 Corinthians names fourteen living persons, but only two of these are specified as married couples: Cephas/Peter and his wife (1:12; 9:5) and Aquila and Prisca/Priscilla (16:9; other texts name Prisca first; also see 5:1, where a man who is living with his father's wife is mentioned). Much more numerous are single men (Timothy, 16:10–11; Apollos, 16:12) and male pairs (Paul and Sosthenes, 1:1; Crispus and Gaius, 1:14). We also have the "household" (not "family") of Stephanas with his two male companions Fortunatus and Achaicus (a couple? 1:16 and 16:15–18), which gives us a total of nine unmarried men. (If Stephanas had been married, the emphasis on his household without mentioning his wife would have been strange.) Paul also mentions a single woman, Chloe, probably a merchant like Lydia, with her "people" (not "household"; 1:11, see HCSB note).

Obviously, then, neither the house-churches in Corinth nor Paul with his surroundings in Ephesus reflects an environment dominated by married couples. (→Romans; 1 Thessalonians; Philemon; Philippians; Colossians.) The letter does indicate (9:5) that other missionaries were married (such as Prisca and Aquila; cf. Andronicus and Junia in Rom. 16:7) and that Jesus had married brothers (James and Judas). However, the great majority (ten of fourteen people named) appear to be single or same-sex couples. Of all the New Testament authors only James and Jude appear to have been married (1–2 Peter probably did not come directly from Peter). Given such a context, we may suspect that the good news Paul proclaims in 1 Corinthians is not bad news for sexual minorities. Is it true?

Notably, 1 Corinthians 5–7 (three entire chapters) is the only detailed treatment in the New Testament of what we would call "sexual" matters (a modern category). Apart from this we have only the isolated verses of Jesus (e.g., concerning divorce to remarry and against adultery) and brief texts in the epistles (→1 Thess. 4:3–8, the most detailed). In the Hebrew scriptures we have an entire book of erotic poetry, the Song of Solomon, with a focus on sexual love not matrimony (much less is it an allegory of God's love for Israel or Christ's love for the church, the traditional interpretations for two thousand years). The obvious question is whether Paul's teaching reflects basic continuity with his Hebrew Bible (especially the Song of Songs' erotic love poems), or if the Greco-Roman and oriental influences subverted this perspective toward a negativism regarding physical expressions of sexual love. Does Paul speak in these chapters as a defender of the poor, vulnerable, and marginalized, or does he place himself on the side of the strong and a controlling and oppressive patriarchal sexual ideology?

Historically, 1 Corinthians 5–7 has been of considerable importance as the purported basis for St. Augustine's sexual ideology (sexual relations only within marriage and only for procreation), the dominant paradigm in most churches almost until the present. Furthermore, from the Reformation until the present, Protestants commonly have interpreted 1 Corinthians 5–7 as representing matrimony as the Christian norm. Here St. Augustine and the medieval tradition are more faithful to Paul than modern Protestants, since they recognized that Jesus' single life is the norm for Paul and the majority of his colleagues.

The ideological prejudice is noted in the common tendency to put "marriage" as the topic title of 1 Corinthians 7 in most Bibles, when in fact the chapter deals in much greater detail with virginity (7:25–40), directs widows not to remarry because of the proximity of Jesus' second coming (7:8–9, 29–35; →1 Tim. 5:11–14), and underscores the great superiority of celibacy for those who want to serve God (7:7). However, contrary to St. Augustine's sexual ideology, procreation never enters into Paul's (apocalyptic) perspective when dealing with sexual matters.

In Paul's discussion of marital sexual relations in 7:1–5 he transcends his patriarchal culture by insisting on justice, equality, and mutuality of conjugal rights. However, sexual relations in matrimony are described only as an "obligation," not as pleasure! Neither procreation of children (Genesis 1–2) nor love appears in Paul's perspective at this point (1 Corinthians 13). Matrimony is reduced to a type of control technique to deal with sexual passion (7:9; cf. the exaltation of the husband's love in Ephesians 5, which is deutero-Pauline).

When Paul deals with married men, who had money to pay prostitutes (6:9–20), he starts from a concept of the individual Christian's body as the temple of the Holy Spirit and points out the great danger for this body in having sexual relations with a pagan prostitute. If Christian wives insisted in a great deal of sexual abstention for ascetic motives (7:5), we may understand why their husbands paid prostitutes. However, Paul's teaching in 6:9–20 presents many problems.

- The notion that contamination of the Christian body by contact with a prostitute appears to contradict another of Paul's convictions: a Christian woman married to a pagan man would have a more powerful effect in making holy not only the pagan husband but also in producing "holy" children (i.e., "not contaminated" by paganism, 1 Cor. 7:14).
- Jesus also gave example of the sanctifying power of the Holy Spirit (purifying lepers and bringing cadavers back to life by touching them), and taught that it was not exterior things that contaminate us but evil thoughts that proceed out of the heart (Mark 7; Matthew 15; see the affirmations in Rom. 14:14, 20 and Titus 1:15 that all *things* are clean). Does Paul here fall into the error of thinking that sex is something dirty and impure or that prostitutes do not also bear the image of their Creator?
- Jesus was a friend of prostitutes and toll collectors (Luke 5:30; Matt. 11:19; 21:31–32), whom he treated with loving respect and chose as special instruments in the proclamation of his dominion (Luke 7; John 4). Resurrected, he appeared first to Mary Magdalene. For Paul, however, the pagan prostitute does not appear as a person, much less as a potential disciple of Jesus, but as unclean, a threat to Christian purity that must be avoided. Nevertheless, Paul's condemnation is not directed to the prostitutes but to Christian husbands who exploited them.

Perhaps, as in the case of the supposed inferiority of women, their head coverings in worship, and his acceptance of slavery and monarchies, we should question Paul's teaching on sexuality when aspects of his thought appear incoherent to us. But Paul's praxis as a single man, follower of Jesus (unmarried), his continual formation of intimate partnerships with other males (→John, Jesus and his Beloved Disciple), and his establishment throughout the Roman Empire of ecclesiastical communities dominated not by traditional households but by sexual minorities, enable us to see in the apostle Paul a paradigm of Christian freedom (1 Cor. 9:1) with a gospel that is just as much good news for sexual minorities as it is for women and the poor.[10]

In part, our contemporary problems with Paul's teachings in 1 Corinthians 5–7 arise because we do not note the fundamental place that oppression and liberating justice play in this text. Paul makes it clear that oppression and injustice (*adikoi*) are incompatible with God's just new order that Christian communities should manifest (1 Cor. 6:9–11). Paul then presents the use of prostitutes by wealthy husbands as something unacceptable. Sexual uncleanness is reinterpreted in the first place as injustice and the loss of freedom (cf.

---

10. Martin, *Corinthian Body*, 250–51.

Torah). *Porneia* is understood as the sexual filth that results from unjust, oppressive, irresponsible sexual exploitation, without mutual freedom, respect, knowledge, and love (6:12–20).

As we may observe in →1 Timothy, the modern tendency to translate *arsenokoitai* ("bed-males," 1 Cor. 6:9) as "homosexuals" is totally mistaken. The term does not refer to the modern concept of sexual orientation, nor to lesbians, but to males who engaged in exploitative, abusive, and oppressive sexual practices, be it with women, other males, or youths. In 1 Cor. 6:9, the previous word, *malakoi* (lit., "soft"), at times was a metaphor for effeminate men. However, in ancient times an "effeminate" male could be someone who spent excessive time in the company of women and in frequent sexual relations with them. Throughout almost all of church history *malakoi* has been misinterpreted as a condemnation of masturbation.[11]

Bibliography

Bassler, Jouette M. "1 Corinthians." In *The Women's Bible Commentary*, ed. Carol A. Newsom and Sharon H. Ringe, 411–19. Louisville: Westminster John Knox, 1998.

Betz, Hans Dieter, and Margaret M. Mitchell. "Corinthians, First Epistle to the." *ABD*, 1:1139–48.

Castelli, Elizabeth A. "Disciplines of Difference: Asceticism and History in Paul." In *Asceticism and the New Testament*, ed. Leif E. Vaage and Vincent L. Wimbush, 171–85. New York: Routledge, 1999.

Collins, Raymond F. *First Corinthians*. Sacra Pagina 7. Collegeville, Minn.: Liturgical Press, 1999.

Deming, Will. "The Unity of 1 Corinthians 5–6." *Journal of Biblical Literature* 115, no. 2 (1996): 289–312.

Fee, Gordon D. *The First Epistle to the Corinthians*. NICNT. Grand Rapids: Eerdmans, 1987.

Fisk, Bruce N. "PORNEUEIN as Body Violation: The Unique Nature of Sexual Sin in 1 Corinthians 6:18." *New Testament Studies* 42 (1996): 540–58.

Foulkes, Irene. *Problemas pastorales en Corinto: Comentario exegético-pastoral a 1 Corintios*. San José, Costa Rica: DEI/SEBILA, 1996.

Furnish, Victor Paul. *The Theology of the First Letter to the Corinthians*. Cambridge: Cambridge University Press, 1997.

---

11. Dale B. Martin, "*Arsenokoites* and *Malakos:* Meanings and Consequences," in *Biblical Ethics and Homosexuality: Listening to Scripture*, ed. Robert L. Brawley (Louisville: Westminster John Knox, 1996), 117–36. Frederick Danker acknowledges "the impropriety" of the RSV's translation "homosexuals"; see Walter Bauer, *A Greek Lexicon of the New Testament and Other Early Christian Literature*, 3d ed., rev. by Frederick W. Danker (Chicago: University of Chicago Press, 2000), 135. Above all, see David Fredrickson's case for translating "soft ones" and "bed-males" in 1 Corinthians 6:9–10 as "those who *lack self-control*, nor the arrogant who penetrate boys" (p. 197). Fredrickson takes us considerably beyond Dale Martin's essay, since Martin leaves "soft ones" with the translation "effeminate," which then still requires more explaining; see David E. Fredrickson, "Natural and Unnatural Use in Romans 1:24–27: Paul and the Philosophic Critique of Eros," in *Homosexuality, Science, and the "Plain Sense" of Scripture*, ed. David L. Balch (Grand Rapids: Eerdmans, 2000), 197–222).

Glancy, J. A. "Obstacles to Slaves' Participation in the Corinthian Church." *Journal of Biblical Literature* 117 (1998): 481–501. Concerning slaves as sexual property of their owners.

Hays, Richard B. *First Corinthians.* Interpretation: A Bible Commentary for Teaching and Preaching. Louisville: Westminster John Knox, 1997.

Horsley, Richard A. *1 Corinthians.* Abingdon New Testament Commentaries. Nashville: Abingdon, 1998.

Johnson, Luke Timothy. "Glossolalia and the Embarrassments of Experience." *Princeton Seminary Bulletin* 18, no. 2 (1997): 113–34.

Martin, Dale B. *The Corinthian Body.* New Haven: Yale University Press, 1995.

———. "*Arsenokoites* and *Malakos:* Meanings and Consequences." In *Biblical Ethics and Homosexuality: Listening to Scripture,* ed. Robert L. Brawley, 117–36. Louisville: Westminster John Knox, 1996.

———. "Tongues of Angels and Other Status Indicators." *Journal of the American Academy of Religion* 59 (1991): 547–89.

Mitchell, Alan C. "Rich and Poor in the Courts of Corinth." *New Testament Studies* 39 (1993): 562–86.

Mitchell, Margaret M. *Paul and the Rhetoric of Reconciliation.* Louisville: Westminster John Knox, 1991.

Moore, Stephen. *God's Gym: Divine Male Bodies of the Bible.* New York: Routledge, 1996.

Payne, Philip. "Fuldensis, Sigla for Variants in Vaticanus, and 1 Cor. 14:34–35." *New Testament Studies* 41 (1995): 240–62.

———. "MS 88 as Evidence for a Text without 1 Cor 14:34–5." *New Testament Studies* 44 (1998): 152–58.

Rosner, Brian S. *Paul, Scripture and Ethics. A Study of 1 Corinthians 5–7.* Arbeiten zur Geschichte des Antiken Judentums und des Urchristentums 22. Leiden, Netherlands: Brill, 1994.

Schrage, Wolfgang. *Der erste Brief an die Korinther.* 3 vols. Evangelisch-katholischer Kommentar zum Neuen Testament. Zurich: Benziger; Neukirchen-Vluyn: Neukirchener, 1991–97.

Von Dehsen, Christian D. "Sexual Relationships and the Church: An Exegetical Study of 1 Corinthians 5–7." Ph.D. diss., Union Theological Seminary, New York, 1987.

———. *Paul on Marriage and Celibacy; The Hellenistic Background of 1 Corinthians 7.* Society for New Testament Studies Monograph Series 83. Cambridge: Cambridge University Press, 1995.

Wire, Antoinette Clark. "1 Corinthians." In *Searching the Scriptures,* vol. 2, *A Feminist Commentary,* Elisabeth Schüssler Fiorenza, 153–95. New York: Crossroad, 1994.

———. *The Corinthian Women Prophets: A Reconstruction through Paul's Rhetoric.* Minneapolis: Fortress, 1990.

Witherington, Ben, III. *Conflict and Community in Corinth: A Socio-Rhetorical Commentary on 1 and 2 Corinthians.* Grand Rapids: Eerdmans, 1995.

Chapter 8

2 CORINTHIANS

God's Solidarity with the Weak and the "Crazy"

Outline

1. Preamble: addressees, greetings, thanksgiving, blessing	1:1–11
2. Paul's motive for changing his travel plans...	1:12–2:13
— *Possible division between letters* —	
3. Digression: the apostolic ministry, from Troas to Macedonia...	2:14–6:13
Purity and Separation (non-Pauline fragment?	6:14–7:1
...Digression concluded	7:2–4
— *Possible division between letters* —	
...Summary of travel plans: Paul in Macedonia, where he meets with Titus	7:5–16
— *Possible division between letters* —	
4. Organization and administration of offering for the poor	8:1–9:15
To Corinth distinct letter?	8:1–24
To Achaia distinct letter?	9:1–15
— *Possible division between letters* —	
5. Paul's defense: human weakness and divine strength	10:1–13:10
Response to the accusation of weakness	10:1–11
Response to the accusation of ambition	10:12–18
Discourse of a "fool": Paul obligated to boast about himself	11:1–12:10
Signs of an authentic apostle	12:11–13
Concern for the Corinthians	12:14–21
Warnings and exhortations	13:1–10
6. Conclusion: recommendations, final greetings	13:11–13

Commentary

Introduction

Although 2 Corinthians was written ca. 57 C.E., without doubt by Paul, perhaps from Macedonia (or in part, from Ephesus), most specialists question the document's unity and believe 2 Corinthians to be a collection of Paul's letters. However, no consensus has been achieved regarding the number of letters, their order, and their mutual relationship. Johann Salomo Semler's research (1776) marked the beginning of a long history of hypotheses concerning the number and order of the letters.

Now, surprisingly, in the last decade, the possibility of 2 Corinthians' unity has gained support. Recent studies of the techniques of ancient rhetoric point out that abrupt changes in emotional tone do not necessarily indicate seams signaling distinct documents. Consequently, especially for an initial approach to 2 Corinthians, it seems preferable to accept tentatively the tradition of the unity of the letter. At the same time, we should recognize that certain divisions in the letter are so abrupt that they may indicate seams of originally distinct letters from Paul.

1. The Poor and Poor Paul

Paul had made it clear in 1 Corinthians that the Corinthian church was primarily poor (1:26–29; with many women and slaves, 11:1–21), but nevertheless able to participate in the ecumenical offering for the "poor saints" (Christian Jews) in Jerusalem (16:1–4). In 2 Corinthians the apostle dedicates two entire chapters to the theme of the administration of this offering (chaps. 8–9), which some consider originally to have been two distinct letters. In 8:9 Paul portrays Jesus as one who though rich "became poor" (through the incarnation) and who thus is the paradigm for the communities of his followers, the poor and those expressing solidarity with them in love: "For you know the generous act of our Lord Jesus Christ, that though he was rich, yet for your sakes he became poor, so that by his poverty you might become rich."

Notably, in church history 2 Corinthians 8 and 9 have been cited to solicit economic support for innumerable projects from pastors' and missionaries' salaries to the construction of (often luxurious) buildings. However, the institutional church has tended to suffer amnesia regarding the original context and purpose of the offering. Churches continue citing texts from 2 Corinthians 8 and 9 to encourage generosity in offerings while overlooking the fact that the offering requested by Paul was solely to help the poor in Jerusalem (Jewish Christians who were persecuted and oppressed; cf. Rom. 15:25–28; Acts 11:29–30; 24:17; Gal. 2:10; 1 Cor. 16:1–4). Similarly, we cite Paul's words concerning the Lord's Supper (1 Cor. 11:23–26) but omit the original context, where the supper clearly was a gesture of solidarity with the poor (1 Cor. 11:17–22).

In 2 Corinthians Paul faces a church crisis, deploying an entire repertory of administrative instruments: personal visits, sending of delegates, and letters with memorable rhetoric. Concerning the "fool's speech" (2 Cor. 11:1–12:10), Hans Dieter Betz comments: "In this wild and brilliant self-parody, the apostle demolishes the presumptions of his adversaries. He restores his credibility by discrediting theirs through the use of his entire arsenal of irony, sarcasm and parody. . . . In the role of the fool he performs—without actually doing—that which he judges to be inappropriate [boasting, in order to defend himself against slander]."[1] This "fool's speech" is the culmination of the defense that Paul makes of his office as apostle, the dominant theme of the letter.

For the administration of the offering, Paul seeks to avoid accusations of misappropriation of funds (2 Cor. 12:16–17) by insisting on scrupulous supervision by three men. This group included a brother of the Corinthian church, elected democratically by the majority (who showed their approval *cheirotonētheis,* lit., "with the hand," 2 Cor. 8:18–20). Thus the three delegates are called "apostles" (8:23), a term that for Paul means only "missionary, messenger, delegate," and does not refer to the twelve men of the Gospels (1 Cor. 9:5; Rom. 16:7).

Material riches frequently are denounced in the Gospels as a spiritual force that corrupts (Mark 10:17–25; Matt. 6:25–33; Luke 6:20; see James 2:2–6; 1 Tim. 6:6–10). In 2 Corinthians, however, Paul presents the other side of the dialectic: wealth may be a divine blessing that ends degrading dependence and empowers us to serve others (2 Cor. 9:8). Paul does not ask the Christian community in Corinth to practice the primitive communism of the first church in Jerusalem; nor does he demand that everyone sell all and give the proceeds to the poor (see Acts 2:44–45). Rather, Paul describes the Corinthians as partakers of divine riches (9:8–11; 8:7) and exhorts them to be generous with those who are in need (see 1 Tim. 6:17–20).

Of the seven "catalogs of suffering" that commentators have discovered in Paul's letters, four are in 2 Corinthians (4:8–10; 6:4b–10; 11:23b–29; 12:10; see 1 Cor. 4:10–13a; Rom. 8:35; Phil. 4:12; cf. 2 Tim. 3:10–13). In fact, these "catalogs of suffering" might better be called "catalogs of *oppression,*" since the sufferings enumerated by Paul are mainly consequences of the injustices and violence of the authorities and the socially powerful groups.[2] Specific vocabulary for oppression is common in 2 Cor.: 1:4–10, 24 ("lord it over"); 4:8, 17; 6:4; 7:2 ("oppressed . . . harmed . . . defrauded"), 4–5 ("oppressed"), 12 ("one oppressing . . . one suffering oppression"); 8:2, 13–15; 11:20, 23b–33; 12:10, 13, 18.

As in the Exodus paradigm and commonly throughout the Hebrew Bible, Paul sees oppression as the fundamental cause of poverty: 6:4, 10; 8:2, 13–15;

---

1. Hans Dieter Betz, "Corinthians, Second Epistle to the," *ABD,* 1:1149.

2. Thomas D. Hanks, "Poor/Poverty (New Testament)," *ABD,* 5:417; cf. J. T. Fitzgerald, *Cracks in an Earthen Vessel: an Examination of the Catalogs of Hardship in the Corinthian Correspondence,* Society of Biblical Literature Dissertation Series 99 (Atlanta: Scholars Press, 1988). For common mechanisms of oppression, see also the important doctoral dissertation of Young Ihl Kim, "The Vocabulary of Oppression in the Old Testament" (Drew University, Madison, New Jersey, 1981).

11:9 with 23b–33. And since poverty is most commonly caused by oppression, liberating justice (both divine and human) is the appropriate response:

- as in the Exodus, liberating justice characterizes God's actions in history, and this God is described not as a blindfolded passive goddess, but as a warrior, responding militantly to oppression with power and weapons of liberating justice (6:7, 14);
- "indignation . . . readiness to see liberating justice accomplished" (7:11; similarly, 10:6);
- Paul's hope for the church reflects God's distribution of manna (Exodus 16) and land (Joshua 13–21; the Jubilee Year, Leviticus 25), so liberating justice is to result in basic equality (*isotēs*) in the new community (8:13–15);
- giving to the poor is not viewed primarily as charity, but as liberating justice (9:8–10, citing Ps. 112:9);
- perhaps Paul's reference to those who masquerade as "just" reflects Jesus' ironic description of "self-righteous" hypocrites who promise freedom but actually enslave (11:15, 20; →Mark 2:17);
- for Paul "salvation" includes deliverance from oppression (1:6, 10–11);
- liberating justice is the fundamental work of God's Spirit (3:8–9), and where the Spirit of the Liberator God is present, liberation and freedom result (3:17);
- Jesus was made sin (or sin offering) "that we might experience God's liberating justice in him" (5:21).

From his seven catalogs of oppression we may see that Paul, more than any other figure in the New Testament, approaches Jesus' life style: a poor itinerant prophet with neither home nor wife (for the case of Jesus, see the Luke and Matthew texts attributed to Q). The only notable difference is that Jesus apparently depended totally on the hospitality and support of others (women in Luke 8:1–3), while Paul performed manual labor (making leather tents) in order to not overburden the struggling new communities in less hospitable Gentile territories.

In 2 Corinthians Paul's enemies who slander him appear to differ from those of 1 Corinthians. During the brief interval between the two letters (56 and 57 C.E.), apparently another group of "false apostles" arrived who were more dangerous than those referred to in 1 Corinthians. In Galatians Paul had opposed a sector of Jewish Christians who wanted to impose circumcision and Moses' law on the Gentiles. And he spoke in 1 Corinthians of factions among the Corinthians themselves who threatened the unity of the church. In 2 Corinthians, however, those who created problems were intruders from outside the church (although apparently connected with someone in Corinth; see "the one who did the wrong," 2 Cor. 7:12). The Jewish-Christian missionary intruders emphasized Jesus' miraculous powers and demanded miracles and revelations from Paul to authenticate his ministry as an apostle (2 Cor. 12:1, 7, 12; 13:3). They also accused him of misappropriating offering funds for personal enrichment.

2. *The Weak, Sick, and Physically Challenged*

More than any other book of the New Testament, 2 Corinthians emphasizes human weakness—especially that of Paul himself—and God's solidarity with the weak (see *sarx,* "flesh," which is weak):

- suffering, affliction, tribulation, oppression, condemned to death (Paul and co-workers) (1:3–11)
- a veil over their minds (image of the blind) (3:14–18)
- the veiled gospel . . . the god of this age blinds them [image] . . . darkness (4:3–4, 6)
- clay jars . . . we always carry in our bodies the death of Jesus (4:7–10)
- "our outer nature is wasting away" (4:16)
- "if the earthly tent we live in is destroyed" (5:1)
- "we regard no one from a human point of view . . . Christ from a human point of view . . . in Christ there is a new creation" (5:16–17)
- Paul's body is weak (according to his critics) (10:10)
- Paul: five times received forty lashes minus one . . . three times beaten with rods (11:23–25)
- Paul: "I will boast . . . of my weaknesses . . . a thorn was given me in the flesh [an eye affliction?]. . . . *'My grace is sufficient for you, for power is made perfect in weakness'. . . . whenever I am weak I am strong*" (12:5–10)
- Christ "was crucified in weakness, but lives by the power of God. For we . . . weak . . . with him by the power of God" (13:4)

In patriarchal culture, women were considered to be "the weaker vessel" (1 Pet. 3:7). However, in 2 Corinthians Paul himself admits to having his "thorn in the flesh" (12:7), and to being someone "weak" but strengthened by divine grace: "[God] said to me, 'My grace is sufficient for you, for power is made perfect in weakness'. . . . for whenever I am weak, then I am strong" (12:9–10). The entire theology of 2 Corinthians is summarized in this dialectic between human weakness (not only of women) and divine power. And God's power manifests itself in history in liberating justice, salvation, forgiveness, reconciliation, and healing—provisionally in the church, but eventually for the entire cosmos.

3. *Women*

With the exception of the symbolic/theological usage of the church and of Eve (11:2–3), 2 Corinthians does not explicitly speak of women. Nevertheless, from 1 Corinthians we know that women played an important role in church leadership (1 Cor. 1:11; 11:2–16; 12–14). Therefore, we may conclude that when Paul spoke to "the church" in 2 Corinthians (1:1, etc.), he included the women. One exhortation might seem to be directed only to men: "be men of courage [*andrizesthe,* lit., 'play the man' = have courage], be strong" (1 Cor. 16:13). However, in reality it is directed to the entire church, women included, and thus indicates flexibility in gender roles (see Priscilla, Rom. 16:3–4). Such flexibility complements the apparent rigidity in Paul's teaching concerning women's head coverings (1 Cor. 11:2–16).

Furthermore, 2 Corinthians provides us with the most explicit example of inclusive language in the New Testament. In 6:18 Paul quotes 2 Sam. 7:14, where the original Hebrew speaks solely of "sons." But Paul modifies the citation in 2 Corinthians to explicitly include women, giving us a kind of "feminist rereading": "I will be your father, and you shall be my sons *and daughters,* says the almighty Liberator God" (cf. Isa. 43:6). If Paul could exhibit such freedom and flexibility when citing and interpreting sacred scriptures, do we not follow him most faithfully when (to achieve greater clarity concerning God's liberating justice and the inclusivity of the new order) we do the same? In 2 Corinthians, as in Galatians, Paul insists that the mark of the authentic "charismatic" Christian (guided and empowered by God's Spirit) is not passive conformity to oppressive traditions and structures, but freedom: "where the Spirit of the Lord is, there is freedom" (2 Cor. 3:17; cf. Gal. 5:1; 2:4).

The theology of suffering in 2 Corinthians is amply discussed in feminist theology. Jouette Bassler concludes that 2 Corinthians' theology of the cross is powerful, but also potentially dangerous for women. We may appreciate Paul's interpretation of the cross here as an astute defense against rivals in Corinth, effectively subverting their slander. Paul's theology of suffering, however, does not justify passivity in the face of meaningless suffering or oppression.[3] Bassler points out that Paul also used the figure of Eve (the only woman named in 2 Corinthians) as the deceived (11:3) to strengthen the patriarchal prejudices in regard to women and their supposed susceptibility to deception (1 Tim. 2:14). In the same text Paul speaks of being jealous with a "divine jealousy," although in his lists of vices the apostle describes jealousy as a work of the flesh and sinful (illustrating the error of reading the vice lists as if they were universal absolutes of Greek "ethics," cf. Gal. 5:20).

4. *Sexual Minorities*

The catalogs of suffering demonstrate that Paul frequently was the victim of slander, injustice, oppression, and violence. As in the case of widows, orphans, and single women, an itinerant foreigner like Paul could not count on relatives' protection. Therefore, he suffered defamation and slander that caused the authorities to punish him unjustly. Unlike most Protestant missionaries today, Paul remained unmarried. 2 Corinthians comes from Paul and his companion Timothy (1:1, 19), does not name any contemporary woman (cf. Eve in 11:1–3), and, aside from Timothy, speaks only of Titus (also deeply

3. Jouette M. Bassler, "2 Corinthians," in *The Women's Bible Commentary,* ed. Carol A. Newsom and Sharon H. Ringe (Louisville: Westminster John Knox, 1992), 420–22.

loved, 2:13; 7:6–16; 8:23), Silvanus (1:19), and two unnamed men elected as apostles-delegates (8:18–23).

Although today we often hear the Bible cited in support of traditional family values, nuclear families are virtually nonexistent in the New Testament, where the single life of Jesus and his followers like Paul is presented as the new norm (cf. the patriarchal households dominant in the Hebrew Bible). In Genesis (1:28) the *couple* Adam and Eve constitute God's image, but in the New Testament the *unmarried* Jesus is God's image, sometimes with his followers, also primarily persons without families or those who had abandoned their families to follow Jesus (Luke 14:26; 18:29; →Colossians; Ephesians). As elsewhere in the New Testament, in 2 Corinthians not the patriarchal family but the church constitutes the center of God's presence and praxis in the world. This church, whose members primarily are not married couples but sexual minorities, is a counterculture community characterized by friendship and love.[4] (→1–3 John.)

5. Anti-Judaism: The Hebrew Scriptures and the "Old Testament"

It has been customary since Melito, bishop of Sardis (ca. 190 C.E.), to call the Hebrew scriptures the "*Old* Testament," with the implication of something inferior and surpassed. The New Testament itself, however, *never* refers to the Hebrew scriptures with this pejorative term (see 2 Tim. 3:14–17). Rather, the New Testament books refer to the Hebrew Bible simply as "the scriptures" and uses similar honorific expressions (the "sacred letters"). The contrary tradition of dismissing the Hebrew Bible as the "Old" Testament is but one of many manifestations of anti-Judaism, almost always unconscious, in the history of the church, which culminated in the Nazi Holocaust with the deaths of six million Jews and other minority groups (homosexuals, Gypsies, communists, Jehovah's Witnesses, etc.). Such pejorative verbal expressions that cause offense commonly form part of our standard vocabulary and the very structure of our language. We use them without thinking of their destructive impact (God only as Father, Old Testament, queer, fairy, blind, son of a bitch, faggot, etc.; →James's discussion of the tongue).

Many mistakenly attribute to 2 Corinthians the tradition of referring to the Hebrew scriptures as the "Old Testament." However, when Paul mentions the "old covenant" (2 Cor. 3:14), he refers not to the books of the Hebrew scriptures but to the covenant God made with *Moses,* in contrast to the new covenant prophesied by *Jeremiah* (Jer. 31:31–34), a prophecy that also forms part of the Hebrew scriptures (see the quotations in Hebrews 8 of the New Testament).

Beginning with the disdain for the Hebrew scriptures as the "Old" Testament (the only "Bible" that Jesus and Paul knew), for centuries many churches customarily stand in respect for the reading of the Gospels but remain seated

---

4. For love in 2 Corinthians see 2:4, 8; 5:14; 6:6; 8:7–8, 24; 9:6–15; 11:11, 13; 12:15; 13:11, 13; →1 Corinthians 13.

for the reading of the Hebrew Bible (and also for the other books of the New Testament). Standing to honor Jesus during the reading of the Gospels may be an appropriate Christian gesture, but since Jesus himself and Paul recognized only the Hebrew scriptures as "Bible," is it respectful to remain seated for their scriptures, the Hebrew Bible? The terminology today varies: some prefer to speak of the "First Testament" instead of the "Hebrew scriptures," and "Second Testament" instead of the "New Testament." If we decide to maintain the traditional terminology and ritual (standing), at the least we need to be aware of the dangers in this tradition and recognize that such a tradition has no basis in the New Testament (→2 Tim. 3:14–17). In contrast, in 2 Corinthians, Paul (always a Jew), dedicates two chapters (8–9) to his project of carrying an offering from the Gentiles to the poor saints (fellow Christian Jews) in Jerusalem (multiple identities were common in the New Testament).

Bibliography

Barnett, Paul. *The Second Epistle to the Corinthians.* NICNT. Grand Rapids: Eerdmans, 1997.

Bassler, Jouette M. "2 Corinthians." In *The Women's Bible Commentary,* ed. Carol A. Newsom and Sharon H. Ringe, 420–22. Louisville: Westminster John Knox, 1998.

Belleville, Linda L. *2 Corinthians.* Downers Grove, Ill.: InterVarsity, 1996.

Betz, Hans Dieter. "Corinthians, Second Epistle to the." *ABD,* 1:1148–54.

Furnish, Victor Paul. *II Corinthians.* AB 32A. New York: Doubleday, 1984.

Martin, Ralph P. *2 Corinthians.* WBC 40. Dallas: Word, 1986.

Matthews, Shelley. "2 Corinthians." In *Searching the Scriptures,* vol. 2, *A Feminist Commentary,* ed. Elisabeth Schüssler Fiorenza, 196–217. New York: Crossroad, 1994.

Murphy-O'Connor, Jerome. *The Theology of the Second Letter to the Corinthians.* Cambridge: Cambridge University Press, 1991.

Thrall, Margaret E. *2 Corinthians.* 2 vols. ICC. Edinburgh: T. & T. Clark, 1994–2000.

Chapter 9

GALATIANS

Christ Liberated Us from the Law That We Might Remain Free

Outline

Introduction, 1:1–10

Pained greeting (omitting Paul's usual expression of gratitude), 1:1–5

Admonition (amazement and denunciation against adversaries), 1:6–10

1. Paul's Defense (Personal Experience, History), 1:11–2:14

    Paul's divine call/vocation (not "conversion"), 1:11–24

    Paul's meeting with leaders in Jerusalem (= Acts 15?), 2:1–10

    Paul confronts Peter in Antioch, 2:11–14

2. Debate with Adversaries: A Liberating Gospel, 2:15–21

3. Justification by Faith Alone: Six Arguments, 3:1–4:31

    The Galatians' experience of the Spirit, 3:1–4

    God's promise to Abraham, 3:5–18

    God's purpose with the law, 3:19–29

    Sons and heirs of God, 4:1–11

    Friendship and solidarity with Paul, 4:12–20

    An allegory: Hagar and Sarah, 4:21–31

4. Exhortation (Praxis), 5:1–6:10

    Christians, free of the Law, 5:1–12

    Freedom, love, walking in the Spirit, 5:13–26

    Solidarity in an inclusive, viable community, 6:1–10

Conclusion, 6:11–18

Commentary

1. Judaism, Anti-Judaism, and Paul the Jew

While 1 John reveals that "God is love" and James teaches us to practice liberating justice in the face of oppression, Paul in Galatians proclaims an even more fundamental truth—liberty: "For freedom Christ has set us free (from the law)" (5:1). Love presupposes freedom (divine and human), and the goal of biblical justice is the liberation of the oppressed. Therefore, according to the Exodus paradigm, liberation and freedom constitute a truth even more fundamental than love and justice.

However, considering liberation and freedom more basic than justice and love does not mean that they are more important or more valuable. Freedom can only create a framework or foundation for many possibilities, and it is easily abused: "As slaves of God, live as free people, yet do not use your liberation as a pretext for oppression" (1 Pet. 2:16). In Galatians Paul puts it this way: "You were called to freedom, brothers and sisters, but do not use your freedom as an opportunity for selfish indulgence; rather through love become slaves to one another" (5:13).

The Bible does not distinguish between "moral" law and "cultic" law, but it does distinguish those dimensions and uses of the law that manifest love and promote liberating justice (Rom. 8:4; 2 Tim. 3:16; 1 Tim. 1:9). Cultic and national dimensions, such as circumcision, are not applicable to the Gentiles as are love and discipline, the fruit of the Spirit.

Despite the clarity of Galatians' liberating message, Bible scholars differ somewhat in specifying the letter's precise geographical and historical context.

- The majority identify the meeting that Paul mentions in Gal. 2:1–10 with the council of Acts 15; they understand that the Galatians were the ethnic people of that name in the *north* near the modern city of Ankara in Asia Minor (now Turkey), whom Paul also visited (Acts 16:6; 18:23); thus they date the letter around 55 C.E., shortly before Romans.

- Others, however, point out that the Roman province of Galatia extended to the *south* and included the cities of Iconium, Lystra, and Derbe (where Paul established churches, according to Acts 14:1–23); they identify the meeting of Gal. 2:1–10 with the early visit to Jerusalem to alleviate famine (Acts 11:27–30; 12:25) and thus suggest a date for the letter around 48–49 C.E., making it the earliest of Paul's letters.

To think that in Galatians Paul speaks as a "Christian" attacking "Jewish" enemies would be mistaken, since the juxtaposition of these categories in that period of time is anachronistic. Paul never thought or spoke of himself as being "converted" from Judaism to Christianity. Rather he considered himself a Hebrew of the Hebrews (Phil. 3:5) *called,* not converted, to proclaim the good news of Jesus to the Gentiles (Gal. 1:15; Acts also always speaks of Paul's *calling,* not his "conversion" [Acts 9; 22; 26]). The division between "synagogue" and "church" occurred after Paul's ministry, not unlike the case of John Wesley, who died an Anglican clergyman, and whose successors then established the Methodist denomination as a distinct and separate institution.

Paul had founded the churches in Galatia (1:2; 4:13–14), whether the ethnic region in the north or the entire Roman province, including cities further south. However, behind the apostle certain Judeo-Christian teachers had arrived who required pagan converts to be circumcised and also to keep other prescriptions of Moses' law, such as the Sabbath and the feasts (4:10), and perhaps the food laws (2:12; 4:17). For Paul this teaching was not a religious-theological matter of little importance, much less a discrepancy regarding personal or social "ethics." Rather, it represented a rejection of the truth of the gospel itself (1:6–9; 2:5, 14). Paul became so indignant in the face of the Galatians' swallowing the false teaching that he omitted the expressions of gratitude to God with which he begins his other letters (Rom. 1:8–11; 1 Cor. 1:4–9; 2 Cor. 1:3–7; Phil. 1:3–11; 1 Thess. 1:2–10; Philem. 4–7).

From the beginning Paul underscores his own subversive authority as an apostle (1:1–2, 11–24) and that of Jesus as a liberator (1:3–5). For Paul the word "apostle" itself was almost synonymous with "free" (1 Cor. 9:1), since he itinerated everywhere, using his authority to subvert the oppressive powers of patriarchal households and empire. The apostle aimed for the inclusive communities he founded to embody such freedom, which was Moses' fundamental accomplishment as well as that of Jesus in his death and resurrection. Originally it was thus even with the Galatians, until "false brothers slipped in to *spy on the freedom* we have in Christ" (2:4)—somewhat difficult to imagine in the case of many modern churches where middle-class conformity is the law and the words "liberation" and "freedom" are feared and censured.[1]

Especially in Romans and Galatians, Paul insists that Christian freedom is part of the experience of justification by faith (Gal. 2:15–16; Rom. 3:21–26). That is to say that God, like the father of the prodigal son, embraces and receives us (or like a judge, reclaims us and declares us just) on the basis of our faith and not because of our merits or works. Such teaching was of special importance for those who were marginalized, excluded, weak, poor, and oppressed, and frequently slandered in human courts.[2] The false teachers

---

1. Jacques Ellul, *The Ethics of Freedom* (Grand Rapids: Eerdmans, 1976), 271.

2. Elsa Tamez, *The Amnesty of Grace: Justification by Faith from the Latin American Perspective* (Nashville: Abingdon, 1993). Justification in Galatians results in liberation and freedom (5:1), and thus expresses God's liberating justice (Exodus paradigm); see the works of José P. Miranda and Karen Lebacqz in the general bibliography; also Stephen Charles Mott, "The Partiality of Biblical Justice: A Response to Calvin Beisner," in *Christianity and Economics and the Post-Cold War Era: The Oxford Declaration and Beyond,* ed. Herbert Scholossberg, Vinay Samuel, and Ronald J. Sider (Grand Rapids: Eerdmans, 1994), 81–99. R. A. Kelly summarizes well this recent development: "In the 1970's attention to the meaning of righteousness was expanded through the contributions of Liberation Theology. Theologians such as J. Segundo, G. Gutiérrez and L. Boff challenged definitions of the gift nature of God's righteousness and extended its power from personal justification to historical liberation. In addition Liberation Theology has reinforced justice as the primary meaning of righteousness, pointing to God's liberation of Israel from Egypt as the paradigm. With these challenges of definition, Liberation Theology has raised a significant biblical and theological challenge to traditional concepts of church and morality, including the ideology

undoubtedly would have cited the case of Abraham, to whom God gave the commandment of circumcision (Genesis 17). But Paul responds that Abraham experienced divine justification by faith alone before he was circumcised and thus became the father also of Gentile believers, even though they were not circumcised (Gal. 3:1–18, 29; Gen. 15:6).

2. *Homophobia, Sexism, and Racism: "Another Gospel"?*

Of the ten people named in Galatians (two of whom are women), seven represent sexual minorities. Four are not married: Jesus Christ (1:1), Paul (1:1), Barnabas (2:1, 9, 13), and Titus, a Gentile (2:1, 3). The house of Abraham is not a typical "family"—Abraham, who sent away in divorce his concubine-slave Hagar (plus their son Ishmael, not mentioned here), and Sarah (3:6–18, 29; 4:21–31). Only Isaac (Abraham's son by Sarah, married to Rebecca, 4:28), Cephas/Peter (1:18; 2:8–9, 11–14), and James (1:19; 2:9–11) represent traditional marriages. No wonder Paul struggled so hard to make the Galatian churches inclusive of "unclean" and uncircumcised Gentiles!

Today, Christian struggles in favor of the poor, women, blacks, sexual minorities, and the physically challenged commonly are referred to as "justice issues," which of course they are. However, Paul insists that the false teachers who demanded that Gentile believers be circumcised and keep the law of Moses were not preaching Jesus' good news to the poor, but "another gospel" (Gal. 1:6–9)! Similarly, with all our "justice issues" what we are really up against are false teachers who proclaim "another gospel," however much they may pride themselves on being "evangelical." What is at stake in such struggles is not some minor adjustment in the church's "social ethics" but the very gospel itself.

In the struggle against homophobia, for instance, the issue may become clarified if we can learn to "think left-handedness." Many churches still imagine that they proclaim Jesus' good news to everyone alike, whatever their sexual orientation. But in fact, persons of homosexual orientation who respond soon find that a "circumcision party" is on their case: after simply "believing in Jesus," they learn that they are supposed to start thinking of themselves as heterosexual, submit to all kinds of "ex-gay" tortures to try to change their sexual orientation, get married, produce children, and avoid divorce at all cost. Not surprisingly, depressions, addictions, destructive behavior, and suicides commonly result.

Today, no one would dream of demanding that all left-handed persons "simply accept Christ as Savior and Lord," but then devote decades in tortuous efforts to try to become right-handed, make "recognizing their true right-handedness" essential to their sanctification, and go through life acting

---

that connects Christianity and capitalism in North America" ("Righteousness," *The International Standard Bible Encyclopedia,* vol. 4 [Grand Rapids: Eerdmans, 1988], 195). Kelly indicates his preference for Luther's interpretation, perhaps because he seems unaware of the contributions in biblical exegesis and theology that support the newer, broader interpretation. In the same revised *ISBE,* see A. D. Verhey, "Oppression," one of many subjects strangely omitted in *ABD,* 3:609–11.

(hypocritically) like right-handed people! Anyone today who so pretended to "evangelize" left-handed people would be denounced as proclaiming "another gospel" totally at odds with Jesus' liberating good news. For churches that have spent decades studying and arguing about "homosexuality" rather than repenting of their homophobia, Galatians still has a prophetic word that needs heeding: those who seek to impose heterosexual norms on sexual minorities are preaching "another gospel."

3. *Remembering the Poor*

The liberating Gospel that Paul sought to embody as an apostle and that he preached everywhere included a certain diversity between Peter's ministry to the Jews and that of Paul to the Gentiles. However, as with Jesus' good news ("to the poor," Luke 4:18), one fundamental issue was indispensable—not negotiable—and required unity: James, Peter, and John "asked only one thing, that we remember the poor, which was actually what I was eager to do" (2:10).[3] Christian freedom, according to Paul, never permits us to neglect the needs of the poor, "For in Christ Jesus neither circumcision nor uncircumcision counts for anything; the only thing that counts is faith working through love" (5:6). In his eagerness to remember the poor and his acceptance of apostolic right hands of "fellowship" (*koinōnia,* "solidarity," 2:9), of course, Paul probably had in mind particularly the offering from Gentile churches that he hoped to deliver to the poor Christian Jews in Jerusalem (→2 Corinthians 8–9). The Galatians were expected to provide for their own poor: "let us do good to all people, especially to the household of faith" (Gal. 6:10; →Titus; Eph. 4:28).

Although not specifically said to produce material poverty, oppression in Galatians has diverse and highly significant manifestations. Although not in prison (→Philippians; Philemon), Paul does refer to the violent persecution that he first perpetrated and later suffered (1:13, 23; 4:29; 5:11; 6:17) and that the false teachers sought to avoid (6:12). Above all, in Galatians Paul frequently views the law as an oppressive "yoke of slavery" from which Gentile believers should remain free (5:1; Acts 15:10), since all who are "under the law" (4:5, 21) also are under its "curse" (3:10, 13). And if the law is an oppressor that brings a curse, circumcision of Gentile males represents a kind of violence, an emasculation/castration (5:12; 6:12) fervently to be avoided.

Paradoxically, the cross of Christ in Galatians causes faithful disciples like Paul to suffer persecution and yet also proves to be God's decisive instrument of liberating justice, redeeming those under the oppressive yoke of the law (3:13). Believers come to experience God's liberating justice (*dikaiosynē*) not through the law, but only through Christ's redeeming sacrifice (2:21; see 1:4; 4:5). In his eloquent rhetoric Paul can also suggest a more positive role for

---

3. Thomas D. Hanks, "Poor/Poverty (New Testament)," *ABD,* 5:418. Aside from 2:10, Paul's only other explicit use of "poor/beggarly" (*ptōchos*) in Galatians refers to the "weak and beggarly elemental spirits" (4:9).

the law, compared to a disciplinarian who uses "tough love" to get students to class on time (3:23–26). He can even refer to believers fulfilling "the law of Christ" by bearing one another's burdens in love (6:2), and he speaks of Moses' entire law as summed up in the single command: "Love your neighbor as yourself" (5:14; cf. Lev. 19:18). However, for understanding Paul's view of justice/justification fundamentally as expressions of God's liberation from oppression, we must keep in view Galatians' creative adaptation of the Exodus paradigm: its many negative references to the law as an oppressive yoke, with circumcision as a violent emasculation—and Jesus' death and resurrection as God's decisive acts for human liberation.

4. Baptized Women: Free and Equal

Paul names ten persons in Galatians, but only Abraham's wife, Sarah, and her concubine-slave, Hagar, are women. In Jesus' time it was just as revolutionary to address God as a personal "Father" as it is today to address God as "Mother." In writing this letter, Paul of course used the Greek of the day, which like all traditional languages reflected a patriarchal ideology that took for granted male superiority (see, e.g., "men . . . Father . . . brothers," 1:1–2). Paul also teaches, however, that when women experience the Spirit in baptism, the new community transcends traditional dichotomies with their injustices and rigid roles (only males were circumcised):

> For you are all *sons* of God through faith in Christ Jesus. As many of you as were baptized into Christ have clothed yourselves with Christ. There is no longer Jew or Greek, there is no longer slave or free, *there is no longer male and female;* for all of you are one in Christ Jesus." (3:26–28; see 4:4–7; →1 Cor. 12:13)

If we seek to modify the male chauvinism of the original Greek with inclusive translations ("sons and daughters" instead of "sons"), we run into difficulties. If we translate "sons" inclusively as "sons and daughters," we have the problem that in ancient societies daughters had an inferior status and in general could not inherit properties.[4] Paul, however, insists precisely that in Christ all of us, women and men, have the equally high status, privileges, and freedom of "sons" in patriarchal societies. Christian communities are not to discriminate, treating free men differently from women and slaves—both inferior in status in his culture. Thus, Paul can speak of God as "Father" (4:4–7), while referring to himself as a "mother" for the Galatian Christians (4:19).

Jointly with his use of Abraham as a paradigm of faith, Paul also offers an extensive allegory of Sarah, Abraham's wife, and Hagar, Abraham's slave and concubine who was sent away, that is, divorced (4:21–31, sexual minorities). In accord with patriarchal and prescientific concepts, Galatians (4:26–27, 31, citing the Greek text of Isa. 54:1) speaks of the heavenly Jerusalem as being literally sterile but spiritually very fruitful.

---

4. Carolyn Osiek, "Galatians," in *The Women's Bible Commentary*, ed. Carol A. Newsom and Sharon H. Ringe (Louisville: Westminster John Knox, 1998), 423–27.

Finally, we note that Paul emphasizes that "by *faith* alone" we experience justification and receive the Spirit, but this faith does not remain alone forever. Instead of the patriarchal family with its multiple sons and daughters, and instead of the yoke of the law imposed by an outside authority, Paul focuses on the ninefold "fruit of the Spirit," which is

> love, joy, peace,
> patience, kindness, goodness,
> faithfulness, gentleness, and discipline;
> [concluding with irony] against such things there is no law! (5:22–23)

Scholars continue to be remarkably divided over the translation of a phrase in a text that for many is their favorite in Galatians and even in the entire Bible: "I have been crucified with Christ; and it is no longer I who live, but it is Christ who lives in me. And the life I now live in the flesh I live by faith *in* the Son of God, who loved me and gave himself for me" (2:19b–20; cf. the NRSV note, "Or 'by the faith *of* the Son of God.' " But even though translators disagree regarding the translation of one phrase, they all recognize that the Christian life, according to Paul, is lived because of the faith and faithfulness of Jesus, who inspires in us a personal faith.

5. The Sick and the Physically Challenged

Paul refers to his own literal physical challenge/illness (probably an eye malady) and the strong solidarity that the Galatians had manifested on that occasion. But later he would use metaphors of blindness in which the emotional pain of the apostle would appear to be reflected in language of physical suffering:

- "You foolish Galatians! Who has bewitched you? It was before your eyes that Jesus Christ was publicly exhibited as crucified!" (3:1; see 2:20; 3:13).
- "You know that it was because of a physical infirmity (*astheneian,* lit., "weakness") that I first announced the gospel to you. . . . Had it been possible, you would have torn out your eyes and given them to me" (4:13–15). Cf. 6:11, "See what large letters I make when I am writing in my own hand!" (See also 2 Cor. 12:7; Acts 9:8–18; 22:9, 11–13; cf. 26:18.)
- "My little children, for whom I am again in the pain of childbirth until Christ is formed in you" (4:19). Note the feminine side of Paul (→1 Thess. 2:7).
- "I wish those who unsettle you [by preaching circumcision] would castrate themselves!" (5:12).
- "I carry the marks [*stigmata*] of Jesus branded on my body" (6:17; see HCSB note.)
- Cf. 6:10, "let us do good" (also 6:2; Matt. 25:31–46 includes visiting the sick).

6. *Paul and James*

Especially since Martin Luther and the Protestant Reformation, many have been concerned about the apparent contradiction between Paul's teaching (in Galatians and Romans) and that of →James. James writes,

> You see that a person is *justified* by *works* and not by *faith* alone. (2:24)

Meanwhile, Paul affirms,

> For we hold that a person is *justified* by *faith* apart from *works prescribed by the law* (Rom. 3:28);

> We ourselves are Jews by birth and not Gentile sinners; yet we know that a person is *justified* not by the *works of the law* but through *faith* in Jesus Christ. And we have come to *believe* in Christ Jesus, so that we might be *justified* by *faith* in Christ, and not by doing the *works of the law,* because no one will be *justified* by the *works of the law.* (Gal. 2:15–16)

At first glance these texts would appear to include three elements repeated in a total contradiction impossible to resolve. Consequently, Luther's early reaction was to belittle James's "ravings" as an epistle of "straw" and relegate it to the deuterocanonical books.

In modern times, however, it is Paul, not James, who runs the risk of being jettisoned (see this threat to him in Acts 27), especially by black, feminist, womanist, gay, and liberation theologies. Reflecting on the long history of the use of Pauline texts to insult the dignity and deny the rights of slaves, African Americans, women, sexual minorities, and the poor, one African American pastor commented that Paul never encountered a status quo that he didn't like. Even before the nineteenth century we can trace the history of the use of Pauline texts to disavow astronomy and scientific geography and to support the divine right of kings and monarchies against democracies and constitutional republics.

Defenders of a radical Paul, on the other hand, see the apostle as a subversive who had learned to "choose his battles" (according to modern feminist wisdom). He was not interested in applying Band-Aids to preserve the status quo of the tyrannical Roman Empire but sought rather to subvert it completely. His strategy was to establish counterculture communities throughout the Roman Empire as the first fruits of the just new order that he hoped to see inaugurated even during his own lifetime with the return of Christ to reign on earth (→Jude and 2 Peter, apocalyptic eschatology). In accordance with this more sympathetic reading of Paul, we can appreciate John Calvin's wisdom when he insisted that James and Paul used the same words but with different meanings:

- When speaking of *faith* in 2:24, James refers to a purely intellectual belief, the type of faith that even the demons have, since they also "believe that there is only one God" (2:19). Paul also at times refers to an intellectual faith that believes in correct doctrines. But in Galatians and Romans the decisive faith that justifies and saves involves a complete confidence in Jesus that relies on his work for us, a commitment without reservation to Jesus as liberator and guide in the new life that the Spirit gives us.

- When speaking of *works* in 2:24, James refers to a believer's works of love produced as the fruit of the Spirit and of faith. Paul also often refers to the Christian praxis that results from faith ("faith expressing itself through love," Gal. 5:6; "the fruit of the Spirit," Gal. 5:22–23). However, in Rom. 3:28 and Gal. 2:15–16 the apostle contrasts genuine faith with "works of the law" done before faith, which thus might proudly be claimed as a basis of merit, leading us to despise and reject God's grace and Jesus' sacrifice for us (Rom. 3:27–31).
- When speaking of *justification* in 2:24, James speaks of the final judgment after death, where God takes into account our entire life—our actions and deeds (→Matt. 25:31–46). At times Paul also refers to this justification after death at the final judgment, where God takes into account a person's entire life (Rom. 2:5–11). In Rom. 3:28 and Gal. 2:15–16, however, Paul refers to a justification at the *beginning* of the Christian life, where God declares a person just by faith alone—an *anticipation* of the final judgment (see Jesus' teaching that the humble publican "went down to his house justified," Luke 18:14).

Bibliography

Barclay, John M. G. *Obeying the Truth: A Study of Paul's Ethics in Galatians.* Edinburgh: T. & T. Clark, 1988.

Betz, Hans Dieter. "Galatians, Epistle to the." *ABD,* 2:872–75.

Briggs, Sheila. "Galatians." In *Searching the Scriptures,* vol. 2, *A Feminist Commentary,* ed. Elisabeth Schüssler Fiorenza, 218–36. New York: Crossroad, 1994.

Brooten, Bernadette J. "Paul and the Law: How Complete Was the Departure?" *Princeton Seminary Bulletin* (1990): 71–89.

Cousar, Charles B. "Jerusalem, Council of." *ABD,* 3:766–68.

Dunn, James D. G. *The Epistle to the Galatians.* Peabody: Hendrickson, 1993.

———. *The Theology of Paul's Letter to the Galatians.* Cambridge: Cambridge University Press, 1993.

———. *The Theology of Paul the Apostle.* Grand Rapids: Eerdmans, 1998.

Esler, Philip F. *Galatians.* New York: Routledge, 1998.

Longenecker, Richard N. *Galatians.* WBC 41. Dallas: Word, 1990.

Martyn, J. Louis. *Galatians.* AB 33A. New York: Doubleday, 1997.

Osiek, Carolyn. "Galatians." In *The Women's Bible Commentary,* ed. Carol A. Newsom and Sharon H. Ringe, 423–27. Louisville: Westminster John Knox, 1998.

Tamez, Elsa. *Contra toda condena: La justificación por la fe desde los excluidos.* San José, Costa Rica: DEI/SEBILA, 1991.

———. *Justicia de Dios: Vida para todos: La justificación por la fe en Pablo.* San José, Costa Rica: SEBILA, 1991.

———. *The Amnesty of Grace: Justification by Faith from the Latin American Perspective.* Nashville: Abingdon, 1993.

Valantasis, Richard. "Competing Ascetic Subjectivities in the Letter to the Galatians." In *Asceticism and the New Testament,* ed. Leif E. Vaage and Vincent L. Wimbush, 211–29. New York: Routledge, 1999.

Witherington, Ben III. *Grace in Galatia: A Commentary on Paul's Letter to the Galatians.* Grand Rapids: Eerdmans, 1998.

Chapter 10

EPHESIANS

Liberation from Nihilism and from Anti-Judaism

Outline

1.	Greeting	1:1–2
2.	Praise to God for the Spirit's blessings	1:3–14
3.	Prayer for believers (wisdom, power)	1:15–23
4.	Delivered from death, SEATED with Christ in heaven	2:1–11
5.	Christ tore down the wall separating Jews and Gentiles	2:12–22
6.	God welcomes Gentiles into the universal inclusive church	3:1–13
7.	Prayer and praise for God's cosmic parental love	3:14–21
8.	WALKING worthily: community life (one body: unity and diversity)	4:1–16
9.	New life of those baptized into Christ	4:17–24
10.	Concrete instructions for praxis: walk in love	4:25–5:7
11.	Walk illuminated by Christ's light	5:8–20
12.	Patriarchal households: subversive submission of women and slaves	5:21–6:9
13.	THEREFORE STAND: spiritual warfare against oppressive powers	6:10–20
14.	Tychicus's mission, greetings and final benediction	6:21–24

Commentary

Introduction

Ephesians appears to be an amplification, an expansion, of Colossians, with quite similar style and theology. Like Colossians, Ephesians probably does not come from Paul himself but from a colleague around 80–90 C.E. (but cf. 1:1; 3:1; 4:1; 6:19–20). Although Paul had spent three years in Ephesus (Acts 20), Ephesians makes no reference to anyone there and includes no personal greetings. Moreover, the words "in Ephesus" (1:1) are missing in the earlier Greek manuscripts (see HCSB note). Therefore, the document appears to be more a treatise sent as a circular letter to the churches in Asia (now Turkey), carried by Tychicus (6:21), possibly the actual author (as in the case of Colossians; cf. 4:7).

The structure of Ephesians is similar to that of Paul's letters: the first section (1:3–3:21) consists of prayers (1:3–23; 3:14–21) and theological affirmations (2:1–3:13); the second (4:1–6:20) contains exhortations regarding praxis (see Rom. 1:18–11:36, affirmations; 12:1–15:13, exhortations.) However, Ephesians differs from Paul's letters in that it includes a blessing (1:3–14; cf. 2 Cor. 1:3–11) together with thanksgiving (1:15–23; cf. Rom. 1:8–15; 1 Cor. 1:4–9). Ephesians 1–3 focuses on God's sovereign grace (the good news), while 4–6 speaks of human freedom and responsibilities.

1. Contrast: Ephesians and Paul

In 80–90 C.E., fifteen to twenty-five years after Paul's death (65 C.E.), the hope of Jesus' imminent return had diminished, since it is hardly mentioned in Colossians (3:4), while Ephesians speaks principally of a hope already fulfilled (a "realized eschatology"; 1:12, 18–19; 2:12–13; 4:4; cf. 1:13–14, 21; 2:7; 4:30; 6:17 [cf. 1 Thess. 5:8, "the *hope* of salvation"]), or of God's purpose in creating a new inclusive human community and thus of uniting all things in Christ.

- As a consequence, Ephesians speaks in *spatial* terms of a distinction between earth and heaven (1:20; 2:6; cf. Col. 3:1–2) and not so much of the *temporal* distinction of two ages, characteristic of Paul himself (Rom. 13:11–12; 1 Thessalonians; 1 Corinthians 7).

- For Paul salvation was future ("we *will be* saved through [Christ] from the wrath," Rom. 5:9; cf. 1 Thess. 5:9), while in Ephesians it is past: "For by grace you *have been saved* through faith" (2:5, 8–10; see 1:13; 6:17; cf. Col. 1:13). Ephesians thus speaks of a past experience of salvation by faith, while Galatians and Romans emphasize justification (past) and salvation (future; →liberating justice, below). For Paul the resurrection also was future (Rom. 6:5), while in Ephesians we already share Christ's resurrection (2:6; cf. Col. 3:1).

- For Paul the church was a local assembly in a house and described as "the body of Christ" (1 Cor. 12:12–26; Rom. 12:4–5), but in Ephesians the inclusive church is universal, even cosmic (3:10; cf. Col. 1:18, 24; see 4:15), and the metaphor focuses on Christ as "head/source" of the body (1:22–23; cf. Col. 1:18).

- Paul's own letters never included *Haustafeln* (codes for patriarchal households) but focused on the new institution of the church as a fellowship of equals (Gal. 3:28). The churches were seen as paradigms of the new humanity characterized by freedom, justice/ equality, love, peace and wisdom. Married couples living with their children and slaves appear but rarely (Romans 16). However, in the six pastoral and deutero-Pauline letters, four have *Haustafeln* (Colossians, Ephesians, Titus, 1 Timothy; also see 1 Peter) which recognize hierarchical structures and the submission of wives to husbands and slaves to their masters/owners (also see Romans 13:1–7).

- Paul himself preferred to speak of sin in the singular as a hostile power and the liberating act of God in justification (Romans 5:6–11; 7:8, 11; Galatians), but in Ephesians God simply offers "forgiveness" for sins (plural: 1:7; 2:1; 4:32; similarly, Colossians).

2. *Contrast: Ephesians and Colossians*

Although Colossians and Ephesians thus have much in common that distinguish them from Paul's own letters (and also from 2 Thessalonians and the three →pastoral letters), Ephesians differs significantly from Colossians and thus appears to be a later expansion and probably from a different author.

- While the cosmic Christ is the central theme of Colossians, the central theme of Ephesians is the inclusive cosmic church, the fullness of Christ and God. Ephesians never speaks of a local church (see Col. 1:18, 24) but only of the church universal (Eph. 1:22; 3:10, 21; 5:23–32).
- Colossians is directed to a local congregation (probably Laodicea, not Colossae) and focuses on the specific problem of false teaching. But Ephesians ("in Ephesus," 1:1, omitted in the best manuscripts) is not directed to any specific church, nor does it seek to resolve any concrete local problem. Furthermore, Colossians mentions twelve of Paul's friends while Ephesians refers only to Tychicus, the bearer (and possible author) of the letter (6:21; see Col. 4:7).
- Colossians contains two references to "powers" (2:8, 20, *stoicheia,* "elements, fundamental principles"). The reference in 2:20 appears to have the same meaning as in Gal. 4:3, 9: "elements common to religion, be it pagan or Jewish." However, the reference in 2:8 signifies "the first elements or fundamental principles of the physical universe," since in this context the author attacks human philosophy and traditions (see HCSB note to 2:8). These powers and spiritual forces traditionally were interpreted as descriptions of demons. Anglican evangelical John R. W. Stott continues to defend the literal existence of the devil and demons (while recognizing that they may operate through institutions).[1] Authors like Walter Wink deny that cosmic powers have a distinct spiritual existence and see them as the interior or spiritual essence of institutions, states, and ideologies that oppress and do violence.[2] Andrew T. Lincoln believes that the author of Ephesians accepted the literal existence of the devil and demons but thinks that modern interpretations may help the modern reader "adapt first century mythology."[3]

3. *Comparison: Household Codes*

Colossians includes a *Haustafel* (domestic code) that appears to reflect a large number of slaves in the church, but Ephesians appears to reflect the fulfillment of the hope of 1 Peter (3:1, the conversion of many husbands), since the *Haustafel* in Ephesians is directed primarily to husbands (5:25–33). In this text the extensive development in theology of marriage is unique in the New

---

1. John R. W. Stott, *God's New Society: The Message of Ephesians* (Downers Grove, Ill.: InterVarsity, 1979), 267–75.
2. Walter Wink, *The Powers That Be* (New York: Doubleday, 1998).
3. Andrew T. Lincoln, *Ephesians,* WBC 42 (Dallas: Word, 1990), 64.

Testament. For Paul himself, an itinerant bachelor with the spiritual gift of abstaining from sexual relations with women (1 Cor. 7:7), marriage was an inferior state, a concession to the weakness of the flesh (1 Cor. 7:1, 6–9). However, in Ephesians marriage—although hardly a covenant[4]—almost achieves the status of sacrament ("mystery," 5:32), serving as the great paradigm for the relationship between Christ and the church (5:23–30).

Like all the *Haustafeln,* that of Eph. 5:21–6:9 has been strongly criticized for having functioned in later history as an instrument of oppression and violence against women and slaves. Such a text obviously should not serve as a literal guide for the church in the modern world, where we do not accept the institutions of the Roman Empire, or traditional monarchies, or slavery, or the patriarchal households that assume the inferiority of the woman and her submission to the man/husband. However, to be fair with such texts and not to distort their intention, we must interpret them in their literary and cultural context. In the case of Ephesians the following factors are significant:

- The great theme of Ephesians is not the patriarchal family (5:21–6:9) but the cosmic inclusive church and its place in God's project to unite all things in Christ (1:1–4:16). In this universal inclusive church all are saints (1:1) and equal as sisters and brothers (6:23).

- The *Haustafel* (5:21–6:9) is never presented as universal "morals" or "ethics" (Greek philosophical categories absent from the Bible) but as the way to "walk" (literally so in Greek, *peripateite,* 5:15; see 2:2, 10; 4:1, 17; 5:2, 8) with subversive "wisdom" (5:15) in a specific historical context of oppression.

- To walk in wisdom we must be guided by the Spirit (5:18). The imperative "be filled with the Spirit" in 5:18 is the dominant imperative in Greek grammar. The prophets of the Hebrew scriptures and of the New Testament (2:20; 4:11) show us how sensitive the Holy Spirit is to historical and cultural change.

- The submission that the Ephesians *Haustafel* commands is a *mutual* submission (5:21), which introduces the more traditional text in 5:22–6:4. Just as Jesus took the service expected of slaves and made it a paradigm for all his disciples (Mark 10:35–45; see 1 Cor. 9:19; 2 Cor. 4:5; Gal. 5:13), Ephesians takes the submission characteristic of the *Haustafeln* and makes it a responsibility for everyone in the church. Furthermore, mutual submission, which is the responsibility of everyone in the church, is not equivalent to the mere "obedience" that Ephesians commands of slaves and children (6:1, 5), and standards like truth, justice, wisdom, and

---

4. Gordon P. Hugenberger, *Marriage as a Covenant: Biblical Law and Ethics as Developed from Malachi* (Leiden: Brill, 1994; Grand Rapids: Baker, 1998). This remarkable work of immense erudition and value for reference seeks to demonstrate, building on an exceedingly obscure text in Malachi (2:10–16), that marriage in the *Bible* is a covenant. Limited in scope to the Hebrew scriptures, it fails to explain how such an important dogma receives no mention or support from the New Testament. Its methodology and ideology are reminiscent of the medieval debate about how many thousands of angels could dance on the head of a pin. (Malachi's poor text gets trampled beyond recognition by the hypotheses heaped upon it). Cf. L. William Countryman, *Dirt, Greed, and Sex: Sexual Ethics in the New Testament and Their Implications for Today* (Philadelphia: Fortress, 1988), and other works in the general bibliography.

love (4:17–5:20; 6:10–20) always qualify the submission and obedience of the *Haustafel* in 5:21–6:9.

- The sacrificial love that the Ephesians *Haustafel* requires of husbands is something without parallel not only in the entire Bible but in all of ancient culture. Such love represents a strong critique and radical subversion of the self-love characteristic of patriarchal households and the *Haustafeln* that governed them. The Ephesians text also presents a transcendent vision of Christian matrimony unique in the Bible and in all of ancient culture. (Cf. the preference for celibacy of Paul himself and of Jesus and the prioritizing of procreation in Gen. 1:28.)

That said, we must recognize that the New Testament *Haustafeln,* although to a certain degree subversive in their content, also inevitably reflect their patriarchal context. Obviously, throughout church history these domestic codes have been misinterpreted and have commonly functioned as instruments for the oppression of women and slaves. Hence, we should read and cite them with great caution to avoid promoting the literalist errors of religious fundamentalists, who utilize the Bible as an instrument of oppression rather than of liberating justice.

4. Contrast: Empowerment for Militant Women and Slaves (6:10–20)

Studies that focus exclusively on the domestic code (5:21–6:9) commonly lament its patriarchal tone but tend to forget the surprising text that follows. In Eph. 6:10–20 we discover that the entire church—"submissive" wives and women slaves included—are to crossdress as Roman soldiers (according to the metaphors) and demonstrate more courage and militancy than history's most famous crossdresser, Joan of Arc (1412–31)! The militant command to "stand firm" (6:11, 13–14, repeated three times) is a call to demonstrate the courage appropriate to males, especially soldiers. (In Greek the common expression for courage is "act like a male"; see *andrizesthe* in 1 Cor. 16:13 and the way Prisca courageously risked her neck for Paul in Rom. 16:3–4). While Colossians taught that baptism for both women and men replaces circumcision (of males only) as the sign of God's people (2:11–12), Ephesians transforms the concept of war (violence) and of soldiers (men) to focus on a spiritual struggle where the weak of society (women and slaves) are transformed into frightening militants.

Also surprising is the fact that Ephesians 6:10–20 commands a *nonviolent* Christian militancy, using the Word of God with the good news of *peace* as the only offensive instruments. This proactive Christian militancy, according to Ephesians, struggles to establish an inclusive church, which does not discriminate between Jews and Gentiles, women and men, slaves and free, but welcomes all who trust in God and seek to do the good works that God commands (2:8–10; 4:28).

Ephesians points out that spiritual forces (today we might say "ideologies with their majority propaganda") stand behind every oppressor (persecuting

Roman Empire, slave owners, tyrannical husbands). We may better love our enemy/oppressor if we recognize that evil always transcends any oppressor and that such persons commonly act out of ignorance and fear. Recent studies scrutinize the childhood and family psychological patterns of Hitler and other Nazi leaders, seeking to account for the deluge of evil they produced. Attention might better be paid to the dominant ideologies and majority propaganda supporting homophobia and anti-Judaism (see Luther!), machismo, nationalism, and adoration of technology (including propaganda techniques).

5. *The Poor and Oppressed*

In the domestic code (*Haustafel,* 5:21–6:9) Ephesians pays more attention to slaves (6:5–8) than to their masters (6:9), suggesting that the churches addressed still had more poor slaves than affluent masters (see also manual labor, 4:28; →1–2 Thessalonians). Also, as in Colossians, the "inheritance" (1:14; 5:5) is not limited to the nonmaterial sphere, since "spiritual blessings" (1:3) are not "nonmaterial" (the meaning that René Descartes gave to the word "spiritual" centuries later; →1 Corinthians 15). Spiritual blessings, rather, are all the blessings that come to us through the work of the Holy Spirit (including bodily healing and liberation from oppression).

In Ephesians, as in Colossians, wisdom, which commonly enriches, is recommended (1:17–18; 3:10; 5:15–20), and this wisdom is to be expressed especially in the wise use of time (5:16—not to be confused with the American "efficiency" that ignores persons). Ephesians repeatedly exhorts the community to avoid all greed, the cause of so much social injustice (4:19, 22, 28; 5:3–5). Above all, Ephesians encourages the community to engage in manual labor and "good works" of solidarity that empower the weak (4:12) and help the poor (2:10; 4:28) (→Titus).

Paul himself most often is described as the one suffering oppression (*thlipsis,* 3:13), since he is unjustly detained in prison (3:1; 4:1; 6:20). Since Ephesians speaks of salvation as already experienced (see above), references to God's justification are absent. However, we do find references to God's liberating justice, above all to the "breastplate of liberating justice," part of God's armor in Isa. 59:17, but forming part of the Christian armor in Ephesians (6:14; see justice terminology also in 4:24; 5:9; 6:1; cf. the apparent avoidance of justice terminology in →1 Thess. 5:8).

6. *Sexual Conduct of Christians (→1 Thessalonians 4:3–8; 1 Corinthians 5–7)*

Although Ephesians includes instructions for patriarchal households, it names only Paul and Tychicus, both unmarried. Both Colossians (3:5–7) and Ephesians (4:17–24; 5:1–20), deutero-Pauline letters, follow the tradition of Paul himself and interpret Christian praxis as a *walk* (avoiding the Greek philosophical categories of moral absolutes and ethics; Eph. 2:2, 10; 4:1, 17, 20; 5:1–2, 8, 15; Col. 3:7). They stress the person of Jesus (Col. 3:1–4, 16–17), his teaching of brotherly and sisterly love (Col. 3:14; Eph. 5:1–2), guidance of the Holy Spirit (Eph. 5:18), wisdom (Col. 3:16; Eph. 5:15), and a radical new understanding of uncleanness and holiness (Col. 3:5; Eph. 5:3, 5). Both letters repeat the Pauline prohibition of sexual covetousness (see the last of the Ten Commandments in Exodus 20 and Deuteronomy 5), but they introduce a new dimension when they describe covetousness as a form of idolatry (Col. 3:5; Eph. 5:5; see the first and second of the Ten Commandments).

Ephesians refers to certain sexual sins that may not even be "named" (5:3, 12), which was misinterpreted by Thomas Aquinas (1225–74) as a reference to the sin of lust in the form of "sodomy." This sin of "sodomy" had been invented by Peter Damian (1007–72). However, in the Bible itself, Sodom is the name of a city, never of a sin.[5] Peter's linguistic invention and Thomas's exegetical distortion led to centuries of confusion, oppression, and violence, since "sodomy" always remained a muddled concept: Only anal sex between men? Anal or oral sex with women? Sex with animals? Any kind of sex between men? Masturbation, mutual masturbation, and so forth? It proved to be difficult to explain how one could cite Paul (Rom. 1:27) to explicitly condemn a sin that the apostle supposedly said elsewhere could not even be named! This tradition of not being able to name the favorite sin of supposedly celibate clergy is ending today, after centuries of violence against sexual minorities (see the Nazi Holocaust), with costly legal decisions against Roman Catholic clergy for sexual abuse of boys and adolescents.

The Vatican, meanwhile, finally has decided that the sin that Aquinas considered unnamable in fact can be named and even publishes detailed documents about homosexuality—never about homophobia—full of bad science and worse exegesis. Nevertheless, the pope continues to defend the self-destructing tradition of clergy "celibacy." Ephesians, however, never refers to homoerotic acts or imposes silence regarding sins that the letter itself mentions; it simply seeks to discourage conversation that promotes sin by portraying it as attractive.[6]

7. *The Physically Challenged and the Sick*

As in the case of Colossians, Ephesians makes no explicit references to the physically challenged or the sick but does contain three metaphorical references to darkness and illumination/light:

- "with the eyes of your heart enlightened," 1:18
- a reference to baptism as illumination; light symbolizes "kindness, liberating justice, truth," 5:8–14 (cf. Heb. 6:2–4; 10:32)
- "this present darkness," 6:12 (see the man born blind in John 9).

---

5. Mark D. Jordan, *The Invention of Sodomy in Christian Theology* (Chicago: University of Chicago Press, 1997), 150–51.
6. Lincoln, *Ephesians*, 322.

8. Anti-Judaism in Ephesians?

In Paul's own letters the distinction between Jews and Gentiles was fundamental, and each group appears to have a clear sense of its identity (Romans; Galatians). In Ephesians, however, the Gentile recipients (3:1) appear to have a quite limited perception of their inheritance from Israel and stand in need of instruction (2:11–22). In Colossians the mystery revealed in Christ is that the divine plan of salvation includes the Gentiles, but in Ephesians the mystery is the uniting of Jews and Gentiles in the same body of Christ (3:6–7) and even the union of the cosmos (heaven and earth) in Christ (1:9–10). Andrew T. Lincoln points out how Eph. 2:11–22 differs from other New Testament texts concerning the relationship between Israel and the church (Romans 9–11, etc.). In Ephesians 2 the terminology "have been brought near" (2:13) does not mean coming to the point of forming part of Israel but having access to God and being members of the new humanity: "Ephesians 2 describes the church as a new identity that transcends the old identities of Jew and Gentile. Such a perspective differs from that of Romans 9–11, but it has strong affinities with the acute Pauline controversy in Galatians (e.g., 3:28; 6:15–16)."[7] The law, the mark that distinguishes Israel from the Gentiles, is abolished (Eph. 2:15).

9. Ephesians and Modern Nihilism

Jewish and Christian traditions are characterized by their "metanarratives," those great narrations that seek to discern some meaning in human history and personal life: the creation, the Exodus, the birth and ministry of Jesus. While post-Enlightenment modernity sought to substitute other metanarratives for the traditional ones, it still clung to the presupposition that human history and the life of each person have meaning. Jean-François Lyotard classically defined "postmodernity" as "incredulity toward metanarratives."[8]

Perhaps more so than any other book in the Bible, Ephesians insists that human history and our individual lives do have meaning, since all that exists and everything that happens is "for the praise of the glory of God" (1:6, 12, 14; vv. 3–14 constitute a single prayer in the original Greek; cf. Rom. 8:28–38; 11:33–36). But, is it coherent and logical to ask questions about and investigate a supposed "meaning" in life and history if a personal and infinite God does not exist (or at least personal and finite "gods")? If we enter a disordered room that shows evidence of having been robbed, we may investigate and offer hypotheses about the meaning of the disorder; but if we enter a house that has been completely destroyed by a hurricane, we do not inquire about the meaning of the disorder but simply affirm the cause (impersonal).

---

7. Ibid., 163.

8. Brian D. Ingraffia, *Postmodern Theory and Biblical Theology* (Cambridge: Cambridge University Press, 1995), 2.

Even in our "postmodern" era each catastrophe (e.g., an airplane crash) prompts frantic searches on all sides to discover meaning in what has occurred. If the crash proves to have been a terrorist act, we become indignant with the perpetrators, but we have the satisfaction of having found some meaning in what has occurred, and society tries to find and punish the perpetrators. But if the cause is simple mechanical failure, most likely we speak only of the cause but not of the meaning of the tragedy.

For many people today, the great "masters of suspicion" (Friedrich Nietzsche, 1844–1900; Karl Marx, 1818–83; and Sigmund Freud, 1856–1939) have undermined the veracity of the metanarratives that in the West traditionally gave meaning to life. However, authors like Brian D. Ingraffia have demonstrated that the questions and criticisms that these great masters of suspicion hurled against religion in fact discredit only the traditional Platonic-Christian syncretism but fail to address the theology of the Bible itself.[9] Moreover, Latin American theologies of liberation have produced their devastating critiques against traditional theologies and the elitist philosophies inherited from the Greeks and René Descartes (with their dualisms and dichotomies between body and soul, individualism, rationalism, etc.). As we reflect on Ephesians, we may well ask whether it really supports the traditional dominant ideologies of oppression (as traditionally read) or whether it is not better read in fundamental continuity with the subversive and liberating praxis of Moses, Jesus, and Paul himself.

Bibliography

Barth, Markus. *Ephesians*. 2 vols. AB 34, 34A. New York: Doubleday, 1974.

Best, Ernest. *Ephesians*. ICC. Edinburgh: T. & T. Clark, 1998.

Fong, Bruce W. "Addressing the Issue of Racial Reconciliation According to the Principles of Eph. 2:11–22." *Journal of the Evangelical Theological Society* 38, no. 4 (1995): 565–80.

Furnish, Victor Paul. "Ephesians, Epistle to the." *ABD*, 2:535–42.

Ingraffia, Brian D. *Postmodern Theory and Biblical Theology*. Cambridge: Cambridge University Press, 1995.

Johnson, Elizabeth E. "Ephesians." In *The Women's Bible Commentary*, ed. Carol A. Newsom and Sharon H. Ringe, 228–42. Louisville: Westminster John Knox, 1998.

Lincoln, Andrew T. *Ephesians*. WBC 42. Dallas: Word, 1990.

MacDonald, Margaret Y. "Citizens of Heaven and Earth: Asceticism and Social Integration in Colossians and Ephesians." In *Asceticism and the New Testament*, ed. Leif E. Vaage and Vincent L. Wimbush, 269–98. New York: Routledge, 1999.

Russell, Letty M. *Imitators of God: A Study Book on Ephesians*. New York: Mission Education and Cultivation Program Department of the United Methodist Church, 1984.

9. Ibid., 225–41. For a fascinating modern anthropological treatment of such questions, see Nancy Scheper-Hughes, "Undoing: Social Suffering and the Politics of Remorse in the New South Africa," *Social Justice* 25, no. 4 (1998): 114–42.

Stott, John R. W. *God's New Society: The Message of Ephesians*. Downers Grove, Ill.: InterVarsity, 1979.

Tanzer, Sarah J. "Ephesians." In *Searching the Scriptures,* vol. 2, *A Feminist Commentary,* ed. Elisabeth Schüssler Fiorenza, 325–48. New York: Crossroad, 1994.

Wink, Walter. *Naming the Powers: The Language of Power in the New Testament.* Philadelphia: Fortress, 1984.

———. *Unmasking the Powers*. Philadelphia: Fortress, 1986.

———. *Engaging the Powers*. Philadelphia: Fortress, 1992.

———. *The Powers That Be*. New York: Doubleday, 1998.

See also Colossians, "Excursus: House-churches versus *Haustafeln* (Codes for Patriarchal Households)," below p. 151.

Chapter 11

PHILIPPIANS

The Contagious Joy of a Political Prisoner

Outline

1.	Greeting	1:1–2
2.	Thanksgiving and entreaty	1:3–11
3.	Paul's personal situation in prison	1:12–26
4.	The praxis of Christ and his followers	1:27–2:18
5.	Timothy and Epaphroditus's mission	2:19–30
6.	Concerning circumcision and the law	3:1–11
7.	Paul's exemplary praxis	3:12–4:1
8.	Exhortation to Euodia and Syntyche	4:2–3
9.	Joy and peace in prayer	4:4–7
10.	Paul's values and virtues	4:8–9
11.	Thanks for manifestations of solidarity	4:10–20
12.	Greetings and benediction	4:21–23

Commentary

1. Contagious Joy

Philippians, a literary jewel written by Paul from a prison (1:7, 13–14, 17), focuses on the believer's joy in every circumstance. Such joy is the second in his list of the fruits of the Spirit in Gal. 5:22 ("love, *joy,* peace . . . "). We cannot identify the location of this imprisonment with certainty, but its unjust and oppressive character, in opposition to the free proclamation of the good news, is obvious (1:12–18). As in the case of →Philemon, the traditional place of the imprisonment is Rome, which would imply a late date for the letter (60–62 C.E.). Now, however, scholars more commonly propose an imprisonment in Ephesus, with an earlier date (56 C.E.). The city of Philippi was a colony in the province of Macedonia (to the north of Greece), so the church there was the first in what we know as Europe.

In Philippians Paul is a paradigm for the kind of joy in the midst of persecution and oppression that Jesus commanded in the eighth and most extensive Beatitude (Matt. 5:11–12 // Luke 6:22–23; Phil. 2:17–18). Paul and Silas already had manifested such joy when they established the church in Philippi and were imprisoned for their preaching (Acts 16:11–40; see "singing hymns," v. 25, with the jailer's conversion following the earthquake). Paul prays for the church with gratitude and joy (Phil. 1:4) and rejoices whenever the gospel is proclaimed, even when done from malicious motives (1:18); he commands the church: "Rejoice in the Liberator always; I'll say it again: Rejoice!" (4:4; see 2:2, 18, 28, 29; 3:1; 4:10; cf. 4:1).

Paul's joy, ever paradigmatic for the oppressed and the depressed, is thus not the escapist variety common in Eastern religions of his day; nor was it the "contented cow" materialist variety (3:19), be it of capitalist, Marxist, or even Pentecostal ideological species. Paul's joy is that of a believer persecuted and imprisoned because of his proclamation of Jesus' good news. He hopes to be liberated by Jesus, either from jail (1:19; cf. Luke 4:18–19; Acts 16:22–40) or from this life, to live always with his Liberator, "for that is far better" (1:22–23). Paul's joy flows from his commitment to the priority of the gospel (1:7, 12, 16–17, 27; 2:22; 4:3); the centrality of the resurrected Christ (2:5–11; 3:10–11); God's liberating justice (3:6–9; 1:11; 4:8); the solidarity in mutual love of friends in the international, multicultural network of new communities (2:1–4; 3:10; 4:10–19); and a firm hope that encompasses the individual, the church, the new humanity, and the universe (1:6; 2:14–16; 3:11–14; 4:3–7). In addition, Paul felt free to express his indignation against injustice and oppression (3:2, 18–19; cf. Rom. 1:18); perhaps for this reason Paul here did not fall into the depression typical of those who continually seek to repress their anger.[1]

2. *"Prison Letters" and Prisoners*

Traditionally the New Testament was thought to contain seven letters from Paul himself while in prison. Now, however, five of the traditional seven "prison letters" (three →pastoral letters plus →Colossians and Ephesians) are thought to have been written later by the apostle's co-workers. Thus, only Philippians and Philemon of the Pauline letters actually come directly from the apostle during an imprisonment. However, John the Baptist was killed in prison, Jesus himself was taken prisoner before his crucifixion, and his apostles Peter and John were imprisoned (Acts 3–5; 12). Thus, not surprisingly, the New Testament strongly emphasizes solidarity with prisoners, either to free them (Luke 4:18–19; Acts 5:1–21; 12:1–19; 16:16–40) or simply to visit them (Heb. 13:3; Matt. 25:31–46, repeated four times). Such courageous solidarity with prisoners contrasts markedly with many churches today whose only "ministry" to prisoners is to promote the death penalty and ever more

1. Thomas D. Hanks, "The Theology of Divine Anger in the Psalms of Lament" (Th.D. thesis, Concordia Seminary, St. Louis, 1972), 482–506.

severe sentences for them (cf. the spiritual traditions that still produce political prisoners like Gandhi, Martin Luther King, and Nelson Mandela!).

3. Women Leaders

During his second missionary journey (50 C.E.), when Paul and his companions Timothy and Silas sought to establish the church in Philippi, Lydia, a woman and traveling merchant, head of her own household, first welcomed the Word and offered hospitality to the missionaries (Acts 16:11–15). Philippians shows that prominent women continued as leaders in this first "European" church. Paul's principal aim in writing the letter apparently was to achieve reconciliation between two such women, Euodia and Syntyche, church leaders, whose dispute threatened to split the church (4:2–3; cf. 2:2).[2] Since Paul, like Jesus (Luke 8:1–3), depended on the generosity of prosperous and independent women, what the apostle least wanted was a church debilitated by division and thus unable to support his mission work financially (Phil. 4:10–19; cf. Rom. 15:22–29, with tensions between Gentiles and Jews).

4. The Oppressed Poor, Physically Challenged, and Ill

Explicit words for "poverty" do not appear in Philippians, but the letter abounds in other expressions that refer to such realities, reflecting especially Paul's experience: "loss," *zēmia,* 3:7–8; "lack," 4:11–12; "be humbled," 4:12; "to hunger," 4:12; "need," *chreia,* 2:25; 4:16, 19.[3] Paul himself was not of the poor class, and in addition to his elitist religious education with Gamaliel he had a respectable secular trade as a tentmaker (Acts 18:3). But the circumstances of his itinerant life and the persecution he suffered repeatedly left him impoverished (→2 Cor. 11:21b–29). The church in Philippi, directed in part by women, repeatedly had demonstrated economic solidarity to alleviate Paul's needs (Phil. 4:10–19). With such solidarity the church embodied anew the paradigm of Jesus, who was not poor but out of love became poor (2:5–11; cf. 2 Cor. 8:9). The oft cited promise, "My God will fully satisfy every need of yours according to God's riches in glory in Christ Jesus" (4:19), is thus not a universal truth ("dogmatic theology") but an assurance addressed to a specific community that had demonstrated solidarity with the apostle in his need.

The only case of a sick person in Philippians is Epaphroditus, the church's emissary ("apostle") to Paul (2:25–30; 4:18), whom God had healed. However, as happened with the →Galatians (Gal. 5:12), Paul's fury against "those of the circumcision" carries him to the point of interpreting circumcision as a

---

2. On these women, see N. A. Dahl, "Euodia and Syntyche and Paul's Letter to the Philippians," in *The Social World of the First Christians,* ed. L. M. White and O. L. Yarbrough (Minneapolis: Fortress, 1995), 3–15. Also helpful, for a feminist treatment of the problem of language, is Sheila Briggs, "Can an Enslaved God Liberate? Hermeneutical Reflections on Philippians 2:6–11," *Semeia* 47 (1989): 137–53.

3. Thomas D. Hanks, "Poor/Poverty" (New Testament), *ABD,* 5:415.

type of mutilation and disability that the apostle felt the false teachers deserved to suffer (3:2).

5. God's Liberating Justice

In Philippians Paul emphasizes his prisoner status (1:7, 13–14, 17) and explicitly recognizes his imprisonment for the gospel as an experience of "oppression" (*thlipsis,* 1:17); so, given his keen awareness of his Jewish heritage (3:4–6; see the Exodus and Jesus' promise to liberate prisoners and heal the sick, →Luke 4:18–19), it is not surprising that the apostle confidently expected that God would faithfully save/liberate him from prison (1:19). Like Jesus (→Mark 2:17), Paul, of course, recognized that the term "justice" used by the self-righteous and oppressors (Phil. 3:6, 9a) could mean virtually the opposite of God's liberating justice as experienced by the oppressed poor and others who share their faith commitment (3:9b). The latter is what should characterize Jesus' followers (1:7, 11; 4:8).

6. Sexual Minorities and Anti-Judaism

As in Galatians (and later in Romans), for the church community of the marginalized in Philippi, Paul made the good news resound with the justification and vindication that God gives, not through the law but by Jesus' faithfulness until death and by the faith that unites us with him (3:9–10). Therefore (also as in Galatians), Paul fiercely opposed rival missionaries who sought to impose circumcision and the law on Gentile believers. The apostle even classified these rivals as "dogs . . . evil workers . . . those who mutilate the flesh [by circumcision]" (3:2) and as "enemies of the cross of Christ" (3:18). Paul's outburst of "political incorrectness," however, was not anti-Semitic, since Paul, ever a Jew himself, circumcised Timothy (whose mother was Jewish) and never opposed circumcision as a ritual for the Jews (Rom. 2:25–29). However, by rejecting the circumcision of male Gentiles and by accepting the baptism of both sexes as a new sign and the entry point to the people of God (Gal. 3:26–29; Col. 2:11–12), Paul also subverted the entire patriarchal system, which took male superiority for granted, as well as the male right to dominate the woman, and the value of maximum fertility. Especially noteworthy is Lydia's decision (as an unmarried professional woman) to submit to baptism along with the members of her household, without seeking the approval of any man. Circumcision signified not only the patriarchal dominance by males but also the goal of maximizing the propagation of the nation: Abraham's circumcision in Genesis 17 concerns the promise of innumerable descendants (cf. "uncircumcised" fruit trees producing little fruit, Lev. 19:23–25).

When Paul rejected circumcision for Gentile converts and recognized the equality of baptized women leaders in the new people of God, he liberated both genders from viewing sexuality as having only procreative ends (see similarly Jesus: God prunes vine branches [disciples] that do not bear the "fruit" of mutual love, →John 15:1–17). In the new inclusive community the norm is no longer the married couple that procreates (Philippians does not contain a single example) but Jesus and his disciples (such as Paul and Timothy, Clement, Epaphroditus, Lydia, Euodia, and Syntyche)—men and women whose "fruit" was not procreated physically but consisted of new disciples characterized by mutual love. Circumcision, as a sign of patriarchal control of human sexuality, is thus forever rendered null and void.

Instead of Moses' external law, with its commandments to circumcise and be fruitful, Paul exhorts Christians to manifest love with discernment, which comes from the Spirit (Phil. 1:9–11). Such love with discernment, which in Galatians represents the fruit of the Spirit (5:22–23), Philippians prefers to describe as virtues, things "worthy of praise" and of reflection:

> Whatever is true, whatever is honorable, whatever is just [*díkaia*], whatever is pure, whatever is pleasing, whatever is commendable, if there is any excellence and if there is anything worthy of praise, think about these things. (4:8; cf. 2 Pet. 1:5–8)

However, according to Acts, when Paul first met the young Timothy (of a Jewish mother and Greek father) and decided to take him with him as his missionary companion, he immediately proceeded to circumcise him to make him acceptable to the Jews (Acts 16:1–5; cf. Phil. 2:19–24)!

For several centuries it has been common to find in the praxis and the teachings of Paul what appear to be contradictions (as in the entire Bible). The apostle is exposed to such an accusation in Philippians, where he expresses this paradox in two verses:

> Work out your own salvation with fear and trembling; for it is God who is at work in you, enabling you both to will and to work for his good pleasure. (2:12b–13)

Jesus similarly expressed himself in paradoxical language: "For the Human One is going as it has been determined [divine omnipotence], but woe to that one by whom he is betrayed [Judas's guilt]!" (Luke 22:22). Furthermore, quite early the Hebrew scriptures describe the paradox between the omnipotent God who "hardened Pharaoh's heart" and Pharaoh who "hardened his own heart" (Exodus 5–11; cf. Gen. 45:5–8; 50:20). In Romans 9–11 Paul proclaims divine sovereignty in three sections (9:1–29; 11:1–16, 25–32); but he intersperses two other sections affirming human responsibility and faith (9:30–10:21; 11:17–24), concluding with a doxology to the infinite God whom no finite human being can comprehend (11:33–36).

Consequently, French theologian Jacques Ellul concluded that "dialectical" thinking is not a creation of Marx, or of Hegel and Kierkegaard, or of the Greek philosophers, but of the biblical authors (Ellul cited Phil. 2:12b–13 as the exemplary text).[4] Discerning this dialectical characteristic of Paul, together with his priorities and pragmatism in specific contexts, enables us to understand how the apostle (and the Bible) has been cited both in favor of and

---

4. Thomas D. Hanks, "Jacques Ellul: The Original 'Liberation Theologian'?" *Cross Currents* 35, no. 1 (1985): 17–32.

against such diverse elements in modern ideologies—for and against: monarchies, slavery, racism, homophobia, anti-Semitism, liberation/submission of women, and so forth.

Discerning the dialectical character of Paul's thought also enables us to better appreciate the moving affirmation of the apostle, unjustly imprisoned and threatened with death, yet always hoping to be liberated in order to be able to fulfill his calling:

> For to me, living is Christ [human/God, paradox par excellence] and dying is gain. (Phil. 1:21)

Only in his young companion, Timothy, did Paul find someone who shared his total dedication and sacrificial love:

> I have no one like him [Timothy] who will be genuinely concerned for your welfare. All of them are seeking their own interests, not those of Jesus Christ. (Phil. 2:20–21)

This paradigmatic, intimate friendship, however, was but one in the new multicultural, international network of communities—communities of friends that were beginning to subvert and supplant the old orders of patriarchal households and empire ("Caesar's household," Phil. 4:22). Luke Timothy Johnson shows how Paul appropriated the language of friendship from his Greco-Roman cultural context but then used it to develop a particularly Christian understanding of friendship expressed in self-sacrifice and self-emptying love toward others.[5] However, for friends in an elitist male circle to "have all things in common" (share books?) is one thing; friendship in communities that are quite diverse, with prosperous and poor sharing a common weekly meal, commonly results in much more radical challenges (→3 John; Acts 2; 4; 1 Corinthians 11; Jude; 1 Timothy).

Bibliography

Bruce, F. F. *Philippians*. New International Bible Commentary 11. Peabody, Mass.: Hendrickson, 1989.

Fee, Gordon D. *Paul's Letter to the Philippians*. NICNT. Grand Rapids: Eerdmans, 1995.

Fitzgerald, John T. "Philippians, Epistle to the." *ABD*, 5:318–26.

Hawthorne, Gerald F. *Philippians*. WBC 27. Waco, Tex.: Word, 1983.

O'Brien, Peter T. *Philippians*. NIGTC. Grand Rapids: Eerdmans, 1991.

Osiek, Carolyn. "Philippians." In *Searching the Scriptures*, vol. 2, *A Feminist Commentary*, ed. Elisabeth Schüssler Fiorenza, 238–49. New York: Crossroad, 1994.

Perkins, Pheme. "Philippians." In *The Women's Bible Commentary*, ed. Carol A. Newsom and Sharon H. Ringe, 433–36. Louisville: Westminster John Knox, 1998.

---

5. Luke Timothy Johnson, *The Writings of the New Testament*, rev. ed. (Minneapolis: Fortress, 1999), 372–79.

Portefaix, L. *Sisters Rejoice: Paul's Letter to the Philippians and Luke-Acts as Received by First-Century Philippian Women.* Coniectanea Biblica: New Testament Series 20. Uppsala and Stockholm: Almqvist, 1988.

Scroggs, Robin. "Paul the Prisoner: Political Asceticism in the Letter to the Philippians." In *Asceticism and the New Testament,* ed. Leif E. Vaage and Vincent L. Wimbush. New York: Routledge, 1999.

Witherington, Ben, III. *Friendship and Finances in Philippi: The Letter of Paul to the Philippians.* Valley Forge, Pa.: Trinity, 1994.

Chapter 12

COLOSSIANS

Sophia-Wisdom and Liberation from Elitist Patriarchal Philosophies

Outline

1.	Greeting	1:1–2
2.	Thanksgiving supplication	1:3–8 1:9–14
3.	Hymn: Sophia-Wisdom and the Cosmic Christ	1:15–23
4.	Paul's unique apostolate	1:24–2:5
5.	Authentic faith versus vain human philosophies	2:6–23
6.	Praxis within the new community: vices, virtues	3:1–17
7.	Code for patriarchal households (*Haustafel*)	3:18–4:1
8.	Evangelization and discretion with outsiders	4:2–6
9.	Tychicus and Onesimus's trip with personal news	4:7–9
10.	Final greetings and blessing	4:10–18

Commentary

1. Author: Tychicus?

Biblical scholars today commonly conclude that Colossians and Ephesians do not come from Paul himself but from younger colleagues. They also consider Colossians to be the first deutero-Pauline letter (80 C.E.) and think that Ephesians represents a later expansion (90 C.E.), probably by a different author. Colossians and Ephesians possess similar styles and theologies. Since the city of Colossae was destroyed by earthquake in 60–61 C.E. without being reconstructed, no church was there when the letter was written. Perhaps Tychicus (4:7) writes the letter in the name of Paul ("absent" corporally not only in space but also in time, 2:5). Laodicea (2:1; 4:15–16) may be the church to which the letter is directed (some six miles from the destroyed Colossae in what is now Turkey).

2. *Paul, Colossians and Ephesians*

If we compare the theology of the seven letters written by Paul himself (Romans, 1–2 Corinthians, Galatians, 1 Thessalonians, Philippians, and Philemon) with Colossians and Ephesians, these significant differences appear:

- Paul spoke of the church as the "body" of Christ in which all share certain charismatic gifts (1 Cor. 12:12–27; Rom. 12:3–8; see also 1 Cor. 6:12–20); Colossians and Ephesians, however, change the metaphor and speak of Christ as the "head" of the body (Col. 1:18; 2:19; cf. 2:10 = universe; Eph. 1:22–23; 4:15–16).

- Paul described believers as liberated from sin (singular, a power; Romans 6) and emphasized justification (Romans 3–4; Galatians); Colossians and Ephesians speak rather of forgiveness of sins (plural; Col. 1:14; 2:13; 3:13; Eph. 2:1; 4:32);

- Paul himself (the "least of the apostles") humbly acknowledged the importance of the other apostles (1 Cor. 9:5; 12:28–29; 15:7–9; Gal. 1:17, 19) and refused to enter into or claim authority in territories evangelized by others (Rom. 15:20); in Colossians, however, God has entrusted the preaching of the Gospel uniquely to Paul, who undertakes to assure that it is preached to every person in the entire world (1:23–24, 28); this Paul of Colossians has apostolic authority over churches he never visited (1:25; 2:1–2), and his sufferings and oppressions, like Christ's, even have a substitutionary dimension for all (1:24; cf. 4:3, 10, 18)!

- For Paul himself, Christian hope refers to the very act of waiting (Rom. 5:2–5), focused on the future resurrection; Paul insists that the believers have died with Christ but they have not yet been resurrected with him (Rom. 6:5, 8; Phil. 3:11–12). In Colossians and Ephesians, however, eschatology is something already basically "realized," affirming that believers are already raised and ascended with Christ (Col. 2:12–13; 3:1–4; Eph. 2:6; cf. 1 Cor. 4:8; 2 Tim. 2:17–18).

3. *Women and the Cosmic Christ*

Colossians at first appears to address only males ("brothers," 1:2). The domestic code, however, exhorts wives before husbands (3:18–19), and the church in Laodicea appears to have met in a house headed by a woman (Nympha, 4:15). Moreover, in Jewish tradition, divine Wisdom (Sophia, Colossians' central theological focus) is a feminine figure, and Colossians presents Jesus as her incarnation (1:15–20).

Nevertheless, Colossians, the first deutero-Pauline letter, also is the first to include a domestic code (*Haustafel*) for patriarchal households (3:18–4:1) and consequently has received much critical examination in modern feminist studies. We should note that the letter also includes lists of virtues and vices (adaptations of the Ten Commandments to the preferred Greco-Roman genre; 3:5–9, 12–17). Probably we should interpret the specific domestic code exhortations as subordinate to the general advice directed to the house-churches. Nympha's house (4:15), headed by a woman and also the place where the church met, would not have had a patriarch and could represent an alternative model. In later Greek manuscripts the female name Nympha was changed to the masculine form Nymphas!

The household code is directed to three human pairs: wives-husbands, children-parents, and slaves-owners. The code addresses the weaker persons first and gives most detail for slaves (3:22–25), probably because the church consisted primarily of slaves, women, and other socially weak persons. Notably, children are to obey both parents (3:20), but only fathers need to be exhorted to treat their children kindly (3:21). For some reason, the husbands addressed tended to be "bitter" with their wives also (3:19). Perhaps the patriarchs' bad mood with their children and wives was due in part to the practice of sexual asceticism, especially on the part of the women (2:20–23; cf. 1 Cor. 7:1). Moreover, as "heads" of patriarchal households in tension with house-churches often headed by women, the males could have felt insecure, like captains of sinking ships.

The inclusion of the domestic codes (*Haustafeln*) in 1 Peter, the deutero-Pauline letters (Colossians and Ephesians), and the pastorals (1 Timothy and Titus) indicates that a growing number of husbands and slave owners were converted and formed part of the house-churches (often headed by women). One can discern a certain dialectical tension between the house-churches, which reflected the liberty and radical equality of early Christianity (Col. 3:11), and the traditional patriarchal households with their hierarchies of power and traditions of submission (3:18–4:1). The same dialectic may be seen in Paul's letter to the Romans, where the apostle's instructions to the house-churches in Rome (12:1–21) create a highly subversive context for his instructions concerning submission to imperial authorities (13:1–7).

The letters like Colossians, which include submission codes, also give evidence of maintaining the priority of the radical and subversive tradition of the gospel. The church in Laodicea met in a household headed by the woman Nympha (Col. 4:15), while Onesimus, a slave voluntarily freed by Philemon, was a co-worker with Paul (4:9). The supreme authority of Jesus, in whom dwells the fullness of divine Sophia-Wisdom, makes all claim of human authority relative (see "in the Lord," 3:18; cf. 3:20, 22–24).

Neither the codes for patriarchal households nor the virtues and vices lists in Colossians give us universal "morals" or "ethics" (Greek philosophical concepts absent from the Bible). The letter instead speaks of Christian praxis as a "walk" (1:9–10; 2:6–7; 4:5; see also 3:7; see the chapter on Ephesians) guided by the search for complete divine wisdom (4:2–6). To emphasize that Wisdom (Greek: *Sophia;* cf."philo-sophia") was a feminine figure in Hebrew tradition, Mary Rose D'Angelo[1] suggests the following translation:

> She is the image of the unseen God (Genesis 1:26–27),
> first-born of all creation (Proverbs 8:22).
> In/by her was created everything
> in the heavens and on earth (Proverbs 3:19–20; 8:22–30),
> seen and unseen:

1. Mary Rose D'Angelo, "Colossians," in *Searching the Scriptures,* vol. 2, *A Feminist Commentary,* ed. Elisabeth Schüssler Fiorenza (New York: Crossroad, 1994), 318.

> whether thrones or principalities, rules or authorities.
> All things were created through her and for her,
> and she is before all and the all subsists through her;
> She is the head/source of the body, the church/assembly;
> she is the beginning/rule,
> that she might be preeminent among all
> because in her the *pleroma* [divine fullness] was pleased to dwell,
> and through her to reconcile the all to her,
> whether on heaven or on earth (Colossians 1:15–20a).

D'Angelo concludes that in Colossians this hymn to the feminine Sophia-Wisdom is applied to the historical man Jesus, who "made peace through the blood of his cross" (1:20b) and was resurrected (1:18b). In Colossians this divine Sophia-Wisdom, who was revealed fully in the man Jesus Christ, stands opposed to all purely human philosophies (syncretistic mixtures of legalistic Judaism and Eastern religions) that promoted an extreme asceticism, insisting on abstention from sexual relations and certain foods and that demanded circumcision and observance of the Jewish Sabbath (2:8, 16, 21–23; see 1 Cor. 7:1; 1 Tim. 4:1–5, 5:23).

4. *Slaves (the Poor) and Liberating Justice*

In Colossians the domestic code (*Haustafel,* 3:18–4:1) suggests that the church addressed (1:2) consisted mainly of women (3:18) and slaves (3:22–25), since women are the first group mentioned and slaves receive the most attention (see 1 Cor. 1:26–29). The instructions to slaves seek to dignify their person and manual labor (3:23–24). Slaves as well as masters are to avoid oppressing (*adikō;* →Philemon) and to remember that God's just judgment is impartial, without "respect of persons" (3:25). The standards for slave owners include justice (*dik-* term) in the sense of "equality" (*isotēta,* 4:1) with their slaves (James 1:9?). Such pastoral attention dedicated to slaves was not designed to maintain them in their status as slaves (1 Cor. 7:21) but to free them from shame in their manual labor, something looked down on in the Greco-Roman culture (3:23–24), and to give them hope for the future. The "inheritance" (3:24) promised to the slaves (mainly Gentiles) would not be so much a celestial immortality as the world's "land" justly distributed among all, just as in Israel at the time of Joshua (Joshua 13–21; cf. Matt. 5:5; Rom. 4:13).

Slavery most commonly resulted from overwhelming debts. Perhaps for this reason in Colossians Jesus' message of forgiveness replaced Paul's emphasis on justification (1:14; 2:13; 3:13). In accord with the provisions of the Jubilee that Jesus proclaimed (Luke 4:18–19), every fifty years slaves had to be freed, debts canceled (forgiven), and the land justly redistributed ("the inheritance"; Leviticus 25). While slaves waited for the Jubilee Year to come, they could acquire wisdom (according to Prov. 8:1–21, wisdom enriches).

In the Roman Empire slaves commonly were freed after some years of good service or at the death of their masters. Ancient systems were not based on the racism that was foundational to the slavery better known to us from more recent European and American history. Colossians gives us evidence that Philemon had voluntarily freed his slave Onesimus, as Paul had requested (Philem. 8–22; Col. 4:9). Therefore, in the house-churches the traditional distinctions between "slave and free" ceased to exist for the baptized, and in the community of equals the only recognized Lord was Jesus Christ (Col. 3:11; 1 Cor. 12:12–13; cf. the original, radical form in Gal. 3:27–28, where even the distinction between "male and female" is transcended).

However, slaves still were expected to obey their masters "in everything" (Col. 3:22), which in Greco-Roman culture would include complying with the sexual demands of their masters (cf. the prohibitions of irresponsible and unjust sexual activities in 3:5).

5. Sexual Minorities and Anti-Judaism

Although feminist and African American studies have examined the domestic codes for patriarchal households with a critical eye, they have not sufficiently scrutinized the place of sexual minorities (an overlapping category) in the house-churches. In Romans 16 Paul greets only three married couples in a chapter that names twenty-nine people. However, even more remarkably, among twelve persons mentioned by name in Colossians (eleven men, not counting Jesus, and one woman) *not one* is married. The only household named explicitly is that of Nympha, a woman (4:15). The patriarchal code exhorts wives to be submissive to their husbands, but the only woman mentioned by name is the head of her own household and a leader of the church that met in her house in Laodicea!

Moreover, the situations of all twelve persons named in Colossians (single/widowed/divorced) shows that the church (like Jesus' original circle) represents an alternative to the patriarchal households—in effect, the deconstruction of such households. The letter comes from "Paul" and his longtime companion, Timothy (1:1). Although patriarchal codes emphasized the submission of slaves, the conclusion of Colossians reveals that Onesimus, Philemon's slave (Philem. 10–11), has been set free (voluntarily, as Paul had requested) and is Paul's emissary (Col. 4:9). Onesimus, Luke, and Tychicus are called Paul's "beloveds" (4:7, 9, 14). Tychicus (4:7–8), bearer of the letter (perhaps the author), and Epaphras (1:7–8; 4:12–13; Philemon 23) appear to follow the lifestyle of Paul and Timothy as an itinerant same-sex pair.

In addition, Colossians names three colleagues of Paul and Timothy who also continue being Jews (literally "of the circumcision"): Aristarchus, Mark (Barnabas's cousin), and Jesus/Justus (4:10–11), single men with the lifestyle of unmarried itinerants. Obviously, like Paul in Galatians and Philippians, the author of Colossians does not oppose circumcision of male Jews but rather the imposition of circumcision and the law on Gentile males. According to Colossians, baptism, of both women and men, now takes the place of circumcision (males only), as a sign of belonging to the people of God (2:11–12). Neither Paul (1 Corinthians 7) nor Colossians was interested in promoting the physical fertility that God had commanded in Gen. 1:26–28, but rather, in the multiplication of the house-churches (1:6) and the fruit of the Christian character (1:10). Inasmuch as baptism in the early centuries was performed with the baptized naked, having taken off their old clothing to dress in new clothes, Colossians speaks of the new life in Christ as stripping off the vices of the previous life to be clothed with the virtues of the new life (3:9–10).

In the early years the house-churches probably met primarily in houses headed by women or itinerant couples (like Prisca and Aquila) and not in traditional households (Romans 16). Colossians appears to represent a second stage where more household patriarchs were converted, and that prompted the development of household codes (radically modified by the lordship of Jesus Christ, with priority given to weaker members). Nevertheless, Colossians demonstrates that the nonpatriarchal ecclesiastical structures continued and formed the basic context for the patriarchal household codes. Colossians' inclusion of so much information "subversive" to patriarchy demonstrates that the letter does not represent a type of male conspiracy to place every Christian in a patriarchal household.

Although Colossians by style and theology is closely related to Ephesians, also remarkable is the way it includes references to situations and nine persons mentioned in Paul's letter to Philemon:

- *Paul* in jail plus *Timothy,* co-sender (1:1; Philem. 1)
- *Epaphras,* founded the church (1:7–8) and intercedes for her (4:12–13; Philem. 23, jailed with Paul)
- *Onesimus,* now colleague (4:9), before slave (Philem. 10–18)
- *Archippus,* minister (4:17); not a son of Philemon(?) (Philem. 2)
- *Aristarchus,* jailed with Paul, and *Mark,* Barnabas's cousin (4:10; Philem. 24)
- *Luke,* beloved physician, plus *Demas* (4:14; Philem. 24)

(Also Tychicus, 4:7–9, "bearer" of the letter, may have been its actual author; cf. Eph. 6:21; Titus 3:12; 2 Tim. 4:12; Acts 20:4).

Of eleven men named in Colossians, nine had already been named in Philemon (exceptions: Tychicus and Barnabas). Philemon names a woman, Apphia (v. 2), traditionally considered to be Philemon's wife but most likely an unmarried leader in the church. Colossians speaks of Nympha and the church in her house (4:15) but includes the first of the codes for patriarchal households (*Haustafeln*), commanding submission on the part of wives. None of the eleven men named in Colossians is married, six are mentioned in pairs, and the patriarchal household (not the same as today's "nuclear family") is mentioned only in the code. If Archippus (4:17), like Onesimus, earlier formed a part of Philemon's patriarchal household (Philem. 2), he now, also like Onesimus, has been freed of this structure.

6. *The Physically Challenged*

Colossians makes no reference to the physically challenged or the sick, but see the metaphor of darkness in 1:13 and the opening of the eyes in Eph. 1:18.

7. *Colossians and Postmodernity*

> See to it that no one takes you captive through philosophy and empty deceit, according to human tradition, according to the elemental spirits of the universe, and not according to Christ. (Col. 2:8).

Modernity begins with the individualistic and rationalist philosophy of René Descartes ("*I think,* therefore *I* exist") and the classical Greek philosophies with their dualisms and dichotomies (see above all the positivism of the nineteenth and twentieth centuries with its claims to autonomy, supposed objective and definite knowledge, totally positive evaluation of knowledge, and its blind faith in technology and the myth of progress). Postmodernity questions or rejects all these articles of faith so universally accepted for centuries in the West. And above all, postmodernity is characterized by the negation of all "metanarrations" that traditionally gave meaning to human life in the West (see under Ephesians).

Dealing with Colossians, evangelical theologian Brian D. Ingraffia concludes that "the condemnation of 'empty and deceptive philosophies' should not be read as a rejection of wisdom and intelligence (*against* Nietzsche)." Rather, Colossians "rejects the dualist philosophy of the earliest Gnostics in Colossae, which is, ironically, a philosophy similar to the nihilist defamation of the world that Nietzsche condemns in his attack against Christianity." Nietzsche's attack against Christianity cannot be used to condemn biblical theology, since Colossians "attacks the same type of other-worldly philosophy."[2]

Further, we may suggest that Col. 2:8 is similar to the intent in postmodern thinking of rejecting modern claims of having achieved objective knowledge, a supposed "neutrality" without presuppositions and without faith. On the contrary, according to Col. 2:8 all human thought proceeds either from purely human traditions or from Christ. Objectivity and neutrality are myths of humans who idolatrously claim to take over God's unique role (Genesis 3). Both science and postmodern philosophy recognize that all human thought begins with certain assumptions, from an ideology or a faith that we cannot demonstrate scientifically.

For Colossians, only two types of philosophy exist:

1. those that start with accepting Christ's authority (a subversive authority that frees from all oppression and injustice); and
2. philosophies dominated by human traditions, which aid oppression with their elitist ideologies and their majority propaganda (note contemporary discourse

---

2. Brian D. Ingraffia, *Postmodern Theory and Biblical Theology* (Cambridge: Cambridge University Press, 1995), 75.

that speaks incessantly of morals, ethics, family values—categories and terms utterly foreign to biblical theology). A Dutch Reformed philosophical current exists that anticipated postmodernism by insisting on a recognition of the presuppositions behind all human thinking.[3]

Excursus: House-churches versus *Haustafeln* (Codes for Patriarchal Households)

Colossians 3:18–4:1 (80 C.E.)	*Ephesians (90 C.E.)*
	5:21, mutual submission
3:18, wives submit	22–24, wives to husbands
19, husbands love	25–33, husbands love wives
20, children obey	6:1–3, children obey
21, parents do not provoke	4, parents do not provoke
22–25, slaves obey	5–8, slaves obey
4:1, owners be just	9, owners do not threaten

1 Peter 2:11–3:12 (80 C.E.)
(*Community* Code; see 2:13–17)

[Cf. the dialectic in →Romans with the instructions to the five house-churches (12:1–21 and 16:1–27) with submission to the Roman Empire in 13:1–7.]

SUBMISSION
2:13–17, all, to authorities
18–25, servants to masters
3:1–6, wives to husbands
(but religious freedom)

HONOR
3:7, husbands to wives

MOTIVES/PURPOSES
2:13, "for the Lord's sake"
15, "silence the ignorance of the foolish"
2:21, Christ's example
3:1, win the husbands (evangelism); cf. 3:15
3:7, prayers without hindrances

Titus 2:1–10; 3:1–2 = *(90 C.E.)* =	*1 Timothy 2:8–15; 6:1–2*
(*Congregational* Codes: widows, the rich)	
2:1, introduction	
2, older men	2:8, men
3–5, women, older and young	9–15, women
6–8, young men	
9–10, submission of slaves	6:1–2, slaves
3:1–2, submission to authorities	

3. See the works of Abraham Kuyper and Hermann Dooyeweerd; also in the United States, Cornelius Van Til and Nicholas Wolterstorff. For the growing opposition to homophobia in this tradition see the works of Hendrik Hart and James Olthuis cited in William D. Dennison, "Dutch Neo-Calvinism and the Roots for Transformation: an Introductory Essay," in *Journal of the Evangelical Theological Society* 42, no. 2 (June 1999): 287.

Bibliography

House-Churches versus Haustafeln

Balch, David L. "Household Codes." *ABD,* 3:318–20.

Fitzgerald, John T. "Haustafeln." *ABD,* 3:80–81.

Martin, Clarice J. "The *Haustafeln* (Household Codes) in African American Biblical Interpretation: 'Free Slaves' and 'Subordinate Women.' " In *Stony the Road We Trod: African American Biblical Interpretation,* ed. Cain Hope Felder, 206–31. Philadelphia: Fortress, 1991.

———. "Womanist Interpretation of the New Testament: The Quest for Holistic and Inclusive Translation and Interpretation." *Journal of Feminist Studies in Religion* 6 (1990): 41–62.

Meeks, Wayne A. "The Haustafeln and American Slavery: The Hermeneutical Challenge." In *Theology and Ethics in Paul and His Interpreters,* ed E. H. Lovering and J. L. Sumney, 232–53. Nashville: Abingdon, 1996.

Schottroff, Louise. *Lydia's Impatient Sisters: A Feminist Social History of Early Christianity.* Trans. Barbara and Martin Rumscheidt. Louisville: Westminster John Knox, 1995. See esp. 69–78 concerning "Oppression of Women and Hatred of Women's Liberation (1Timothy 2:9–15)."

Postmodernism

Grenz, Stanley J. *A Primer on Postmodernism.* Grand Rapids: Eerdmans, 1996.

Ingraffia, Brian D. *Postmodern Theory and Biblical Theology.* Cambridge: Cambridge University Press, 1995.

Lakeland, Paul. *Postmodernity: Christian Identity in a Fragmented Age.* Minneapolis: Fortress, 1997.

Thistleton, Anthony C. *Interpreting God and the Postmodern Self.* Grand Rapids: Eerdmans, 1995.

Colossians

Barclay, John M. G. *Colossians and Philemon.* Sheffield: Sheffield Academic Press, 1997.

Barth, Markus, and Helmut Blanke. *Colossians.* AB 34B. New York: Doubleday, 1994.

D'Angelo, Mary Rose. "Colossians." In *Searching the Scriptures,* vol. 2, *A Feminist Commentary,* ed. E. Schüssler Fiorenza, 313–24. New York: Crossroad, 1994.

Dunn, James D. G. *Colossians and Philemon.* NIGTC. Grand Rapids: Eerdmans, 1996.

Furnish, Victor Paul. "Colossians, Epistle to the." *ABD,* 1:1090–96.

Horgan, Maurya P. "Colossians." In *The New Jerome Biblical Commentary,* ed. Roland E. Murphy et al, 876–82. Englewood Cliffs, N.J.: Prentice Hall, 1990.

Johnson, Elizabeth E. "Colossians." In *The Women's Bible Commentary,* ed. Carol A. Newsom and Sharon H. Ringe, 437–39. Louisville: Westminster John Knox, 1998.

Lohse, Eduard. *Colossians and Philemon.* Trans. William J. Poehlmann and Robert J. Karris. Hermeneia. Philadelphia: Fortress, 1971.

MacDonald, Margaret Y. " "Citizens of Heaven and Earth: Asceticism and Social Integration in Colossians and Ephesians." In *Asceticism and the New Testament,* ed. Leif E. Vaage and Vincent L. Wimbush, 269–98. New York: Routledge, 1999.

O'Brien, Peter T. *Colossians, Philemon.* WBC 44. Dallas: Word, 1982.

Schweizer, Edward. *The Letter to the Colossians.* Trans. Andrew Chester. Minneapolis: Augsburg, 1982.

Chapter 13

1 THESSALONIANS

The Missionary-Nurse in Paul

Outline

1.	Greeting	1:1
2.	Thanksgiving for the new church	1:2–10
3.	Paul recalls his ministry in Thessalonica	2:1–16
4.	Paul's desire to visit again	2:17–20
5.	Paul sends Timothy	3:1–10
6.	Paul prays to visit again	3:11–14
7.	The *walk* of the Thessalonians: holiness and love	4:1–12
8.	Their living hope: Jesus' return	4:13–5:11
9.	Guidelines for community life	5:12–22
10.	Blessings and farewell	5:23–28

Commentary

Introduction

1 Thessalonians, written by Paul 50–51 C.E., probably is the earliest book of our New Testament (→James; Jude; Galatians). Thessalonica, capital of the Roman province of Macedonia, maintained its Greek culture but devoted itself to the Roman imperial cult. Fleeing persecution in Philippi (2:2; Acts 16:11–40), Paul, Silvanus (Silas), and Timothy arrived in Thessalonica, where they established a predominantly Gentile church (Acts 17:1–10; 1 Thess. 1:9). Further persecution soon caused them to flee again, first to Beroea, where Silvanus and Timothy stayed while Paul continued on to Athens (Acts 17:10–15).

When Timothy met Paul in Athens, the apostle immediately sent him back to Thessalonica to check on the new church (1 Thess. 3:1–2). Paul then went to Corinth, where Timothy (again with Silvanus) brought him a favorable report (3:6–7). However, Timothy apparently reported the Thessalonicans' concern that Paul had not returned to them. Timothy's report, then, motivated Paul to write 1 Thessalonians from Corinth. The new church in Thessalonica had been in existence less than a year. The church's "leaders" (5:12) worked pastorally but without constituting a formal group, and worship was unstructured and charismatic (5:16–22, "prophecies"), as expected when educated elites do not dominate (see 1 Cor. 14:26).

1. The Oppressed Poor, Sick, and Physically Challenged

Thessalonica was an important commercial city, and from the beginning the church included prosperous women (Acts 17:4). Most members, however, were working class artisans (1 Thess. 4:11–12) who only through their work could avoid poverty and achieve a certain independence (5:14). Evidently there were few if any slaves, since the manual labor that Paul commands would not have been a matter of choice for them. Oppression (*thlipsis,* 1:6; 3:3, 7; and *thlibō,* 3:4), especially expressed in religious persecution due to rejection of idolatry (1:9; cf. Acts 19), had been their common experience and undoubtedly contributed to their economic hardship.[1] The exhortation to help the "weak" (5:14) probably includes the sick, the physically challenged, and the poor.

2. Liberating Justice and Future Salvation

Philip Esler reminds us that although prominent in both Galatians and 2 Thessalonians, the concepts of justice/righteousness (*dik-* words) and references to the law are both almost absent from 1 Thessalonians.[2] Esler takes this as evidence that 1 Thessalonians represents a more pristine form of Paul's theology than Galatians and Romans, which with their emphasis on justice, justification, and law represent a contextual response to Judaizing Christians and that righteousness for Paul signifies basically "legitimate [community] identity."[3]

Not only is justice/righteousness notably rare in 1 Thessalonians, but it even seems to be purposely avoided. Thus in 1 Thessalonians Paul cites Isa. 59:17, "[God] put on liberating justice [*dikaiosynē*] as a breastplate and placed the helmet of liberation/salvation [*sotēia*] on his head," but changes the phrase "breastplate of liberating justice" to "breastplate of faith and love" (1 Thess. 5:8). This substitution reflects Paul's theological focus on "faith, hope, and love" in 1 Thessalonians (1:3; 3:6, 12–13; 4:9–10, 13–14), which contrasts remarkably with the emphasis on justice, justification, and law in Galatians and

---

1. Thomas D. Hanks, *God So Loved The Third World: The Biblical Vocabulary of Oppression,* trans. James C. Dekker (Maryknoll, N.Y.: Orbis, 1983), 49.

2. Philip F. Esler, *Galatians* (New York: Routledge, 1998), 154–59, 178. Even attentive Bible readers commonly fail to note that the virtual absence of justice terminology (*dik-* words) in pristine Pauline theology is paralleled by the scarcity of such terms in Q and →Mark, our earliest sources of Jesus' teaching. In Q (the sayings material common to Matthew and Luke), the only example is Luke 7:35: "Wisdom is justified [*edikaiōthē*] by all her children" (// Matt. 11:19, "by her works"). Mark employs *dikaios* once to report Herod's view of John the Baptist as "just and holy" (6:20), but from Jesus' lips only in the triple tradition saying: "I did not come to call the *dikaious* (just/righteous), but sinners" (2:17b // Matt. 9:13 // Luke 5:32, where Luke adds "to repentance"). →Mark.

3. Ibid., 178, 143.

Romans, usually taken as normative for Paul's theology. *Dik-* words in 1 Thessalonians occur only in 2:10 ("how holily and *justly* and blamelessly we were among you"), and in 4:6, the reference to God as the "avenger/vindicator" (*ekdikos*) of those who sexually defraud a Christian brother (or sister? see below).

In 4:15–17 Paul indicates that he expects the second coming of Jesus before his death ("*we* who are alive"; cf. 1 Cor. 15:52), but later he changed his perspective (2 Cor. 4:14). Jesus' final intervention constitutes liberation both from the coming (divine) wrath (1 Thess. 1:10; 5:9) and from all human oppression and violence (1 Thess. 1:6; 2:2, 14–16; 3:3–4, 7; 4:6; →James 4:13–5:11; "apocalyptic hope," →Jude). While in 1 Thessalonians Paul appears to expect that believers may be caught up, or "raptured," at any moment (4:13–18; imminence), →2 Thessalonians (2:1–12; deutero-Pauline) indicates the necessity of precursory signs.

3. *Paul's Guidelines for (Male?) Sexual Behavior*

> For you know what instructions we gave you through the Lord Jesus. For this is the will of God, your sanctification: that you abstain from sexual misbehavior [*porneia*]; that each one of you know how to possess your own vessel [*skeuos*] in holiness and honor, not with covetous passion, like the Gentiles who do not know God; that no one transgress against a brother [or sister?] or defraud him [or her?] in this matter, because the Lord is an avenger in all these things, just as we have already told you beforehand and solemnly warned you. For God did not call us to uncleanness but in holiness. Therefore whoever rejects this rejects not human authority but God, who also gives the Holy Spirit to you. (1 Thess. 4:2–8; →1 Corinthians 5–7)

3.1. Paul here bases his instructions on Jesus' teachings, which, with the exception of adultery and divorce to remarry, said nothing specific about sexual misconduct (see below on *porneia*). Jesus appears to have found sins in the economic and religious sphere (especially hypocrisy) to be much more serious. Especially if we compare the Pentateuch's detailed laws (Leviticus 15; 18; 20), the simplicity of Jesus' and Paul's teaching is impressive. A few basic guidelines for those who "walk" in Jesus' way (1 Thess. 4:1) take the place of detailed legal codes.

3.2. The fact that both Jesus and Paul use some terms common in the legal codes of the Hebrew scriptures ("purity," "holiness") has confused many readers. However, Jesus and Paul each insisted on giving new meaning to the traditional words: "Blessed are the pure *in heart,* for they will see God" (Matt. 5:8; cf. the circumcision of the heart in Rom. 2:25–29; similarly, "impurity" stands for injustice and oppression in Romans 6:19). In the Hebrew scriptures, many activities that made participants "impure, unclean, or dirty," and thus unfit to enter the temple and participate in worship, were not sinful. For example, God had commanded, "Be fruitful and multiply, and fill the earth" (Gen. 1:28). But on seeking to fulfill this commandment of the Creator, after having sexual relations, even a married couple remained "unclean/dirty" until the evening, even after taking a ritual bath (Lev. 15:18). In contrast, Jesus broke with Moses' legal regulations to declare all *food* clean (Mark 7:19). Thus, Jesus' praxis (touching lepers, corpses, and hemorrhaging women) and his teaching that the real "filth" comes from within, from the heart, simply becomes explicit in Mark 7:20–23. Paul went even further, writing that "All *things* in truth are clean" (Rom. 14:14, 20; cf. Titus 1:15, "To the pure all *things* are pure").

3.3. Commentators have debated much about Paul's intended meaning when he uses the word *skeuos* ("vessel, container, implement, tool," 4:4), which could refer metaphorically either to a person's (male or female) own "body" (NRSV, NIV; possibly even a euphemism for one's genitals) or to a man's "wife" (1 Pet. 3:7, see NRSV note). If Paul uses this metaphor to speak of the wife, he reflects his patriarchal context, since the text, written by a man, is then directed only to men (all apparently married), and the woman is seen as male sexual property. "Sexual misbehavior" (*porneia,* 4:3) would then refer to adultery, understood as the theft of sexual property belonging to another married man (4:6), contrary to the Ten Commandments (seventh and tenth). However, Paul and his most intimate friends (1:1), along with Jesus and almost all of his apostles, did not have wives. Consequently, Paul probably deliberately utilized an *ambiguous metaphor* (*skeuos,* "vessel" = either body/genitals or wife) that would be relevant to all readers, male or female, whether unmarried (like himself) or married.

3.4. Paul stresses the principle of the tenth commandment: not coveting that which belongs to one's neighbor (see Col. 3:5; Eph. 5:3, 5), not defrauding one's brother (perhaps with a reference to adultery), and abstaining from *porneia* ("sexual misbehavior"). Originally, *porneia* referred only to prostitution, but traditionally has been mistranslated as "fornication" or as "sexual immorality," infamously ambiguous terms. Neither the word "sexual" nor the word "immorality" is in the Greek, since "morals" (like ethics) is a Greek philosophical concept and not biblical. Moreover, "sexual" is a concept that was not developed until the eighteenth century (Song of Songs refers only to "love," not "sex"). Perhaps the best translation of *porneia* today would be "sexual misbehavior," but in the New Testament various meanings are found: at times it refers to adultery or incest rather than prostitution. Before modern inventions of more dependable contraceptive methods, heterosexual intercourse more commonly produced children, involving parental responsibility, so "irresponsible/unjust sexual behavior" would be another alternative translation of *porneia.*

3.5. In dealing with the sexual sphere, rather than starting from the countless laws of the Hebrew scriptures, Paul begins with Jesus' teaching, his redefinition of traditional concepts of impurity and holiness, the Holy Spirit's guidance, and the importance of avoiding harm to a brother or sister in the community. Paul makes no explicit reference to Moses' law but may allude to several of the Ten Commandments as relevant. In 4:3–8 we may detect allusions to the seventh commandment, prohibiting adultery; the eighth, prohibiting theft; and the ninth, prohibiting false witness (4:6, "defrauding the brother").[4] Above all, Paul emphasizes the importance of brotherly and sisterly love (1 Thess. 4:9–10; cf. Rom. 13:8–14). As in all the Bible, the life of the people of God is not defined by Greco-Roman philosophical concepts of morals and ethics, but is perceived as a "walk" in specific historical contexts (1 Thess. 4:1, 12; 2:12; 3:11; cf. "praxis" in 4:11).

4. The Woman (Feminine Side) in Paul and His Companions

> ...though we might have made demands as apostles of Christ. But we were gentle among you, *like a nurse tenderly caring for her own children.* So deeply do we care for you that we are determined to share with you not only the gospel of God but also our own selves, because you have become very dear to us. (1 Thess. 2:7–8)

At times, Paul seems to reflect his contemporaries' common gender ideologies regarding rigid differences between men and women, proper social roles, the supposed inferiority of women, and their corresponding submission to men (1 Cor. 11:2–16; Rom. 1:26–27 [cf. the textual problem of 1 Cor. 14:34–35]). This traditional side of Paul's thought became even more strongly developed in the deutero-Pauline and pastoral letters. As a result, the diversity and complexity of Paul's own dialectic in this area became obscured.

First Thessalonians 2:7–8 is perhaps the best example among many where Paul transcends the dominant male chauvinist ideology of his culture (see also Paul as mother in Gal. 4:19; Philem. 10, *egennēsa,* "birthed," not "begat"). As always, gender ideology had been built into the very structure of the language, making it difficult to discern and overcome. For example, *andrizomai,* "act like a man" was the common Greek way of referring to the virtue of courage. Paul, however, exhorted the entire church at Corinth, women included, to thus "act like men" (*andrizesthe,* 1 Cor. 16:13). In Romans he expressed his gratitude to Priscilla (Prisca) for demonstrating such courage in saving his life (Rom. 16:3–4). The fact that Paul typically mentions Priscilla first and her husband second does not give the impression that he is describing a timid, submissive woman, but rather a church leader who even corrected the theology of the erudite and eloquent Apollos (author of Hebrews? Acts 18:24–26).

When Luke indicates that at the founding of the church in Thessalonica "not a few of the leading women" were among those who responded to Paul's teaching (Acts 17:4), probably he refers to upper-class Greek women attracted to Judaism who attended the synagogue. Notably, 1 Thessalonians names only men (Paul, Silvanus, and Timothy, all single) and is addressed primarily to men (see section 3.3 above on the possible reference to women in 4:4 under the ambiguous image of a *skeuos,* "vessel, implement").

---

4. See also: the tenth, on not coveting (2:5; but cf. strong desire in 2:17); the sixth, on not killing (2:15); the fourth, on working (4:11–12; 5:14, 6–7; but nothing about the Sabbath rest).

5. Anti-Semitism/Anti-Judaism (from a Comma?)

Modern readers often express concern regarding Paul's supposed anti-Semitism (more precisely, nonracist anti-Judaism):

> For you, brothers and sisters, became imitators of the churches of God in Christ Jesus that are in Judea, for you suffered the same things from your own compatriots as they did from those *Jews* [, (?)] who killed both the Lord Jesus and the prophets, and drove us out; they displease God and oppose everyone. . . . " (1 Thess. 2:14–15)

Many such texts in the New Testament give a similar impression and have been interpreted in ways that foment anti-Semitic violence throughout the history of the church, culminating in the Holocaust under Hitler, in which six million Jews were killed along with thousands of other minorities persecuted by the Nazis (homosexuals, communists, Jehovah's Witnesses, Gypsies, etc.). The original Greek, however, has no commas, since Paul refers only to some Jews (those responsible for Jesus' death), not to all Jews.

Moreover, in Rom. (9:3–5; 11:17–31) Paul explicitly presents a different perspective concerning Jews (Israel, Abraham's descendants). Hence, some commentators argue that Paul presents contradictory views in 1 Thessalonians and Romans, while others even conclude that 1 Thess. 2:15–16 is a later, non-Pauline addition.

However, the distinction and separation between synagogue and church, and between Judaism and Christianity, occurred only at the end of the first century, after the books of the New Testament were written. When Paul wrote (50–58 C.E.), he and his compatriots were considered and called "Jews" or "Israelites," and those who followed Jesus' "Way" were viewed simply as one of many Jewish sects (as had been the case of Jesus and his followers).

Therefore, as conservative evangelical commentator Leon Morris concludes, "Paul is not writing here about all Jews, but only those involved in the activities he names."[5] Similarly, I. Howard Marshall says, "Paul is writing here about particular Jews, those who have shown hostility to God's messengers, and not about the Jews in general."[6] This ought to be obvious. Notably, however, such common sense often is not applied when commentators read Rom. 1:26–27 and interpret the text in a way that foments homophobia and violence against all "homosexuals." Such use of the text, of course, links Paul to Nazi homophobia and contradicts his intention of following Jesus. To interpret an ancient text that condemns specific harmful activities in the service of racism (against all Jews or blacks) or homophobia (against all homosexuals) is to abuse both the text and the individuals discriminated against.

---

5. Leon Morris, *The First and Second Epistles to the Thessalonians,* NICNT (Grand Rapids: Eerdmans, 1991), 83.

6. I. Howard Marshall, *1 and 2 Thessalonians,* NCBC (Grand Rapids: Eerdmans, 1983), 82.

Bibliography

Donfried, Karl P. "The Cults of Thessalonica and the Thessalonian Correspondence." *New Testament Studies* 31 (1985): 336–56.

Fatum, Lone. "1 Thessalonians." In *Searching the Scriptures,* vol. 2, *A Feminist Commentary,* ed. Elisabeth Schüssler Fiorenza, 250–62. New York: Crossroad, 1994.

Gaventa, Beverly Roberts. *First and Second Thessalonians.* Interpretation: A Bible Commentary for Teaching and Preaching. Louisville: Westminster John Knox, 1998.

Hock, Ronald F. "God's Will at Thessalonica and Greco-Roman Asceticism." In *Asceticism and the New Testament,* ed. Leif E. Vaage and Vincent L. Wimbush, 159–70. New York: Routledge, 1999.

Krentz, Edgar M. "Thessalonians, First and Second Epistles to the." *ABD,* 6:515–23.

Marshall, I. Howard. *1 and 2 Thessalonians.* NCBC. Grand Rapids: Eerdmans, 1983.

Morris, Leon. *The First and Second Epistles to the Thessalonians.* NICNT. Grand Rapids: Eerdmans, 1991.

Perkins, Pheme. "1 Thessalonians." In *The Women's Bible Commentary,* ed. Carol A. Newsom and Sharon H. Ringe, 440–41. Louisville: Westminster John Knox, 1998.

Wanamaker, Charles A. *Commentary on 1 and 2 Thessalonians.* NIGTC. Grand Rapids: Eerdmans, 1990.

Chapter 14

2 THESSALONIANS

Preventing Poverty by Diligent Labor

Outline

1.	Greeting	1:1–2
2.	Thanksgiving and petition (Jesus' return, 6–10)	1:3–12
3.	Six precursory signs of Christ's return	2:1–12
4.	Perseverance of the Christians	2:13–17
5.	Prayer and evangelization	3:1–5
6.	Praxis: the obligation to work	3:6–15
7.	Farewell and benediction	3:16–17

Commentary

The first scholar to seriously question whether Paul himself actually wrote 2 Thessalonians was J. E. C. Schmidt in 1798. Although Paul undoubtedly wrote 1 Thessalonians about 50–51 C.E., making the first letter quite possibly the earliest document of the New Testament, most scholars now conclude that 2 Thessalonians was written a generation later (80–90 C.E.) by a disciple of Paul. This conclusion (despite 2 Thess. 3:17) has become increasingly common since 1972, when German scholar E. Trilling published his first detailed research.

Whatever our conclusions about authorship and date, 2 Thessalonians represents a rather queer bird in the New Testament canon. It differs enormously from the pastoral letters (1–2 Timothy, Titus) and the other deutero-Pauline letters (Colossians, Ephesians), and it does have most in common with 1 Thessalonians. Nevertheless, when 1 Thessalonians is compared closely with 2 Thessalonians, significant differences, both theological and stylistic, become apparent. Most contemporary investigators conclude that superficially similar elements that 2 Thessalonians shares with the earlier letter give the impression that a later Pauline disciple is seeking to imitate the apostle. This later writer does lay claim to the inspiration of Paul's own spirit (see 3:17) and in a later crisis seeks to communicate apostolic "traditions" (2:15; 3:6). His emphasis on the readers being "counted worthy" of God's realm and call (1:5, 11) need not imply that they acquired merit by their suffering and so deserved divine acceptance, but rather as pointing to God's providential ordering of their lives (including the persecution) and their gracious inclusion in the new humanity (see Luke 17:10; 20:35). However, in all probability Paul himself did not write 2 Thessalonians (cf. Mark 7:3, 8, Jesus' critique of the oppressive, purely human traditions of the elders).

1. *Eschatology*

2 Thessalonians is the only Pauline/deutero-Pauline letter that has as its primary theme eschatology, the events related to Jesus' second coming. Although the eschatology in this letter is of the abrupt apocalyptic type, the author does insist that before the climactic second coming six other events must occur first (2:1–12; cf. 1 Thessalonians, where the second coming appears to be imminent without the necessity of preceding signs). The first chapter focuses on the revelation of Jesus in his second coming (1:5–12), the second (2:1–12) speaks of a lawless oppressor (similar to the antichrist of John's letters), while the third (3:6–14) insists that the Christian praxis appropriate to the time is diligent manual labor to avoid poverty, coupled with good works expressing solidarity with the weak and poor (→Titus).

The "lawless one" (2:3, 7–8) is not presented as an anarchist but as a totalitarian tyrant-oppressor (note *adikia,* "injustice," 2:10, 12). 2 Thessalonians' affirmation that "he takes his seat in the *temple* of God, declaring himself to be God" (2:4b) has perplexed interpreters of all persuasions (regarding authorship and date). If we assume Paul himself to be the author (50 C.E.), the prophecy of a desecration of the Jerusalem temple never was fulfilled literally, and that temple was destroyed in 70 C.E. However, if we accept that 2 Thessalonians was written around 80–90 C.E., fifteen to twenty-five years after Paul's death (ca. 65 C.E.), then the author is describing a future desecration of a temple that no longer existed!

Some, therefore, have proposed that 2 Thessalonians must refer figuratively to the church as God's temple (1 Cor. 3:16–17; 2 Cor. 6:16; Eph. 2:21), but the New Testament never teaches that the church as a whole would become apostate. In 1646 the Westminster Confession (xxv:6) still identified the lawless tyrant as the pope in Rome (the common Protestant interpretation during the Reformation). More recently, dispensationalist interpreters (see below) have insisted that the temple in Jerusalem must be reconstructed before the revelation of the lawless one (the antichrist) and Jesus' second coming (see Luke's reference to "the times of the Gentiles," 21:24; but such a reconstructed temple still would not be the one literally intended by Paul, if writing around 50 C.E.). For the majority of interpreters today, therefore, we should not understand such apocalyptic images so literally, but recognize them as metaphors: "No specific temple is in mind, but the motif of sitting in the temple and claiming to be God is used to express the opposition of evil to God."[1]

2. The Oppressed Poor and the Physically Challenged

Although 1 Thessalonians also had addressed a church that suffered persecution and oppression (see 1:6; 2:2, 14–16; 3:3, 7), 2 Thessalonians appears to reflect a more serious situation that clamors for the sudden intervention of Jesus as a just judge (1:4–10, with *thlibō/thlipsis,* indicating oppression and affliction, four times; plus "persecutions" one time and "suffer" one time).[2] Eschatological hope for God's liberating justice normally is expressed in a dramatic apocalyptic form in such oppressive contexts (→James 5:1–6; Revelation; cf. the calmer parables of the realm quietly growing in Matthew 13). In all the Pauline and deutero-Pauline literature, only 2 Thessalonians describes the final judgment with its punishment of oppressors as a kind of consolation for the oppressed (1:6–9; cf. 3:2; cf. Paul himself, who usually describes God's justice as a positive liberation from all oppression and suffering, as in the Exodus).

In 1 Thessalonians Paul had addressed a church greatly perplexed about the destiny of those who had already died, and he sought to encourage believers with the hope of Jesus' imminent second coming (4:13–5:11). Second Thessalonians, on the other hand, no longer contemplates an imminent second coming, but rather, focuses on six necessary prior events in the apocalyptic calendar—above all, the revelation of the final oppressor, the lawless tyrant, who seeks to take God's place, sitting in the temple itself and demanding to be worshiped as God. Moreover, the second letter speaks mysteriously of a thing (2:6) or a person (2:7) that acts as an obstacle that restrains the revelation of the lawless one whose characteristic work would be injustice/oppression (*adikia,* 2:10, 12).[3]

In 1 Thessalonians Paul expressed concern about certain unruly believers (5:14) and—contradicting elitist prejudices of the Greco-Roman culture—exalted the value of manual labor for all (4:11) with the goal of helping the needy through good deeds (4:12; cf. 2 Thess. 3:8). Second Thessalonians, however, addresses a more serious problem: many in the church apparently claimed to have already entered their heavenly Sabbath "rest" (1:7) and had stopped working, contrary to the fourth of the Ten Commandments, which commanded six days of work before the seventh day of rest. Therefore, 2 Thessalonians exhorts at length (3:6–15), referring to Paul's own example, and sets forth a severe principle: "Anyone not willing to work should not eat" (3:10). The warning concerns only those "unwilling" to work, since the plight

---

1. I. Howard Marshall, *1 and 2 Thessalonians,* NCBC (Grand Rapids: Eerdmans, 1983), 192; cf. "some material building" (Leon Morris, *The First and Second Epistles to the Thessalonians,* NICNT [Grand Rapids: Eerdmans, 1991], 224).

2. Thomas D. Hanks, *God So Loved The Third World: The Biblical Vocabulary of Oppression,* trans. James C. Dekker (Maryknoll, N.Y.: Orbis, 1983), 49.

3. See Thomas D. Hanks, "Poor/Poverty (New Testament)," *ABD,* 5:418.

of those who had lost their land and become urban unemployed was well known in New Testament times (see Matt. 20:2–7). This teaching, then, was not directed against the unemployed, nor should it be applied with any legalistic literalism to children, the sick, or the physically challenged. However, in cases of persons who refused to work, 2 Thessalonians recommends a kind of "tough love" that still insisted on acknowledging the unruly as brothers and sisters in the faith (3:14–15; cf. 1 Corinthians 5 and the incestuous man). With our common tendency to regard as "enemies" those who disagree with us (on controversial ideological issues such as abortion, and equality for women and sexual minorities), much may be learned from this letter.

3. *Judaism*

Like Yahweh (the Liberator God of the Exodus), Jesus comes to liberate his people (2 Thess. 1:4–9) from their oppression and from the persecutor/tyrant ("the lawless one," soon to appear, 2:1–12). Additional continuity with Judaism is evident in the allusions to the Ten Commandments: work and rest (fourth commandment, 2 Thess. 3:6–13—but without legalistic Sabbatarianism), truthfulness (ninth commandment, 2:9–10), and idolatry, the ideology of the oppressors (first and second commandments, 2:4). The law is understood as teaching love (1:3; 3:5), justice, and good works, and sin is understood as oppression/injustice (see Rom. 8:1–4; 2 Tim. 3:14–17). However, the traditions with greatest authority come from Paul himself (oral instruction and letters), not from the law (2:15; 3:14). (See also the comments in this chapter about the Jerusalem temple and regarding dispensationalism.)

4. *Women and Sexual Minorities*

When Paul established the church in Thessalonica (Greece), his co-workers included prominent women (Acts 17:4), and in 1 Thessalonians Paul compares himself with a nursing mother (2:7–8). In 2 Thessalonians, however, although the "brothers" (1:3; 2:1; 3:1, 15) undoubtedly included many women, specific references to women do not appear. The same tranquil restfulness and eagerness to listen (*hēsychia*) that 1 Timothy (2:11–12) counseled for women, as well as men (2:2), 2 Thessalonians (3:12) recommends to all (note "peace" as the frame of the letter's theology, 1:2; 3:16).[4] "Busybodies" of both genders are encouraged to respect the privacy rights of others (2 Thess. 3:11; see 1 Tim. 5:13; 1 Pet. 4:15; Luke 12:13–14). The images of Jesus in his second coming (1:7–10) who destroys the oppressive tyrant (2:3–10) are militant (masculine?) figures. Each letter presents itself as coming from Paul, Silvanus, and Timothy, all unmarried (1 Thess. 1:1; 2 Thess. 1:1).

4. Jouette M. Bassler, "Peace in All Ways: Theology in the Thessalonian Letters," in *Pauline Theology*, vol. 1, *Thessalonians, Philippians, Galatians, Philemon*, ed. Jouette M. Bassler (Minneapolis: Fortress, 1991), 71–85. Bassler points out that in the Greek tradition peace commonly indicated the state of rest following war, strife, or tribulation (*thlipsis*, "oppression, affliction") and that in 2 Thessalonians peace has ecclesiological, social, and eschatological dimensions (p. 77). As in the prophets, cosmic eschatological (and ecological!) peace is the fruit of God's decisive act of liberating justice (Isa. 32:15–17).

5. Dispensationalism

This contemporary theology and hermeneutic had antecedents in the eighteenth century, but its principal "ecclesiastical father" was the lawyer and Anglican cleric, John Nelson Darby (1800–1882) of London and Dublin. In 1828 Darby left the Anglican Church to join the Plymouth Brethren. However, the movement soon split into the "exclusive" Brethren (under Darby's leadership), who did not permit persons from other denominations to partake with them in the Lord's Supper, and the more "open" Brethren (following B. W. Newton).

Soon far transcending Plymouth Brethren circles, dispensationalist hermeneutics became widely promulgated in fundamentalist circles in the Americas through the Bible annotated by Cyrus I. Scofield (1843–1921, an American Congregationalist layman and, like Darby, a lawyer) and the works of Lewis Sperry Chafer and Charles C. Ryrie. This interpretation of the Bible (hermeneutics) tends to be quite literalistic, but its most fundamental characteristic is the emphasis on a *strong distinction—or dichotomy—between Israel and the church*. The primary question asked regarding any New Testament text is whether it is addressed to Jews (e.g., Jesus in the Sermon on the Mount, the Lord's Prayer) or to the church (which includes Jews who believe in Jesus). With such criteria, Paul's letters come to have more authority for Christians than do the Gospels, where Jesus addresses primarily his fellow Jews.

The term "dispensationalism" comes from the practice of dividing the Bible into seven "dispensations" (administrations). A dispensation, according to Scofield, is "a period during which man is proved with respect to his relative obedience to some *specific* revelation of God's will." Seven dispensations are thus delineated in the Bible:

1. Innocence: before the fall of Adam and Eve, Genesis 1–2 (see Gen. 1:28)
2. Conscience: from the fall to Noah, Genesis 3–5 (3:7)
3. Human Government: from Noah to Abraham, Genesis 6–11 (8:15)
4. Promise: from Abraham to Moses, Genesis 12—Exodus 19
5. Law: from Moses to Christ, Exodus 20—Malachi and the Gospels
6. Grace: the period of the church, Acts 2 to the rapture
7. Realm: the millennium, when the Hebrew Bible promises of an earthly realm for the nation of Israel will be fulfilled (Rev. 20:1–6)

For most dispensationalists, the church was born on the day of Pentecost (Acts 2), and they continue practicing water baptism and the Lord's Supper. Nevertheless, some ("hyperdispensationalists") follow E. W. Bullinger (1837–1913), insisting that the church began only with Paul (Acts 9/13 or 28). Therefore, they practice neither sacrament (if they accept Acts 28) or only the Lord's Supper (if they accept Acts 9/13). Such a diversity of conclusions results from assuming that only certain later Pauline letters have direct authority for the church under the dispensation period of grace.

Traditionally the church taught that Christians would have to endure a great tribulation before Jesus' second coming (Mark 13; Luke 21; Matthew 24–25). Nevertheless, beginning with their sharp distinction between Israel and the church, dispensationalists insisted that Jesus' teachings in the Gospels were addressed only to his fellow Jews, but that Jesus would return *before* the great tribulation to rescue Christians (the secret "rapture" of the church, from the Latin *rapio,* "snatch away"; see 1 Thess. 4:15–17). Nonbelieving Jews would then have to endure the great tribulation of seven years (Revelation), after which Jesus would descend to earth to reestablish the national kingdom of Israel (the millennium, Revelation 20), in accord with Hebrew Bible promises. This new doctrine of a secret rapture of the church seven years before the second coming (in effect, dividing Jesus' second coming into two stages) appears to have its origin in a prophetic vision of Margaret MacDonald in Scotland (1830) and a charismatic service of Edward Irving (1832), which then influenced John Darby's notion of a secret rapture and his strange interpretation of Jesus' second—and third!—comings.

Dispensationalism has enjoyed enormous success in spreading its literalistic interpretation of the Bible by means of annotated Bibles (especially that of C. I. Scofield, 1909, revised 1917; revised by others, 1967), Bible institutes for the training of evangelists, missionaries and pastors (without university training), and popular books (most prominently, Hal Lindsey). Rather than dispensations, the Bible itself prefers to speak of covenants/alliances and manifests a fundamental continuity (the history of salvation/liberation that culminates in the gospel).

Nevertheless, dispensationalism has made significant contributions in the following ways:

1. rejecting the traditional Neoplatonic tendency of excessively "spiritualizing" many texts (although still tending to overlook *materialistic interpretation* now more coherently developed in Latin American liberation theologies);
2. breaking with elitist educational traditions to pioneer forms of theological education by extension;
3. underscoring something of the *diversity* in the scriptures (note the biblical theology movement, beginning in the nineteenth century);
4. anticipating contemporary emphasis on *canonical interpretation* (developed especially in the works of Brevard Childs); Scofield wrote, "It is impossible to understand any portion of the Scriptures without having some conception of its place in the total context of the Bible";
5. recognizing the importance of *distinguishing between Israel and the church* (without going to the extreme of creating artificial dichotomies). The great twentieth-century theologian Karl Barth was influenced by the writings of E. F. Stroüter, a dispensationalist who returned from America to Switzerland and insisted in the importance of distinguishing between Israel and the church in the

interpretation of the New Testament, an approach that has become fundamental for proper interpretation, especially of books such as Romans.

Dispensationalists and other fundamentalists exercise an important influence on contemporary international politics, since (starting from their literalistic interpretation of biblical prophecy) they strongly support the state of Israel against its Arabic neighbors, while at the same time aggressively proselytizing to convert Jews to fundamentalist Christianity.

Bibliography

Beavis, Mary Ann. "2 Thessalonians." In *Searching the Scriptures,* vol. 2, *A Feminist Commentary,* ed. Elisabeth Schüssler Fiorenza, 263–71. New York: Crossroad, 1994.

Jewett, Robert. *The Thessalonian Correspondence: Pauline Rhetoric and Millenarian Piety.* Philadelphia: Fortress, 1986.

Johnson, E. Elizabeth. "2 Thessalonians." In *The Women's Bible Commentary,* ed. Carol A. Newsom and Sharon Ringe, 442–43. Louisville: Westminster John Knox, 1992.

Knust, Jennifer Wright. "2 Thessalonians and the Discipline of Work." In *Asceticism and the New Testament,* ed. Leif E. Vaage and Vincent L. Wimbush, 255–67. New York: Routledge, 1999.

Menken, Maarten J. J. *2 Thessalonians.* New Testament Readings. New York: Routledge, 1994.

See also bibliography for chapter 13, 1 Thessalonians.

Dispensationalism and Neodispensationalism

Bock, Darrell L. "Why I Am a dispensationalist with a Small 'd'." *Journal of the Evangelical Theological Society* 41, no. 3 (1998): 383–96.

Blaising, Craig A. and Darrell L. Bock, ed. *Dispensationalism, Israel and the Church: The Search for Definition.* Grand Rapids: Zondervan, 1992.

Jewett, Robert. *Jesus against the Rapture.* Philadelphia: Westminster, 1979.

Ladd, George Eldon. *A Theology of the New Testament.* Grand Rapids: Eerdmans, 1974; rev. ed., 1994.

Ryrie, Charles. *Dispensationalism Today.* Chicago: Moody, 1965.

See also Charles Cosgrove, unpublished paper on E. F. Stroüter and Karl Barth, presented at the annual meeting of the Society for Biblical Literature, San Francisco, November 22–25, 1997.

Chapter 15

1 TIMOTHY

Merry News for Widows: "You May Remarry"

Introduction to the Pastoral Letters

Thomas Aquinas in the thirteenth century first pointed out the pastoral character of 1 Timothy, which D. N. Berdot in 1703 designated as "pastoral." P. Anton, however, in commentaries published in 1753–55, was the first to designate all three (1–2 Timothy and Titus) as "pastoral letters," a designation now universally accepted. The letters are not directed to churches but to Timothy and Titus, apostolic emissaries responsible for appointing pastoral leadership ("elders/bishops" and "deacons") in Ephesus and Crete. The letters deal with themes related to this responsibility.

Author and Date

Beginning with the studies by Friedrich Schleiermacher (1 Timothy, 1807) and Johann Gottfried Eichhorn (1812), modern studies have achieved a broad consensus that the pastoral letters in their final form were not written directly by Paul. The three letters share a distinctive common style and theological perspective and appear to come from a colleague of Paul, writing in Rome around 85 C.E.

Situation

Titus and 1 Timothy refer to Paul as free and traveling from the isle of Crete, by way of Ephesus and Macedonia, toward Nicopolis in Greece (Titus 1:5; 3:12). Titus is written to the apostle's emissary in Crete, and 1 Timothy to the other emissary in Ephesus (1:3, in present-day Turkey). Both Timothy and Titus, Paul's emissaries according to these letters, appear to function more like later bishops, since they exercise a certain authority over local church elders. This phenomenon could explain the development of the distinct office of bishop/overseer in the patristic era, following the death of the apostles and their personal emissaries.

According to 2 Timothy, Paul is in Rome and his martyrdom imminent (4:6–8). The apostle addresses Timothy, still in Ephesus (4:12–13), asking him to come promptly to Rome. Titus, because of its more concise form, appears to have been written before 1 Timothy. Second Timothy, as Paul's testament facing martyrdom, has its own character, but shares *stylistic and theological characteristics* with Titus and 1 Timothy. For example:

1. "The saying is sure and worthy of full acceptance," an expression characteristic of the pastorals (five times) but that does not occur in any other part of the New Testament (1 Tim. 1:15; 3:1; 4:9; 2 Tim. 2:11; Titus 3:8).[1]

2. *Eusebēs,* "godly, religious," with its cognates, thirteen times in the pastorals, but never elsewhere in the Pauline literature (1 Tim. 2:2; 3:16; 4:7–8; 6:3, 5–6, 11; 2 Tim. 3:5; Titus 1:1; cf. 1 Tim. 5:4; 2 Tim. 3:12; Titus 2:12); also characteristic of 2 Peter, 1:3, 6–7; 3:11; cf. 2:9; also see Acts 3:12; 10:2, 7; 17:23; and "ungodly" in Jude 4, 15 (four times!), 18; 1 Tim. 1:9; Rom. 1:18; 4:5; 5:6; 11:26.[2]

3. In the letters from Paul himself "faith" normally is the dynamic act of trusting and committing oneself with Christ, but in the pastoral letters "the faith" refers to sound faith or teaching (correct ideas, beliefs, things to believe), a "deposit" (1 Tim. 6:20; 2 Tim. 1:12, 14; cf. Jude 3).[3]

Outline: 1 Timothy

1.	Greetings	1:1–2
2.	False teachers, the law, and the gospel	1:3–11
3.	Paul's calling and Timothy's responsibility	1:12–20
4.	Public prayer and a peaceable life	2:1–8
5.	Women and peaceful worship	2:9–15
6.	Qualifications for bishops and deacons	3:1–16
7.	Refutation of spurious asceticism	4:1–5
8.	Timothy's praxis and teaching	4:6–16
9.	Instructions for elders and widows	5:1–16
10.	Qualifications for elders	5:17–25
11.	The yoke of slavery and the dangers of wealth	6:1–10
12.	Exhortations to Timothy and to the prosperous	6:11–21a
13.	Benediction	6:21b

1. George Knight, *Commentary on the Pastoral Epistles* (Grand Rapids: Eerdmans, 1992), 99–100; Jerome D. Quinn, *The Letter to Titus,* AB 35 (New York: Doubleday, 1990).
2. Quinn, *Titus,* 282–91.
3. Ibid., 271–76.

Commentary

1. Widows: Women and Poverty

First Timothy mentions no women by name, but their leadership in the early churches is emphasized, since only here in the New Testament do we find a lengthy section devoted to the order of widows (5:3–16). Such women, independent of the patriarchal households, consecrated themselves to Christian ministry but needed economic assistance from the churches. Paul himself had counseled that widows should *not* remarry (1 Cor. 7:8–9), since he apparently expected Christ's second coming shortly (7:26, 29–31). First Timothy, to the contrary, counsels remarriage, especially for young widows (1 Tim. 5:11–15), to avoid having the church become overburdened economically with the support of too many widows. Here again we see that the Bible does not offer universal "ethics" or "morals" but wise counsel reflecting concrete and distinct historical contexts.

On the other hand, 1 Timothy teaches that to be enrolled on the list of widows supported economically by the church, one requirement was to have been married only once (5:9). However, this would make it impossible for a remarried young widow who was widowed again to be supported by the church. As in the case of widows of Hellenic households in Jerusalem, for whom the church instituted the order of deacons (Acts 6:1–7), the widows' poverty makes it evident that this condition was particularly common in the case of women (see the poor, widows, and orphans in the Hebrew scriptures, and Yahweh's wrath against their oppressors, Exod. 22:21–24).

A related concern in 1 Timothy is tranquillity in community and public life (2:2) and that prayers for all humans be expressed in peaceful worship, without interruptions caused by fighting between the men (2:8) or by women determined to correct their husbands publicly during worship (2:9–15). Recognizing that when we speak we are not listening, 1 Timothy insists that the most profound worship occurs in moments of quietness, when we wait silently and listen to the Holy Spirit (2:2, 11–12; cf. James 1:19; Ps. 46:10; Hab. 2:20). In the Christian tradition the Quakers have most developed this "sacrament of silence." The tranquillity/silence that 1 Timothy recommends for women (2:11–12; cf. 1 Pet. 3:4) is also indicated as a norm for all, men included (2:2; cf. 1 Thess. 4:11; 2 Thess. 3:12; the same Greek root can even indicate Sabbath rest, Luke 23:56).

The "submission" that 1 Timothy recommends to wives (2:11) is also a responsibility of husbands (Eph. 5:21, 25–33). However, the prohibition against women teaching men (1 Tim. 2:12) differs from Paul's teaching. In his own letters Paul recognized and accepted women who, with all liberty, prophesied (1 Cor. 11:5) and taught (Phil. 4:2–3), and traveled as "apostles" (Junia in Rom. 16:7; see also Prisca, 16:3; Acts 18:26). Even John Calvin acknowledged that 1 Timothy's argument to support the prohibition of women teaching men (Adam's creation prior to Eve in Genesis 2) was not convincing, since John the

Baptist came before Jesus but had less authority (and the animals were created before humans in Genesis 1!)

The conclusion of the argument in 1 Tim. 2:15 also is quite problematic because many women are saved without ever marrying or having children, and the scriptures—especially Paul's writings—insist that we are saved through faith and not by works. 1 Timothy here may speak with casual hyperbole, not meant to be taken literally, to refute those who prohibited marriage (4:3). In other words, a woman need not be a virgin or abstain from sexual relations in order to be saved, but we should not suppose that every Christian woman is going to marry and have children.

2. *The Affluent and the Oppressed Poor*

First Timothy takes a less radical position than Paul's own letters and Jesus' praxis, not only regarding liberation and equality for women, but also regarding the poor and the wealthy. The letter reflects a situation in which more affluent people had joined the churches in Ephesus (note the women with costly attire, 2:9–10) but were still a minority in communities where most were poor and vulnerable (widows, 5:9–16; slaves under a "yoke," 6:1–2; etc.). Timothy is exhorted to address the affluent boldly, underscoring the spiritual danger of money ("For the love of money is a root of all kinds of evil," 6:10), and also to insist on solidarity and generosity with the poor (6:17–19; cf. 2:10). Because of these texts 1 Timothy, along with the other pastorals, has been deprecated as "bourgeois," deviating seriously from Jesus' and Paul's radical teaching and praxis.

The New Testament consistently insists on expressions of solidarity with the poor, the weak, and the oppressed. However, the documents, given their diverse historical contexts, reflect considerable variety regarding specifics. In Q, our earliest source for Jesus' teaching (ca. 60 C.E.), solidarity with the poor is expressed in the lifestyle of itinerant prophets who were homeless. Mark, our earliest Gospel (ca. 70 C.E.), addresses communities of disciples in stable households, but still exalts Jesus' radical demand that a rich young man leave *everything* in order to become a disciple (10:17–31). Luke preserves this radical tradition (18:18–30), but then immediately counterbalances it (for his more affluent churches) with the paradigm of the rich Zacchaeus, who gave only *half* of his belongings when he became Jesus' disciple (19:1–10; cf. Acts: a primitive communism, Paul's Q-style itinerancy qualified by his tentmaking, etc.).

First Timothy represents a further accommodation, exhorting the rich simply to be generous, demonstrating a degree of solidarity, without specifying this more precisely. Nevertheless, a church composed *primarily* of the poor (widows, slaves, and deacons who help the poor) and with only a small minority of rich (who are generous and show solidarity with the poor) should not be deprecated as a "bourgeois" church. We may observe this same diversity of historical contexts and teachings in the Hebrew scriptures (cf. the Hebrew slaves of the Exodus with the moderate teaching of Proverbs). Again, the Bible does not offer universal "morals" or "ethics" but how to walk in wisdom, guided by teachings reflecting diverse historical contexts but also with historical continuity in its norms of liberation/freedom, justice, and love in solidarity. Avoiding foolish and cruel expressions of asceticism, 1 Timothy stands in continuity with the Hebrew Bible, opposing those who forbid marriage (4:3), and emphasizing the goodness of God's entire creation (4:3–5; 6:17; see Genesis 1; Song of Songs).

Even more than Titus, 1 Timothy is concerned with the *structures and government of the churches,* representing a further step in the process of institutionalization (→Titus and the effect on the poor). Titus speaks of the churches in Crete directed by a body of "elders/ presbyters" who had oversight functions (1:5–9). First Timothy, however, speaks of elders (plural) in Ephesus, but with a "supervisor/president/bishop," perhaps one member, chosen by them (3:1–7; 4:14; 5:17–22). First Timothy also speaks of deacons and orders of "women deacons" (3:11) and widows (5:3–16). For 1 Timothy, the church is "the household of . . . the living God, the pillar and bulwark of the truth" (3:15), which replaces the patriarchal family as the foundation of society. This household of God is the fruit of Jesus' radical good news (3:16; 1:12–17). First Timothy adapts its teaching to a later context (see the conduct of women, slaves, and the rich), but seeks to maintain and strengthen the new counterculture structures in the face of false teachers who sought to undermine them. Considered in isolation, 1 Timothy's adaptations may seem to be ill-advised political compromises, but interpreted as part of a more radical canon, we may recognize a certain wisdom in the diversity and the dialectic.

3. Liberating Justice, Law and Judaism

In continuity with the Exodus paradigm of the Hebrew Bible, 1 Timothy views justice primarily from the perspective of the oppressed as liberating justice. Thus Jesus, a victim of cruel injustice, oppression, and the violence of the crucifixion, experienced his resurrection as liberating justice ("justified/vindicated by the Spirit," 1 Tim. 3:16; see HCSB note). Similarly, since Moses' law prohibited violence and oppression of the weak, it is superfluous for the person whose praxis is already characterized by liberating justice and solidarity with the weak and poor (1:8–11). And Timothy in his own ministry is exhorted to flee the self-indulgent lifestyle typical of wealthy oppressors and to pursue liberating justice (6:11; see Matt. 5:6, 10–12). Throughout the letter, this liberating justice is complemented with frequent exhortation to good works as expressions of solidarity with the weak, the poor, the vulnerable, and the oppressed (2:10; 3:2; 5:8–10 [note *thlibō,* "oppress/afflict," v. 10], 16, 25; 6:2, 18). In Paul's own letters (Romans, Galatians) we may observe a critical/dialectic posture in terms of the law (Torah). In Galatians and Romans Paul teaches that Christians are "free" from the law (Galatians 5; Romans 7), since the law functions negatively to convict of sin, enabling us to see our need of the gospel and of salvation by grace and faith alone. In Galatians Paul refers to "the fruit of the Spirit," not obedience to the law (Gal. 5:19–23).

First Timothy 1:8–11, however, reformulates the fifth through the ninth of the Ten Commandments into a vice list (a genre popular in the Greco-Roman literature) that specifies fourteen vices. In this list the fourth commandment (concerning work and Sabbath rest) does not appear (but see rest/tranquillity in 2:2, 11–12; →1–2 Thessalonians).

4. Sexual Sins or Sexual Minorities?

Although 1 Timothy mentions no women by name, five men are named: Paul, Timothy, and Christ Jesus (1:1–2, unmarried); Hymenaeus and Alexander (1:20; unmarried?); and Pontius Pilate (6:13, married; cf. Matt. 27:19; →2 Timothy). In 1 Timothy's vice list (1:9–10) the seventh commandment (prohibition of adultery) becomes a prohibition of prostitution/sexual misbehavior (*pornois*) and also of "bed-males" (*arsenokoitais,* from *koitē,* "bed"—here a euphemism for sexual intercourse—and *arsēn,* "male").

Since 1946, when the Revised Standard Version of the New Testament was published, this term frequently has been mistranslated as "homosexuals." Although a rare word whose precise meaning has long been disputed, obviously it is formed from two simple and common words: male + bed. It is also clear that "bed" here is not literal but instead has a metaphorical sense signifying some type of sexual activity (see the negative use of "beds" alone in Rom. 13:13 and the positive reference to the marriage "bed" in Heb. 13:4). The position of "bed-males" in 1 Tim. 1:10 helps us determine the meaning, since it occurs between a reference to unjust and irresponsible sexual behavior (*pornois*) and a word that signifies "slave traders." The translation of "bed-males" as "homosexual" is inadmissible, since "homosexual" is a word invented toward the end of the nineteenth century with reference to the new understanding of "sexual orientation," a modern scientific concept. Moreover, "homosexual" includes women of this orientation, lesbians, and does not necessarily imply any sexual activity. Heterosexual and bisexual men could involve themselves in the slave trade and prostitution that 1 Timothy may have in view. "Bed-males" in 1 Tim. 1:10 apparently views as a vice male-male anal sexual relations (without condoms) that involved exploitation, oppression, and abuse, probably related to the purchase/kidnapping of boys for use in male prostitution.[4] However, terms in vice lists commonly lack legal precision, since they are used rhetorically to denounce enemies (compare in modern English similar vulgar male denunciations). To take such a vulgar term of abuse and seek to exegete it literally with legal precision ("persons—or only males?—of homosexual orientation who engage in any expression of same-gender sexual relations") is ludicrous. The only other use of *arsenokoitai* in the New Testament is by Paul

4. Dale B. Martin, "*Arsenokoites* and *Malakos:* Meanings and Consequences," in *Biblical Ethics and Homosexuality: Listening to Scripture,* ed. Robert L. Brawley (Louisville: Westminster John Knox, 1996), 117–36; on the relationship of the sexual exploiters with slave trade and prostitution, see J. Albert Harrill, "The Vice of Slave Dealers in Greco-Roman Society: The Use of a Topos in 1 Timothy 1:10," *Journal of Biblical Literature* 118, no. 1 (1999): 97–122. See in addition p. 108, n. 11, above.

himself, where its use with a related term may suggest a somewhat different connotation (→1 Corinthians 6:9).

Bibliography

The Pastoral Letters

Bassler, Jouette. *1 Timothy, 2 Timothy, Titus.* Abingdon New Testament Commentaries. Nashville: Abingdon, 1996.

Davies, Margaret. *The Pastoral Epistles.* New Testament Guides. Sheffield: Sheffield Academic Press, 1996.

Johnson, Luke Timothy. *Letters to Paul's Delegates: 1 Timothy, 2 Timothy, Titus.* Valley Forge, Pa.: Trinity, 1996.

Knight, George W., III. *Commentary on the Pastoral Epistles.* NIGTC. Grand Rapids: Eerdmans, 1992.

Maloney, Linda M. "The Pastoral Epistles." In *Searching the Scriptures,* vol. 2, *A Feminist Commentary,* ed. Elisabeth Schüssler Fiorenza, 361–80. New York: Crossroad, 1994.

Marshall, I. Howard. *The Pastoral Epistles.* International Critical Commentary. Edinburgh: T. & T. Clark, 1999.

Mounce, William D. *Pastoral Epistles.* WBC 46. Nashville: Thomas Nelson, 2000.

Quinn, Jerome D. "Timothy and Titus, Epistles to." *ABD,* 6:560–71.

Quinn, Jerome D., and William C. Wacker. *The First and Second Letters to Timothy.* Eerdmans Critical Commentary. Grand Rapids: Eerdmans, 1999.

Streete, Gail Corrington. "*Askesis* and Resistance in the Pastoral Letters." In *Asceticism and the New Testament,* ed. Leif E. Vaage and Vincent L. Wimbush, 299–315. New York: Routledge, 1999.

Young, Frances. *The Theology of the Pastoral Epistles.* Cambridge: Cambridge University Press, 1994.

1 Timothy

Dewey, Joanna. "1 Timothy." In *The Women's Bible Commentary,* ed. Carol A. Newsom and Sharon Ringe, 444–49. Louisville: Westminster John Knox, 1998.

Kidd, Reggie M. *Wealth and Beneficence in the Pastoral Epistles: A "Bourgeois" Form of Early Christianity?* Society of Biblical Literature Dissertation Series 122. Atlanta: Scholars Press, 1990.

Martin, Dale B. "*Arsenokoites* and *Malakos:* Meanings and Consequences." In *Biblical Ethics and Homosexuality: Listening to Scripture,* ed. Robert L. Brawley, 117–36. Louisville: Westminster John Knox, 1996.

Schottroff, Luise. *Lydia's Impatient Sisters: A Feminist Social History of Early Christianity.* Trans. Barbara and Martin Rumscheidt. Louisville: Westminster John Knox, 1995.

Thurston, Bonnie Bowman. *The Widows: A Women's Ministry in the Early Church.* Minneapolis: Fortress, 1989.

Chapter 16

2 TIMOTHY

Good News for Those Condemned to Death

Outline

Commentary

1. Paul Oppressed, Imprisoned, Impoverished

Just as 2 Peter comes to us as Peter's testament before his martyrdom in Rome under Nero (64–65 C.E.), so 2 Timothy is presented as Paul's testament prior to his martyrdom, also in Rome during the same period. Second Timothy in its final form probably was written later by a younger colleague (80–85 C.E.) but may well contain historical memories and teachings from Paul himself that were adapted to a later context.

Facing winter without adequate clothing (4:13), an impoverished Paul had been unjustly imprisoned and then abandoned by all his friends and colleagues, with the exception of Luke (4:9–12, 16). Paul's situation portrayed here reflects the circumstances of oppression and poverty of many who faced the death penalty, often innocent (imprisoned for debt or by religious bigots).

Paul's entire missionary career had been one of persecution and continual oppression (3:10–13; see 1:8, 12, 16; 2:9; 4:5, 14, 17). Jesus' followers were to distance themselves decisively from all such oppressive tendencies (*adikia,* acts totally opposed to the just character of the Liberator God of the Exodus, 2 Tim. 2:19, citing Num. 16:5) and seek to incarnate God's liberating justice and solidarity with the weak and poor (2:20–22).

2. God's Liberating Justice through Jesus

Although the Gospels themselves present no evidence of fulfillment, according to Luke, Jesus had presented himself as the liberator of prisoners (Luke 4:18–19; see John the Baptist's cruel martyrdom and cf. Acts 4 and 12). The New Testament stresses the Christian responsibility of visiting prisoners, without assuming that a miraculous liberation would follow (Matt. 25:36, 39, 43–44; Heb. 13:3). In 2 Timothy Paul faces realistically his imminent execution (4:6). Nevertheless, he still insists that Jesus—like Yahweh in the Exodus—is the liberator who had repeatedly liberated him in the past (3:11; 4:17) and who also, as just judge, would finally liberate him from all oppression and save him for God's just new order expected to descend soon from heaven (4:18; cf. 1:10). God would then reward the apostle's faithfulness with a crown as a token of vindication and reward from the Exodus God of liberating justice (4:7–8; cf. Savior/Liberator and salvation in 1:9–10; 2:8–10).

Many who advocate the death penalty support their arguments by citing Gen. 9:6, God saying to Noah, "Whoever sheds the blood of a human, by a human shall that person's blood be shed; for in God's own image God made humankind." The Torah includes many such provisions in which crimes are punishable by death. However, we easily forget that in the diversity of biblical teachings other texts demonstrate how frequently the state tragically errs by seeking to punish a human being with the death penalty. In the Hebrew Bible, for example, we have the cases of Moses and Daniel, and in the New Testament, Jesus, Stephen, James, Peter, and Paul. See also the case of the adulterous woman in John 8:1–11, where Jesus subversively sets aside the death penalty that the Mosaic law had stipulated for adultery.

3. Judaism

According to 2 Timothy, even awaiting execution, Paul does not concern himself with ecclesiastical structures to preserve the churches—not a word about hierarchies, popes, cardinals, and bishops! Rather, he gives us the classical affirmation of the inspiration of the scriptures as an always valid authority following his death (3:14–17).[1] The letter encourages Timothy to study and interpret responsibly the scriptures (2:15) and to communicate the gospel to other "faithful people who will be able to teach others as well" (2:2). Today,

1. Raymond E. Brown, *An Introduction to the New Testament* (New York: Doubleday, 1997), 678–80; Kevin J. Vanhoozer, *Is There a Meaning in This Text? The Bible, the Reader, and the Morality of Literary Knowledge* (Grand Rapids: Zondervan, 1998), 367–468.

many reject any idea of inspired Scriptures, while others cite Paul to support a legalistic fundamentalism far from the reality that 2 Timothy seeks to affirm. Four aspects easily are overlooked:

1. Second Timothy 3:14–17 does *not* refer to the New Testament but to the Hebrew scriptures that Timothy had known from early childhood. Consequently, Christians may apply the text to the New Testament only by analogy (see 2 Pet. 1:19–21; 3:15–16).
2. Second Timothy interprets the Hebrew scriptures as texts that testify to Jesus and indicate the way of forgiveness, health, and liberation from oppression—all of which are indicated by the word "salvation"—not by works of the law of Moses but by faith in Jesus as the Anointed One, whom God empowered to be the Savior, Healer, and Liberator.
3. The Hebrew scriptures offer neither "ethics" nor "morals" but "wisdom" for life's journey, instruction in "liberating justice" (solidarity with the oppressed), and "good works" that empower the weak and the poor (cf. 4:17; →Titus).
4. Second Timothy's strong teaching concerning the inspiration of the Hebrew scriptures contradicts the anti-Judaic tendency common in church history of depreciating the Hebrew Bible as an "Old" Testament (→2 Corinthians). On the other hand, the insistence of the text that the Hebrew scriptures themselves point toward an integral liberation through a commitment with Jesus, God's Anointed One, supports the validity of the church's testimony concerning God's saving acts in the person of Jesus. Theologically we may affirm that the same liberating God of the Exodus (Yahweh) is revealed in Jesus' praxis and person. For that reason, both the Hebrew scriptures and the New Testament attest to the same liberating God and seek to transform individuals and create viable communities that manifest God's liberating justice in their good works (Matt. 25:31–46).

4. Women and Sexual Minorities

Although 2 Timothy names twenty-five men and only four women, the prominence of the women is notable. This recognition reflects Timothy's personal experience, since he was first instructed in the Hebrew faith by his mother, Eunice, and grandmother Lois (1:5). With his Jewish mother, Timothy had followed the Jesus way since shortly before his first contact with Paul, who chose him as his companion (in Lystra, 49–50 C.E.). Acts 16:1–3 indicates that Timothy's father was a Gentile but not necessarily married to Timothy's mother. Paul sends greetings to Timothy from a woman companion in Rome, Claudia (2 Tim. 4:21). The apostle also salutes Prisca (Priscilla) and Aquila for the last time (4:19), naming Prisca first, as was common (the only exception is →1 Cor. 16:19, written for a situation where women were overturning patriarchal traditions; see 1 Cor. 11:2–16; cf. the scribal gloss, 14:34–35). In a letter that stresses the positive importance of women, many find shocking the pejorative reference to "weak women" easily misled by false teachers (*gynaikaria*, 3:6).

Timothy himself seems to have been somewhat timid (2 Tim. 1:7–8), insecure (1 Tim. 4:12), quite emotionally attached to Paul (2 Tim. 1:4), and of delicate health (1 Tim. 5:23), all perhaps consequences of continual emotional repression. Paul treats him as his own beloved child (2 Tim. 1:2), although Timothy must have been thirty-five to forty years old, according to chronology presupposed in the letter (with Paul's imminent death in 65 C.E. some fifteen years after Timothy's call in Lystra). Timothy's timidity may have resulted from a sense of shame, a theme Paul repeatedly returns to in the letter (1:8, 12, 16; 2:15).

Of twenty-nine persons named in 2 Timothy, six probably had been married: Prisca and Aquila are the only married couple named (4:19a), but Lois and Eunice, Timothy's grandmother and mother respectively, probably also had been married (1:5, possibly widows later). Reference is also made to Jesus' ancestor David (2:8, who had nine wives, two concubines + Abishag), and to Onesiphorus's household (probably his widow and children, perhaps also with slaves), since he apparently had recently died (1:16–18; 4:19). If such was the situation, only here does the New Testament encourage prayer for someone deceased.

Second Timothy names twenty-two other men plus Claudia (a woman) as individuals. Six men are mentioned in pairs: four because they had abandoned either Paul (Phygelus and Hermogenes, 1:15) or the truth (Hymenaeus and Philetus, 2:17), plus Jannes and Jambres (3:8, Egyptian magicians who opposed Moses, according to a Jewish tradition). Also named are Demas, who had abandoned Paul (4:10), and Alexander the coppersmith, who had done him much harm (4:14–15). In more positive contexts, in addition to Timothy and Jesus (1:1–2), Paul names Crescens, Tychicus, Titus, and Carpus (4:10–13), plus Erastus and Trophimus (4:20, the latter left sick in Miletus); also Mark, who was with Timothy in Ephesus (4:11). With Paul in Rome when he pens his last testament are four men (Luke, 4:11; Eubulus, Pudens, and Linus, 4:21) plus the woman Claudia (4:21). →Romans 16 presents a similar picture, naming only three married couples among thirty-eight persons. Obviously, sexual minorities were dominant in these contexts, a perspective suppressed in traditional commentaries (→Titus; Philippians; Colossians).

With his martyrdom imminent, the Paul of 2 Timothy focuses especially on God's promise of life (1:1, 10), which includes not only the Greek concept of immortality (1:10), but also the Hebrew concept of bodily resurrection (2:8, 11–12; see JB note at 2:18). In the face of his death, Paul shows himself fully confident of having fulfilled God's purpose in his life (4:7) and anticipates being rewarded in eternal life with the crown of a winning athlete (4:8). However, by the grace of God no one need be a "loser" and all may be winners (4:8b), even someone who was "the foremost of sinners" (1 Tim. 1:15).

Bibliography

Aageson, James W. "2 Timothy and Its Theology." In *Society of Biblical Literature 1997 Seminar Papers*, 692–714. Atlanta: Scholars Press, 1997.

Dewey, Joanna. "2 Timothy." In *The Women's Bible Commentary*, ed. Carol A. Newsom and Sharon Ringe, 450–51. Louisville: Westminster John Knox, 1998.

Donelson, Lewis R. "Studying Paul: 2 Timothy as Remembrance." In *Society of Biblical Literature 1997 Seminar Papers*, 715–31. Atlanta: Scholars Press, 1997.

Fee, Gordon D. "Towards a Theology of 2 Timothy from a Pauline Perspective." In *Society of Biblical Literature 1997 Seminar Papers*, 732–49. Atlanta: Scholars Press, 1997.

Murphy-O'Connor, Jerome. "2 Timothy Contrasted with 1 Timothy and Titus." *Revue biblique* 98 (1991): 403–18.

See also the 1998 SBL Seminar Papers on the pastoral letters and the bibliography for the pastoral letters, p. 173 above.

Chapter 17

TITUS

Good News with Good Works for the Marginalized

Outline

1.	Greetings from Paul to Titus	1:1–4
2.	Designation of presbyters/overseers (bishops)	1:5–9
3.	False teachers incapable of good deeds	1:10–16
4.	Subversive submission in patriarchal households	2:1–10
5.	Praxis (good works) and the blessed hope of liberating justice	2:11–15
6.	Subversive submission to authorities	3:1–7
7.	Personal advice to Titus: good works	3:8–14
8.	Farewell and blessing	3:15

Commentary

Surprisingly, Titus, a "Greek" (Gentile and uncircumcised, Gal. 2:3), does not appear in the Acts of the Apostles. Nevertheless, as administrator of offerings from the Gentile churches for the impoverished Jewish saints in Jerusalem (2 Cor. 8:6), he was an outstanding companion of Paul. The apostle sent him to mediate between factions in the Corinthian church (2 Cor. 7:5–7) and expressed profound affection for his loyal collaborator (2 Cor. 2:13). In Acts, Luke almost overlooks the important offering for the saints in Jerusalem (24:17) and avoids supplying details concerning the local controversies that might create a bad impression of Paul for the Roman authorities. Perhaps because Titus was Paul's emissary in controversial situations, Luke does not mention him in Acts.

The letter to Titus, as the other two pastorals (1–2 Timothy), probably was not penned directly by Paul but by a colleague. The three pastoral letters appear to have been written no earlier than 85 C.E., some twenty years after Paul's death. The language and the theology of the pastoral letters differ a great deal from the letters by Paul himself. However, inspired by God's Spirit and preserving a certain unity with Paul's spirit (1 Cor. 5:3–5) and continuity with apostolic teaching, they may well preserve many traditions and memories of the apostle himself.

1. The Poor and the Physically Challenged

Just as Titus strove to assure the arrival of the offering for the impoverished saints in Jerusalem, the letter directed to him details the Christian praxis manifested in "good works" for needy people (the poor, the physically challenged, the sick, the elderly, 1:16; 2:7, 14; 3:8, 14). Good works, in fact, constitute the purpose itself of Christian redemption (2:14; see Eph. 2:8–10) and are understood as a response to concrete and material human needs (3:14; see Matt. 25:31–46; Eph. 4:28).[1] The letter even speaks of God as a "philanthropist," referring to God's "goodness" and "love for human beings" (*philanthrōpia,* 3:4). Titus, like the other pastoral letters, commends a praxis that avoids the interminable verbal disputes characteristic of so many religions and ideologies (1:10, 14; 3:9–11; see 1 Tim. 1:4; 4:7; 5:13; 6:4–5, 20–21; 2 Tim. 2:14–19, 23–24; 4:3).

Crete was a prosperous island, and its large Jewish community flourished under Roman hegemony and rule. However, the Christian assemblies commended to Titus's care included mainly older women (many apparently widows or unmarried, 2:3–5), young men (apparently unmarried, 2:6–8), and slaves (2:9–10; cf. aged men, 2:2; →Colossians, household codes). Despite the negative comments about the Cretan pagans and certain Jewish teachers (1:12–14), Titus says nothing explicitly about persecution. However, the Cretan churches' constituency and the letter's emphasis on good works to the needy suggest Christian communities somewhat marginalized that did not share fully in Cretan prosperity. Titus's teaching on justification by grace (3:7) may thus well echo Paul's emphasis on God's vindication of the oppressed and inclusion of the marginalized (see "Liberator/Savior," 1:3–4; 2:10–11, 13 ["redeem/free," 14]; 3:4–6; →Galatians; Romans). God's liberating justice was to be reflected in qualifications of the churches' leaders ("elders/overseer-bishops," 1:3–9), who were to be "just" (1:8), in the sense of avoiding violence ("not a striker," 1:7) and showing solidarity with visiting strangers ("hospitable," 1:8; cf. Sodom's inhospitality, the attempted gang rape of visiting angels! [Genesis 19]). God's liberating justice and faithful solidarity with the needy also were to be reflected in the lives of the entire baptized, Spirit-empowered community (2:12), thus avoiding the complacent "self-righteousness" to which Jesus ironically referred (3:5; →Mark 2:17). Titus also maintains the common apostolic apocalyptic "blessed hope" of God's final decisive intervention with liberating justice, putting an end to all oppression and violence (2:13; →James 5:1–6).

---

1. José P. Miranda, *Marx and the Bible: A Critique of the Philosophy of Oppression,* trans. John Eagleson (Maryknoll, N.Y.: Orbis, 1974), 144–45.

2. *Women*

Much of Titus's practical instruction is included in a domestic code (*Haustafel*) for patriarchal houses (2:1–10; for other examples, see Colossians, Ephesians, 1 Peter; the word "family" never occurs in the original texts of the Bible). The socioeconomic level of the churches may be indicated by the fact that the code primarily is directed toward women (2:3–5) and slaves (2:9–10), weak and poor elements in patriarchal societies (also note the young men in 2:6–8). The absence of instructions for the owners of the slaves may indicate churches with few wealthy members. No woman is mentioned by name in Titus (see the chapter on 2 Timothy).

Feminist interpreters commonly criticize Titus's instruction to the young women to be submissive to their husbands and work in the home (2:5). However, the Bible nowhere pretends to provide us with universal "morals" or "ethics" unrelated to specific historical contexts, and such instructions, like those directed toward slaves, are wisdom only for their specific historical context. Other biblical texts give quite different teaching to women, slaves, and other oppressed groups in other historical contexts. The canon should function *inclusively* to insist that we examine all the pertinent texts and not limit ourselves to those texts that most reflect the customs of the patriarchal cultures (see the chapter on Jude). Women and slaves, by rejecting the religious authority of kings and patriarchs in order to affiliate with Christian base communities, actually had demonstrated shocking freedom and independence. Domestic codes in the pastoral letters seek to assure the authorities that in the house meetings the leaders exhorted the women and the slaves not to foment further rebellion, but uphold the tradition of submission in certain areas. In the house-churches members even prayed for the kings and the patriarchs (1 Tim. 2:1–2). Consequently, many discern a kind of "subversive" submission in such instructions that made survival possible for the minority communities threatened with persecution and violence. Such contextual teaching regarding submission in certain areas does not constitute a universal "ethic" for all times and places.

Modern readers commonly consider the domestic codes (*Haustafeln*) offensive, but it is important to interpret them in the light of:

1. their literary context in each book where they occur: 1 Peter's defense of immigrants; Titus's emphasis on good works for the poor, the physically challenged, and the sick; 1 Timothy's unique emphasis on widows' importance in the churches;

2. their historical-cultural context, where the decision of women and slaves to affiliate with the house-churches constituted a remarkable expression of freedom and rebellion against the empire's authority, with its idolatrous homage to Caesar, and also against the patriarchal houses, where the father determined the religion of all members;

3. the context of the entire biblical canon, the text for instruction in the new communities, where slaves and women could learn of books with other teachings, such as the Exodus, a virtual manual of liberation for slaves!

We cannot enter into the minds of the codes' authors who taught submission, but we may perceive a certain wisdom in their tactic of "choosing battles": they sought to strengthen the base communities and help them to grow and to protect them from persecution. They insisted that house-churches maintain their right to exist as a counterculture, subversive to both empire and patriarchal houses. In their contexts, however, in the cases of women and slaves, they accepted limitations in the expressions of freedom.

3. *Sexual Minorities and Foreigners*

Although Titus speaks of marriages with submissive women (without naming any), the letter mentions by name only seven single men: Paul himself, Titus, and Jesus Christ (1:1–4); Artemas and Tychicus (3:12); and the lawyer Zenas and Apollos (a couple on a mission, 3:13). In a letter that stipulates that each elder should have one wife and believing children (1:5–6; cf. 1 Tim. 3:2), Paul, his emissary Titus, and his four colleagues in mission (as Jesus' emissaries) did not conform to this norm (not universal ethics!).

Moreover, although Jude (v. 14) cites the apocryphal Jewish 1 Enoch, the letter to Titus goes even further, citing the *pagan* Cretan poet Epimenides of Knossos, Crete (sixth century B.C.E.), even describing him as a "prophet" who testified against his own countrymen truth significant for the churches (1:12–13, see HCSB and NIV notes). William Percy[2] points out that, according to Greek sources, Epimenides was a kind of Cretan gay shaman who traveled to Athens to help the magistrate Solon in his reforms, including the institution of homoerotic love, in accord with the Cretan model—yet Paul's famous sermon in Acts (17:28) also cites him favorably! Commonly the Titus citation from Epimenides is taken as a kind of ethnic slur:

> Cretans are always liars, vicious brutes, lazy gluttons. (Titus 1:12)

In the Hellenic world Cretans were considered liars, since they claimed that Zeus's tomb was in Crete. The letter to Titus apparently exploits the readers' xenophobic prejudice to support its argument against false teachers in Crete (2:10–14). The caricature's bitter hyperbole makes it difficult to believe that the author of Titus had any hope of persuading the Cretans to submit to his authority.

In patriarchal societies prohibitions of various types of sexual "uncleanness" were usual, since such societies sought to guarantee maximum fertility and legitimate heirs. As with Jesus (Mark 7:1–23; Matt. 15:10–20; John 13:10) and Paul (Rom. 14:14–23), Titus subverts traditional sexual ideologies regarding "uncleanness" with its radical affirmation, "To the pure all things

---

2. William A. Percy, *Pederasty and Pedagogy in Archaic Greece* (Urbana: University of Illinois Press, 1996), 174–76.

are pure" (1:15). According to this letter, when we refuse solidarity with the poor and fail to help them with good works, that is what now constitutes an "abomination" (1:16).

4. *Praxis: Piety and Wisdom*

In Titus and 1–2 Timothy the favorite word to describe Christian behavior is "pious/reverent/devoted/respectful/godly" (*eusebēs* and its cognates—five times in Titus 1:1; 2:2, 7, 12). The use of this term, popular in the imperial ideology, was not common in earlier New Testament writings, and its adoption as a preferred term in the pastoral letters indicates a desire to demonstrate common ground between the Christian communities and their cultural context. Like the mandates of submission to kings, patriarchs, and slave owners, the insistence on "piety" sought to demonstrate that the communities were not as extremist as their enemies said.

Another emphasis in the letter is that all should be "sensible/prudent" (*sōphron-* words, 1:8; 2:2, 5–6, 12) and have common sense. Therefore, its lists of virtues should not be understood with a rigid and legalistic literalism but with a wisdom that knows how to interpret them appropriately according to their context. As was common in Greek philosophy, the letter counsels avoiding "excesses": demonstrating self-control, not being a slave to any vice, having only one wife, not being a drunkard or violent or greedy for gain (1:6–8; the last reflected also in the last of the Ten Commandments, "Do not covet"; see also Titus 2:12, 3:3).

5. *Health and Ecology*

Especially in Titus, good teaching is characterized by being "healthy" or "sound" (1:9, 13; 2:1–2, 8; cf. 1 Tim. 1:10)—creating health for individuals, communities, and the cosmos. In Titus the gospel sounds like Paul (2:11–14; 3:4–7), since it speaks of justification, but it is a justification "by grace" (3:7) rather than by faith (see the chapters on Romans and Galatians). Jesus is described both as Savior/Liberator and as God (2:13; cf. 1:3–4; 2:10–11; 3:4–6). The "blessed hope" (2:13) is not some Neoplatonic escape from the material world, but the apocalyptic hope that God will soon embrace and renew the entire cosmos, including the earth. "Eternal life" (1:2; 3:7) refers to "abundant life" (see John 10:10), involving bodily resurrection and a renewed earth and cosmos characterized by justice and peace ("rebirth," 3:5; see Matt. 19:28; 2 Pet. 3:13; Rom. 4:13; 8:18–39; Revelation 20–22; Isa. 11:1–9; 65:25; Hos. 2:18).

6. *Democracy and Hierarchy*

Titus is an important document in the process of institutionalization in the churches. Significant above all is the fact that at this early stage the term "bishop/overseer" (*episkopos,* 1:7) simply describes the function of the "elders" (*presbyteros*) but does not designate a distinct superior hierarchical position (see Acts 20:17, 28, and HCSB note to v. 28). That is, on the one hand, Titus's designation of "elders" to "oversee" the churches represents a step in the institutionalization of the churches. Although the elders of the churches were all at the same level, without the hierarchy of a bishop above them, in fact Paul and his emissaries, Titus and Timothy, exercised an authority superior to that of local elders. Therefore, soon after the death of that generation the elders probably chose one of their members as "chair/presider," who later appropriated the name of bishop/overseer.

On the other hand, during the Reformation, in opposition to the papal hierarchy, John Calvin and his followers utilized the pastorals and Acts 20 to call for a dismantling of traditional church structures and a return to a more simple, democratic ecclesiastical government (with elders, or bishops/overseers, at the same level). Before Calvin, Luther had rejected the authority of the pope, but maintained a hierarchy with bishops superior to the other clergy. In the centuries after the Reformation, in the Calvinist countries (Holland, Scotland, and later the United States) it occurred to political leaders to take the Calvinist ecclesiastical model and apply it to the national political level, establishing democratic republics instead of monarchies supported by hierarchical churches. Thus, texts such as Titus and 1 Timothy, undoubtedly rather "conservative" in their original historical contexts, later became instruments of radical sociopolitical change, and church polity transformed national political structures.

Bibliography

Dewey, Joanna. "Titus." In *The Women's Bible Commentary*, ed. Carol A. Newsom and Sharon Ringe, 452. Louisville: Westminster John Knox, 1998.

Percy, William Armstrong. *Pederasty and Pedagogy in Archaic Greece*. Urbana: University of Illinois Press, 1996.

Quinn, Jerome D. *The Letter to Titus*. AB 35. New York: Doubleday, 1990.

See also the bibliography for chapter 15, the pastoral letters.

Chapter 18

PHILEMON

Liberating Solidarity with a Slave

Outline

1. Paul and Timothy's salutation to Philemon and house-church leaders Apphia and Archippus — vv. 1–3
2. Paul's thankful prayers for the faith and love of an affluent Christian slave-owner — vv. 4–7
3. Paul's diplomatic plea for Onesimus's forgiveness and manumission — vv. 8–22
4. Greetings from Paul's five single male colleagues; benediction — vv. 23–25

Commentary

1. The Poor and Oppressed

The traditional reading of Paul's letter to Philemon now appears somewhat novelistic: Onesimus, an unbelieving slave and a fugitive from Philemon, a Christian leader in Colossae, robbed something from his owner and managed to travel to distant Rome, where (miraculously?) he finds Philemon's good friend Paul in prison (Acts 28:16–31). Through Paul's preaching Onesimus converts to Christianity, but Paul then sends the slave back to Philemon with this letter asking forgiveness and freedom for the slave. Such an interpretation is not impossible, but in the light of new research an alternative reading appears more probable. According to either reading, the book clearly reflects the perspective of the oppressed and marginalized: Paul is unjustly imprisoned in some city, and the slave Onesimus, property of the affluent Philemon, is returned to his owner, to whom this personal letter is directed, requesting Christian solidarity with Paul the prisoner and with Onesimus the slave (cf. Matt. 25:31–46).

The novelistic traditional interpretation was based on a limited knowledge of Roman law, which did require that fugitive slaves be returned to their owners (who then usually punished the slave severely, at times including crucifixion). For Paul, a Jewish Roman citizen, the Roman law stood in direct conflict with God's law in Deuteronomy:

> Slaves who have escaped to you from their owners shall *not* be given back to them. They shall reside with you, in your midst, in any place they choose in any one of your towns, wherever they please; you shall *not oppress* them. (Deut. 23:15–16)

Deuteronomy thus expresses the same solidarity with oppressed slaves that God had shown by freeing the Hebrew slaves in the Exodus from Egypt. In Onesimus's case, Paul for some time had obeyed this Deuteronomic law, but now, by returning him with this letter to Philemon, the apostle appeals to Philemon's conscience and risks submitting himself, along with the slave, to the severe Roman law. Philemon, an affluent Christian, probably was neither a Jew nor a Roman citizen, had a church using his home as a meeting place, and eagerly awaited the visit of his dear friend and mentor Paul. What could he do with such a letter and with his penitent slave Onesimus, now truly "useful" (the meaning of his name, v. 11) and a brother in the faith?

Recent research on Roman law reveals another possible scenario, somewhat similar but less novelistic (that is, without inventing or exaggerating miraculous elements). Roman law refers to common cases of "triangular" situations: a slave having difficulties with his owner seeks out a third party to serve as legal counsel against the angry owner. The slave's goal, then, was not to become a permanent fugitive but to return to the owner's house with a legal defender's support in order to better his working conditions. In such cases under Roman law the slave would not be punished as a fugitive.

This new scenario better accounts for the details of this letter. We then no longer need suppose that Onesimus somehow encountered Paul by chance in distant Rome. If he really intended to escape as a permanent fugitive, why would he intentionally seek out his angry master's dear friend? Advocates of the revised scenario propose that Paul was jailed rather in Ephesus, the closest large city to Colossae, and that the letter is one of Paul's earliest (54–55 C.E., not from Rome, 60–62, as previously supposed). We have no information concerning Paul's supposed imprisonment in Ephesus (but see 1 Cor. 15:32; 2 Cor. 1:8); hence, others would link the letter to Paul's imprisonment in Caesarea (57–59 C.E.; Acts 24:26–27), but this appears less likely. Similarly, we may now better understand that Onesimus easily could have pilfered enough to travel by donkey to Ephesus. Much more difficult was the traditional supposition that he stole enough to travel by boat as a tourist all the way to Rome (he was a provincial slave, not a politician!).

Notable in this new revised scenario is the transformation of the concept of evangelism, the proclamation of Jesus' good news to the poor, oppressed, and marginalized. According to the traditional interpretation, Onesimus was converted only by Paul's preaching. But we can now see how Paul's verbal proclamation was backed up by his praxis of solidarity with Onesimus: Paul, unjustly imprisoned, risks his friendship with the affluent Philemon in order to serve as the slave's legal defender. The letter is thus remarkably relevant for modern churches that seek numerical growth only through verbal evangelization (preaching, literature, television, etc.). The letter presents an evangelistic paradigm consistent with Jesus' ministry and the Bible in general (note Moses in the Exodus). We may also perceive how Paul not only achieved the slave's conversion but also addressed the affluent owner, insisting on a just, wise, and merciful solidarity with the oppressed, consistent with Jesus' praxis and teaching.

In light of the newer reading of the letter, we may profitably consider the tragic history of its misinterpretation, especially in the eighteenth and nineteenth centuries, when Philemon came to be the favorite book of the defenders of cruel racist slavery in the British Empire and in the southern United States.[1] This history shows how easily we impose our cultural and ideological prejudices to turn the Bible into an instrument of torture and violence instead of a proclamation of liberation, justice, and love. Modern study of Philemon uncovers three errors in the use of the book to defend racist slavery: (1) failing to distinguish two different types of slavery; (2) failing to distinguish between letters written by Paul himself (including Philemon) and other writings by his later disciples (the deutero-Pauline and the pastoral letters); and (3) not appreciating Paul's apocalyptic perspective and theology in opposing oppressive institutions.

1. The recourse to Philemon to defend racist slavery erred from being simplistic, fundamentalist, and cruel; in reality, however, a genuinely literal interpretation was never achieved. Those who misinterpreted Philemon to defend racist slavery failed to perceive that, in spite of using the same word, in the ancient Near East (including the Bible) "slavery" differed significantly from the racist slavery of the eighteenth and nineteenth centuries. For example, in ancient times usually one became a slave because of debts and was not sequestered because of belonging to a certain race; also, a slave could save from wages to buy freedom, or could wait a few years and be freed (usually before thirty years of age), or at least gain freedom when the owner died. Thus, although "slavery" designated systems with common elements (permitting ownership not only of the work but also the body of another, including the right to abuse sexually), the differences were significant.

2. As a letter from Paul himself, Philemon should first be interpreted in the light of the apostle's other letters. (See Gal. 3:28, where being in Christ subverts the differences between Greek and Jew, slave and free, man and woman; and 1 Cor. 7:21, where slaves are encouraged to seek freedom and where the slave's new identity in Christ transcends social or legal status.) Therefore, nineteenth-century defenders of slavery committed a methodological error when they began with the deutero-Pauline and pastoral letters, with their patriarchal household codes (Col. 3:18–4:1; Eph. 5:21–6:9; 1 Tim. 6:1–2; Titus 2:2–10; cf. 1 Pet. 2:18–25, probably by a later disciple of Peter). This same methodological error of prioritizing the pastorals and deutero-Pauline letters

1. Peter J. Gomes, *The Good Book: Reading the Bible with Mind and Heart* (New York: William Morrow, 1996), 84–101.

while neglecting the closer and most pertinent contexts has created tremendous distortion regarding Paul's teaching about women (→Galatians; 1 Corinthians; Romans 16).

3. A fundamental factor for appreciating Paul's approach to human institutions such as slavery is his apocalyptic theology, according to which the apostle anticipated Jesus' second coming during his own lifetime or shortly thereafter (see 1 Thessalonians; cf. Jude). Consequently, since it was impossible to envision an effective political strategy to abolish the institution of slavery immediately in the Roman Empire, Paul's approach was to establish throughout the empire house-churches that served as counterculture paradigms anticipating God's expected just new order ("realm").

In the long run, Paul's strategy, proclaiming Jesus' liberating good news and establishing ecclesiastical communities in houses throughout the Roman Empire, turned out to be more effective than any violent alternative (in antiquity slave revolts always failed). The early churches sought to transform the lives of people from diverse socioeconomic backgrounds and unite them in communities characterized by liberty, justice, and love. Notably, in this letter, although both Paul and Epaphras are prisoners (vv. 1, 9–10, 23) and Onesimus a slave (v. 16), the only unjust/oppressive act mentioned (v. 18, *ēdikēsen*) is that of Onesimus against his owner, not the owner's abuse of his slave! That Paul viewed Onesimus's act not simply as harmful but as unjust is indicated by the apostle's promise to "repay" (v. 19). Such linguistic data does not contradict the fact that Onesimus, as a slave, undoubtedly suffered worse injustices than anything he committed (pilfering and fleeing?). But Paul evidently did not view the institution of slavery as intrinsically unjust/oppressive, and his linguistic usage here reminds us that virtually everyone has some power (strength, youth, intelligence, sexual attractiveness) and is, even though economically, socially and politically disadvantaged, capable of acts of oppression. If Onesimus had fallen into debt and thus sold himself into slavery, Philemon's purchase might be viewed as more just and compassionate than our modern indifference to unemployment.

2. *Women and Sexual Minorities*

Patriarchal interpretations assume that Paul addressed a "family": Philemon with his wife, Apphia, and son Archippus (v. 1). However, feminist theology points out the probability that Apphia and Archippus were not Philemon's wife and son but other house-church leaders who would help assure that Philemon carried out all that Paul proposed. In other words, Paul takes the "private" matter between Philemon and his runaway slave and makes it a public concern for consideration by everyone in the little church community in Colossae, as well as Paul's six male companions in Ephesus (vv. 23–24 + Onesimus, vv. 10–12).

The fact that the letter comes from Paul and Timothy, accompanied by five other single men, supports the interpretation of Apphia and Archippus as individual church leaders, not Philemon's wife and son. Moreover, Paul rarely refers to married couples in his letters (three couples among thirty-eight persons named in Romans 16). The identification of Archippus as a "fellow soldier" hardly suggests that he is Philemon's son. If Archippus is independent and since the house is Philemon's (singular "your" in v. 2), it is unlikely that "sister" Apphia is Philemon's wife (see Priscilla and Aquila and "*their* house," Rom. 16:5; 1 Cor. 16:19; cf. Col. 4:15). The patriarchal identification of Philemon, Apphia, and Archippus as a "family" (a couple with an unmarried adult son) would make them the only nuclear family named by Paul in his letters. In that case, we would have to ask whether the "son" Archippus, an unmarried, mature adult, was gay! Paul addresses the male Philemon as "beloved" (literally; cf. NRSV, "our dear friend") and refers to Onesimus as his "child" (v. 10, not "begotten," but "birthed," *egennēsa,* as by a woman; cf. Gal. 4:19; 1 Thess. 2:7; James 1:18), also deeply loved ("my own heart," *splanchna,* lit., "bowels/intestines," v. 12). The explicit "love triangle" in this letter consists of three men, not any supposed nuclear family. Quite possibly Onesimus much later became Bishop Onesimus of Ephesus. Such a leadership capacity could explain in part Paul's zeal to free him from slavery.

Studying Philemon, Paul's shortest letter, together with its ghastly history of racist and patriarchal misinterpretation, can provide us with a helpful shove down the path of divine truth. Black theologian Peter J. Gomes, for example, points out that in contemporary debates concerning sexual minorities, the church today repeats the same errors in biblical misinterpretation that so many committed in the past when the Bible was used to promote violence against Jews, slaves, blacks, and women. In the light of modern biology and psychology, we no longer believe that our compassion flows from our "bowels/intestines" (*splanchna* in Philemon 7, 12, 20; "heart" in modern translations, but that also is prescientific). The presence of such prescientific elements in the Bible (as Galileo demonstrated regarding astronomy/cosmology) warns us against the fundamentalist practice of taking isolated scriptural texts as pretexts to oppress women, blacks, and sexual minorities.

3. The Sick and Physically Challenged

Although Paul acknowledges being elderly (v. 9, and hence weak), in Philemon he makes no other explicit reference to the sick or physically challenged. Quite possibly such persons also participated in the church in Colossae that met in Philemon's house (see Luke, the physician, v. 24; cf. Col. 4:14). Healing would be included within "every good thing" (v. 6; cf. emotional healing, vv. 7, 20).

Bibliography

Bartchy, S. Scott. "Philemon, Epistle to." *ABD*, 5:305–10.

———. "Slavery (Greco-Roman), New Testament." *ABD*, 6:65–73.

Callahan, Allen Dwight. *Embassy of Onesimus: The Letter of Paul to Philemon.* Harrisburg, Pa.: Trinity, 1997.

Dunn, James D. G. *Colossians and Philemon.* NIGTC. Grand Rapids: Eerdmans, 1996.

Finley, M. I. *Ancient Slavery and Modern Ideology.* New York: Viking, 1980.

Glancy, J. A. "Obstacles to Slaves' Participation in the Corinthian Church." *Journal of Biblical Literature* 117 (1998): 481–501. Concerning slaves as sexual property of their owners.

Harrill, J. A. *The Manumission of Slaves in Early Christianity.* Tübingen: Mohr, 1995.

Hock, R. F. "A Support for His Old Age: Paul's Plea on Behalf of Onesimus." In *The Social World of the First Century Christians: Essays in Honor of Wayne A. Meeks,* ed. L. M. White and O. L. Yarbrough, 67–81. Minneapolis: Fortress, 1995.

Lewis, L. A. "An African American Appraisal of the Philemon-Paul-Onesimus Triangle." In *Stony the Road We Trod: African American Biblical Interpretation,* ed. Cain Hope Felder, 232–46. Philadelphia: Fortress, 1991.

Martin, Dale B. *Slavery as Salvation: The Metaphor of Slavery in Pauline Christianity.* New Haven: Yale University Press, 1990.

Perkins, Pheme. "Philemon," In *The Women's Bible Commentary,* ed. Carol A. Newsom and Sharon H. Ringe, 453–54. Louisville: Westminster John Knox, 1998.

Petersen, Norman R. *Rediscovering Paul: Philemon and the Sociology of Paul's Narrative World.* Philadelphia: Fortress, 1985.

Winter, S. C. "Philemon." In *Searching the Scriptures,* vol. 2, *A Feminist Commentary,* ed. Elisabeth Schüssler Fiorenza, 301–12. New York: Crossroad, 1994.

See also the bibliography for chapter 12, "Colossians."

Chapter19

HEBREWS

Subversive Hermeneutics and Jesus' Liberating Purpose

Outline

1. God's final, decisive revelation: Jesus (not Leviticus or Paul)	1:1–4
2. Angels as a sexual minority in the Bible (and Jesus' superiority to them)	1:5–2:4
3. Humanity's glorious origin and destiny (and Jesus' death that defeats evil)	2:5–18
4. Faithfulness: Moses and Jesus as authentic paradigms	3:1–6
5. Listening to God's voice in the midst of the AIDS crisis: God's wrath against the oppressors, not against the oppressed and ill	3:7–19
6. Coming out of the closet to enter into God's rest (God's Word as a sword to convict oppressors, not a club to clobber the oppressed)	4:1–13
7. Prayer: our bold approach to the throne of grace (God's loving solidarity in welcoming sexual minorities without discrimination)	4:14–5:10
8. Stern warning for times of persecution (when our solidarity with the oppressed falters)	5:11–6:12
9. God's promises and vows: our anchor of hope in time of crisis (our holy unions: celebrations of freedom without vows?)	6:13–20
10. Melchizedek, patron saint for sexual minorities: how God revised Moses' law to ordain a priest who is different/queer	7:1–28
11. Jesus, lay minister of a better covenant with superior promises (whose law of love is inscribed on our hearts)	8:1–13
12. Jesus' death (1): earthly defeat, celestial triumph (our sins of ignorance today: racism, sexism, anti-Semitism, homophobia)	9:1–28

Commentary

The book traditionally known as "The Epistle of Paul the Apostle to the Hebrews" is neither a letter nor from Paul. Hebrews is anonymous. The author may well have been Apollos (Acts 18:24–26), unmarried and itinerant, like Paul (18:24, 27; see high priority concerns about hospitality and imprisonment in Heb. 13:2–3). The author represents a cultured and educated elite and addresses well-informed readers recently impoverished by persecution (10:32–34). Although traditionally known as a letter, Hebrews does not have the typical introductory patterns of that genre. Rather, it is a sermon, an exhortation (13:22), and only at the end (13:23–25) includes the news and personal greetings characteristic of a letter.

Hebrews probably was written ca. 65–66 C.E., shortly after Paul's martyrdom and the great fire in Rome (64 C.E.), but before the war and the destruction of Jerusalem (67–70 C.E.), thus, almost forty years after Jesus' death and resurrection (30 C.E.; see the "forty years" in 3:17).

Hebrews appears to address a house-church (twenty to fifty people) in Rome (Heb. 13:24). Romans 16 had indicated some five such house-churches in Rome (58 C.E.). Emperor Claudius's edict (49 C.E.) expelling Jews (including Jewish Christians) from Rome resulted in confiscation of their property

(10:34), and the city's great fire (64 C.E.) had led to persecution and imprisonment (10:32–33). Christian Jews suffered this persecution first from emperors (who viewed them as a Jewish sect), but also from Jewish compatriots (for whom they were heretics).

Of all the New Testament books, Hebrews most frequently makes use of the Hebrew scriptures, especially the radical Exodus traditions, the forty years in the wilderness, the conquest (followed by the just distribution of land). Nevertheless, Hebrews represents an extreme among the writings of the New Testament because of the evident degree of Neoplatonism in its language and theology. Furthermore, the numerous citations from the Hebrew Bible never simply reflect the original meaning but continually propose new interpretations, often Christological, and appropriate to the readers' context.[1]

1. The Oppressed Poor and Liberating Justice

Concerning poverty and its causes, Hebrews follows the Exodus paradigm: oppression as the fundamental cause of poverty.[2] The question still debated is whether liberation/salvation is conceived in purely Neoplatonic terms (a "way out" similar to the Exodus but with a spiritualized, immaterial, heaven as the goal); also whether the eschatology of Hebrews is consistent with the apocalyptic and utopian perspective common to the rest of the New Testament: a cosmic hope that includes a *new earth* characterized by justice (see 2 Pet. 3:13).

Passages referring explicitly to poverty are few but significant and eloquent. The great "faith chapter" culminates with triumphalistic references to militarism and political victories in Israel's history (11:32–35), but then realistically acknowledges,

> Others, however, suffered mocking and flogging, and even chains and imprisonment. They were stoned to death, they were sawn in two, they were killed by the sword; they went about in skins of sheep and goats, impoverished [*hysteroumenoi*], oppressed [*thlibomenoi*], tormented—of whom the world was not worthy. They wandered in deserts and mountains, and in caves and holes in the ground. (11:36–38)

The persecution that brutalized and impoverished these people left them without homes and adequate clothing, while they suffered violence, torture, and mocking. However, like the elect in James (2:5), they were rich in faith (Heb. 11:39–40). In other references to the poor, Hebrews speaks of the impoverished Christians whose properties were plundered (10:32–34) and of the Israelite slaves in Egypt (11:24–26; see Exodus 1–15).

Since Hebrews begins by emphasizing that God spoke through the prophets (1:1), the focus on oppression and persecution as fundamental causes of poverty is not surprising (10:33; 11:25, 37). The oppression targeted a persecuted

1. Harold W. Attridge, *The Epistle to the Hebrews,* Hermeneia (Philadelphia: Fortress, 1989). For an excellent summary of the transformation of Platonism in Hebrews, see Luke Timothy Johnson, *The Writings of the New Testament,* rev. ed. (Minneapolis: Fortress, 1999), 464–67.

2. Thomas D. Hanks, *God So Loved the Third World: The Biblical Vocabulary of Oppression,* trans. James C. Dekker (Maryknoll, N.Y.: Orbis, 1983), 44–46.

group and also threatened any who showed solidarity with them (10:33, *koinōnia;* 11:25; cf. those in solidarity with the poor whom Jesus called the "poor in spirit" [→Matt. 5:3; 25:31–46]).

Hebrews shares with the rest of the New Testament the understanding that the church's ministry provides partial and provisional response to the suffering of the poor. Thus, in Hebrews the "assembling together" is both to meet the material needs and for spiritual edification (10:24–25). The church's ministry to the oppressed may be seen theologically as the internalization of God's just law in the new covenant/alliance (8:8–12; note *adikia,* "oppression," v. 12; cf. 6:10; 10:17; Jer. 22:16). Externally this ministry is manifested in the good works for the needy, the solidarity of *agape*-love and the service (*diakoneō*) to the saints (6:10). Mutual love (*philadelphia*) is manifested in the hospitality to homeless visitors (13:1–2, itinerant prophets and evangelists like Apollos?), visiting those who suffer imprisonment (13:3, 23), physical solidarity with those "excommunicated" from their traditional spiritual community (13:12–13), good works, and shared sacrifice (*koinōnia,* 13:15–16, 21). The basic prerequisite for such sacrificial actions is to be free of the "love of money" (13:5).

The new covenant of Hebrews 8 (see Jeremiah 31) internalizes the Torah as a whole, including its considerable sociopolitical justice dimension, not just select compassionate and reformist elements. Consequently, Hebrews 8 implies a "structural" approach to eliminate oppression (see 8:12, *adikia;* cf. 6:10) and to instill a praxis of liberating justice ("know me," 8:11; see Jer. 22:16–17). The traditions of the Exodus and the conquest in 3:1–4:11 and the political-military triumphalism of 11:32–35 also are pertinent, but all were past realities, not contemporary. Although not as explicit as Luke in presenting the gospel as good news "to the poor," Hebrews similarly proclaims a gospel that involves an integral salvation-liberation. For Hebrews, however, as for our other New Testament documents, inclusive house-churches represented the first fruits of God's anticipated just new order.

A Neoplatonic reading of Hebrews would contradict the other utopian-apocalyptic writings of the New Testament (Revelation 20–22; 2 Pet. 3:13). Nevertheless, despite tendentious translations, we may detect, even behind Neoplatonic mistranslations, teachings coherent with the materialism of Hebrew thought and that of the other New Testament books. Above all, "Mount Zion" and "the heavenly Jerusalem" (12:22–24; cf. 11:10, 16) should not be misinterpreted as an immaterial realm eternally separated from the earthly scene, but rather as "near" *in space* as well as in time (13:14). The Jerusalem that is heavenly in origin will finally (as in Revelation 21–22) *descend to earth* to consummate God's realm ("earth . . . heaven . . . we are receiving," 12:26–28; cf. Matt. 6:10, "on earth").

Whatever the correct reading (Neoplatonic-spiritual or Hebrew materialist), the consummation of God's realm represents, as in other parts of the New Testament, the glorious resolution for the suffering of the poor and the oppressed. Without doubt, the teachings of Hebrews about creation (1:1–4;

12:27) and bodily resurrection (11:35; 13:20) are more consistent with a Hebrew materialist reading of the book. However, even though an intermediate state and the celestial sphere receive greater development and emphasis than in other New Testament books, this reading does not necessarily contradict the apocalyptic material and earthly dimension. Hebrews' description of Moses' decisive option for solidarity with the poor and oppressed provides us with our most vivid and explicit paradigm of this fundamental element in contemporary liberation theologies:

> By faith Moses, when he was grown up, refused to be called a son of Pharaoh's daughter, choosing rather to share *ill-treatment* with the people of God than to enjoy the fleeting pleasures of sin. He considered *abuse suffered* for the Christ to be greater wealth than the treasures of Egypt, for he was looking ahead to the reward. (11:24–26)

Undoubtedly, the erudite and eloquent author of Hebrews identified with this portrait of Israel's great liberator, who established Torah to exemplify God's liberating justice and maintain the liberated community free from enslavement.[3] Given Hebrews' deep grounding in the Hebrew Bible and the Exodus paradigm of poverty caused by oppression, we are not surprised to find throughout the book repeated references to liberating justice. The first chapter sets the tone with its portrayal of Jesus as messianic Son, whose divine rule is characterized by rectitude, liberating justice and detesting of oppression (1:8–9, citing Ps. 45:6–7; cf. Psalm 72). In the great faith chapter, Noah (not Abraham!), *saved* from the flood that extinguished violent contemporaries, exemplifies God's liberating justice (*dikaiosyne*) that comes by faith (11:7). In Hebrew, Melchizedek's very name ("king exemplifying *liberating justice*") and city ("king of [Jeru]salem," *peace*) unite two fundamental characteristics of God's rule (7:1–2; similarly, the "harvest of liberating justice and peace" resulting from divine discipline in 12:11; cf. Isaiah's apocalyptic hope for liberating justice resulting in peace, 32:15–18). Hospitality for the homeless (itinerant prophets, disciples fleeing persecution) and solidarity with oppressed prisoners are described as expressions of mutual love (13:1–2) but, in the context of the book, may also be understood as expressions of liberating justice (see 12:23; 11:33; cf. 2:2; 5:13; 9:1, 10; 11:4; Matt. 25: 31, 46).

2. *Women and Sexual Minorities*

Hebrews mentions only two women by name: Abraham's wife, Sarah (11:11; see her involvement in bigamy and promoting divorce in Genesis 16 and 21), and Rahab the prostitute (11:31; cf. various unnamed women of faith in 11:35). Concerning Sarah Hebrews says, "It was equally by faith that *Sarah*, although past the age, *was empowered to conceive* [lit., "deposit seed"], because *she* trusted that God who had made the promise would be faithful to

3. Strangely ignored by Jorge Pixley and Clodovis Boff's excellent study, *Opción por los pobres* (Buenos Aires: Paulinas, 1986).

it" (11:11). The Greek text thus attributed to Sarah the male role of "depositing seed" (even though the existence of the feminine ovule fertilized by semen was not scientifically recognized until the nineteenth century). To avoid anachronism, our translations commonly change Sarah's role and reduce her to a parentheses: "By faith he [Abraham] received power of procreation, even though he was too old (Sarah herself being barren) because he considered God faithful who had promised" (11:11, cf. NIV and NRSV).

Given the marginalization of women in Hebrews, the exaltation of Rahab, the Gentile prostitute who showed solidarity with the Israelites in the conquest of Jericho, is notable (11:31; Joshua 2). Just as James places Rahab and Abraham on an equal footing as examples of sexual minorities with faith (2:25), Hebrews presents Rahab as comparable to Sarah in faith (Matt. 1:5 includes Rahab in Jesus' genealogy). This exaltation of Rahab in the Bible is consistent with the presentation of Jesus as a "friend of toll collectors and prostitutes" and with the teaching of Paul, who did not rebuke the prostitutes but Christian husbands who paid for their services (1 Cor. 6:12–20). Churches that condemn sex workers deviate widely from the teaching and example of Jesus and the New Testament authors (Matt. 21:31–32).

Furthermore, according to the Hebrew scriptures, Sarah herself must be reckoned among the sexual minorities: first, she is called "sterile" (a patriarchal and prescientific perspective); second, she arranges for Abraham to take as concubine her slave Hagar (putting her in a kind of *ménage à trois* that endured several years); and third, she demands the dismissal (divorce) of Hagar with her son Ishmael, Abraham's firstborn. Genesis even accuses Sarah of "oppressing" Hagar (Hebrew: *ʿānāh,* Gen. 16:6). First Peter depicts Sarah as a pious, submissive wife (3:5–6), but in Genesis she is strong, not always submissive, and is the first person in the scriptures accused of "oppression."[4]

Nevertheless, for many contemporary readers, more problematic than Hebrew's omission of heroic women of faith (like Deborah) is the interpretation of Christ's death as a kind of child abuse, a sacrifice in which God (like Abraham threatening Isaac in Genesis 22) cruelly abuses his son. Mary D'Angelo concludes that Hebrews implies divine approval for child abuse (2:10; 5:8; 12:4–11).[5] Similarly, with reference to Hebrews 12:5–11, which cites Prov. 3:11–12, Donald Capps maintains that the author of Hebrews gives evidence of having suffered abuse as a child (which may have included sexual abuse).[6] Capps recommends as preferable Jesus' teaching that God is a kind Father (see Q, the Sermon on the Mount, and the parable of the prodigal son) and the teaching of Matthew, where Jesus introduces a new era in adult-child relationships in which children are treated with dignity and respect (18:1–5 // Mark 9:33–37 // Luke 9:46–48; similarly Isa. 11:1–9 and Psalm 8). Also, Heb. 12:8

---

4. Hanks, *God So Loved the Third World,* 49; "Poor/Poverty (New Testament)," *ABD,* 5:126.

5. Mary Rose D'Angelo, "Hebrews," in *The Women's Bible Commentary,* ed. Carol A. Newsom and Sharon H. Ringe (Louisville: Westminster John Knox, 1992), 366.

6. Donald E. Capps, *The Child's Song: The Religious Abuse of Children* (Louisville: Westminster John Knox, 1995).

easily leads to child abuse with its pejorative reference to those who are "bastards and not sons," another example of the patriarchal culture supporting an ideology through language control (→James).

Hebrews' focus on Christ as high priest may be manipulated to prohibit the ordination of women. Nevertheless, Jesus was a lay person and not descended from the priestly tribe of Levi, but he exercised a priesthood similar to that of Melchizedek (see below). Consequently, we may understand Jesus' priesthood as involving a rejection of traditional patriarchal ordination and a basis for accepting the spiritual leadership of women, sexual minorities, and the physically challenged (7:11–19; 8:3–5; see Isa. 56:3–5).

Hebrews defends the integrity of heterosexual marriage against those who despised it (13:4 [adherents of some Neoplatonic philosophy?]; note the use of "bed" as a sexual euphemism with a positive sense; cf. "bed-males" [→1 Timothy, 1 Corinthians]). However, the homeowners expected to practice hospitality and resist the temptation to love money (13:2, 5) may have included many who were not married (→Romans 16). Sexual minorities certainly receive the strongest affirmation throughout the book. Above all, Jesus, unmarried and not of priestly descent, is the new high priest whose sacrifice, "once and for all time" (10:12), puts an end to all previous sacrifices and priesthoods. Since Jesus was a lay person, not descended from Aaron or from the tribe of Levi, Hebrews portrays his priesthood as prefigured by the Gentile king and priest Melchizedek of Jerusalem, whom the scriptures present not only as never married but even as having neither parents nor descendants (7:1–3, sexual minority, really "queer"!).

Melchizedek's story clarifies antiquity's prescientific concept of procreation, since Hebrews even affirms that when Melchizedek went out to encounter the patriarch, Abraham already carried in his loins descendants (such as Levi) who were born centuries later (7:9–10)! Often the Bible is cited against abortion because the unborn are already viewed as human beings (Psalm 139; Luke 1, etc.). However, should we also then conclude that all semen in male "loins" contains real human beings destined to be born even generations later? Campaigners against abortion must assume rather a modern scientific understanding of procreation. They cannot start simply from biblical texts that affirm the existence of life before birth, because such biblical texts also presume that human life exists in semen even centuries *before* conception.[7]

In fact, not only isolated cases (Rahab, Sarah, Abraham, Melchizedek) but the great majority of persons named in Hebrews represent sexual minorities of some type. In the list of heroes of the faith in Hebrews 11, for example, only two, Enoch and Joseph, appear to be heterosexuals legitimately married

7. Therein lies the significance of Hillary Clinton's point at the women's conference in Beijing: in the most populous nations, respecting women's decisions rather than invoking patriarchal state intervention is more effective in reducing abortions, since with modern medical technology widely available, husbands commonly require women to keep aborting females until a male is conceived. Both Hebrews and Hillary Clinton's observation are fatal to popular patriarchal fundamentalist polemics that argue that to respect women's decisions implies advocating abortion.

to only one wife. Nevertheless, unmarried Abel died by violence at the hands of his brother Cain, who apparently incestuously married a sister. Noah had only one wife, but became drunk after the flood, lay naked, and apparently was raped by his son Ham (Gen. 9:18–28, euphemistic language; see HCSB note). Isaac and Jacob married close relatives (incest, according to Leviticus), and even Moses was the son of an incestuous relationship (Exod. 6:20; Lev. 18:12).

3. The Weak, Physically Challenged, and Sick: Divine Healing and Empowerment

The people of God are perceived in Hebrews as debilitated, "weakened" by so much persecution and oppression (4:15; 5:1–3; 11:34–35), but even more as "exhausted" (12:12) and consequently yearning to ascend to the new Jerusalem (12:22, 28) and enter their heavenly "rest" (4:1–11). Much more than other New Testament books, Hebrews utilizes the vocabulary and certain Neoplatonic concepts common among educated persons in the Greco-Roman culture. The book nevertheless remains deeply rooted in the fundamental Hebrew concepts of God's creation, liberating acts in history, and the dynamic understanding of the life of God's people as walking on *a way* (3:10; 9:8; 10:20) or "running a race" (12:1–3).[8] Like the rest of the Bible, Hebrews never employs the static, ahistorical concepts of "ethics" or "morals" dominant in Greek philosophy and the Neoplatonized traditional theologies. The weak, tired, and physically challenged are not a marginalized class in Hebrews, but represent all of God's people, who should, nevertheless, "run with perseverance the race that is set before us" (12:1):

> Therefore lift your drooping hands and strengthen your weak knees, and make straight paths for your feet, so that what is lame may not be put out of joint, but rather be healed. (12:12–13; cf. Isa. 40:27–31)

Bibliography

Attridge, Harold W. *The Epistle to the Hebrews.* Hermeneia. Philadelphia: Fortress, 1989.

———. "Hebrews, Epistle to the," *ABD*, 3:97–104.

Bruce, F. F. *The Epistle to the Hebrews.* Rev. ed. NICNT. Grand Rapids: Eerdmans, 1990.

Capps, Donald E. *The Child's Song: The Religious Abuse of Children.* Louisville: Westminster John Knox, 1995.

D'Angelo, Mary Rose. "Hebrews." In *The Women's Bible Commentary,* ed. Carol A. Newsom and Sharon H. Ringe, 455–59. Louisville: Westminster John Knox, 1998.

de Silva, David A. *Despising Shame: Honor Discourse and Community Maintenance in the Epistle to the Hebrews.* Society of Biblical Literature Dissertation Series 152. Atlanta: Scholars Press, 1996.

8. Robert Jewett, *Letter to Pilgrims: A Commentary on the Epistle to the Hebrews* (New York: Pilgrim Press, 1981).

Eisenbaum, Pamela. "The Virtue of Suffering, the Necessity of Discipline, and the Pursuit of Perfection in Hebrews." In *Asceticism and the New Testament,* ed. Leif E. Vaage and Vincent L. Wimbush, 331–53. New York: Routledge, 1999.

Ellingworth, Paul. *The Epistle to the Hebrews.* NIGTC. Grand Rapids: Eerdmans, 1993.

Eller, Vernard. *Christian Anarchy: Jesus' Primacy over the Powers.* Grand Rapids: Eerdmans, 1987.

Gordon, Robert P. *Hebrews.* Sheffield: Sheffield Academic Press, 2000.

Hagner, Donald A. *Hebrews.* New International Bible Commentary 14. Peabody, Mass.: Hendrickson, 1990.

Hanks, Thomas D. *Hebrews: Encouragement for Sexual Minorities.* St. Louis: Other Sheep, 1998.

Jewett, Robert. *Letter to Pilgrims: A Commentary on The Epistle to the Hebrews.* New York: Pilgrim Press, 1981.

Kittredge, Cynthia Briggs. "Hebrews." In *Searching the Scriptures,* vol. 2, *A Feminist Commentary,* ed. Elisabeth Schüssler Fiorenza, 428–54. New York: Crossroad, 1994.

Lane, William L. *Hebrews 1–8.* WBC 47A. Dallas: Word, 1991.

———. *Hebrews 9–13.* WBC 47B. Dallas: Word, 1991.

Pfitzner, V. C. *Hebrews.* Nashville: Abingdon, 1997.

Chapter 20

JAMES

The Priority of Praxis Guided by Wisdom

Outline

1. Greetings, 1:1

2. Introduction: aphorisms, 1:2–27

    Joy in the midst of oppression, 1:2–4 (→5:7–11)

    Democratization of wisdom, 1:5–8 (→3:13–18)

    Destiny of the rich, 1:9–11 (→2:1–7; 4:13–5:6)

    God, source only of the good, 1:12–18 (→3:13–4:10)

    Diligence in listening, 1:19–21 (→3:1–12)

    The word and praxis: authentic religion, 1:22–27 (→2:14–26)

3. Essays, 2:1–5:18

    Respect for the dignity of the poor, 2:1–9

    The law that preserves the liberated community free from oppression, 2:10–13

    Faith and sacrificial good works for the poor and vulnerable, 2:14–26

    Tongues that murder the poor and vulnerable, 3:1–13

    Wisdom democratized, 3:14–18

    Violence of covetous oppressors, 4:1–12

    Warnings to prosperous oppressors, 4:13–5:6

    Imminent advent of the Liberator and Judge, 5:7–11

    Avoid oaths, but dialogue with the Creator, 5:12–18

4. Conclusion: mutual correction, 5:19–20

Commentary

1. The Poor, Sick, Women, and Sexual Minorities

With its condemnation of oppression as the fundamental cause of poverty, James is the New Testament book that most closely reflects the Exodus paradigm and prophetic denunciations of wealthy oppressors common in the Hebrew Bible. This should not surprise us if James is the earliest writing of the New Testament (45–50 C.E.) and written by James of Jerusalem, the brother of Jesus (see Mark 6:3; Matt. 13:55; 1 Cor. 15:7; Gal. 1:19; Acts 15:13; 21:18). Many argue for another author and a later date (70–90 C.E.), pointing out that the structure of the assembly (church) was more like that of the pastoral letters (with teachers and elders) than of the Pauline congregations (James 3:1; 5:14–15; cf. 1 Corinthians 12–14, having spiritual gifts rather than offices).[1] This characteristic of James, however, may reflect the Jewish synagogue tradition, a cultural difference rather than a temporal one (see *synagōgē*, "synagogue," 2:2; "assembly," NRSV; cf. HCSB note). Most of those addressed by James were neither poor beggars (2:2) nor wealthy (2:6; 5:1–6). As a Judeo-Christian minority ("Diaspora/Dispersion," 1:1; see HCSB note), the community was composed mainly of small farmers and artisans who possessed little and had to live frugally.

In addition to the term used for the "beggarly poor" (*ptōchos*, four times, 2:2–6), James's vocabulary includes "the humble poor" (*tapeinos*, 1:9; cf. 4:6, 10), "the workers," "the harvesters," and "the just" (5:4, 6; "innocent," NIV). The beggarly poor are characterized as wearing shabby clothes (2:2) or being without clothes and daily food (2:15–16). The weak, marginalized, and needy also included women (2:15), the sick (5:14–16), and sexual minorities: widows (1:27, with orphans) and the sex worker Rahab (2:25; cf. Matt. 1:5; Josh. 2:1–21; 6:22–25; Heb. 11:31). The presentation of Rahab as a paradigm of hospitality and faith together with Abraham (2:21–26; also note that Abraham divorced his concubine, Hagar, Gen. 21:14) demonstrates how close James's perspective is to that of his brother Jesus and the Q source in terms of women and sexual minorities (see John 4; Luke 7). "The composition shows no interest . . . in sexual morality, or the ethics of marriage, or domestic arrangements."[2] The only women specified (widows, 1:27; poor sisters, 2:15; and Rahab, 2:25) represent sexual minorities.

Regarding the fundamental cause of so much poverty, weakness, and marginalization in the world, James never blames the victims for such things as sloth, vices, or genetic inferiority. Rather, James focuses the spotlight on oppression (see Luke 4:18–19).[3] According to James, oppression of the poor and the weak appears to take place basically in three ways:

---

1. Raymond E. Brown, *Introduction to the New Testament* (New York: Doubleday, 1997), 742.
2. Luke Timothy Johnson, *The Letter of James*, AB 37A (New York: Doubleday, 1995), 119.
3. Thomas D. Hanks, *God So Loved the Third World: The Biblical Vocabulary of Oppression*, trans. James C. Dekker (Maryknoll, N.Y.: Orbis, 1983), 45–47.

1. Economic-legal mechanisms, especially against poor debtors (2:1–12)
2. Ambitious and arrogant business people (4:13–17; coveting, 1:14–15; 4:2)
3. Wealthy landowners withhold wages, a very generalized method of oppression (5:4)

The rich "oppress" (*katadynasteuō,* 2:6) those to whom the letter of James is addressed, using false witnesses (note "the tongue," 3:1–12) to drag them into court. Such injustice/oppression (*adikia*) is what basically characterizes the entire worldly system (2:6; cf. 4:4 and "trials," 1:2, 12). The "distress" (*thlipsis,* 1:27) that widows and orphans suffer also relates specifically to oppression (see Mark 12:40; 2 Tim. 3:6).[4]

James (like Jesus) appears to ignore Paul's teaching about Adam's "fall" (Rom. 5:12–21) but expounds a more authentically Jewish doctrine concerning creation (3:9) and sin's origin (1:13–15): everyone is "Adam" (*2 Bar.* 54:19). James does not call for evangelism as it is commonly understood. Nevertheless, a poor person who entered the meeting would be attracted by the honor shown by a welcome without discrimination (2:1–4), by the good news of God's preferential option for the poor (2:5), by the prophetic denunciation of wealthy oppressors (2:6–7), by the praxis of loving solidarity with the poor and weak (1:27; 2:14–17), by testimonies of healing (5:14–15a; see HCSB notes), by the promise of divine forgiveness (5:15b), and by the shared hope of God's decisive final judgment against the oppressors and the violent to create a new world of justice and peace (5:1–6; 3:18). Our quite limited concepts of evangelism fail to recognize that prophetic denouncement of oppression is an essential element of evangelization, biblically conceived as a proclamation of the good news in a preferential way for the poor (Luke 4:18–19; 3:10–14; 6:20–26). James projects the vision of communities of disciples whose attractive lifestyle embodies the proclaimed word (1:18, 21; 4:6; 5:19–20). In a world characterized by greed, tyranny, and oppression, the community, like "a city set on a hill" (Matt. 5:14–16) beckons with love to the poor, the weak, and the oppressed (Isa. 2:2–4).

James is especially concerned about the sins of the tongue that create a false feeling of importance and security for the affluent and deny dignity, honor, and justice for the poor and the weak. Above all, the Bible denounces the sin of false witnesses who, many times bribed by the powerful and the rich, take away land, house, and even life itself from the weak and poor (2:6–7). With his strong emphasis on the sins of the tongue (3:1–13), James reminds us of the destructive use of words to insult, express contempt, and, with gossip, destroy the good reputation ("name") and dignity of human beings. Modern studies about the power of words and labels demonstrate how such negative and destructive elements form part of the vocabulary and grammar of language itself. (Note the negative charge in common English words: whore, prostitute, faggot, queer, blind.) Some interpreters conclude that Jesus' prohibition of calling

4. Ibid., 47–50.

someone *raka* ("insult," NRSV; →Matt. 5:22) would be similar to "sissy" or "faggot" in English.

James presents justification as the divine response of vindication that dignifies and honors the oppressed in the face of the condemnation of the imperial courts and the false accusations of lying and bribed witnesses (2:12–13; 3:8–9; 4:11–12; 5:6). Therefore, James provides two examples: Abraham, an emigrant (note the recipients of the letter, 1:1); and Rahab, the sex worker who offered her hospitality as a gesture of solidarity with the slave ancestors of Israel, emigrants who escaped from Egypt.

As in any other part of the New Testament, becoming a "doer of the word" in fulfillment of the "good news" implies above all responding in a practical way to the material needs of indigent neighbors and one's brothers and sisters in the faith (1:22–25; 4:17, cf. forgiveness and illness in 5:14–16). To refuse to be a doer of the word—helping the poor, the oppressed, and the marginalized—means to kill (murder the poor, 5:6) and also to enter into an adulterous alliance with the oppressive world system (4:4–6; cf. 1 John 3:17).

Although James recommends peace (3:17–18) and approves the nonviolent resistance of the oppressed harvesters, he is not passively indifferent to such injustice and oppression. On the contrary, he energetically denounces the cruel oppression and violence that impoverishes and kills (2:11; 3:8; 5:5–6). For their historical context, nonviolent resistance forms part of the "wisdom that comes from above" that James recommends to all his readers as a critical reflection in the practice of good works (3:13–18). Other dimensions of this divine wisdom include prayer and "militant patience" (1:5–7; 5:13–17).[5] The fervent expectation of Jesus' second coming as God's liberating justice for all the oppressed continues to focus hope for direct imminent divine intervention (5:7–9; "apocalyptic eschatology"). Thus will God fulfill the promise of a new order ("realm") characterized by liberation, justice, love, peace, and wisdom (1:12; 2:5).

Despite his closeness to the Hebrew scriptures, James already is at a certain distance from the oldest traditions of the New Testament that deal with the poor, the weak, and the marginalized: the Christian Jews he addresses are in exile (1:1), but are not itinerant prophets like Jesus and his closest disciples. James's readers live in an established community of "sisters and brothers" (2:6–7, 15; 1:27; 2:25–26), although shaken by conflicts ([of class?] 4:1–3). James is one of three New Testament authors who are married (Peter and Jude are the others; see 1 Cor. 9:5). Nevertheless, his exaltation of Rahab (an unmarried sex worker) and Abraham (a bigamist who divorced his concubine) and his disregard for common family values and responsibilities place him closer to the original ideal of itinerant prophets than to the teaching of some later writings (1 Peter, and the deutero-Pauline and pastoral letters). James prophetically denounces oppression and the abuse of wealth, but does not

5. Elsa Tamez, *The Scandalous Message of James: Faith without Works Is Dead,* trans. John Eagleson (New York: Crossroad, 1990), 51–56.

advocate totally abandoning household, possessions, and business (cf. Luke 14:26; 18:29).

2. *Liberating Justice*

Addressing communities that catered to wealthy visitors and had become indifferent to the poor, James may well have been the pioneer in the incorporation of Hebrew Bible and Jewish justice vocabulary into standard church discourse. Reflecting God's liberating justice in the Exodus paradigm, James uses *dik-* vocabulary with relative frequency (eight times + *adikia,* "oppression/injustice," one time in five chapters):

- "Human wrath does not accomplish God's liberating justice" (*dikaiosynē,* 1:20);
- Abraham and Rahab were "justified" (four uses in 2:21, 23–25) by their authentic faith manifest in their works;
- "Peacemakers who sow in peace raise a harvest of liberating justice" (*dikaiosynē,* 3:18);
- "You murdered the just person [*dikaion*], who did not resist you" (5:6, see 5:1–6);
- "The prayer of a just person [*dikaiou*] is powerful and efficacious" (5:16).

James focuses on the tongue as an instrument of violence in a world characterized by oppression: "The tongue is a fire, a world of oppression/injustice (*adikias*) among the body's parts" (3:6). But he also employs other terms for oppression and violence:

- "Do not the rich men oppress [*katadynasteuousin*] you, and they drag you to tribunals?" (2:6);
- "The wages you failed to pay the workers who mowed your fields . . . You have lived daintily and indulgently on the earth, you have fattened your hearts for a day of slaughter. You condemned [*katedikasate*], you murdered the just person [*dikaion*], who did not resist you" (5:4–6).

3. *James and Jesus: Parallel Texts (//) in Matthew 5–7*

James //	Matthew	
1:2	5:11–12	Great joy . . . on being surrounded by . . . trials.
1:4	5:48	That you may be perfect and complete.
1:5	7:7	Ask God, who gives generously to all.
1:19–20	5:22	Slow to anger.
1:22	7:24	Put the word into practice.
2:5	5:3	Has not God chosen the poor?
2:10	5:19	Whoever keeps the whole law yet stumbles at just one point.
2:13	5:7	Mercy triumphs over judgment.
3:12	7:16	Can a fig tree bear olives, or a grapevine bear figs?
3:18	5:9	Those who seek peace sow in peace.
4:4	6:24	Friendship with the world is hatred toward God.
4:10	5:5	Humble yourselves before God, and God will lift you up.
5:2–3	6:19–20	Your wealth has rotted, and moths have eaten your clothes.
5:9	7:1	Do not grumble against each other, in order not to be judged.
5:10	5:12	Prophets as models of suffering.
5:12	5:34–37	Do not swear, either by heaven or earth.

In addition to the Sermon on the Mount, see James 1:6 // Matt. 21:21; 2:8 // 22:39; 3:1 // 23:8; 3:2ff. // 12:36–37; 5:7 // 24:13; 5:9 // 24:33. At times James is closer to Luke (James 2:5 // Luke 6:20) and apparently knew not Matthew's text but a text similar to the early source Q.

Such data support an early date for James. Were it from another author late in the first century we might expect it to reflect more closely the texts of Luke (80 C.E.) or Matthew (85 C.E.) rather than Q (60 C.E.).[6] The Matthew and Q parallels also indicate how James's Christology focuses primarily on Jesus' teaching and praxis rather than his titles (but see 1:1, and "our glorious Lord" in 2:1).

4. James's Theology for Dialogue with Other Religions

The nineteenth century witnessed the great missionary expansion of the church (in Africa and Asia), and in the twentieth century we have experienced an incomparable ecumenical movement involving dialogue between the Christian confessions. The new millennium, however, appears destined to be above all an epoch of dialogue between the world's religions and ideologies (see the expansion of Islam in traditionally Christian nations). For such a dialogue James offers us highly relevant perspectives and guidelines:

1. "Let everyone be quick to listen, slow to speak" (1:19). Therefore, the dialogue is not some "liberal" invention but a *biblical mandate* and should generally *precede* any effective proclamation of the good news.

2. James carefully describes *religion* (not a biblical category) in terms of a liberating praxis (1:26–27, visit "widows and orphans"), and thus transcends the Marxist critique of religion. See James's texts on good works, oppression, and God's coming judgment of oppressors.

3. The solidarity of James with the *poor* and his focus on *oppression* as the fundamental cause of their poverty (1:27; 2:6; 5:1–6) manifest his continuity with the most profound perceptions of the Hebrew scriptures (the Exodus paradigm). James thus avoids any tendency toward the Neoplatonic asceticism so common in many religious traditions, including Christianity.

4. James faithfully represents the *theocentric* (God-centered) theology of Jesus rather than the *Christocentric* theology of Paul (and most other New Testament authors). For any dialogue with people of other religions, such a point of departure (God, not Christ) has the obvious advantage of focusing first on shared elements of belief (note even Paul in Acts 17; cf. 1 Corinthians 1). We may thus question the traditional Protestant tendency of seeing the few references to Jesus in the book of James as an indication of a theological "weakness." Moreover, by simply calling him "Lord" (1:1; 2:1), James affirms the identity of Jesus with Yahweh, the Liberator God of the Exodus. Although Protestants, beginning with Luther, point out the lack of references in James to the cross, the resurrection, and justification by faith, James appears more concerned about the faith *of* Jesus in a God who does not discriminate against

---

6. Brown, *Introduction*, 734–36; Johnson, *The Letter of James*, 118–23.

the poor, the oppressed, and the marginalized than faith *in* Jesus (2:1; cf. Gal. 2:20).

5. James severely denounces the arrogance of the oppressors and affirms the basic *dignity of the oppressed,* the weak, and the marginalized (1:9–11; 2:1–13; 4:13–17; including sexual minorities, 2:21–25). Such support for and solidarity with the weak and oppressed constitute a fundamental element for authentic religious truth in any culture. (Consider the concern for self-image and dignity in contemporary psychology and in the liberation movements that focus on the pride of women, blacks, sexual minorities, the physically challenged, etc.)

6. James seeks to focus exclusively on the *goodness of God* (1:13, 16–17) instead of preserving the primitive concepts of divinities that incorporate elements of evil and the demonic (see the healing ministry of Jesus, Matthew 9–10; cf. the plagues of the Exodus supposedly sent by Yahweh). Like the good doctor in Jean-Paul Sartre's *The Plague,* Jesus is able to battle against illness because he affirms the pure goodness of his heavenly Parent and does not portray God as author of the plagues that afflict humanity.

7. In his *anthropology* James avoids the Pauline myth of Adam's fall (Rom. 5:12–21; cf. Genesis 3, which does not speak of a "fall" of the race but simply of the disobedience of two persons). Instead, James seeks to present a more realistic and balanced vision of good and evil in human nature (1:14–15; 3:9; 4:11–12). Such insistence on human responsibility for the evil that we ourselves commonly produce would appear more compatible with insights from modern science (biological evolution and evolutionary psychology).

8. By James's *democratization of wisdom* (1:5–8; 3:13–18) and insistence on the indisputable place of reason (3:17, *eupeithēs*), James avoids the extremes of bibliolatry and anti-intellectual fideism so common in traditional theologies. James's understanding of wisdom also subverts elitist tendencies in traditional education (3:1) and the sterile polemics that disguise themselves as "purer theologies" (3:17–4:3).

9. James portrays the *apocalyptic hope* of Jesus' second coming as God's judgment that puts an end to all oppression (5:1–6). He also counsels a militant patience (5:7–11) so disciplined that one can suffer violence without practicing it (5:6; see 3:18).

10. James avoids any concept of *evangelism* that involves aggressive proselytism. Rather, he insists on a praxiological approach (2:1–26) accompanied by honoring with pastoral encouragement all who begin to identify with the community of faith (1:27; 2:2; 5:19–20; cf. Jude 20–23; 1 John 5:16–17; Isa. 2:2–4). In many contexts Paul's more Christocentric but conflictive approach may be more appropriate. However, James, more a wise teacher than an apostle, enables us to appreciate the diversity that exists in the New Testament. He reminds us that the fundamental conflict always should be not with certain mistaken ideas but with oppressive and violent practices and the lies that seek to mask and rationalize them.

Bibliography

Religions

Ariarajah, S. Wesley. *The Bible and People of Other Faiths.* Maryknoll, N.Y.: Orbis, 1989.

Bosch, David J. *Transforming Mission: Paradigm Shifts in Theology of Mission.* Maryknoll, N.Y.: Orbis, 1991.

Esack, Farid. *Qur'an, Liberation and Pluralism: An Islamic Perspective of Interreligious Solidarity against Oppression.* Oxford: One World, 1997.

Knitter, Paul F. *No Other Name? A Critical Survey of Christian Attitudes toward the World Religions.* Maryknoll, N.Y.: Orbis, 1985.

James

Batten, Alicia. "An Asceticism of Resistance in James." In *Asceticism in the New Testament,* ed. Leif E. Vaage and Vincent L. Wimbush. New York: Routledge, 1999. See especially James's critique of the patronage system, 364–67.

Dowd, Sharyn. "James." In *The Women's Bible Commentary,* ed. Carol A. Newsom and Sharon H. Ringe, 460–61. Louisville: Westminster John Knox, 1992.

Eisenman, Robert. *James the Brother of Jesus.* London: Faber and Faber, 1997.

Johnson, Luke Timothy. *The Letter of James.* AB 37A. New York: Doubleday, 1995.

Laws, Sophie. "James, Epistle of." *ABD,* 3:621–28.

Maynard-Reid, Pedrito. *Poverty and Wealth in James.* Maryknoll, N.Y.: Orbis, 1987.

Moo, Douglas J. *The Letter of James.* Grand Rapids: Eerdmans, 2000.

Tamez, Elsa. *Santiago: Lectura latinoamericana de la epístola.* San José, Costa Rica: DEI, 1985.

———. *The Scandalous Message of James: Faith without Works Is Dead.* Trans. John Eagleson. New York: Crossroad, 1990.

———. "James." In *Searching the Scriptures,* vol. 2, *A Feminist Commentary,* ed. Elisabeth Schüssler Fiorenza, 381–91. New York: Crossroad, 1994.

Chapter 21

1 PETER

Persecuted Immigrants in a Xenophobic Empire?

Outline

1. Greeting, 1:1–2

   How Jesus' resurrection creates living hope for persecuted immigrants, 1:3–12

   The dignity and holy identity of (unclean) Gentile Christians, 1:13–25

   Homeless immigrants welcomed into God's household: coheirs with Israel, 2:1–10

2. Community responsibilities (*Haustafel*) in a patriarchal empire, 2:11–3:7

   Thwarting slander by good works to the poor, 2:11–12

   The subversive submission of community to authorities, 2:13–17

   The way of the cross for slaves under unbelieving masters, 2:18–25

   Subversive submission of wives, 3:1–7 (believing husbands' role, v. 7)

3. The way of the cross in the face of persecution and violence, 3:8–4:11

   Nonretaliation in the face of oppression and violence, 3:8–12

   Share the reason for your hope with those who oppress, 3:13–17

   Christ's exemplary suffering of oppression and triumph over violence, 3:18–22

   Spiritual warfare and Jesus' good news of peace, 4:1–6

   Inclusive community and spiritual gifts, 4:7–11

4. Oppressed like Christ, confident of God's liberating justice, 4:12–19

   Presbyter Peter to his fellow elders, to the young, and to all, 5:1–11

   Farewell: the kiss of love, 5:12–14

Perhaps no modern scholar would agree with the traditional Roman Catholic view that 1 Peter represents the first encyclical of the first pope. Scholars now commonly conclude that 1 Peter does come from the Petrine circle in Rome, but not before 80 C.E., at least fifteen years after Peter's martyrdom there (65

C.E.) and thus not from the hand of Peter himself (perhaps from Silvanus/Silas, 5:12). Thus, just as "Babylon" really is Rome (5:13), "Peter" is the symbolic name for the apostle's disciple who wrote the letter. Probably he included actual Petrine traditions but adapted them for persecuted Gentile Christian communities in five Roman Empire provinces (1:1) in what is now Turkey (Asia Minor).

Commentary

1. Oppressed Immigrants (Literal?) and Slaves and God's Liberating Justice

First Peter refers to converted Gentiles who formerly had sufficient means for an affluent and excessive self-indulgent lifestyle (4:3) and among whom some wives still had to resist temptations to flaunt wealth (3:3–4). Obviously a certain diversity of economic level is thus indicated, despite the impoverishment resulting from discrimination, oppression, and persecution. However, 1 Peter is addressed to "visiting strangers of the Dispersion" (1:1; cf. 1:17), whom the author later amplifies to "resident aliens and visiting strangers" (2:11). Here the question of selectivity in literal interpretation notably affects our understanding of the letter. Everyone recognizes that "Babylon" (5:13) is not literal but after 70 C.E. became a symbol or metaphor for Rome. Traditionally, however, "Peter" as author was taken literally, while "resident aliens and visiting strangers" were taken as metaphors for Christians everywhere, envisioned as pilgrims traveling in this world en route to their true heavenly home (cf. Heb. 11:13; 13:14). Today, in contrast, "Peter" commonly is interpreted as a symbol for a later author, while "resident aliens and visiting strangers" commonly are taken literally as immigrants who suffered the oppression common to their class due to the xenophobia (fear of strangers) dominant throughout history and in every culture.[1]

Paul Achtemeier agrees in rejecting the traditional Neoplatonic interpretation of the readers as "souls" exiled from their true heavenly home, but argues that in the context of the letter's controlling metaphor (Israel), persecuted Gentile converts are viewed as becoming like Israel, "exiled" from their surrounding pagan culture and thus suffering the same discrimination, oppression, and violence that literal immigrants and strangers suffer (4:4).[2] Whether 1 Peter addresses literally exiled immigrants or Gentile converts figuratively (but brutally) "exiled" and persecuted by their society, the letter places great emphasis on the injustices, oppression, and violence the recipients suffered. In addition to the many general references to the persecution suffered by the recipients (1:6; 4:1, 12–19; 5:8–10), note especially

---

1. John H. Elliott, *A Home for the Homeless: A Social-Scientific Criticism of 1 Peter, Its Situation and Strategy* (Philadelphia: Fortress, 1990), 714; cf. Moses Chin, "A Heavenly Home for the Homeless: Aliens and Strangers in 1 Peter," *Tyndale Bulletin* 42 (1991): 94–112.

2. Paul J. Achtemeier, *1 Peter,* Hermeneia (Minneapolis: Fortress, 1996), 55–57, 71, 173–75; see also Thomas D. Hanks, "Poor/Poverty (New Testament)," *ABD*, 5:420.

- 2:19, *adikōs,* oppression of household slaves suffering unjustly
- 3:9–12, citing Ps. 34:12–16, where the poor experience oppression and liberation
- 3:13–14, referring to →Matt. 5:6, 10–12, solidarity with the oppressed
- 3:16–18, Christ's suffering on behalf of the unjust/oppressors, *adikōn*
- 5:3, religious leaders who "lord it over" their flock
- 5:13, Babylon = Rome, the oppressive empire

In such a context of persecution, oppression, poverty, and violence, God's justice is understood preeminently as a liberating justice to be decisively expressed in a final judgment that will put an end to all oppression while rescuing, vindicating, and rewarding the oppressed (1:17; 2:14, 23–24; 3:12–14, 18; 4:6, 17–19; →James 5:1–6).

Some believe that the reference to "an inheritance that is imperishable, undefiled, and unfading, kept in heaven for you" (1:4) supports the traditional metaphorical interpretation of pilgrims making their way toward heaven. But in the early Christian apocalyptic eschatology the new Jerusalem descends finally to earth.[3] Traditionally the misinterpretation of 1 Peter as a Neoplatonic document portraying the Christian soul's "salvation" in its pilgrimage towards its true heavenly home has been supported by the common mistranslation of the Greek *psychē* as "soul," which occurs six times in the book (cf. psychology, "the word concerning the soul or life"). Both NIV and NRSV commonly mistranslate *psychē* as "soul" (1:9, 22; 2:11, 25), but in 3:20 they correctly translate it as "people/persons," and in 4:19 as "themselves," properly reflecting the anthropology we would expect from a Jewish writer influenced by the Hebrew Bible and Septuagint Greek.[4] Latin American theologians have emphasized that the mission of the church is not to "save souls" but to bring an integral liberation (forgiveness, healing, liberation from oppression) to the whole person, introducing them by baptism into viable communities. Thus, 1 Peter 1:9, with its reference to the Hebrew prophets, is best translated "obtaining the goal of your faith, the *integral liberation* of your *lives*" ("salvation" understood as the future apocalyptic "integral/cosmic liberation" in 1:5, 9–10; 2:2; see 2 Pet. 3:13; Revelation 17–19).

First Peter thus probably addresses communities with a considerable nucleus of literal exiles and immigrants but may well apply the terms metaphorically to these communities as embracing other elements marginalized and rejected by the dominant pagan culture. Abraham, father to both Israel and the church, was an immigrant (Genesis 12); the Israelites became immigrant slave laborers in Egypt (Exodus); and after Babylon destroyed Jerusalem (586 B.C.E.), most Jews became exiles. Not surprisingly, then, Israel's "Apostolic Creed" (Deut. 26:4–9) emphasized their immigrant roots, and the law repeatedly commanded that justice and mercy be shown to immigrants,

3. Achtemeier, *1 Peter,* 175 (see 2 Pet. 3:13, from the Petrine school, perhaps a decade later).
4. Ibid., 104.

widows, and orphans (Exod. 22:21; 23:9; Lev. 19:33–34; Deut. 24:17–18, 27:19). In Jerusalem at Pentecost we find representatives from three of the five provinces that 1 Peter names (1:1; Pontus, Cappadocia, and Asia in Acts 2:9), and soon persecution arose that forced many believing Jews to immigrate (Acts 8:1–4). In Romans 16 Paul greets twenty-eight immigrants in the churches whom he had known elsewhere (see especially Priscilla and Aquila). As marginalized and oppressed, in many places immigrants are among the first to respond to the good news (note Rahab in Joshua 2; cf. Matt. 21:31). Early Christian communities often developed from a nucleus with a large proportion of Jews and immigrants. First Peter's extension of the terms metaphorically to entire communities was thus quite natural and appropriate.

2. *Xenophobia, Homophobia, and Sexual Minorities*

Throughout human history we find immigrants as strangers accused of importing strange sexual practices. The Hebrew Bible itself warns against certain sexual abominations as typical of the Egyptians and Canaanites (Lev. 18:3, 24–30; 20:23). In European and Latin American history we find descriptions of "sodomy" as a vice imported by the Italians, the French, the English, and various indigenous peoples. In Africa homosexuality commonly has been attributed by one tribe to another, to the Arabs, or to Europeans and Americans.[5] John Boswell has demonstrated how homophobia and anti-Semitism developed in the twelfth century, eventually culminating in the Nazi Holocaust that killed thousands of homosexuals and other minorities together with some six million Jews.[6]

In 1 Peter the apostle is portrayed as accompanied only by Silvanus/Silas (5:12) and his spiritual "son" Mark (5:13), both unmarried. In the entire New Testament, James, Jude (Jesus' brothers), and Peter are the only married authors (see 1 Cor. 9:5), but Peter's wife (unnamed in the New Testament) is not mentioned in 1–2 Peter. If these two letters were not written by Peter personally, then James and Jude would be the only books in the New Testament written by married authors. But even if Peter, James, and Jude really wrote the books that bear their names, only 5 percent of the New Testament would come from married authors, while 95 percent would come from sexual minorities. The emphasis in 1 Peter on the churches as a "household of God," then, has a special significance not only for persons who were literally pilgrims and immigrants (see Elliott, note 1 above) but also for persons who did not have literal spouses and children. A new household ("family"), the community of the disciples of the unmarried Jesus, replaces patriarchal households in God's cosmic liberation project (Mark 3:31–35; Rom. 8:18–39).

For the "unclean" Gentile immigrants whom this letter addresses, many of them sexual minorities (unmarried), 1 Peter focuses on the people of God

5. Stephen O. Murray and Will Roscoe, eds., *Boy-Wives and Female Husbands: Studies of African Homosexualities* (New York: St. Martin's Press, 1998), xi–xxii, 267.

6. John Boswell, *Christianity, Social Tolerance, and Homosexuality* (Chicago: University of Chicago Press, 1980), 15.

as a "spiritual house" (2:5) and "household of God" (4:17). As in the entire Bible, and contrary to dominant modern ideologies reflected in some translations (such as the NIV), 1 Peter never talks about "family" but about "house(hold)s." In accord with this focus on the "house," 1 Peter uses other words of the same root: "construction of a building" (2:5), with a foundation (5:10) and "house servants" (2:18). Even when 1 Peter addresses married couples (3:7), his use of the phrase "live in the same house/under the same roof" (*synoikountes*) reminds us that it was common to include slaves, widows, orphans and other unmarried relatives under such a roof. Such couples did not live alone or only with their own children. In God's new community, the unmarried Jesus' new household, persecuted immigrants without shelter could find a home and feel accepted. God's people throughout the world constitute a "brotherly/sisterly household" (*adelphotēs,* 2:17; 5:9 [only in 1 Peter]) whose principal characteristic is mutual love (1:22; 2:17; 3:8; cf. 4:8–9; 5:14). This brotherly/sisterly love, 1 Peter reminds us, implies respect for privacy rights (4:15, "meddler," NIV). Even if the Greek word *allotriepiskopos* is not interpreted as one who pries into other people's affairs, but as one who commits fraudulent acts ("mischief maker," NRSV), other texts insist on respect for privacy (2 Thess. 3:11; 1 Tim. 5:13; Luke 12:13–14; see Jesus' "messianic secret" in Mark; cf. modern privacy invasions by state, technology, and media).[7]

Despite the sexual minority status of many in 1 Peter and the bias reflected in many translations, the letter says remarkably little about sexual sins. When allusion is made to the Ten Commandments, the condemnation refers to murder and theft but not adultery (4:15). When the recipients' former pagan lifestyle is recalled, three terms refer to the use or abuse of alcohol but only one possibly to accompanying sexual misbehavior (4:3–4; *epithymiais* may simply mean "desire" or "covet," not necessarily sexual "lust"). For 1 Peter, angels and infants may experience strong desire without sin, but the author emphasizes the danger of undisciplined desire that gives rise to unjust acts that harm others (1:12–14, 22; 2:1–3, 11; 4:1–5; 5:2–3; →James).

3. Submissive Wives, the "Weaker Vessel"?

Much controversy in 1 Peter's theology stems from its domestic code (*Haustafel,* "household table"), which exhorts slaves to submit to their masters (2:18–25) and women to their husbands (heads of extended households, 3:1–6; cf. Col. 3:18–4:1; Eph. 5:22–6:9; Titus 2:1–10). The absence of any mention of believing masters and the presence of only one verse addressing believing husbands (3:7) may indicate that 1 Peter was written to communities in which immigrants, poor slaves, and women constituted the basic nucleus. Such New Testament household codes commonly have been interpreted as promoting a conformity with the oppressive patriarchal world and as undermining the equality and radical justice of early Christian communities (Gal. 3:28). However, Paul Achtemeier points out that the intention of the letter

7. Achtemeier, *1 Peter,* 310–13.

and its domestic code was not to urge accommodation, but rather, to warn *against* accommodation, even though it meant suffering.[8]

Although "wives" occupy the second place in the household code (3:1–6), no woman is specifically named in 1 Peter. Because of the general exhortation to submit to imperial authorities (2:13–17; →Rom. 13:1–7), in the case of 1 Peter some prefer to speak of 2:13–3:7 as a "community code" (not limited to patriarchal households). However, when it refers to Rome as "Babylon" (5:13), 1 Peter at the same time anticipates the prophetic denunciation against imperial injustice, oppression, and violence in Revelation (13; 17–19). Paul Achtemeier helpfully delineates 1 Peter's critique of the Roman imperial state as midway between Romans 13 (imperial rulers bear divine authority) and Revelation 13 (the Roman Empire as antichrist to be resisted).[9] First Peter's call for tactical submission to purely human authorities bears witness to the diversity in biblical teaching stemming from changing historical contexts (increasing persecution: Romans, 58 C.E.; 1 Peter, 80 C.E.; Revelation, 95 C.E.).

The strategy of 1 Peter concerning immigrants, slaves, and women who suffer oppression is dialectic: first the letter seeks to encourage, strengthen, and empower them in their dignity (1:1–2:10), but later it calls them to voluntary and subversive submission relative to the dominant imperial and patriarchal structures (2:11–4:18). This submission is not presented as a universal "ethic" but as a subversive strategy or tactic in the face of a concrete oppressive situation and as a wise expression of Christian liberty in this historical context (2:16).

Women and people of color properly have protested against the traditional use of this letter to bolster oppressive structures. But we should not confuse later abuse of the letter with its original intent. The exhortations to submission occur as a tactic to dignify and empower the new community (1:1–2:10) in an empire at that moment invincible (see Rev. 13:4) and as a part of a canon of books that address other historical contexts and give us very different advice (cf. Exodus, and prophetic denunciations of oppression).

4. *Anti-Judaism in First Peter?*

Although Peter's ministry was directed mainly toward his Jewish compatriots (Gal. 2:7), 1 Peter addresses predominantly Gentile communities (2:12; 4:3), perhaps reflecting Peter's decisive role with Cornelius (Acts 10–11; 15). Surprisingly, however, the letter speaks of these Gentiles who professed faith in Jesus as Messiah as if they had become Jews. The letter's controlling metaphor speaks of its Gentile recipients now identified with Israel: they had participated in the Exodus; they now live in the "Dispersion" (1:1); and they are now called to live as God's holy people (1:16; cf. Lev. 19:2), heirs to Israel's titles and privileges (2:9–10).[10] This perspective may stem from the fact that Christians of this era were still viewed simply as one more sect within Judaism (like the

8. Ibid., 51–57.
9. Ibid., 180–82.
10. Ibid., 69–73.

Pharisees, the Sadducees, and the Qumran community). The letter comes from the community of believers in Rome ("Babylon," 5:13), which now appears to be *one* community, not several as earlier (58 C.E.) when Paul wrote Romans 16 (cf. Hebrews 13). In 1 Peter the common oppressor and persecutor of both Jews and new Gentile converts is "Babylon" (Rome). The letter gives no evidence of the type of conflict between traditional Jews and those others who, together with certain Gentiles, had followed the "way" of Rabbi Jesus (cf. Galatians; Philippians; Romans; Matthew; John). First Peter speaks serenely to the Gentiles as heirs of all the privileges of Israel without any suggestion of having taken such privileges from the Jews.[11] The letter warns against unbelief and the lack of commitment but without specifying "Jews" as being especially guilty (2:4–8; cf. Peter's words in Acts 4:11–12) (→Ephesians; Romans 9–11).

5. *The Weak, Physically Challenged, and Sick*

First Peter's recipients share with all humanity the weakness of the flesh (1:24), and prior to their conversion they had lived in "darkness" (2:9; that is, as "the blind"). In addition, however, as immigrants and not Roman citizens in the empire they were socially and economically weak, and as a minority sect within Judaism their weakness was even greater. Furthermore, since so many were slaves and women, they commonly suffered violence, persecution, and oppression. Violent persecution and slave beatings obviously would have left many wounded and physically challenged. Specific references to such people are lacking, but the healing of wounds (2:24, "with his wounds we are healed") is a metaphor that undoubtedly reflected the literal reality of many of the letter's recipients.

6. *Redemptive Suffering: Jesus' and Ours*

First Peter continually reminds readers how the kind of oppression, persecution, and violence they suffered was first suffered by Jesus, in whose steps they are to follow (1:2, 11, 18–21; 2:4, 7, 21–25; 3:18; 4:1, 13; 5:1). Like other New Testament books, 1 Peter offers a diversity of perspectives and metaphors to remind readers how the oppression and violence Jesus suffered on the cross has redemptive power of cosmic significance. 1 Peter portrays Jesus' death as

- a *payment* of great price for the redemption and liberation of slaves (1:18–19)
- a *weakness* ("flesh") that, with divine help, triumphs over all forces of evil (3:18–19)
- an efficacious *sacrifice* to clean sin's interior filth (1:2)
- a *demonstration of solidarity* of love that we should follow and imitate in our relationships with the weak and oppressed (2:21–23)
- the suffering of *punishment* by an innocent person (2:24a)
- and as *wounds* that heal us (2:24b).

---

11. Ibid. See also J. Ramsey Michaels, *1 Peter*, WBC 49 (Dallas: Word, 1988), xlix–lv.

The interpretation of Jesus' death as a cultic sacrifice to expiate sin and propitiate God's wrath has provoked strong criticism, especially from many feminist and African American theologians. They object that powerful oppressors always promote sacrifices on the part of the oppressed while refusing to sacrifice any of their own privileges. We may recognize that certain biblical images of suffering (Abraham sacrificing his son Isaac, or the propitiation of divine wrath) carry such high risks of misinterpretation and abuse that often they are best avoided. However, if our fear of possible abuse of such texts prompts us to oppose all language that speaks of sacrifice, then the sacrificial commitment and solidarity of figures like Martin Luther King, Che Guevara, Nelson Mandela, and Mother Teresa also are disqualified. Like Jesus in the Gospels, 1 Peter does not call its readers simply to self-fulfillment in seeking comfortable and prosperous lives, in the style of much popular modern religion. Despite the diversity of interpretations and emphases, we cannot eliminate the centrality of Jesus' cross without undermining the Christian faith. 1 Peter is one of several New Testament books that makes this especially clear (see Job, Psalm 22, and Isaiah 53 in the Hebrew Bible).

Two texts in 1 Peter used to provoke much discussion (3:18–20 and 4:6), and commonly were used to support the phrase in the Apostle's Creed "He descended into hell" (cf. Matt. 27:52; Eph. 4:8; Phil. 2:10; Col. 2:15). Now, however, the "proclamation to the spirits" (3:19) is taken as referring to Jesus after his resurrection, pronouncing condemnation to angels/evil spirits (Gen. 6:1–4). Interpreted thus, 3:18–20 has nothing to do with 4:6, where the evangelized "dead" are believers (Israelites or Christians) who died before the second coming (see HCSB notes; cf. 1 Thess. 4:13–18).[12]

In opposition to "Babylon" (the cruel and oppressive Roman Empire), 1 Peter's subversive strategy is to consolidate and strengthen the new base communities. Notably, therefore, the letter that represents the Petrine tradition from Rome does not speak of Peter as "first pope," with resplendent cardinals, privileged Vatican City, hierarchy of archbishops, bishops, and priests, and with countless properties throughout the world. The "apostle Peter" of this letter speaks through his later disciple with subversive humility, someone who is but one "elder/presbyter" among many (5:1–2), fervently opposed to all ecclesiastical tyranny (5:3), and addressing Gentile ecclesiastical communities where all members are "priests and kings" (2:9) with their gifts and abilities for ministry (4:10–11).

First Peter shares the common New Testament apocalyptic perspective that "the end of all things is near" (4:7), when Jesus will return to consummate his universal order of justice and peace (1:5–9). After two thousand years we cannot interpret literally such words about the imminence of Jesus' coming. However, in contexts of oppression, torture, and pain we can maintain the

12. Raymond Brown, *An Introduction to the New Testament* (New York: Doubleday, 1997), 714–16; Achtemeier, *1 Peter*, 252–62, 290–91; William J. Dalton, *Christ's Proclamation to the Spirits: A Study of 1 Peter 3:18–4:6*, Analecta Biblica 23 (Rome: Pontifical Biblical Institute, 1965; rev. ed., 1989).

hope that "*after you have suffered for a little while,* the God of all grace, who has called you to share the eternal glory in Christ, will personally restore, support, strengthen, and establish you" (5:10), so "to God be the power forever and ever. Amen" (5:11).

With its final command to express mutual greetings with a "kiss of love" (5:14; mouth to mouth, including males to males in ancient culture), 1 Peter concludes with a kind of integration of spirituality and sexuality.

Bibliography

Achtemeier, Paul J. *1 Peter.* Hermeneia. Minneapolis: Fortress, 1996.

Balch, David L. *Let Wives Be Submissive: The Domestic Code in 1 Peter.* Society of Biblical Literature Monograph Series 26. Chico, Calif.: Scholars Press, 1981.

Boring, Eugene M. *1 Peter.* Abingdon New Testament Commentaries. Nashville: Abingdon, 1999.

Corley, Kathleen E. "1 Peter." *Searching the Scriptures,* vol. 2, *A Feminist Commentary,* ed. Elisabeth Schüssler Fiorenza, 349–60. New York: Crossroad, 1994.

Davids, Peter H. *The First Epistle of Peter.* NICNT. Grand Rapids: Eerdmans, 1990.

Dowd, Sharyn. "1 Peter." In *The Women's Bible Commentary,* ed. Carol A. Newsom and Sharon Ringe, 462–64. Louisville: Westminster John Knox, 1998.

Elliott, John H. *A Home for the Homeless: A Social-Scientific Criticism of 1 Peter, Its Situation and Strategy.* Philadelphia: Fortress, 1990.

———. "Peter, First Epistle of." *ABD,* 5:269–78.

Martin, Clarice J. "The *Haustafeln* [Codes for Houses/Families] in African American Biblical Interpretation: 'Free Slaves' and 'Subordinate Women.' " In *Stony the Road We Trod: African American Biblical Interpretation,* ed. Cain Hope Felder, 206–31. Minneapolis: Fortress Press, 1991.

Michaels, J. Ramsey. *1 Peter.* WBC 49. Dallas: Word, 1988.

Perkins, Pheme. *Peter: Apostle for the Whole Church.* Columbia: University of South Carolina Press, 1994.

Ramírez Kidd, José E. *Alterity and Identity in Israel: The "ger" in the Old Testament.* Beihefte zur Zeitschrift für die alttestamentliche Wissenschaft 283. Berlin and New York: W. de Gruyter, 1999.

Talbert, Charles H., ed. *Perspectives on First Peter.* Macon, Ga.: Mercer University Press, 1986.

Chapter 22

2 PETER

Christian Virtues for a Renewed Green World

Outline

Greeting, 1:1–2

1. Two transfigurations (and God's liberating justice):

   of Christians: the virtues, gifts of God, 1:3–11

   of Jesus: testimony of Peter and the prophecies, 1:12–21

2. False teachers (and God's punishment of oppressors), 2:1–22 (// →Jude 4–19)

3. Jesus' second coming: why the delay? 3:1–16

Exhortation and doxology, 3:17–18

Commentary

Almost all scholars now conclude that 2 Peter does not originate from Peter himself but from an author after the martyrdom of the apostle in Rome (64/65 C.E.). However, even if 2 Peter does not come directly from the hand of Peter, it may well include traditions from the apostle preserved in Petrine circles in Rome, where it probably was written around 80–90 C.E. First Peter uses the place name "Babylon" as a symbol and metaphor for Rome (5:13; cf. Rev. 17:5, 18). Second Peter uses the personal name of Simon Peter to communicate the apostolic message to a later generation, a literary procedure common to the era (see Mark 9:13; Matt. 11:13–14; 17:12; cf. the rejection of literalism in John 1:21; Luke 1:17). The language and teaching of 2 Peter is not similar to that of 1 Peter. However, 2 Pet. 2:1–3:3 is characterized by a close parallelism of ideas and expressions with the letter of Jude, which was probably written before 2 Peter and served as its source. The person who wrote 2 Peter, claiming the name and spirit of Simeon Peter (including the Hebrew name Simeon), sought to be faithful to the apostle's teaching but aimed to communicate the Petrine tradition to communities, perhaps in Asia Minor, threatened more by their own greed and seducers within, rather than oppressors without.

1. Hebrew Apocalypticism, Christianity, and Hellenism

Second Peter adapts the very Jewish perspective of Jude to more Hellenized congregations of a later generation. Specifically, 2 Peter *juxtaposes Hebrew apocalypticism with the Hellenism of a postapostolic generation,* which gives the letter its special character.[1] This Hellenism of 2 Peter is manifest in 1:1–11, where Hellenistic readers would have found especially appealing the emphasis on sharing the divine nature (v. 4), eight virtues, including knowledge (vv. 5–8) and escape from the world (v. 4) to enter into Christ's eternal realm (v. 11). The relationship between this Hellenism and the Hebrew and Christian traditions is especially evident in the list of eight virtues in 1:5–7, where the typically Greek virtues (goodness, knowledge, self-control, perseverance, and piety) occur in a list that begins with faith and ends with mutual affection and love, virtues characteristic of the Judeo-Christian tradition. The Greek virtue of knowledge (vv. 5–6) becomes supremely the Hebrew "knowledge of God" and the Christian "knowledge of Jesus Christ" (1:2–3, 8; see below). This list seeks to avoid creating a dichotomy between Christian praxis (practice) and the admirable aspects of the lives of other human beings created in God's image.

Similarly, a Greek anthropology may be suggested by the concept of the body as a "tent" to be left behind at death (1:13–14, NIV), the reference to Lot as a "tortured soul" (2:7–8), and the description of animals as "irrational" (2:12, 22; cf. man [but not woman] as a rational being in Aristotle). The Hebrew concept of time in 3:8 (Ps. 90:4) has a Hellenistic counterpart in 3:18 ("the day of eternity"). Above all, Hellenistic influence is evident in the consigning of sinning angels to "Tartarus" (2:4), and in 1:4, which affirms that we "may become participants of the divine nature," language lending itself to an impersonal pantheistic interpretation but probably intended only to stress gaining immortality.

However, the apocalyptic hope of Jesus' Parousia has not disappeared in 2 Peter, since the letter is directed to readers who still expect to witness Jesus' second coming (1:19; 3:14). The apparent delay in the final judgment of oppressors is not a sign of God's weakness but of a goodness, love, and patience that seeks the repentance of all persons (3:8–9; see below).

2. The Oppressed, Weak, and Poor

2.1. "The Way." Although markedly more Hellenistic than Jude, the Hebrew character of 2 Peter is evident in its avoidance of the Greek philosophical categories of "ethics" and "morals" and its insistence in the priority of praxis, describing life in terms of a "way" (→1–3 John, on the "way" and walking in the light/truth). "The way" is a favorite biblical metaphor for divine actions in history and for the praxis of God's people and of individuals in collaboration

1. Richard Bauckham, *Jude, 2 Peter,* WBC 50 (Dallas: Word, 1983), 228–35. Although many allusions to the Hebrew Bible may be detected, 2 Peter contains only three citations: 2:22 = Prov. 26:11; 3:8 = Ps. 90:4; 3:13 = Isa. 65:17.

with God's purpose and project in history. In 2 Peter the way is characterized by "truth" (2:2) and as the "straight path" of liberating justice (2:15, 21; cf. Balaam's "way of exploitation/oppression," *adikia,* 2:15; the violent "way of Cain," Jude 11).

2.2. Oppression as Violence. While Jude (v. 5) maintained the fundamental character of the Exodus paradigm, in 2 Pet. 2:5 the flood story replaces the Exodus. Second Peter thus reverts to the chronological order of Genesis 6 and 19: (1) sinning angels, 6:1–4; (2) flood, 6:5ff., (3) Sodom, 19. However, just as the sin of oppression was fundamental in Exodus, so violence (the extreme expression of oppression in the Hebrew Bible) is the fundamental sin provoking the judgment of the flood and Sodom (2 Peter 2:5–6). This connection tends to be lost in translations that prefer to translate the Greek root *aseb-* weakly as "impious/ungodly." However, in the Genesis narrative, the cause of the flood clearly is "violence" (Hebrew *ḥāmās,* 6:11, 13). The Septuagint here rendered "violence" by *adikia* ("injustice, oppression"), but in the Septuagint 2 Peter's preferred *aseb-* root also commonly translates the Hebrew term for "violence."[2]

2.3. Oppression as Injustice. In addition to linking the violent oppression that brought on the divine judgments of the flood and Sodom's destruction, 2 Peter also refers to oppression with the Greek root *adik-* ("injustice, oppression," 2:9, 13 [twice], 15). Especially instructive is the affirmation that "The Liberator God knows how to deliver the pious from trials and to keep oppressors (*adikous*) under punishment until the day of judgment" (2:9). Second Peter 2:13 indicates that the false teachers are characterized by injustice and oppression and will be paid back with harm for the injustice they have done. 2 Peter 2:15 qualifies Balaam's sin as "*loving* injustice/oppression," suggesting that even when we "love" (*agapaō*) this may prove sinful if wrongly directed. Second Peter 2:7 describes just Lot as "being oppressed" (*kataponoumenon,* 2:7), a word used elsewhere describing an Israelite slave whom Moses delivered from violence (Acts 7:24; cf. Exod. 2:11), thus reminding us of Lot's immigrant, marginalized status in Sodom.

2.4. Oppression and Covetousness. Injustice and oppression are also related to 2 Peter's repeated condemnations of greed (*epithymia,* 1:4; 2:10; 3:3; *pleonexia,* 2:3, 14), prohibited in the last of the Ten Commandments (Exod 20:17; Deut. 5:21). After the just distribution of land to all (Joshua 13–21), to covet and plot to acquire a neighbor's property was condemned as injustice and oppression. Such sin is also characterized as "excess" (*aselgeia,* 2:2, 7, 18), especially with reference to violence, oppression, and harm to neighbor in the sexual sphere. Adultery was a consequence of coveting a neighbor's wife. Originally it was conceived as a sin involving the sexual property of another male in a patriarchal society, since a woman was the property of her father

---

2. Jacques Pons, *L'oppression dans l'Ancien Testament* (Paris: Letouzey et Ané, 1981), 166; H. Haag, "chāmās [Violence]," *Theological Dictionary of the Old Testament,* ed. G. Johannes Botterweck and Helmer Ringgren, vol. 4 (Grand Rapids: Eerdmans, 1980), 478–87.

or husband. For 2 Peter the most fundamental sin is precisely such "greed" or "covetousness" (1:4), whether of humans generally, or perhaps interpreting Adam and Eve's original sin. Pride leads us to imagine that we may freely appropriate our neighbor's goods, leaving them deprived of life's necessities (see 1:3).

2.5. Justice That Liberates from Oppression. In the light of the emphases on the "way," violence, injustice, and oppression, in 2 Peter justice basically refers—as in the entire Bible—to liberating justice exercised on behalf of the weak and oppressed (2:7–9; the Exodus paradigm). Although 2 Peter substitutes the flood for Jude's reference (v. 5) to the Exodus, liberating justice flows as a powerful stream through 2 Peter (1:1, 13; 2:5, 7, 8 [twice], 21; 3:13 [a total of eight *dik-* terms]—"righteousness" is the misleading common English translation; note also four references to oppression/injustice with *adik-* terms in 2:9, 13, 15). God's liberating justice is linked to the "equality" (*isotimon*) in status enjoyed by later Gentile readers in the inclusive community, where they share equal status with Jewish apostles like Peter (1:1). Noah heralds God's liberating justice that delivered him and his household from their violent contemporaries (2:5). Lot's justice and solidarity (2:7–8) were expressed in his hospitality to the visiting angels and by his efforts to protect them from the attempted gang rape by the men of Sodom (→below, "women").

2.6. Liberating Justice and the Knowledge of God. Second Peter thus appears to reflect Jeremiah's teaching (22:13–16): to practice liberating justice manifest in solidarity with the weak and oppressed is "*to know* Yahweh," the Liberator God. To refuse to practice liberating justice results in not being acknowledged and honored by God (see Matt. 7:21–23; 25:31–46). Personal knowledge of God and Christ in 2 Peter, then, is closely related to the praxis of liberating justice (1:2–3, 8; 2:20–21; 3:18). Such knowledge is not equivalent to the later Gnostic emphasis on knowing secret truths, nor is it equivalent to the concept of "knowing" orthodox doctrines, the common emphasis in so much of traditional Christianity. For 2 Peter, fully knowing Jesus Christ involves following faithfully the way of liberating justice (2:20–21). And just as Isaiah envisioned the new earth as characterized as becoming "full of the knowledge of the Liberator God as the waters cover the sea" (11:9), so 2 Peter anticipates a new earth characterized by liberating justice (3:13).[3]

2.7. Liberating Justice and the Hope of the Poor. Second Peter's Jewish roots are clearly evident in its "materialism" and its emphasis on God's promises (1:4; 3:13) that describe the historic divine project: a just new order for the world. Such an order is not an escape from this world to live in a "spiritual" (in the later sense of "nonmaterial") celestial sphere, but "a renewed heaven *and a renewed earth*...characterized by liberating justice" (3:13; Matt. 5:3,

---

3. A sad but revealing indication of the unbiblical character of much theology that prides itself on being "conservative evangelical" is the fact that James I. Packer, a highly respected scholar, could devote an entire book to the theme of *Knowing God* (Downers Grove, Ill.: InterVarsity, 1973), yet make no reference to doing justice—or to Jeremiah 22:13–16. Packer's well-written book has been considered an evangelical "classic," widely circulated for decades.

5; Rom. 4:13; 8:20–22). This Hebrew apocalyptic hope is distinct from the individualistic and spiritualized hope of elitist Greek philosophy (the liberation of the spiritual "soul" from the material body).

In the light of 2 Peter's reaffirmation of the fulfillment of God's promises regarding material hopes for a new earth, we may properly understand what the implied author means by speaking of his death as an "exodus" (*exodos,* 1:15). This exodus involves a metaphorical use of the literal exodus referred to by Jude (v. 5), but in the context of 2 Peter's apocalyptic hope for a new earth, it cannot be interpreted as an individualistic, spiritualizing reductionism. Rather, it must be understood as similar to Paul's affirmations of individual immortality, as an anticipation (not a substitute) of the resurrection of the body (Phil. 1:21–23; 1 Cor. 15:50–57; 2 Cor. 5:1–10; cf. Jesus' death as an Exodus, Luke 9:31). Modern readers will recognize that 2 Peter includes in its vision mythical elements concerning the creation of the world out of water and a future cosmic conflagration that destroys the "elements" (3:5–10).[4]

On dealing with the false teachers (2:1), 2 Peter in 2:1–3:3 uses the letter of Jude as a source but adapts it for the later historical context. The false teachers in 2 Peter's churches appeared to have much in common with elitist Epicurean philosophy, which denied life beyond the grave and divine judgment and promoted the search for pleasure (hedonism, 2:13) in this life. Second Peter omits the references in Jude concerning aspirations of possessing the Spirit and receiving revelations (Jude 8, 19) and also the reference to a perversion of grace (Jude 4). The characteristic that the false teachers in 2 Peter seem to have in common with those of Jude is covetousness (Jude 16, 18). The elitist false teachers in 2 Peter demonstrate an eschatological skepticism that led them to mock God's promises to the poor (2 Pet. 3:3–4, 13; 1:11, "richly"; see Matt. 5:3 // Luke 6:20) and to reject God's judgment against oppressors (2:9).

Second Peter responds that the same God who judged the world in the past (2:3–16) will judge present oppressors (2:17–22). Delay in God's judgment does not signal divine weakness but reveals the patience and love of God, who desires that all repent (3:8–10). Surprisingly, in both 2 Peter and Jude the false teachers are present at the very heart of the community, regularly participating in the Lord's Supper. Despite the strong language against them, however, 2 Peter does not recommend that the false teachers be expelled from the community (see Matthew 13; cf. Paul in 1 Corinthians 5), but even appears to maintain hope for their repentance (3:9).

3. Women and "Early Catholicism"

Some feminist scholars criticize 2 Peter for not giving explicit attention to women in the text. True, 2 Peter focuses on the transfiguration of Jesus, where he appeared in a glorified form, together with Moses and Elijah, and was

4. Bauckham, *Jude, 2 Peter,* 302; Jerome Neyrey, *2 Peter, Jude,* AB 37C (New York: Doubleday, 1993), 240–45.

accompanied by three male apostles (1:16–18; see Luke 9:28–35). However, 2 Peter does not focus on the transfiguration in order to exclude women but because this event, witnessed by Peter, strengthens hope for a time of crisis, presenting Jesus as already installed by God and at work to establish God's just new order. In addition, the Hebrew scriptures included not only the Law ("of Moses") and the Prophets (such as Elijah) but also a third component, the sapiential (wisdom) Writings, where the feminine figure of Sophia/Wisdom is central. (See also the women prophets in the Bible and in the early churches.) Any reader of the Gospels will recall how the male apostles abandoned Jesus at the end (see Peter's triple denial), while the women disciples were faithful and end up proclaiming the good news to the male apostles.

In the style of Luke, 2 Peter (2:22) balances the proverb of a dog (masculine gender in Greek; see Prov. 26:11) with a sow (feminine gender in Greek). In addition, 2 Peter (2:15–16) points out how God used a donkey (neuter in Greek but feminine in Hebrew in the narrative in Num. 22:21–35) to reprimand the unfaithfulness of the prophet Balaam. Notably, in Numbers the donkey (as so many women in all ages) accuses the man of violence against her: "What have I done to you, that you have struck me these three times?" (Num. 22:28). It does not require much imagination to see in the donkey, which according to its animal nature should be irrational (2 Pet. 2:12) and mute (see 1 Cor. 14:34–35), the figure of abused women, whose voices demand justice, like the blood of Abel.

Although some scholars consider 2 Peter to be an example of "early Catholicism" with its institutionalization of the faith, in fact the letter contains not a word about ecclesiastical offices. Instead, the direct and personal knowledge of God is open to all (3:18), and all may even become partakers of the divine nature (1:4; see John 1:9). The only leadership 2 Peter mentions is that of the prophets and teachers, who could be either false or authentic, men or women (2:1). Second Peter speaks of certain uninformed and weak persons in the faith who "twist" the Scriptures, which by that time included some of Paul's letters (3:15–16), but does not single out women as especially prone to misinterpret Paul. This reference to a collection of Paul's letters represents a first step in the formation of the New Testament canon. (Second Peter's elimination of references in Jude to two noncanonical Jewish books is also pertinent.) Although Peter himself suffered a rebuke from Paul (Gal. 2:11–20), 2 Peter insists on the fundamental unity between Paul (properly interpreted) and Peter. The letter insists that Paul's teaching concerning justification by faith and Christian freedom should not be misinterpreted ("twisted") as libertinism.

Many understand 2 Pet. 1:20 to insist on the need for an orthodox, official interpretation by church *authorities* ("early Catholicism"), and they oppose the right of *individuals* to interpret the scriptures according to personal criteria. However, 1:20 may refer to the *origin* of prophecies, not to their *interpretation:* "no prophecy of scripture came about by the prophet's own interpretation. For prophecy never had its origin in the will of humans, but men and women spoke from God as they were carried along by the Holy Spirit"

(1:20–21, NIV; also HCSB note on 1:20).[5] True, New Testament authors start from the concept of their base communities, not with modern individualism. But even if we accept an alternative ("the interpretation of scriptural prophecy is never a matter for the individual"; 1:20 JB), an interpretation guided by the Spirit and by fidelity to apostolic tradition may be carried out by the entire community, women included (1 Cor. 14:29; 1 John 2:20, 26–27), and not by some assumed ecclesiastical authorities. Second Peter anticipates later Catholicism only in this general sense of affirming the fundamental unity between Peter and Paul and of achieving a certain unity also between Hebrew apocalypticism and Hellenism. However, this is a Hellenism of a Judaism already adapted to its Greek cultural context, especially outside of Palestine.

4. *Sexual Sins and Sexual Minorities*

Despite the misleading language of many translations and commentaries, 2 Peter says little explicitly regarding the sexual sphere. Second Peter 2:4 refers to the angels who sinned (the "sons of God" of Gen. 6:1–4), but does not specify that their sin consisted in having sexual relations with women ("giants" resulting in the Genesis myth, a unique kind of sexual minority!). Although 2 Peter omits Jude's explicit reference to the men of Sodom going after "strange flesh" (of angels), 2 Pet. 2:5–6 links the violence that provoked the flood with the violence that brought judgment on Sodom (*aseb-* words). This would remind readers that the sin of inhospitable Sodom involved attempted gang rape of the visiting angels (the sin of violence, not of "homosexuality" as in popular homophobic misinterpretations).

Although 2 Peter refers three times to Lot as exemplifying liberating justice (2:7–8), Lot's efforts to placate Sodom's rapists with the offer of his two virgin daughters, being part of his cruel patriarchal culture, goes unnoticed (see similarly Judg. 19:24–26). In Genesis Lot's two virgin daughters return the father's "compliment" by getting him drunk and committing incest (19:30–38; see similarly Noah, evidently anally raped by his son, 9:18–27). Second Peter 2:10 speaks of coveting (possibly a neighbor's wife), but not necessarily sexual "lust." In 2 Peter, sexual sin is explicit only in the metaphorical reference to "eyes full of adultery," possibly the book's only explicit reference to a woman (*mestous moichalidos* in 2:14 may refer to eyes "full of [desire for] an adulteress" rather than eyes "of an adulteress").

Although Peter as implied author was the only one of the twelve apostles known to be married, modern "family values" find no support in 2 Peter. The focus on the flood and Noah (one of the few Hebrew Bible heroes who was monogamous not polygamous) might be cited in support of contemporary "family values," but this is more than offset by the emphasis on Lot's "justice" (despite trying to placate rapists by offering his virgin daughters and then fathering children by incest), and the elimination of Jude's sexual focus in

5. Bauckham, *Jude, 2 Peter*, 154.

describing Sodom's sin. The sexual sin of the infiltrating false teachers is specified as the (heterosexual) sin of adultery, while Jesus Christ and the apostle Paul (both single) are set forth as exemplary paradigms (1:1–2; 3:15–16) by 2 Peter's actual author, who, like them, may well have been unmarried.

Other references to sexual sin in 2 Peter are alluded to only in general terms of injustice, covetousness, oppression, and violence, and the author refrains from imposing any detailed legal code (cf. Leviticus). Law in 2 Peter is used only in the singular (2:21; 3:2), perhaps with reference to Jesus' new command (John 13:34–35) or the "royal law" of love to neighbor (James 2:8; cf. Lev. 19:18; Mark 12:31; Luke 10:35–37; Rom. 13:8–10).

5. Doing Theology

Certainly one of 2 Peter's most important lessons is its theological method: a paradigm of creativity that seeks to be faithful to prophetic and apostolic traditions, yet struggles to maintain and communicate faith in a new historical context. Faced with the threat of false teachers, 2 Peter first cites the *experience* of Peter at the transfiguration (1:16–18), supported by the Hebrew scriptures (1:19–21) and by Paul's *letters*. By this time a collection of Paul's letters already had come to be reckoned as "scripture," but they were characterized as "wisdom" for the way, not as inculcating "morals" or providing "ethical absolutes" (3:15–16).

We may ask ourselves, however, how we can be faithful to God after the Holocaust, where the Nazis murdered millions of Jews and thousands of homosexuals, Gypsies, Jehovah's Witnesses, communists, and other minorities. Can we continue to insist with 2 Peter that God is the Sovereign of history and that soon God will punish the oppressors and the violent? When the Parousia (second coming) of Jesus has been delayed not only for two generations but for two millennia, can we still affirm that this is evidence of the patience and love of God who waits for all to come to repentance? Faced with an ecological disaster that threatens to make the planet uninhabitable, can we continue to hope for a renewed world characterized by justice? Those who today seek to follow Jesus in "the way" may sense as acutely as anyone the difficulties in their faith, but perhaps conclude that common alternatives present not difficulties, but impossibilities. Second Peter reminds us that false prophets may "exercise" or "have" a "love" (2:15) and claim a "liberation" (2:19) that are spurious: "They promise them freedom, but they themselves are slaves of corruption; for people are slaves to whatever masters them" (2:19). This encourages vigilance in the face of so much modern ideology and propaganda that promise paradise but deliver purgatory.

6. The Handicapped and the Sick

Second Peter includes only a metaphorical reference to one who is "nearsighted and blind" and is forgetful of having been purified (1:9, baptism?). Ancient rhetoric makes no provision for modern concerns about politically correct language in such cases. To refer more sensitively to the "visually challenged" here would contradict the intent of the rhetoric (→Babylon the "harlot," not "sex worker," in Revelation 17). Although the divine promises (1:4) refer to virtues and holiness (1:5–8), not to health, in the final analysis they include the redemption of the body from all uncleanness and "corruption" (→Jude).

Bibliography

Bauckham, Richard. *Jude, 2 Peter,* WBC 50. Dallas: Word, 1983.

Dowd, Sharyn. "2 Peter." In *The Women's Bible Commentary,* ed. Carol A. Newsom and Sharon H. Ringe, 465. Louisville: Westminster John Knox, 1998.

Elliott, John H. "Peter, Second Epistle of." *ABD,* 5:282–87.

Heide, Gale Z. "What is New about the New Heaven and the New Earth? A Theology of Creation from Revelation 21 and 2 Peter 3." *Journal of the Evangelical Theological Society* 40, no. 1 (March 1997): 37–56.

Neyrey, Jerome H. *2 Peter, Jude.* AB 37C. New York: Doubleday, 1993.

Rakestraw, Robert V. "Becoming Like God: An Evangelical Doctrine of Theosis," *Journal of the Evangelical Theological Society* 40, no. 2 (June 1997): 257–69.

Rosenblatt, Marie-Eloise. "2 Peter." In *Searching the Scriptures,* vol. 2, *A Feminist Commentary,* ed. Elisabeth Schüssler Fiorenza, 399–405. New York: Crossroad, 1994.

Chapter 23

1 JOHN

God's Pure Love in Solidarity with the Poor

Outline

Introduction/Prologue: The Word Creates Community Life, 1:1–4

1. God is Light, Walk in the Light, 1:5–3:10

    Break with injustice, oppression, violence, 1:5–2:2

    Keep Jesus' commandment(s) (love your sister and brother), 2:3–11

    Guard against the oppressive world system, 2:12–17

    Guard against antichrists, who shatter solidarity, 2:18–27

    The purifying hope: Jesus' triumph over injustice, 2:28–3:10

2. God is Love, Walk in Love, 3:11–5:12

    Avoid violence (Cain), practice solidarity with the poor, 3:11–24

    Guard against antichrists and the oppressive world system, 4:1–6

    Love as God, who "is love," sacrificially loved us, 4:7–21

    The power of faith to overcome the oppressive world system, 5:1–13

    The efficacy of prayer in the face of oppression, 5:14–17

Conclusion/Epilogue: Three Final Certainties, 5:18–21

Commentary

In all the Bible, we find the great affirmation "God is *love*" only in 1 John, where it occurs twice in the fourth chapter (1 John 4:8, 16). However, the first chapter of the same book also affirms that "God is *light*" (1:5). The Gospel of John gives us a third affirmation of fundamental importance: "God is *spirit*" (John 4:24). The perception that God is love represents the culmination of all truth in the Bible, and as such, provides us the pinnacle from which we can contemplate, understand, and properly interpret all that the Bible says.

1. Love as Solidarity with the Weak and Poor

What does John mean when he affirms that God is love? John wrote his letters around 95 C.E. to combat the teachings of certain persons who had left the Christian community (2:18–27, 4:1–3). Because of their denial of the incarnation they were similar to (1) the Docetists, who claimed that Jesus was a spirit and only *appeared* to be a human of flesh and blood; and (2) the Gnostics of the second century, who asserted that salvation came through proper knowledge (*gnōsis*).

Faced with these Docetic and Gnostic tendencies, John emphatically insisted on the physical reality of the incarnate Jesus (1:1–2), stating, "We declare to you what we have seen and heard so that you also may have *koinōnia* with us; and truly our *koinōnia* is with the Parent and with the Son Jesus Christ" (1:3). The Greek word *koinōnia* is rendered several ways in our translations of the scriptures (e.g., "fellowship," "communion"). The basic meaning is "to have in common," as in our word, "commun-ism," but often the best translation today would be "solidarity." Certain persons had shattered the solidarity and abandoned the Christian community. They denied the reality of the incarnation and proclaimed salvation by means of their elitist and spiritual philosophy, which had nothing to do with the injustices and sufferings in the material world. Early Christian communities included many poor people, and John made it quite clear what was involved for all those who wanted to live in solidarity with these communities: "We know love by this, that he laid down his life for us—and we ought to lay down our lives for one another. How does God's love abide in anyone who has the world's goods and sees a brother or sister in need and yet refuses to help?" (3:16–17).

Jesus (early source Q, Matt. 5:44 and Luke 6:27), as well as Paul (Rom. 12:14–21), commands us to love our enemies, but in John, Jesus limits himself to the commandment of mutual love between disciples (John 13:34; 15:12, 17; cf. 17:9). Nonetheless, experience and church history remind us that to love those with whom we live can be more difficult.

2. Sin as Injustice, Oppression, Violence

Sin, according to John, is all that oppresses and does damage to our weak and poor brother or sister: "If we confess our sins, God who is faithful and just will forgive us our sins and cleanse us from all *adikia* ("injustice, oppression," 1:9; see 5:17).[1] The sins of injustice, oppression, and lack of solidarity and love represent "darkness" (1:6; 2:9–11). These sins characterize "the world," and disciples of Jesus should stop conforming themselves to this corrupt, cruel, and violent system (2:15–17; 3:15).

At the same time, "darkness" represents ignorance (2:11). Thus, when John states that "God is light" (1:5), he declares that God is the source of all justice and truth. The elitist Greek philosophies placed much emphasis on *knowing*

1. Tom Hanks, "Liberation Theology after 25 Years: Passé or Mainstream?" *Anvil* 10, no. 3 (1993): 200.

the truth. But John, as is common in the Bible, speaks of a praxis, a practice, of *walking* in the truth. The Bible never speaks of "ethics" or "morals" (dominant concepts of the Greek philosophies) but of human life, both individual and communal, as a "walk." This walk always implies a concrete historical context necessary for proper understanding of the divine instructions (see 1:6–7; 2 John 4, 6; 3 John 4).

3. The "Epistemological Privilege of the Poor": Why John Wrote This Letter

At the beginning John indicated that his purpose in proclaiming (1:3) and writing (1:4) his message was to promote *koinōnia* (solidarity) among the Christians, both poor and rich, so that the *joy* of all would be fulfilled. However, at the end of the letter we find another purpose that receives even greater emphasis: "I write these things to you who believe in the name of the Son of God, so that you may *know* that you have eternal life" (5:13).

We can trace the importance of this purpose (of knowing, of being certain of our relationship with God) throughout the entire letter:

> "By this we may *know* that we *know* him, if we keep his commandments" (2:3).
>
> "You have an anointing from the Holy One, so all of you *know* the truth" (2:20).
>
> "If you *know* that he is just, you may *know* that everyone who practices liberating justice has been born of him" (2:29).
>
> "We *know* that we have already passed from death into the sphere of life, because we love the brothers and sisters; the one not loving remains in the sphere of death" (3:14).
>
> "All who keep [Christ's] commandments remains in him and he in them; and by this we *know* that he remains in us, by the Spirit he gave us" (3:24).
>
> "By this we *know* that we remain in him and he in us, because of the Spirit he has given us" (4:13).

In this way John answers the Gnostic types, who were so proud of possessing knowledge (*gnōsis*) superior to "common," ignorant people. Faced with the arrogance of the elitists who had broken the community's solidarity, leaving to establish their ghettos of privilege, John seeks to remind the humble community of believers that they are the ones who really have authentic knowledge of God. In the same way today many think that true knowledge comes through studies and university degrees or becoming wealthy in order to know "important" people and to have all the modern technology that gives access to the great libraries of the world. But John continues the teaching of the carpenter of Nazareth, who insisted that God hides himself from the wise and learned of the world and reveals herself to the humble and poor (Matt. 11:25–30; 1 Cor. 1:18–31).

For this reason many theologians in Latin America have spoken of the "privilege" that the poor and humble have in the matter of knowledge of

God and God's will (Matt. 5:3–6; Luke 6:20–26). Since this privilege refers to the matters of knowledge (which philosophers call "epistemology"), many theologians now insist on the "epistemological privilege" of the poor. With their perspective, from below, the oppressed, marginalized, and victims of violence cry out to the God of the Exodus to liberate and save them. They may suffer every type of evil, but can know that oppression and injustice are not God's will.

John also thus wants to insist on the epistemological privilege of his humble community. Through the testimony of the apostles, their obedience and practice of justice and love, and the divine Spirit who dwells within them, the believers reach full knowledge and assurance of their relationship with God and of the character of God as a God of truth, liberating justice, and love. The elitists had left the community in order to protect their privileges, but they lost this epistemological privilege of knowing God and God's liberating purposes.

John's Gospel speaks of readers who already possess and participate in "eternal life," not in the philosophical sense of a celestial life without material dimension, but in a community life in solidarity that begins in this life and continues after death: "This is eternal life, that they may *know* you, the only true God, and Jesus Christ whom you have sent" (John 17:3; cf. Jer. 22:16, "to know Yahweh" is to practice liberating justice; Matt. 25:31–46).

4. *Textual Problem: 1 John 5:7*

See NRSV, HCSB, and JB notes. The very late Trinitarian addition of the Greek Textus Receptus, followed by the Authorized (King James) Version, is unanimously rejected by modern scholars. It occurs in none of the earlier and reliable Greek manuscripts and versions and was not cited by the Greek church fathers in their efforts to establish the Trinitarian doctrine. What was apparently a gloss (marginal commentary) mistakenly was copied into later manuscripts as part of the text.

Bibliography

1, 2, and 3 John

Brown, Raymond E. *The Community of the Beloved Disciple.* New York: Paulist Press, 1979.

———. *The Epistles of John.* AB 30. New York: Doubleday, 1982.

Countryman, L. William. "Asceticism in the Johannine Letters." In *Asceticism and the New Testament,* ed. Leif E. Vaage and Vincent L. Wimbush, 383–91. New York: Routledge, 1999.

Edwards, Ruth B. *The Johannine Epistles.* New Testament Guides. Sheffield: Sheffield Academic Press, 1996.

Hutaff, Margaret D. "The Johannine Epistles." In *Searching the Scriptures,* vol. 2, *A Feminist Commentary,* ed. Elisabeth Schüssler Fiorenza, 406–27. New York: Crossroad, 1994.

Kysar, Robert. "John, Epistles of." *ABD,* 3:900–912.

Lieu, Judith. *The Second and Third Epistles of John: History and Background.* Edinburgh: T. & T. Clark, 1986.

Marshall, I. Howard. *The Epistles of John.* NICNT. Grand Rapids: Eerdmans, 1978.

O'Day, Gail R. "1, 2, and 3 John." In *The Women's Bible Commentary,* ed. Carol A. Newsom and Sharon H. Ringe, 466–67. Louisville: Westminster John Knox, 1998.

Perkins, Pheme. *The Johannine Epistles.* New Testament Message 21. Wilmington, Del.: Michael Glazier, 1984.

Rensberger, David. *1 John, 2 John, 3 John.* Abingdon New Testament Commentaries. Nashville: Abingdon, 1997.

Sloyan, Gerard S. *Walking in the Truth: Perseverers and Deserters—The First, Second, and Third Letters of John.* The New Testament in Context. Valley Forge, Pa.: Trinity, 1995.

Strecker, G. *The Johannine Letters.* Trans. Linda J. Maloney. Hermeneia. Minneapolis: Fortress, 1996.

Chapter 24

2 JOHN

The Limits of Tolerance to Make an Inclusive Community Viable

Outline

1. Greetings to the Elect Lady and her children, vv. 1–3
2. The bond of inclusive love that unites, vv. 4–6
3. The limits of tolerance: antichrists, vv. 7–11
4. Greetings from the Elect Sister and her children, vv. 12–13

Commentary

1. Women and Sexual Minorities

Second John is the only New Testament book addressed to a "woman." While 3 John names three unmarried males and speaks of the church as a community of "friends/beloveds," 2 John prefers the image of a "lady" with her children (vv. 1, 4–5, 13), perhaps because the author addresses a house-church (v. 10) led by a woman, such as Lydia (Acts 16:13–15), or Priscilla (Rom. 16:3–5), or the apostle Junia (Rom. 16:7). Both 2 and 3 John thus subvert the patriarchal model of a family headed by a male. The contrast with an all-male hierarchy in the later institutionalized church is impressive. Nevertheless, 2 John's exhortation not to allow imposters to enter and teach in the house-church may reflect the notion already evident in the pastoral letters that women were more easily led astray (1 Tim. 2:14; 2 Tim. 3:6–7).

2. The Way: (a) Truth and (b) Love: A Fundamental Dialectic for the Weak and Poor

In both 2 and 3 John the same juxtaposition of truth and love is fundamental, but in 2 John the emphasis falls more on "truth" (five times in vv. 1–4, plus "teaching," three times in vv. 9–10) rather than on "love" (vv. 1, 3, 5–6, plus "grace, mercy," v. 3). John the elder addresses the ecclesiastical community under the figure of an "elect lady and her children, whom I love in the *truth,* and not only I, but also all who know the *truth,* because of the *truth* that abides in us and will be with us forever.... *truth* and love" (vv. 1–3). Truth is also expressed in reference to the "teaching" (vv. 9–10) of the incarnation ("flesh," v. 7; cf. 1 John 2:18–19; 4:1–2), affirming the complete humanity of Jesus and demonstrating his basic solidarity with the weak (cf. 1 John 1:1–4; 3:17).

While 1 John juxtaposes *light* and love, 2 John juxtaposes *truth* and love, and 3 John reverses the emphasis to juxtapose *love* and truth. All three letters describe the recipients not just as believing the truth, but primarily as *walking* in the truth:

> I was overjoyed when some of the friends [*adelphoi,* "brothers"] arrived and testified to your faithfulness to the truth, namely, how you *walk* in the *truth.* I have no greater joy than this, to hear that my children are *walking* in the *truth*.... Everyone has testified favorably about Demetrius [the bearer of the letter?], and so has the truth itself. We also testify for him, and you know that our testimony is true. (3 John 3–4, 12)

The Bible never speaks of "ethics" or "morals," which are categories of the Greek elitist philosophies. Instead, the Bible describes the Christian life as a "walk":

> If we say that we have *koinōnia* ["solidarity/fellowship"] with God yet *walk* in the darkness, we lie by word and deed. But if we *walk* in the light, as God is in the light, then we have *koinōnia* with one another, and the blood of Jesus, God's Son, cleanses us from all *adikia* ["injustice/oppression"]. (1 John 1:6–8)

In 2 John 4–6 the elder refers to members of the community who walk in the truth, fulfilling the divine commandment(s) to walk in mutual love, which involved solidarity with the many weak and poor members of the community (see 1 John 3:16–18).[1]

3. *Safe Space for the Elect Lady and Her Children*

The inclusive, welcoming solidarity of love has its norms and limitations (vv. 7–11). When those who pretend to be progressives "progress" right off the road of truth and of mutual love, John says that we should neither follow nor receive them. We can never make common cause with the oppressors in their oppression of the weak, nor with the violent in their violence against the poor. Certain conflictive contexts demand a choice in favor of the oppressed and against the injustice and lies of the oppressors (the "option for the poor").

This intimate link between love and truth that the Bible teaches is not much appreciated today. But only in that way can we maintain viable communities and safe places in an often hostile and violent world. Consequently, in Romans Paul similarly sought to strengthen tolerant and hospitable communities (15:7–13), but at the same time he recognized that tolerance and hospitality have their limits (16:17–20; cf. 2 Cor. 6:14–7:1 with its context; Titus 3:10–11; Rev. 2:2; Matthew 18). Undoubtedly many would prescribe particular

---

1. Thomas D. Hanks, "Poor/Poverty (New Testament)," *ABD,* 5:421.

norms and standards differently than John, but in our modern world, characterized by terrorism and violence, with even children shooting their classmates in small towns, we can appreciate the importance of the elder's concern for safe space.

4. Judaism and Anti-Judaism?

It appears that 3 John and 2 John present a marked contrast regarding the relation of the Johannine communities to Judaism.

Third John is the only New Testament book that does not refer explicitly to Jesus Christ and seems to contain nothing that a pious Jew might not write or accept:

- Life is presented simply as "walking" in "the way," a favorite metaphor in the Hebrew Bible.
- Even more than James, 3 John is theocentric rather than Christocentric, naming God three times (vv. 6, 11), and speaking literally of "the name" (*onoma*, v. 7), probably intending reference to Jesus, but which a Jewish reader could easily understand as referring to the sacred name of Yahweh, the liberator of the Exodus.
- Outsiders are referred to literally as "Gentiles" (v. 7), which suggests a sense of Jewish identity for those inside the community.
- Third John contains neither an opening nor closing greeting that is specifically Christian (cf. 2 John 3), but concludes with the traditional Hebrew greeting of "peace" (v. 15; Heb., *shālôm*).
- Although 3 John contains the only explicit references to the "church" in the Johannine writings (vv. 6, 9–10), the Greek term (*ekklēsia*) literally means "assembly" and may refer to any political or religious gathering.
- Above all, the theology of 3 John is emphatically ecumenical, affirming that all humans who do good are of God (v. 11); that is, the criterion that distinguishes human beings is not some creed or certain titles attributed to Jesus, but an "orthopraxis" of solidarity with other humans in their need (similarly Jesus in Matt. 25:31–46).

By its sensitive, cautious language, 3 John thus gives the impression that the elder John and Gaius have profound Jewish roots, maintain an ecumenical spirit, and seek to avoid unnecessary offense to Jewish readers.

Second John, on the other hand, reflects more the Christocentric theology and style characteristic of Paul:

- An explicitly Christian greeting opens the letter (v. 3).
- Jesus' "new commandment" is now cited as no longer new (vv. 5–6; cf. John 13:34–35).
- Jesus' incarnation is the decisive point for determining a policy of solidarity or separation (vv. 7–11).
- Jesus Christ is named explicitly in an emphatically doctrinal context.

Nevertheless, the separation policy set forth is directed only against heretical Christians (Docetic and proto-Gnostic types) who accepted Jesus' deity but denied the full humanity of the incarnation (see under 1 John). The refusal of hospitality (2 John 10), therefore, is not directed against needy travelers in general or Jews in particular, but against imposters who sought to infiltrate the house-churches, proclaiming elitist teachings that damaged the welfare of the community.

Thus, 3 John and 2 John proceed from the same Jewish author. Gaius (3 John) apparently was Jewish, but the "Elect Lady" (2 John) may well have represented a largely Gentile house-church.

5. The Conflictive History of the Johannine Community

To better understand the great diversity between the emphatic recommendation of hospitality in 3 John and the strong prohibition of hospitality in 2 John, Raymond Brown's reconstruction of the Johannine Community history in five stages is of great help.[2] While this precise reconstruction is hypothetical, it provides a helpful framework for interpretation. Something like this development must be presupposed as these early disciples struggled to establish inclusive, welcoming communities that would be viable in an often hostile world.

5.1. Formation. Before the Gospel of John was written, the Beloved Disciple and other Jews in Palestine, followers of John the Baptist (John 1:35–40), accepted Jesus as the Davidic Messiah. They joined with other Jews who made disciples in Samaria (John 4) and who understood Jesus to be a new Moses, but preexistent (John 1:1–28).

5.2. Rejection. Certain Jewish leaders threw Jesus' disciples out of the synagogues (John 9:22; 16:2) under the accusation that they, contradicting Jewish monotheism, made Jesus a second God (5:18). As a result, this community of the Beloved Disciple became quite hostile toward these leaders and their followers (8:44) and stressed the magnitude of the fulfillment of the promises of God now in this life (abundant eternal life, the gift of the Holy Spirit).

5.3. Emigration. To escape the persecution in Palestine, the community of the Beloved Disciple moved to Ephesus, where the Beloved Disciple (or a more Hellenized colleague) wrote the Gospel of John 1–20. The Gospel placed emphasis on Jesus' deity (1:1; 20:28) and full humanity (1:14), and on mutual love as the only commandment (13:34; 15:12, 17; concerning love toward enemies, see under Matthew, Luke, and Romans).

5.4. Separation. Some of the more prosperous members decided not to practice solidarity with the weak (*koinōnia,* 1 John 1:3, 6–7) or share their possessions with the poor (3:16–18), so they separated themselves from the community (2:18–19). The letters of 1 and 2 John were written to combat the Docetic and proto-Gnostic errors and exaggerations of this separatist elitist group.

---

2. Raymond E. Brown, *Introduction to the New Testament* (New York: Doubleday, 1997), 374–76, 404–5.

5.5. Institutionalization. The letters of 3, 2, and 1 John and the Gospel of John 21 (the appendix) were written as responses to the crisis of authority in the communities, probably in that order (the canonical order of 1–3 John, as in the case of Paul's letters, was determined by length, not chronology). In John 21 Jesus gives Peter pastoral authority, although in John 10 Jesus himself is the only true pastor (see 1 Pet. 5:1, "fellow elder," and Peter in Matt. 16:13–23). Diotrephes, apparently wealthy, with a house-church meeting in his ample home, is criticized in 3 John for abusing his authority as owner of the house, expelling members and refusing hospitality to the elder John's emissaries. Diotrephes' authority simply as homeowner is remarkably different from that of the elders in 1 Tim. 5:17–18, lacking spacious homes, but with salaries and authority to teach. Perhaps in Timothy's context affluent women owned the large homes, and the power struggle with poorer elders provoked the male effort to reduce their influence by prohibiting their teaching and authority over males (1 Tim. 2:11–15). Diotrephes' apparent egotism may have stemmed from excessive fear of the influence of unknown itinerant teachers and prophets whom he sought to silence by prohibiting all contact with them (3 John 7–11). With his ambition to dominate instead of serve (cf. Mark 10:45), Diotrephes may anticipate the institution of monarchical bishops, first attested in the letters of Ignatius of Antioch (died ca. 135; see the "Nicolaitans" ["conquering the people"?] later in Ephesus, Rev. 2:6, 14–15; cf. Balaam ["devours the people"]). In the face of Diotrephes' fears and abuse of authority, the elder John responds only with exhortation, evidently lacking authority for more forceful action.

Bibliography: Freedom and Subversive Authority

Eller, Vernard. *Christian Anarchy: Jesus' Primacy over the Powers.* Grand Rapids: Eerdmans, 1987.

Ellul, Jacques. *Anarchy and Christianity.* Trans. Geoffrey W. Bromiley. Grand Rapids: Eerdmans, 1991.

See also the bibliography for chapter 23, "1 John."

Chapter 25

3 JOHN

Hospitality as Making an Inclusive Community of Friends

Outline

1. Greetings to the beloved Gaius, vv. 1–2
2. Praise of *Gaius* for his hospitality, vv. 3–8
3. Criticism of *Diotrephes* for his lack of hospitality, vv. 9–11
4. Testimony in favor of *Demetrius* (carrier of the letter?), v. 12
5. Farewell: churches as communities of friends, vv. 13–15

Commentary

Third John is the shortest book of the New Testament (219 words; cf. 2 John, 245; Philemon, 355; Jude, 457). The author refers to himself simply as "elder/presbyter" (1:1), not as an "apostle." If not the apostle John, he may have been a disciple who preserved and adapted the Beloved Disciple's teachings for a future generation. Third John was written probably around 95 C.E., perhaps in Ephesus, by the same writer as 2 and 1 John (note "the elder" also in 2 John 1).

1. The Way: (a) Love and (b) Truth

Despite its brevity, 3 John helpfully illuminates fundamental facets of *love* (vv. 1–2, 5–6, 11; cf. "friends," v. 15) and of *truth* (vv. 1, 3–4, 8, 12; cf. "testimony," vv. 3, 6, 12). In John's three letters, love and truth maintain a dialectical relationship and constitute the two poles for their teaching ("theology"). A disciple's life must move ahead like a train, always on these two tracks. In these letters, as in the Bible in general, truth is not so much to be "believed" as to be "done" (v. 8).

Truth is understood metaphorically as a *way,* and the disciples are always to "walk" on this path (vv. 3–4, literal translation). Third John is directed to the leader of a church, Gaius, whom the author calls, literally, "beloved" (vv. 1–2, 5, 11) "whom I love in the truth" (v. 1). John also describes the exaggerated self-love of Diotrephes, "who *loves* to put himself first" (v. 9; see below).

2. For Poor Strangers: Hospitality

To walk in truth, as when we manifest love in acts of hospitality to homeless strangers, is to do good (v. 11; Matt. 25:31–46). Gaius, like John, is characterized by authentic love: instead of xenophobia (the fear and hatred of strangers and foreigners), Gaius is famous for his hospitality and love for strangers (vv. 5–6). However, in this case they are not prosperous tourists but emissaries of Jesus, same-sex pairs, who followed his example of voluntary poverty ("taking nothing") in order to share the good news (vv. 6–8).

Hospitality is presented in the Bible as a fundamental manifestation of divine and brotherly love (Rom. 12:13; 15:23–24; 16:1–2; 2 John 9–11; Heb. 13:1–2). Often it was a matter of life or death because of the cultural context in the ancient Near East (Judges 19). Instead of hospitality, travelers often suffered violence and sexual abuse. For such offenses God had to judge the men of Sodom and Gomorrah, who sought to rape God's angel messengers (Genesis 19; cf. the good Samaritan in Luke 10:29–37). Those who traveled in "the name [of Jesus]" (*onoma,* v. 7) were impoverished persons who depended on the hospitality and solidarity of well-to-do persons like Gaius to meet their needs and enable them to fulfill their mission (v. 8).

3. Integral Salvation: Forgiveness, Healing, Liberation

Reflecting Jesus' purpose in his ministry of healing the sick to manifest God's inbreaking new order, the elder John prays for Gaius's physical health and prosperity, which would facilitate his offer of hospitality (v. 2; cf. James 5:13–18). The Johannine letters also provide us images of healthy persons who "walk in the truth" (3 John 3–4; 2 John 4, 6; cf. 1 John 1:7; 2:6) and who are physically healthy and thus able to work (3 John 5, 8). To be "blind" and to "walk in darkness," on the other hand, are metaphors that describe the ignorance of people who live in hate and do not love their brothers and sisters (1 John 2:9–11). John seeks to liberate and protect the church from Diotrephes' tendency to oppress (concerning forgiveness, see 1 John 1:7–2:2).

4. House-churches as Communities of Friends

Usually the New Testament speaks of the church as a community of sisters and brothers (1 John 3:11–17; 2 John 1, 13; Matt. 23:8–12). This image emphasizes the household to which one belongs by birth, not by choice. In 3 John, however, the church (vv. 6, 9–10) is not a hierarchy of officials governing patriarchal families. The image of brothers and sisters (vv. 5, 10) is surpassed by that of the church as a community of "friends" (v. 15). Jesus himself chooses this image when he says, "I do not call you servants any longer, because the servant does not know what the master is doing; but I have called you *friends, because I have made known to you everything that I have heard from my Father*" (John 15:15). In addition to the intimacy, Jesus underscores the depth of commitment toward his friends: "No one has greater love than this, to lay down one's life for one's friends" (John 15:13; cf. "brothers" in 1 John 3:16 [NIV] and "enemies" in Rom. 5:6–11).

In the mid-seventeenth century in Great Britain, a religious movement under the leadership of George Fox (and later William Penn in America) called themselves simply "Friends," but were soon named "Quakers" by their opponents. They were characterized by a rejection of traditional ecclesiastical ordained male hierarchies, the recognition of women as leaders, and opposition to oaths, military service, and slavery. In 1963, six years before the Stonewall riots and more than a decade before the American Psychiatric Association reached similar conclusions (1973), British Quakers concluded that homosexuality is simply "sexual left-handedness" and began to openly welcome sexual minorities within their worship services.

5. *Women and Feminist Theology of Friendship*

Although only males are named in 3 John, women undoubtedly were among the "friends" who exchanged greetings (v. 15) and probably among the poor missionaries whom Gaius welcomed (vv. 5–8; see also "the elect lady and her children" addressed in 2 John). Although friendship is one of the most important themes in philosophy and literature (including the Bible), few theologians have written about it. Thanks to feminist theology, as expressed in works such as those of Carter Heyward, Mary Hunt, and Elizabeth Stuart, this situation is changing. Mary Hunt concludes that friendship, not the family, is society's fundamental institution, and that heterosexual marriage at its best is only one example of friendship.[1] We cannot "define" words so rich and profound as "friends" and "friendship," since it would be presumptuous to try to control their meaning and linguistic use. As in the case of the word "love," each new experience reveals more unimagined facets and nuances. In addition, different historical and cultural contexts profoundly affect our experience of friendship: to have a friend/neighbor in a rural context in ancient times was very different from the friendship between professionals in a modern urban center. Nonetheless, we may indicate certain common dimensions of authentic friendship that the Bible emphasizes.

We like to think that we choose our friends, or, as in the experience of the rich (Proverbs, below), that others choose us. Such freedom is a luxury not enjoyed in many small villages, where to be "neighbor" is to be "friend," with the exception of enemies. Jesus warns us that in the community of his followers, the decision is not our concern, since he has already chosen his friends (John 15:16). Furthermore, since Jesus is "a friend of toll collectors and 'sinners'" (Matt. 11:19 // Luke 7:34 = Q), we may find it difficult to learn to accept and love all whom Jesus befriends.

1. Mary E. Hunt, *Fierce Tenderness: A Feminist Theology of Friendship* (New York: Crossroad, 1991), 9.

We may prefer friends with whom we share interests, but Jesus pointed out that his friends share the common task of proclaiming the good news and constructing new communities as the first fruits of the coming new order (John 15:16). To be a Christian is not to remain isolated (Heb. 10:25) but to form part of one of these communities that transcend patriarchal families (Mark 3:20–21, 31–35; John 19:25–27). However, because we are finite, limited, we are not able to have innumerable friends. Even Jesus avoided taking the entire multitude up to the Mount of Transfiguration (Mark 9:2), nor did he ask that the Twelve keep watch with him, but chose only three (Mark 14:32–34).

The book of Proverbs contains many teachings about friendship. With an almost brutal realism, it notes that the rich have many friends while the poor lose the few they have (Prov. 14:20; 19:4, 6–7). In accord with divine wisdom, a friend should be

- faithful (17:17; 18:24; 27:10)
- true (16:28; 17:9; 27:6; 28:23; 29:5; see Gal. 4:16)
- sensitive, courteous (25:17, 20; 26:18–19; 27:14)
- wise (27:9, 17; see David and Jonathan, 1 Sam. 23:16)

Intimacy with a friend makes us vulnerable. The Psalms remind us that intimacy and vulnerability entail the possibility of betrayal (Ps. 35:11; 41:9; 55:12–14, 20–21; 109:4). Few long-lasting friendships have remained free of some sense of betrayal. Only the capacity to forgive makes it possible for a friendship to endure, but by God's grace a crisis may enable the friendship to reach a new level of commitment and intimacy (→Philippians).

Bibliography

See the bibliography for chapter 23, 1 John.

Bibliography: Friendship

Aelred of Rievaulx [1110–67]. *Spiritual Friendship*. Kalamazoo, Mich.: Cistercian Publications, 1977.

Boyd, Stephen B. *The Men We Long to Be: Beyond Domination to a New Christian Understanding of Manhood*. San Francisco: HarperSanFrancisco, 1995.

Carpenter, Edward, ed. *Ioläus, an Anthology of Friendship*. London: Albert and Charles Boni, [1902] 1935.

Clapp, Rodney. *A Peculiar People: The Church as Culture in a Post-Christian Society*. Downers Grove, Ill.: InterVarsity, 1996.

Fitzgerald, J. T., ed. *Friendship, Flattery, and Frankness of Speech: Studies on Friendship in the New Testament World*. Novum Testamentum Supplements 82. Leiden: Brill, 1996.

———. *Greco-Roman Perspectives on Friendship*. Atlanta: Scholars Press, 1997.

Heyward, Carter. *Touching Our Strength: The Erotic as Power and the Love of God*. San Francisco: Harper & Row, 1989.

Hunt, Mary E. *Fierce Tenderness: A Feminist Theology of Friendship.* New York: Crossroad, 1991.

Konstan, David. *Friendship in the Classical World.* Key Themes in Ancient History. Cambridge: Cambridge University Press, 1997.

Stuart, Elizabeth. *Just Good Friends: Towards a Lesbian and Gay Theology of Relationships.* London: Mowbray, 1995.

Sullivan, Andrew. *Love Undetectable: Notes on Friendship, Sex, and Survival.* New York: Alfred A. Knopf, 1998.

Vasey, Michael. *Strangers and Friends: A New Exploration of Homosexuality and the Bible.* London: Hodder & Stoughton, 1995.

See also the bibliography for chapter 11, "Philippians."

Chapter 26

JUDE

Celebrating the Love-feasts, Subverting the Canon

Outline

1. Greeting, vv. 1–2
2. Reason for the letter: intrusion of ungodly leaders, vv. 3–4
3. False prophets: three paradigms of divine punishment, vv. 5–7

   Their blasphemies: three sinful precedents, vv. 8–11

   Their intrusion into the love-feasts brings judgment: four images, vv. 12–13

   Enoch prophesied against them, 14–16; so did the apostles, vv. 17–19
4. Three virtues (faith, love, hope) and three obligations of community love, vv. 20–23
5. Doxology: walking on the way without falling, vv. 24–25

Commentary

Traditionally, the letter of Jude is attributed to Jude, the brother of Jesus (Mark 6:3; Matt. 13:55) and of James (Jude 1). Jude, James, and Simon Peter were the only three authors of New Testament books said to be married (see 1 Cor. 9:5). That is to say, more than 90 percent of the New Testament represents writings of unmarried men (Matthew, Mark, Luke, John, Paul [plus Apollos, author of Hebrews?]) who, consequently, do not reflect the ideology and values of the modern nuclear family dominant in cultures and churches today.

Jude was not an apostle but a prominent leader and itinerant missionary in the early Palestinian Judeo-Christian movement (1 Cor. 9:5). The letter may be one of the earliest writings of the New Testament, perhaps in the decade of 50–60 C.E. Although Jude differs greatly from James, it reflects well the apocalyptic theology of early Christianity. Many scholars question whether the letter really comes from Jude, but the recent research supports the traditional attribution of the letter to him. (Such is not the case with →2 Peter, which has much in common with Jude but appears to come from a disciple of Peter around 90 C.E.)

1. The Poor: Salvation/Liberation and "Love-Feast" Banquets

Like 2 John, Jude insists on the limits of hospitality in regard to false teachers who had succeeded in infiltrating the community's "love-feasts" (*agapais,* v. 12). In the entire New Testament only Jude calls the Lord's Supper a love-feast (cf. "feasting along with you," 2 Pet. 2:13), but the designation became very common in the patristic literature after the New Testament, reminding us that the eucharist, or the Lord's Supper, was an actual meal. Paul's description shows us how the rich abused the poor and the slaves on such an occasion when love was lacking. When the slaves arrived late from their work, they found that the rich had eaten all the food and gotten drunk after drinking all the wine (→1 Cor. 11:17–22; cf. Acts 2:46). To eliminate such "class struggles" in the very heart of the church, after a few centuries the love-feasts were reduced to a religious ritual, with tiny symbols of the original meal, in almost all the churches until the present day. However, Jude reminds us that the original practice was a love-feast, and Paul enables us to see how the poor enjoyed this banquet before abuses set in.

Reflecting its early Palestinian origin (50–60 C.E.), Jude avoids justice terminology ([*a*]*dik*- terms), containing only one such reference, the fiery "eternal vengeance/punishment" (*dikēn,* v. 7) of Sodom and Gomorrah (see similarly Jesus' teaching in our earliest Gospel, →Mark, and the Q source). Jude prefers to speak of "salvation" in the sense of an integral liberation, as in the Exodus paradigm (vv. 3, 5, 23, 25). In contrast, →2 Peter (80–90 C.E.) refers to injustice/oppression (*adik*- terms) four times and liberating justice (*dik*- terms) eight times, for a total of twelve!

2. Feminist Critique of Jude's "Patriarchal Limitations"

As Marie-Eloise Rosenblatt points out, "Jude typifies a patriarchal focus that excludes the mention of women and renders women's presence, voice, contributions, and roles invisible."[1] She suggests, however, that women prophets were among the false leaders that infiltrated the church! While this is possible, an alternative approach is preferable. Not a word in Jude excludes the possibility that in the inclusive house-churches that he addresses the women prepared and administered the eucharist in its early form as a love-feast, especially since the early churches often met in homes headed by women. Why not insist on the presence of women, quite possibly as the dominant majority in the churches that received this letter and hosted the meals? Jude would then be exhorting mainly women leaders to teach the truth against the errors of male intruders (vv. 3–4; cf. 2 Tim. 3:6–7), and to carry out their pastoral work (vv. 22–23) empowered by the glorious promises of the final doxology (vv. 24–25).

True, Jude's examples of impious sinners are limited to infamous males in Israel's scriptures: Cain, Balaam, Korah (v. 11), and the males of Sodom

---

1. Marie-Eloise Rosenblatt, "Jude," in *Searching the Scriptures,* vol. 2, *A Feminist Commentary,* ed. Elisabeth Schüssler Fiorenza (New York: Crossroad, 1994), 393.

(v. 7). And as positive examples Jude also names only males: Jesus Christ, his brothers James and Jude, Adam, Enoch, Moses, in addition to the angel Michael. However, Jude's "apostles" (v. 17) may well have included leaders such as Mary Magdalene and Junia (Matt. 28:1–10; Rom. 16:7). Jude makes no attempt to blame women (such as Eve or false women prophets) for the existence of evil in human history or in the church, nor does he impose any limitation on women's leadership in the church in response to his letter.

3. The Subversion (Opening) of the Canon

To warn against false teachers (vv. 3–19) who wanted to infiltrate the house-churches where the love-feasts were celebrated, Jude (vv. 6, 9, 14–15) cites two pseudepigraphal books (*1 Enoch* and the *Testament of Moses*) popular among first-century Jews but not part of the Hebrew canon. In this way Jude allows us to see the early Christians' freedom in terms of the canon. The value of the traditional canon could be to avoid the loss or neglect of books normative for Jews and Christians, but such positive, inclusive value does not eliminate the possibility of recognizing significant truths in other books, as various modern feminist and womanist theologians insist (see also Titus 1:12).

4. Jude, Jesus, and Sodom: Homosexuality in Animals, Homophobia in Humans

> And those angels who did not maintain their own position of authority, but left their proper dwelling, God has maintained in eternal chains in deepest darkness for the judgment of the great Day. Similarly, Sodom and Gomorrah and the surrounding cities, which, in the same manner as the angels, indulged in irresponsible sex [*ekporneusasai*] and went in pursuit of different flesh [*sarkos heteras*], serve as an example by undergoing a punishment of eternal fire. (Jude 6–7)

Among our common English translations, only the Authorized (King James) Version preserves the literal meaning of the Greek, which refers to the flesh of angels as "strange flesh" (cf. our modern word "heterosexual," from the Greek *heteros,* "different"). Translated literally in this way, we can see how Jude follows the teaching of his brother Jesus and saw no condemnation of "homosexuality" in the account of the destruction of Sodom and Gomorrah in Genesis 19. Jewish literature of the day commonly cited God's judgment against Sodom as a condemnation of sexual love between persons of the same gender. In this way the Jews sought to make propaganda against the Greek and Roman Empires, which oppressed them for so many centuries. The Jews claimed that such sexual practices were common among their oppressors but not among Jews. Jesus broke with this popular Jewish xenophobic and homophobic tradition and returned to the original meaning of Genesis, where Sodom is punished for refusing hospitality and then attempting violence instead (Matt. 10:14–15; Luke 10:10–12).

Jude is quite clear in the original Greek. In v. 6 he refers to angels who, before the flood, came down to earth and sired children ("giants") with human women (Gen. 6:1–4). Then in v. 7 Jude speaks of the account where the men of Sodom sought to rape the angel visitors (Genesis 19). Jude describes these angels as "other flesh." The dominance of homophobia in society and the church is evidenced by the fact that many who promote violence against sexual minorities cite this text of Jude as a condemnation of "homosexuality" (when the original Greek actually contains the word *heteras,* from which the modern term "heterosexual" is derived!). Both the word and concept of "homosexuality" are of modern origin, dating only from the nineteenth century. However, medieval laws that condemn "sodomy" and modern propaganda that attacks "homosexuals" do not refer to sexual males attempting sexual violation of angels! Unlike the Hebrew scriptures (Old Testament), certain New Testament texts describe "angels" as "spirits" (Heb. 1:7, 14) that do not marry (Mark 12:25). Jude, however, stands closer to early (mythological?) traditions of the Hebrew scriptures, where angels are considered capable of sexual relations with human beings (see also Paul in 1 Cor. 11:10). Homophobic translation of Jude 7 is exemplified in the NRSV, which even drags in the concept of "unnatural" lust (from Romans 1; cf. "perversion" in the NIV). The NRSV admits in a footnote that the original Greek of Jude 7 says "went after other flesh." The original French JB translated Jude 7 properly and the JB footnote in English is correct.

Significantly, Jude does refer to actions done "naturally" (v. 10, "*physikōs*) and to instincts that are "natural" (v. 19, *psychikoi*). However, translations commonly avoid the concepts of nature in these texts (v. 10, "by instinct," NRSV, NIV; v. 19, "worldly," NRSV), where acting according to "nature" is condemned as sinful and (v. 10) "irrational." Confusion is created by the fact that in Romans 1 Paul condemns anal sex (without condoms) as "against nature" (*para physin*), both when females offer themselves to males (1:26), and similarly, when males penetrate other males (1:27). Here in Romans Paul thus implies that to act "naturally" is good, while for Jude, to act "naturally" is characteristic of irrational animals and sinful, implying that humans ought to avoid the natural and act against their natural, animal instincts. However, in Rom. 11:24 Paul himself celebrates the fact that God acts "against nature" (again, *para physin*) by engrafting Gentiles into the olive tree, Israel (note also all of Jesus' miracles). Neither the Hebrew Bible nor Jesus speaks of "nature" (a Greek philosophical concept), but rather of creation and God as creator. When Paul and Jude appropriate the philosophical vocabulary of "nature," modern readers easily get confused by the contradictory senses—all the more when translators (with apparent homophobic bias) introduce the term "unnatural" when it is not in the original Greek, but avoid the term "nature" when it is present in the Greek (→Romans).

As John Boswell's classic study made clear (1980), observation of same-sex erotic behavior and pair-bonding in animals goes back at least to Aristotle. Nevertheless, heterosexist bigotry has so darkened minds that ever since we find brilliant philosophers and theologians continually contradicting themselves about whether such behavior actually occurs in animals and the "moral/ethical" conclusions to be purportedly deduced from it. Bruce

Bagemihl's recent study documents homosexual behavior in more than 450 species of mammals, birds, reptiles, and insects.[2]

German scientist and theologian Volker Sommer has nicely diagrammed the two contradictory affirmations about animals commonly made and the two illogical conclusions to which theologians have leaped:[3]

1. "Homosexuality is against nature (does not occur among animals)"	→	3. "Homosexuality should be rejected"
2. "Homosexuality is natural (does occur among animals)"	→	4. "Homosexuality should be accepted"

The apostle Paul traditionally has been misinterpreted as arguing from affirmation #1 to #3 (Rom. 1:26–27), even though later in the same letter he celebrates God's acts "against nature" (→Romans). Although Jude does not qualify the attempted gang rape of angels as "against nature" (v. 7), his later conclusion that humans should avoid imitating the "natural" behavior of irrational animals (v. 10) logically would make him the church father of later theologians who admitted the occurrence of same-gender erotic behavior in animals, but still leaped to conclusion #3. In this ridiculous history that Boswell and others have traced on these questions, homophobic prejudice has swamped both sound science and coherent theology. Bagemihl's documentation involving 450 species hardly makes a leap from #2 to #4 any more logically compelling than traditional spurious arguments. But the very diversity of meaning and rhetoric in the New Testament involving the term "nature" (Romans 1 versus Romans 11 and Jude 10) ought to warn us against repeating the common simplistic errors of the past. Fundamentalists like to argue that God created Adam and Eve not Adam and Steve, and permitted only heterosexual animal pairs to enter Noah's ark. Now we may at least respond by inquiring where Bagemihl's 450 species came from—undoubtedly from that same place over/under Noah's rainbow where Cain found a wife!

5. Anti-Semitism and Illness

Although traditionally neglected by theologians, Jude ought to have functioned in the church as a bulwark against anti-Semitism. Like James, Jude exemplifies the continuity of the churches with Judaism, with Jude even citing as authorities two Jewish books not in the Hebrew canon (vv. 6, 9, 14–15). Jude includes no reference to illness, but see the reference to strengthening in the final doxology (vv. 24–25).

6. Jude and the Hope of the Poor

Jude kept alive the apocalyptic hope of the early churches (vv. 14–25; →Mark 13; Matthew 24–25; Luke 17:20–37; 21; 1–2 Thessalonians; James; Rev-

2. Bruce Bagemihl, *Biological Exuberance: Animal Homosexuality and Natural Diversity* (New York: St. Martin's Press, 1999).

3. Volker Sommer, *Wider die Natur: Homosexualität und Evolution* (Munich: Beck, 1990), 161.

elation). This apocalyptic perspective and theology is highly significant for evaluating the common New Testament approach to human institutions. New Testament authors looked for the second coming of Jesus shortly after the fall of Jerusalem in 70 C.E. to overthrow the violent and oppressive system of the Roman Empire and to establish on earth God's new order, characterized by freedom, justice, wisdom, and love (2 Pet. 3:13). With this goal in view, New Testament authors carefully "chose their battles." They thought Jesus' return depended on the worldwide establishment of ecclesiastical communities, which would serve as first fruits of the new order and countercultural paradigms in the face of an oppressive empire (Mark 13:10; Matt. 24:14; Romans 11–12, 15–16). Consequently, they did not give priority to applying Band-Aid patches to reform the old order a bit. Having experienced the first fruits of the new order, they struggled wholeheartedly to see it triumph decisively with Jesus' expected triumphal return.

Obviously, for Christians today, such apocalyptic theology has its limitations, but it would be unfair to criticize early Christians as resigning themselves to the continued dominance of the status quo. The prominent Greek philosophies hoped only that the nonmaterial soul would escape from the material body to then participate in the nonmaterial celestial sphere. With similar resignation, pantheistic Eastern religions expected the soul at death to be dissolved in an impersonal divine cosmic sea, perhaps to be reincarnated. In marked contrast, the apocalyptic hope of the Hebrew prophets, in common with the New Testament, is a hope based on (1) a personal God, creator of the entire material cosmos, and (2) the bodily resurrection and ascension of Jesus into a material heaven. Consequently, the apocalyptic Christian hope encompasses the human body together with all the earth and the cosmos (Matt. 5:5; Romans 8; 1 Corinthians 15; Revelation 21–22).

Our long history and the modern sciences obviously enable us to transcend apocalyptic theology in certain aspects. When the biblical authors contemplated the past, they projected a universe created some four thousand years B.C.E.; regarding the future, they hoped for the coming of Jesus within a generation. We can now count nearly two thousand years of history after the life of Jesus and the fall of Jerusalem, with the gradual expansion of the church throughout the world. According to socioeconomic analyses, with churches with millions of members, especially in democratic countries, we are able to accomplish much human liberation and justice that remained outside the early apocalyptic vision that sustained the hope of the tiny persecuted communities in the first century.

However, to recognize such limitations does not justify despising the primitive apocalyptic theology that kept alive the hope of the early Christian communities. The apocalyptic hope motivated these early churches to plant nonviolent counterculture communities throughout the Roman Empire. From the very beginning the new house-churches established a kind of dialectic tension with traditional institutions: first with the temple in Jerusalem (Acts 2) but soon extending to synagogues and imperial institutions elsewhere. As a strategy to upset a powerful empire, it would be difficult to imagine anything more effective than the house-church strategy in this dialectic, since no one wasted any energy struggling to put Band-Aids on an empire doomed to collapse. Early Christian praxis weakened and failed only when it increasingly conformed itself with the injustices, oppressions, and violence of the order it sought to undermine. Jude and other New Testament writers struggled tenaciously against the beginnings of this tendency to conformity to the dominant oppressive world order. In modern history we may compare the nonviolent strategies of Gandhi and Martin Luther King.

7. Intertextuality: The Later Use of Jude in 2 Peter

Jude (50–60 C.E., early Jewish)	→	2 Peter (90 C.E., more Hellenized)
v. 4		2:1–3a
vv. 5–8		2:3b–10a
vv. 8–9		2:10b–11
v. 10		2:12–13a
v. 11 . . .		[2:15–16]
v. 12		2:13b–14
[v. 11] . . .		2:15–16
vv. 12–13		2:17
v. 16		2:18
vv. 17–18		3:1–3

When 2 Peter condemns false teachers (2:1–3:3), the author incorporates thirteen of Jude's twenty-five verses (partly or totally). Only Jude 1–3, 14–15, and 19–25 are left unused! While Jude had denounced certain intruders who denied that God judges sin (vv. 4, 15), 2 Peter condemns mockers who denied that Jesus would return to judge the world (3:3–4; cf. 1:16–17;). Other notable changes include the following:

a. Of Jude's three examples of punishment (vv. 5–8: Israel in the desert, the angels of Gen. 6:1–4, Sodom), 2 Peter substitutes the flood (Gen. 6:5–8:22) for Israel in the desert and also rearranges the three examples to follow the chronological order of Genesis, thus eliminating the Exodus paradigm.

b. Jude 5–8 insists on God's capacity to judge (throughout history and in the final judgment), while 2 Pet. 2:4–9 emphasizes God's capacity to save from judgment (Noah and Lot exemplify those whom God rescues from judgment).

c. Second Peter eliminates Jude's two citations from Jewish pseudepigraphal works (vv. 9, 14–15: the dispute over Moses' body, the prophecy of Enoch); thus, in 2 Peter the importance of the human body after death and the flexibility of the canon disappear (though adding the letters of Paul to the canon is another kind of opening!).

d. Second Peter 2:4 provides for a more Hellenized punishment (NRSV note, "Tartaros," from Greek mythology; cf. Jude 6, "eternal chains in deepest darkness").

e. In the reference to Sodom and Gomorrah, 2 Pet. 2:6–8 eliminates Jude's specific indication of the intent to rape the visiting angels (v. 7, "other flesh"); angelic capacity for sexual relations is thus obscured, while the sins of Sodom become more general and common: impiety, violence, oppression, excesses, lack of scruples and principles, legal infractions (but without reference to Moses' law).

f. Second Peter's "banqueting" (2:13) replaces Jude's specific reference to the *agapē* meal (v. 12).

g. Jude's three examples of sinners from the Hebrew Bible (v. 11: Cain, Balaam, Korah) are reduced in 2 Peter to only Balaam (2:15–16, but with the addition of his speaking donkey's unnatural feat).

h. Second Peter 2:19–22 (with no parallels in Jude) develops certain aspects of the false teachers' sins and adds the proverb about the dog (from Prov. 26:11) and the proverb about the sow (common in Greek literature).

Bibliography

Homosexuality in Animals

Bagemihl, Bruce. *Biological Exuberance: Animal Homosexuality and Natural Diversity.* New York: St. Martin's Press, 1999.

Boswell, John. *Christianity, Social Tolerance, and Homosexuality.* Chicago: University of Chicago Press, 1980.

Linzey, Andrew. *Animal Gospel.* Louisville: Westminster John Knox, 1998.

Sommer, Volker. *Wider die Natur: Homosexualität und Evolution.* Munich: Beck, 1990.

Weinrich, James D. *Sexual Landscapes.* New York: Scribners, 1987.

Jude

Bauckham, Richard. *Jude, 2 Peter,* WBC 50. Dallas: Word, 1983.

———. *Jude and the Relatives of Jesus in the Early Church.* Edinburgh: T. & T. Clark, 1990.

———. "Jude, Epistle of." *ABD,* 3:1098–1103.

Countryman, L. William. "Asceticism or Household Morality? 1 and 2 Peter and Jude." In *Asceticism and the New Testament,* ed. Leif E. Vaage and Vincent L. Wimbush, 71–95. New York: Routledge, 1999.

Dowd, Sharyn. "Jude." In *The Women's Bible Commentary,* ed. Carol A. Newsom and Sharon H. Ringe, 468. Louisville: Westminster John Knox, 1998.

Gamble, Harry Y. "Canon, New Testament." *ABD,* 1:852–61.

Neyrey, Jerome H. *2 Peter, Jude.* AB 37C. New York: Doubleday, 1993.

Rosenblatt, Marie-Eloise. "Jude." In *Searching the Scriptures,* vol. 2, *A Feminist Commentary,* ed. Elisabeth Schüssler Fiorenza, 392–98. New York: Crossroad, 1994.

Thurén, Lauri. "Hey Jude! Asking for the Original Situation and Message of a Catholic Epistle." *New Testament Studies* 43 (1997): 451–65.

Chapter 27

REVELATION

Woe to the Great Sex Worker, Babylon

Outline

1. Introduction 1:1–8
   - Prologue, 1:1–3
   - Greeting, 1:4–8
2. Seven Prophetic Letters to Oppressed Churches in Asia 1:9–3:22
   - Preparatory vision, 1:9–20
   - The seven letters, 2:1–3:22
     - Ephesus, Smyrna, Pergamum, Thyatira, Sardis, Philadelphia, Laodicea
3. Seven Seals Opened by the Victorious Slain Lamb 4:1–8:1
   - Two preparatory visions, 4:1–5:14
     - God the Creator-Liberator on his throne, 4:1–11
     - The Lion/Lamb who directs the course of history, 5:1–14
   - The Lamb breaks the seven seals, 6:1–8:1
4. Seven Trumpets 8:2–11:19
   - Preparatory vision: the prayers of the saints, 8:2–5
   - The first six trumpets, 8:6–9:21
     - Imminence of final catastrophe, 10:1–7
     - The little book devoured, 10:8–11
     - Two martyr-witnesses (Peter and Paul?), 11:1–13
   - The seventh trumpet, 11:14–19
5. Seven Visions: the Oppressed and God's Judgment on Their Oppressors 12:1–15:4
   - Vision of the Woman and the Dragon, 12:1–18
   - The dragon transmits his power to the beast, 13:1–10

The false prophet in the service of the beast, 13:11–18

The marriage feast of the Lamb, 14:1–5

Angels announce the hour of judgment, 14:6–13

The harvest of the nations, 14:14–20

The song of Moses and of the Lamb, 15:1–4

6. Seven Cups (Angels Punish Oppressors) 15:5–16:21

Introduction, 15:5–8

Seven cups (= plagues), 16:1–21

7. God's Judgment against the Great Harlot Babylon (= Rome) 17:1–19:10

The infamous whore and the beast, 17:1–18

The fall of Babylon (= Rome), 18:1–24

Songs of triumph in heaven, 19:1–10

8. God's Final Defeat of the Oppressive, Violent, Idolatrous Empire 19:11–20:15

First eschatological combat, 19:11–21

The martyrs' thousand-year reign (millennium), 20:1–6

Second eschatological combat, 20:7–10

Final judgment against oppressive nations, 20:11–15

9. The Cosmic Goal of Human History 21:1–22:5

New Heavens and Renewed Earth, 21:1–8

The bride, the new Jerusalem descends to earth, 21:9–22:5

10. Epilogue 22:6–21

Commentary

Introduction

Revelation is the only book of the apocalyptic genre in the New Testament (cf. Daniel in the Hebrew scriptures; see also Mark 13; Matthew 24–25; Luke 21; Isaiah 24–27; Zechariah 1–8; Ezekiel 37–39). Apocalyptic literature, a form of prophecy (Rev. 1:3; 22:7, 9–10, 18, 19), is characterized by highly symbolic visions accompanied by interpretations instead of revelation by words alone (Jer. 1:9). The genre arises in times of great crises that clamor for God's abrupt intervention in human history (note the persecutions in Rev. 1:9; 2:10; 12:17; and the martyrs in Rev. 2:13; 6:9–11; 13:15; 17:6; 18:24; 20:4; cf. 11:7–10). Revelation's famous millennium (20:1–6) promises a first resurrection for martyrs only, while the general resurrection occurs "one thousand years" afterwards.

The final edition of Revelation probably was written in Asia Minor (today's Turkey) around 95 C.E. during the local persecutions toward the end of Domitian's reign (81–96 C.E.). This final edition probably was prepared after the destruction of Jerusalem (70 C.E.), since only after that event did the Jews begin to refer to Rome as "Babylon" (the empire that destroyed Jerusalem in 587/6 B.C.E.).

Revelation alludes to legends that the emperor Nero (54–68 C.E.) had returned to life (13:3; 17:9–11), which circulated during the two decades after his death. However, an earlier edition of Revelation may have been written during the Neronic persecution of 64 C.E., since the book speaks of the temple in Jerusalem as still standing (11:1–3), and uses the symbolic number "666" for the beast, which probably symbolizes the name of Nero. Possibly the earlier edition of the book (ca. 64 C.E.) consisted of 1:4–11; 4:1–22:5 (introduction, visions); later, a second edition (ca. 95 C.E.) added 1:1–3; 1:12–3:22; 22:6–21 (introduction, seven letters, conclusion).

Few scholars now defend the tradition that the apostle John, the son of Zebedee (and Beloved Disciple?), was the author of Revelation. Nevertheless, despite many differences, the Gospel of John, the three letters of John, and Revelation do share significant common characteristics. Consequently, scholars now commonly infer the existence of a Johannine community that preserved the teachings of the apostle and wrote them for later ages (see Rev. 1:1, 4, 9; 22:8; cf. 21:14, where the apostles seem to be figures of the past).

1. Anti-Judaism in Revelation?

The references to the Hebrew scriptures in Revelation (in 65 percent of the verses)[1] suggest a Jewish author, while the Semitic characteristics of the Greek style would indicate a Palestinian, perhaps emigrated to Asia Minor during the crisis of 66 to 73 C.E. Revelation generally appears to be the most Jewish book in the New Testament, and Jerusalem plays a central role in its hope. The author directs his fiery denunciation not against Judaism but against the Roman Empire ("Babylon, the great harlot") that oppressed both Jews and Christians.

Two texts, however, do describe "those who say they are Jews and are not" as a "synagogue of Satan" (2:9; 3:9). Nevertheless, instead of agreeing to a general anti-Jewish interpretation, we may understand that the texts speak solely of two local groups of Jews (in Ephesus and Philadelphia, ca. 95). These local groups probably had slanderously denounced Jesus' followers before the Roman authorities, resulting in violent persecution and the imprisonment of many believers in these two cities. The followers of the Lamb

1. Steve Moyise, *The Old Testament in the Book of Revelation,* JSNTSup 115 (Sheffield: Sheffield Academic Press, 1995).

apparently considered themselves to be authentic Jews.[2] Although opposition is expressed to the eating of pagan sacrificial food (2:14, 20), Jewish dietary laws, circumcision, and Sabbath keeping do not surface as controversial concerns.

2. *The Poor and the Physically Challenged*

Modern studies, especially by Latin Americans and feminists, clarify the radical character of the apocalyptic and utopian genres.[3] Such writings usually originate in groups that are poor, marginalized, oppressed, and persecuted (as was John, oppressed and exiled on the isle of Patmos, 1:9). The empire's wars of conquest against the weak peoples and nations produced hunger and plague (6:5–8; 16:1–11). Juan Stam[4] calls attention to the severe denunciation of the imperial oppression and the obscene lust, rationalized with idolatrous religious pretentiousness (Revelation 13; 17–18). Both rich and poor succumbed to the idolatrous socioeconomic demands of the second beast (13:16–17). Elisabeth Schüssler Fiorenza writes, "The promise of triumph assures those who are poor, harassed and persecuted of the essentials for life in the future eschatology: food, clothing, housing, citizenship, security, honor"[5] Consequently, it is understandable that Revelation interested Friedrich Engels and Karl Marx so much and that Engels selected it as the theme of his only article on a biblical book.[6]

Poverty and oppression, however, appear more in images in Revelation than in the technical and explicit vocabulary.[7] The poverty (*ptōcheia*) of the church in Smyrna is attributed to the oppression/persecution coming from certain "Jews" (2:9; better understood as "other Jews," since John and many in the seven churches also were Jews; cf. 3:9; see above). The reference to the "poor" (*ptōchos*) church in Laodicea (3:17–18) is metaphorical, but the context enables us to delineate what poverty literally involves: to have need, be miserable, deplorable, blind, naked, suffer shame. The link between being physically challenged ("blind") and poverty is clear, as in Luke 4:18–19. John does not speak literally of the physically challenged (note the dead idols that can neither see nor walk, 9:20; cf. Dan. 5:4, 23), but one metaphorical ref-

---

2. Peder Borgen, "Polemic in the Book of Revelation," in *Anti-Semitism and Early Christianity*, ed. Craig A. Evans and Donald A. Hagner (Minneapolis: Fortress, 1993), 199–211.

3. Ricardo Foulkes, *El Apocalipsis de San Juan: Una lectura desde América Latina* (Buenos Aires: Nueva Creación; Grand Rapids: Eerdmans, 1989).

4. Juan B. Stam, "El Apocalipsis y el imperialismo," in *Capitalismo, violencia y antivida*, ed. Elsa Tamez and Saúl Trinidad (San José, Costa Rica: DEI, 1978), 1:359–94; "Las sanciones económicas de la Gran Bestia," in *Caminos: Revista Cubana de Pensamiento Socioteológico* 4 (1996): 51–59; *Apocalipsis y profecía: Las señales de los tiempos y el tercer milenio* (Buenos Aires: Kairos, 1998), 62–99.

5. Elisabeth Schüssler Fiorenza, *The Book of Revelation: Justice and Judgment* (Philadelphia: Fortress, 1985), 124–25.

6. Friedrich Engels, "El Libro del Apocalipsis," in *Sobre la religión*, ed. Hugo Assmann and R. Mate (Salamanca, Spain: Sígueme, [1883] 1974), 323–28.

7. Thomas D. Hanks, *God So Loved The Third World: The Biblical Vocabulary of Oppression*, trans. James C. Dekker (Maryknoll, N.Y.: Orbis, 1983), 48.

erence is common: "Let anyone who has an ear listen" (Rev. 2:7, 11, 17, 29; 3:6, 13, 22; 13:9).

Although Jesus "went about doing good and *healing*" the sick, Revelation reflects the old theology of the Exodus: God directly, or through angel messengers, punishes oppressors with plagues and pestilence (6:5–8; 16:1–11). Revelation thus seeks to demonstrate that God remains sovereign in all human suffering and permits suffering only within strict limits (days, weeks, months, years), always with the final purpose of liberating God's people from oppression and all suffering.

John's Gospel refers to Jesus as "the Lamb of God who takes away the sin of the world" (1:29; cf. the Exodus paschal lamb and Isaiah's suffering servant, 53:7). Revelation speaks of Jesus as the "Lamb" (twenty-nine times!). Revelation, however, refers to the slain Lamb (5:6, eternally "physically challenged"),[8] and this slain Lamb is the key to human history (alone "worthy to open the scroll," 5:9). The secret of the triumph of God's project in human history is thus based not on the military power of great empires (with their dead idols, 9:20) but in the voluntary suffering of the Lamb and his persecuted followers.

3. *Oppression, Violence and Liberating Justice*

Vocabulary for oppression, sometimes explicitly linked with poverty, dominates in Revelation 1–13, while God's liberating justice becomes the focus in Revelation 14–22. Technical vocabulary for oppression includes *thlipsis* ("oppression, affliction," 1:9; 2:9 [+ "poverty"], 10, 22; 7:14)[9] and *adik-* words ("injustice, oppression, harm," 2:11; 7:2–3; 9:4, 10, 19; 11:5; 18:5; 22:11). Notable in Revelation is the ecological concern expressed in the condemnation of those who oppress/harm the earth (7:2–3; 9:4, 10, 19; cf. 6:6) and the eventual destruction of those who "destroy the earth" (11:18). The cosmic Creator's heavenly throne is appropriately decked out as if preparing for a Green Party victory celebration (4:3)!

In addition to such explicit vocabulary, Revelation refers to experiences of oppression, persecution, and violence by description and metaphor. Oppressive violence is signified above all by the frequent references to the blood of martyrs and of the slain Lamb (1:5 [cf. "pierced," 1:7; "slain," 5:6, 9, 12]; 7:14; 12:11; 19:2, 13). When God "avenges" the blood of martyred saints (6:10; 19:2), blood commonly results from the lethal punishment (6:12; 8:7–8; 11:6; 14:20; 16:3–4). John experienced oppression and persecution by being exiled to the isle of Patmos (1:9); Antipas was martyred (2:13); martyrs were slain (6:9–11); God's two witnesses are killed in a city characterized by the oppression and violence of Sodom and Egypt (11:7–8); the dragon "makes war" (hardly a just one!) on the seed of the woman (12:17); chap. 13 describes

---

8. Nancy Eiesland, *The Disabled God: Toward a Liberatory Theology of Disability* (Nashville: Abingdon, 1994), 98–100.

9. Hanks, *God So Loved The Third World*, 48.

in detail the economic mechanisms of oppression and the violence characteristic of imperial tyranny (see especially the "mark of the beast" in 13:16–17; cf. 14:9, 11; 15:2; 16:2; 19:20; 20:4); chaps. 17–18 describe in detail the obscene economic wealth of "Babylon" (= Rome), the idolatrous "harlot" (hardly "sex worker" in John's politically incorrect rhetoric!).

Reflecting the Exodus paradigm, God's liberating justice (*dik-* words) is introduced in a reference that relates the song of Moses to the song of the Lamb (15:3–4; similarly 16:5, 7; 19:2, 8, 11; 22:11). The liberating justice of saints and martyrs, who risk their lives to express solidarity with the poor, oppressed, and persecuted, reflects the liberating justice of God and of the slain Lamb (19:8; 22:11). Twice Revelation refers to God's "avenging" the blood of martyred saints (*ekdikeō*, 6:10; 19:2). As in the Exodus (Exod. 22:21–24), so in Revelation, God's wrath consistently reflects just indignation against the oppressors, not against the oppressed, and reminds us that God can never be indifferent to injustice, oppression, and violence against the poor, the oppressed, the weak, and the marginalized (6:16–17; 11:18; 14:10, 19–20; 15:1; 16:1, 19; 19:15; cf. the dragon's wrath, 12:12, 17).[10]

4. *Sexual Minorities*

Reflecting the fact that slaves in antiquity commonly were sexually exploited, John denounces the slave trade in "human *bodies* and souls of men" (18:13, NIV; cf. 19:18; see under 1 Tim. 1:10, where "bed-males, men-stealers" probably refers to sexual exploiters of kidnapped young male slaves in prostitution, not to our modern scientific concept of "homosexuals" with a certain orientation). Sex workers themselves, however, whether male or female, undoubtedly would have felt much more accepted sitting beside the Sea of Galilee at Jesus' feet than in the seven churches of Asia Minor listening to the Seer's insulting rhetoric denouncing the idolatrous empire as the "great whore" (Revelation 17–18).

For centuries the declaration that sexual relations with women "defile" (14:4) inspired inexpressible joy among medieval monks who delighted to fantasize about themselves as "virgins" married to the Lamb.[11] Since the Reformation, pro-marriage Protestants commonly have concluded that this text is one of the most difficult in the New Testament. Adela Yarbro Collins suggests that Revelation here makes clear the author's hatred and fear of women and sexual instincts,[12] which are common in cases of internalized homophobia.[13] As in Paul's letters (→1 Corinthians), a tension exists in Revelation between traditional rigid concepts concerning gender and more flexible concepts. The

10. Thomas D. Hanks, "The Theology of Divine Anger in the Psalms of Lament" (Th.D. thesis, Concordia Seminary, St. Louis, 1972), 501–6.

11. John Boswell, *Christianity, Social Tolerance, and Homosexuality* (Chicago: University of Chicago Press, 1980), 216–18.

12. Adela Yarbro Collins, "Revelation, Book of," *ABD*, 5:694–708.

13. See chapter 4 on John, the Beloved Disciple, in this volume; L. William Countryman, *Dirt, Greed, and Sex: Sexual Ethics in the New Testament and Their Implications for Today* (Philadelphia: Fortress, 1988), 135–38.

undefiled "virgins/celibates" (Rev. 14:4) are masculine,[14] but like good transsexuals, at the end of the book they form part of the feminine bride, wife of the masculine Lamb (21:9–27).

When Revelation speaks of "Sodom" (11:8, with "Egypt" [= Jerusalem]), the city is viewed as a symbol of violence, oppression, and persecution (see the lack of hospitality in Genesis 19), not of homoerotic relations. Likewise, when Revelation refers to certain persons as "dogs" excluded from the new just community (22:15), the reference is to apostate Christians who sacrificed to idols and betrayed their brothers and sisters to the imperial authorities (cf. 21:8).[15] The apocalyptic genre maintains an absolute dichotomy between good and evil (without shades of gray), and in the same way in the sexual sphere portrays only celibates and prostitutes, or contrasts a virgin to the great harlot. Ordinary married couples are conspicuous by their absence in this book.

Appropriately, then, although the Creator's throne is decked in green (4:3), in chap. 10 John has a vision of a mighty angel, described as dressed appropriately to lead a gay pride parade "with a rainbow on his head" (10:1). This rainbow angel's message to the churches (who today are forever studying "homosexuality" instead of homophobia) is "There will be no more delay!" (10:6).

5. Women

As is common in other New Testament books, in Revelation the women mentioned are sexual minorities (see under Matthew, where the only exceptions are Pilate's wife and the mother of James and John, perhaps a widow; 27:19; 20:20). In Revelation, without exception, not only all the women, but also all the men, are sexual minorities. In the symbolism of the book the new Jerusalem, the future yearned for, is presented under the image of a bride adorned for her husband, the Lamb (19:7; 21:1–22:5). In 14:1–5 the "bride" is presented under the image of 144,000 "virgin" males never defiled by sexual relations with women (perhaps a symbol of the economic relations with the empire). All the people of God (Israel + the church, not simply the Virgin Mary) appear under the image of the woman clothed with the sun (12:1–6, 13–17), a single

---

14. Tina Pippin, "The Revelation to John," in *Searching the Scriptures,* vol. 2, *A Feminist Commentary,* ed. Elisabeth Schüssler Fiorenza (New York: Crossroad, 1994), 113.

15. Countryman, *Dirt, Greed, and Sex,* 231–32; Richard B. Hayes, *The Moral Vision of the New Testament* (San Francisco: HarperCollins, 1996), 185. Recently a few commentators have suggested that the "dogs" excluded from the new Jerusalem may be a metaphorical reference to "male homosexuals, pederasts, or sodomites," since in the parallel vice list in 21:8 the equivalent term is "abominable"; see David Aune, *Revelation 17–22,* WBC 52C (Nashville: Thomas Nelson, 1998), 1222–24; cf. 1130–31. However, at most the text refers to sexual acts, not orientation (and only by males, not females); and in keeping with the meaning in Leviticus, if male homoerotic acts are in view, it would only be male-male anal penetration (without condoms; →Romans). Moreover, the equivalent term in the parallel vice list of 9:20–21 refers to idolatry, which also is what Ezekiel usually specifies as the content of the "abomination" related to Sodom. Hence, as in Romans 1, in the case of Rev. 21:8 the context indicates sexual acts undertaken in the context of idolatrous worship, such as cultic prostitution.

mother, who gives birth to her firstborn (without mention of a generative father).

In contrast to the positive images of women, we have the negative images (also of sexual minorities): the great "whore" Babylon (= Rome; chaps. 17–18) and the false prophet Jezebel (2:20–23, recalling the infamous queen who opposed the prophet Elijah; see 1 Kings 16:31; 19:1–3). Adela Yarbro Collins has shown how Revelation functions as a form of "catharsis" (emotional cleansing, as occurs with Greek tragedies and the works of Shakespeare) to reduce the great discrepancy we feel ("the cognitive dissonance") between *what is* (injustice, oppression, violence, persecution) and *what should be* (freedom, justice, love in solidarity, fullness of life).[16]

Revelation also may provoke a catharsis by convincing readers that what should be already exists in reality: the Creator God is majestically seated on his celestial throne, while the slain Lamb opens the seals and directs the course of human history toward a triumphal culmination. For readers staggered by so much oppression and violence, Revelation offers a strategy of psychological transference to alleviate their fury: remarkably, John never suggests that the followers of the Lamb resort to counterviolence, but rather, encourages them with the visions of God and Christ now doing battle for them and defeating their oppressors.

6. *Theological Significance*

Unquestionably, for modern readers Revelation, written in an ancient context of persecution and bitter suffering, has severe limitations. Contemporary scholars continually unmask the errors of literalist, fundamentalist, and dispensationalist interpretations that seek to decipher a scenario of precise predictions concerning the state of Israel and anticipated "antichrists."

Nevertheless, Revelation maintains its value: (1) as a prophetic denouncement of imperial oppression and violence; (2) for its absolute certainty concerning the final triumph of God's liberating justice against all the forces of evil; and (3) for its glorious vision of a hope that encompasses freedom, justice, peace, and fullness of life *on earth*. Like other books of its genre, Revelation insists on the renovation of the entire cosmos (see Romans 8; 2 Peter), earth included, and rejects the comfortable Neoplatonic escapism to some ethereal "spiritual" sphere. God is the creator of the universe (4:11) whose wrath is at work in history to judge luxurious empires with all their collaborators—to "destroy those who *destroy the earth*" (11:18). In his final portrayal of earth restored, John envisions a stream of pure water lined by a species of tree (not extinct, despite previous plagues) whose leaves "are for the healing of the nations" (22:2).

The works of lesbian writer Rachel Carson (especially *Silent Spring*, 1962) have played the key role in communicating the dangers of pesticides to

16. Adela Yarbro Collins, *Crisis and Catharsis: The Power of Apocalypse* (Philadelphia: Westminster, 1984).

the general public and launching the international environmental movement. Moreover, as Engels in the last century realized, far from being some "opiate for the masses," the yearned-for new Jerusalem finally descends to earth to replace every oppressive empire, and God's ultimate dwelling place is here with God's people (not vice versa, 21:3, 10). The choice presented throughout Revelation between Christ or Caesar has been used by Daniel Berrigan, Ernesto Cardenal, and Allan Boesak to denounce nuclear proliferation, Somoza's tyranny in Nicaragua, and the racist segregation system of South Africa. "Revelation is a cathartic text for Christians in oppressive systems."[17]

Bibliography

Aune, David E. *Revelation 1–5*. WBC 52A. Dallas: Word, 1997.

———. *Revelation 6–16*. WBC 52B. Nashville: Thomas Nelson, 1998.

———. *Revelation 17–22*. WBC 52C. Nashville: Thomas Nelson, 1998.

Bauckham, Richard. *The Climax of Prophecy: Studies on the Book of Revelation*. Edinburgh: T. & T. Clark, 1993.

Beale, Gregory K. *The Book of Revelation*. NIGTC. Grand Rapids: Eerdmans, 1998.

———. *John's Use of the Old Testament in Revelation*. JSNTSup 166. Sheffield: Sheffield Academic Press, 1999.

Boesak, Allan A. *Comfort and Protest: The Apocalypse from a South African Perspective*. Philadelphia: Westminster, 1987.

Borgen, Peder. "Polemic in the Book of Revelation." In *Anti-Semitism and Early Christianity*, ed. Craig A. Evans and Donald A. Hagner, 199–211. Minneapolis: Fortress, 1993.

Carson, Rachel. *Silent Spring*. New York: Crest, 1962.

Collins, Adela Yarbro. "Revelation, Book of." In *ABD*, 5:694–708.

———. *Crisis and Catharsis: The Power of Apocalypse*. Philadelphia: Westminster, 1984.

Engels, Friedrich, "El Libro del Apocalipsis." In *Sobre la religión*, ed. Hugo Assmann and R. Mate, 323–28. Salamanca, Spain: Sígueme, [1883] 1974.

Ewing, Ward B. *The Power of the Lamb: Revelation's Theology of Liberation for You*. Cambridge, Mass.: Cowley, 1994.

Fiorenza, Elisabeth Schüssler. *The Book of Revelation: Justice and Judgment*. Philadelphia: Fortress, 1985.

———. *Revelation: Vision of a Just World*. Minneapolis: Fortress, 1991.

Foulkes, Ricardo. *El Apocalipsis de San Juan: Una lectura desde América Latina*. Buenos Aires: Nueva Creación; Grand Rapids: Eerdmans, 1989.

Garrett, Susan R. "Revelation." In *The Women's Bible Commentary*, ed. Carol A. Newsom and Sharon H. Ringe, 469–74. Louisville: Westminster John Knox, 1998.

González, Catherine Gunsalus and Justo González. *Revelation*. Westminster Bible Companion. Louisville: Westminster John Knox, 1997.

Hogan, Steve and Lee Hudson, eds. "Carson, Rachel [Louis] (1907–1964)." In *Completely Queer: The Gay and Lesbian Encyclopedia*, 123–24. New York: Henry Holt, 1998.

17. Pippin, "The Revelation to John," 115–16.

Howard-Brook, Wes, and Anthony Gwyther. *Unveiling Empire: Reading Revelation Then and Now.* Maryknoll, N.Y.: Orbis, 1999.

Kraybill, J. Nelson. *Imperial Cult and Commerce in John's Apocalypse.* JSNTSup 132. Sheffield: Sheffield Academic Press, 1996.

Mounce, Robert H. *The Book of Revelation.* Rev. ed. NICNT. Grand Rapids: Eerdmans, 1998.

Moyise, Steve. *The Old Testament in the Book of Revelation.* JSNTSup 115. Sheffield: Academic, 1995.

Pippin, Tina. "The Revelation to John." In *Searching the Scriptures,* vol. 2, *A Feminist Commentary,* ed. Elisabeth Schüssler Fiorenza, 109–30. New York: Crossroad, 1994.

———. *Death and Desire: The Rhetoric of Gender in the Apocalypse of John.* Louisville: Westminster/John Knox, 1992.

Richard, Pablo. *Apocalipsis: Reconstrucción de la esperanza.* San José, Costa Rica: DEI, 1994.

Stam, Juan B. *Apocalipsis y profecía: Las señales de los tiempos y el tercer milenio.* Buenos Aires: Kairos, 1998.

———. "El Apocalipsis y el imperialismo." In *Capitalismo, violencia y antivida,* ed. Elsa Tamez and Saúl Trinidad, 1:359–94. San José, Costa Rica: DEI, 1978.

———. "Las sanciones económicas de la Gran Bestia," in *Caminos: Revista Cubana de Pensamiento Socioteológico* 4 (1996): 51–59.

Appendix A

Chronological Order of the New Testament

For a more historical order, the books can be read as follows:

From Jesus' Brothers in Palestine (45–60 C.E.)

1. James (45–60)	The Priority of Praxis Guided by Wisdom
2. Jude (50–60)	Celebrating the Love-Feasts, Subverting the Canon

Paul's Seven Unquestioned Letters (50–58 C.E.)

3. 1 Thessalonians (50–51)	The Missionary-Nurse in Paul
4. Philemon (54–55)	Liberating Solidarity with a Slave
5. Galatians (54–56)	Christ Liberated Us from the Law That We Might Remain Free
6. Philippians (56)	The Contagious Joy of a Political Prisoner
7. 1 Corinthians (56)	Use Your Gifts to Strengthen the Body
8. 2 Corinthians (57)	God's Solidarity with the Weak and the "Crazy"
9. Romans (58)	Anti-Judaism and Homophobia Deconstructed

Q (60) and Hebrews (66 C.E.)

Q = "Source" (60)	Texts common to Luke and Matthew but not occurring in Mark
10. Hebrews (66)	Subversive Hermeneutics and Jesus' Liberating Purpose

Synoptic Gospels + Acts (70–85 C.E.)

11. Mark (69–70)	Good News for the Sick and the Physically Challenged
12. Luke (80)	Good News for the Poor and for Women
13. Acts (80)	Queer Couples Collaborate in Mission to the Unclean
14. Matthew (85)	A Log Cabin Publican? Good News for Sex Workers!

Deutero-Petrine Letters (80–90 C.E.)

15. 1 Peter (80)	Persecuted Immigrants in a Xenophobic Empire?
16. 2 Peter (90)	Christian Virtues for a Renewed Green World

Deutero-Pauline Letters (from Pauline Disciples to Later Churches) (75–90 C.E.)

17. Colossians (75–85)	Sophia-Wisdom and Liberation from Elitist Patriarchal Philosophies
18. Ephesians (80–90)	Liberation from Nihilism and from Anti-Judaism
19. 2 Thessalonians (80–90; or 50–51 C.E. from Corinth, if from Paul himself)	Preventing Poverty by Diligent Labor

Pastoral Letters (from "Paul" to His Emissaries) (90 C.E.)

20. Titus (90)	Good News with Good Works for the Marginalized
21. 1 Timothy (90)	Merry News for Widows: "You May Remarry"
22. 2 Timothy (90)	Good News for Those Condemned to Death

Johannine Writings (90–95 C.E.)

23. John (90)	Jesus' Beloved Disciple Subverts Literalism and the Law
24. 3 John (90–95)	Hospitality as Making an Inclusive Community of Friends
25. 2 John (90–95)	The Limits of Tolerance to Make an Inclusive Community Viable
26. 1 John (90–95)	God's Pure Love in Solidarity with the Poor
27. Revelation (95)	Woe to the Great Sex Worker, Babylon

Appendix B

Didactic Reading Order for the New Testament

This is the recommended order for the first reading of the New Testament.

Introductory Reading

1. 3 John — Hospitality as Making an Inclusive Community of Friends (90–95, from Ephesus)
2. 2 John — The Limits of Tolerance to Make an Inclusive Community Viable (90–95, from Ephesus)
3. 1 John — God's Pure Love in Solidarity with the Poor (90–95, from Ephesus)
4. James — The Priority of Praxis Guided by Wisdom (45–60, from Jerusalem)
5. Galatians — Christ Liberated Us from the Law That We Might Remain Free (54–56, from Ephesus)
6. Jude — Celebrating the Love-feasts, Subverting the Canon (50–60, from Palestine)
7. 2 Peter — Christian Virtues for a Renewed Green World (85–90, from Rome)
8. Mark — Good News for the Sick and the Physically Challenged (69, in Rome)
9. 1 Thessalonians — The Missionary Nurse in Paul (50–51, from Corinth)
10. John — Jesus' Beloved Disciple Subverts Literalism and the Law (90, in Ephesus)
11. 1 Peter — Persecuted Immigrants in a Xenophobic Empire? (80, from Rome)
12. Philemon — Liberating Solidarity with a Slave (54–55, from Ephesus)
13. Philippians — The Contagious Joy of a Political Prisoner (56, from Ephesus)

14. Luke — Good News for the Poor and for Women
(80, in Greece or Macedonia)

15. Acts — Queer Couples Collaborate in Mission to the Unclean
(80, in Greece or Macedonia)

16. 2 Corinthians — God's Solidarity with the Weak and the "Crazy"
(57, from Macedonia)

17. 1 Corinthians — Use Your Gifts to Strengthen the Body
(56, from Ephesus)

Deutero-Pauline Letters (from Pauline Disciples to Later Churches)

18. Colossians — Sophia-Wisdom and Liberation from Elitist Patriarchal Philosophies
(75–85, from Ephesus)

19. Ephesians — Liberation from Nihilism and from Anti-Judaism
(80–90, in Ephesus)

20. 2 Thessalonians — Preventing Poverty by Diligent Labor
(80–90, various possibilities; or 50–51 from Corinth if from Paul himself)

Pastoral Letters (from "Paul" to His Emissaries)

21. Titus — Good News with Good Works for the Marginalized
(90, from Ephesus, en route to see Titus on Crete)

22. 1 Timothy — Merry News for Widows: "You May Remarry"
(90, from Macedonia, to Timothy in Ephesus)

23. 2 Timothy — Good News for Those Condemned to Death
(90, from Rome, to Timothy in Troas or Ephesus?)

Longer, Complex Books

24. Matthew — A Log Cabin Publican? Good News for Sex Workers!
(85, in Antioch, Syria)

25. Hebrews — Subversive Hermeneutics and Jesus' Liberating Purpose
(66, anonymous author [Apollos?], to Rome or Jerusalem)

26. Revelation — Woe to the Great Sex Worker, Babylon
(95, from Patmos, to seven churches in Asia)

27. Romans — Anti-Judaism and Homophobia Deconstructed
(58, from Corinth)

Bibliography

General Works

Althaus-Reid, Marcella Maria. *Indecent Theology: Theological Per/versions in Sex, Gender and Politics.* New York: Routledge, 2000.

Balch, David L., ed. *Homosexuality, Science, and the "Plain Sense" of Scripture.* Grand Rapids: Eerdmans, 2000.

Barr, James. *The Concept of Biblical Theology: An Old Testament Perspective.* Minneapolis: Fortress, 1999.

Bauer, Walter. *A Greek-English Lexicon of the New Testament and Other Early Christian Literature.* 3rd ed. Ed. Frederick W. Danker. Chicago: University of Chicago Press, 2000.

Blomberg, Craig L. *Give Me neither Property nor Riches: A New Testament Theology of Material Possessions.* Grand Rapids: Eerdmans, 1999.

———. *Jesus and the Gospels.* Nashville: Broadman & Holman, 1997.

———. *The Historical Reliability of the Gospels.* Downers Grove, Ill.: Inter-Varsity, 1987.

Boff, Leonardo. *Cry of the Earth, Cry of the Poor.* Maryknoll, N.Y.: Orbis, 1997.

Boykin, Keith. *One More River to Cross: Black and Gay in America.* New York: Anchor/Doubleday, 1996.

Brown, Raymond E. *An Introduction to the New Testament.* New York: Doubleday, 1997.

Brueggemann, Walter. *Theology of the Old Testament: Testimony, Dispute, Advocacy.* Minneapolis: Fortress, 1997.

Conlon, James. *Geo-Justice: A Preferential Option for the Earth.* San Jose, Calif.: Resource Publications, 1990.

Corley, Kathleen E. *Private Women, Public Meals: Social Conflict in the Synoptic Tradition.* Peabody, Mass.: Hendrickson, 1993.

Countryman, L. William. *Dirt, Greed, and Sex: Sexual Ethics in the New Testament and Their Implications for Today.* Philadelphia: Fortress, 1988.

Drake, Robert. *The Gay Canon.* New York: Anchor/Doubleday, 1998.

Dunn, James D. G. *The Theology of Paul the Apostle.* Grand Rapids: Eerdmans, 1998.

Eiesland, Nancy L. *The Disabled God: Toward a Liberation Theology of Disability.* Nashville: Abingdon, 1994.

Eiesland, Nancy L., and Don E. Saliers. *Human Disability and the Service of God: Theological Perspectives on Disability.* Nashville: Abingdon, 1998.

Elliott, Neil. *Liberating Paul: The Justice of God and the Politics of the Apostle*. Maryknoll, N.Y.: Orbis, 1994.

Evans, C. A., and Donald A. Hagner, eds. *The New Testament and Anti-Semitism*. Minneapolis: Fortress, 1993.

Felder, Cain Hope, ed. *Stony the Road We Trod: African American Biblical Interpretation*. Minneapolis: Fortress, 1991.

Fiorenza, Elisabeth Schüssler, ed. *Searching the Scriptures*. 2 vols. New York: Crossroad, 1994.

Fishburn, Janet. *Confronting the Idolatry of Family: A New Vision for the Household of God*. Nashville: Abingdon, 1991.

Freedman, David Noel, ed. *The Anchor Bible Dictionary*. 6 vols. New York: Doubleday, 1992.

Germond, Paul, and Steve de Gruchy, eds. *Aliens in the Household of God: Homosexuality and Christian Faith in South Africa*. Capetown and Johannesburg: David Philip, 1997.

Gudorf, Christine E. *Body, Sex, and Pleasure: Reconstructing Christian Sexual Ethics*. Cleveland: Pilgrim Press, 1994.

Habel, Norman, ed. *The Earth Bible: Reading the Bible from the Perspectives of the Earth*. 5 vols. Sheffield: Sheffield Academic Press, 2000–.

Hanks, Thomas D. "Bernadette J. Brooten on Natural Theology and Unnatural Acts in Romans 1." Paper presented at the annual meeting of the Evangelical Theological Society, Claremont, Calif., 20–22 November 1997.

———. "The Theology of Divine Anger in the Psalms of Lament." Th.D. thesis, Concordia Seminary, St. Louis, 1972.

———. *God So Loved the Third World: The Biblical Vocabulary of Oppression*. Maryknoll, N.Y.: Orbis, 1983. (*Opresión, pobreza y liberación: Reflexiones bíblicas*. San José, Costa Rica: Caribe, 1982.)

———. "Jacques Ellul: The Original 'Liberation Theologian'?" *Cross Currents* 35, no. 1 (1985): 17–32.

———. "The Evangelical Witness to the Poor and Oppressed." *Theological Students Fellowship Bulletin* (September–October 1986): 11–20. (Paper presented at the Evangelical Theological Society, 1985, Moody Bible Institute, Chicago.)

———. "Poor, Poverty" (New Testament). *ABD*, 5:414–24.

———. "Vocabulary and Theology of Oppression: The Place of Sexual Minorities?" Paper presented at the annual meeting of the Society of Biblical Literature, San Francisco, November 22–25, 1997.

Hanson, Paul D. *The People Called: The Growth of Community in the Bible*. San Francisco: Harper & Row, 1986.

Harris, Maria. *Proclaim Jubilee: A Spirituality for the Twenty-first Century*. Louisville: Westminster John Knox, 1996.

Hayes, John H., ed. *Dictionary of Biblical Interpretation*. 2 vols. Nashville: Abingdon, 1999. (see especially Ken Stone, "Gay/Lesbian Interpretation," 1:432–34; T. Schmeller, "Liberation Theologies," 2:66–74.)

Hays, Richard B. *The Moral Vision of the New Testament: A Contemporary Introduction to New Testament Ethics*. San Francisco: HarperCollins, 1996.

Helminiak, Daniel A. *What the Bible Really Says about Homosexuality.* Millennium edition, updated and expanded. Tajique, N.Mex.: Alamos Square Press, 2000.

Hopkins, Dwight N. *Introducing Black Theology of Liberation.* Maryknoll, N.Y.: Orbis, 1999.

Hugenberger, Gordon P. *Marriage as a Covenant: Biblical Law and Ethics as Developed from Malachi.* Leiden: Brill, 1994; Grand Rapids: Baker, 1998.

Johnson, Luke Timothy. *The Writings of the New Testament.* Rev. ed. Minneapolis: Fortress, 1999.

Kim, Young Ihl. "The Vocabulary of Oppression in the Old Testament." Ph.D. diss., Drew University, 1981.

Kinsler, Ross, and Gloria Kinsler. *The Biblical Jubilee and the Struggle for Life.* Maryknoll, N.Y.: Orbis, 1999.

Ladd, George Eldon. *A Theology of the New Testament.* Rev. ed. Ed. Donald A. Hagner. Grand Rapids: Eerdmans, 1994.

Lebacqz, Karen. *Six Theories of Justice.* Minneapolis: Augsburg, 1986.

———. *Justice in an Unjust World.* Minneapolis: Augsburg, 1987.

———, ed., with David Sinacore-Guinn. *Sexuality: A Reader.* Cleveland: Pilgrim Press, 1999.

Martyn, J. Louis. *Theological Issues in the Letters of Paul.* Nashville: Abingdon, 1997.

Massey, J. E. "Reading the Bible as African Americans." In *The New Interpreter's Bible,* ed. L. Keck, et al., 1:154–60. Nashville: Abingdon, 1994.

Mauser, Ulrich. *The Gospel of Peace.* Louisville: Westminster John Knox, 1992.

Miranda, José P. *Marx and the Bible: A Critique of the Philosophy of Oppression.* Maryknoll, N.Y.: Orbis, 1974. (*Marx y la Biblia: Crítica a la filosofía de la opresión.* Salamanca, Spain: Sígueme, 1972.)

Mosala, Itumeleng J. *Biblical Hermeneutics and Black Theology in South Africa.* Grand Rapids: Eerdmans, 1989.

Newman, Carey A., ed. *Jesus and the Restoration of Israel: A Critical Assessment of N. T. Wright's "Jesus and the Victory of God."* Downers Grove, Ill.: InterVarsity, 1999.

Newsom, Carol A., and Sharon H. Ringe, eds. *The Women's Bible Commentary.* Louisville: Westminster John Knox, 1992.

Pixley, Jorge, and Clodovis Boff. *Opción por los Pobres.* Buenos Aires: Paulinas, 1986.

Pons, Jacques. *L'oppression dans l'Ancien Testament.* Paris: Letouzey et Ané, 1981.

Regenstein, Lewis G. *Replenish the Earth.* New York: Crossroad, 1991.

Rogers, Eugene F., Jr. *Sexuality and the Christian Body: Their Way into the Triune God.* Oxford: Blackwell, 1999.

Russell, Letty M., and J. Shannon Clarkson, eds. *Dictionary of Feminist Theologies.* Louisville: Westminster John Knox, 1996.

Schaeffer, Francis, with Udo Middelmann. *Pollution and the Death of Man.* Wheaton, Ill.: Crossway, 1992.

Schwantes, Milton. *Das Recht der Armen.* Beiträge zur biblischen Exegese und Theologie 4. Frankfurt: Peter Lang, 1977.

Sider, Ronald J. *Just Generosity: A New Vision for Overcoming Poverty in America.* Grand Rapids: Baker, 1999.

Spencer, Daniel T. *Gay and Gaia: Ethics, Ecology, and the Erotic.* Cleveland: Pilgrim Press, 1996.

Streete, Gail Corrington. *The Strange Woman: Power and Sex in the Bible.* Louisville: Westminster John Knox, 1997.

Swartley, Willard M. *The Love of Enemy and Nonretaliation in the New Testament.* Louisville: Westminster John Knox, 1992.

Tamez, Elsa. *Bible of the Oppressed.* Maryknoll, N.Y.: Orbis, 1982.

Thurston, Bonnie. *Women in the New Testament.* New York: Crossroad, 1998.

Vaage, Leif E., and L. Wimbush, eds. *Asceticism and the New Testament.* New York: Routledge, 1999.

Vasey, Michael. *Strangers and Friends: A New Exploration of Homosexuality and the Bible.* London: Hodder & Stoughton, 1995.

Wilson, Nancy. *Our Tribe: Queer Folks, God, Jesus, and the Bible.* San Francisco: HarperCollins, 1995.

Wright, Nicholas Thomas. *The Climax of the Covenant: Christ and the Law in Pauline Theology.* Edinburgh: T. & T. Clark, 1991; Minneapolis: Fortress, 1992.

———. *The New Testament and the People of God.* Minneapolis: Fortress, 1992.

———. *Jesus and the Victory of God.* Minneapolis: Fortress, 1996.

Yoder, Perry B., and Willard M. Swartley, eds. *The Meaning of Peace: Biblical Studies.* Louisville: Westminster John Knox, 1992.

Bibles Especially Recommended

The HarperCollins Study Bible. New Revised Standard Version, with notes by the Society of Biblical Literature. New York: HarperCollins, 1993. Ecumenical, scholarly.

The New Jerusalem Bible. New York: Doubleday, 1985. Roman Catholic, scholarly, translated/adapted from the French.

The Holy Bible, New International Version. New York: International Bible Society, 1984. Conservative Evangelical. An inclusive language edition is available from Hodder & Stoughton, London (1995).

Holy Bible, Contemporary English Version. New York: American Bible Society, 1995.

The Original African Heritage Study Bible. Ed. Cain Hope Felder. Nashville: James C. Winston, 1993.

"Q" (ca. 60 C.E.)

"Q" (from German *Quelle,* meaning "source") represents texts not found in Mark but common to Luke and Matthew. They are more radical concerning the poor, women, and sexual minorities (see Hanks, "Poor, Poverty" (New Testament), *ABD,* 5:414–24, and Luise Schottroff below).

Hanks, Thomas D. "Poor, Poverty" (New Testament). *ABD,* 5:414–24.

Kloppenborg, John S. *The Formation of Q.* Philadelphia: Fortress, 1987.

Robinson, James M., John S. Kloppenborg, and Paul Hoffman, eds. *Critical Edition of Q.* Hermeneia Supplement. Minneapolis: Augsburg, 2000.

Schottroff, Luise. "The Sayings Source Q." In *Searching the Scripture,* vol. 2, *A Feminist Commentary,* ed. Elisabeth Schüssler Fiorenza, 510–34. New York: Crossroad, 1994.

For annual updates of "Q" bibliography, see David M. Scholer in *The Society of Biblical Literature Seminar Papers.* Atlanta: Scholars Press.